Work and Society
A Reader

Edited by

Keith Grint

Polity

Copyright © Editorial matter and organization Keith Grint 2000

First published in 2000 by Polity Press in association with Blackwell Publishers Ltd

Editorial office:
Polity Press
65 Bridge Street
Cambridge CB2 1 UR, UK

Marketing and production:
Blackwell Publishers Ltd
108 Cowley Road
Oxford OX4 1JF, UK

Published in the USA by
Blackwell Publishers Inc.
350 Main Street
Malden, MA 02148, USA

ISBN 0–7456–2222–4
ISBN 0–7456–2223–2 (pbk)

A catalogue record for this book is available from the British Library and has been applied for from the Library of Congress.

Typeset in 10 on 12 pt Times
by Kolam Information Services Pvt. Ltd, Pondicherry, India
Printed in Great Britain by TJ International, Padstow, Cornwall

This book is printed on acid-free paper.

Contents

CONTENTS

Figures

Tables

Acknowledgements

I would like to thank Rebecca Harkin, Alison Dygnas, Sue Leigh, Gill Motley and Ruth Thackeray at Polity, and Mary Thackeray, Gill Colquhoun, Juanita Foster-Jones, Andy Priestner and Jenny Roberts at Templeton College's ICL, for their usual professional and friendly help and advice with this project. I would also like to record my thanks to Kris and Katy for their help, example, and complete lack of pity for me in karate, Beki for making me laugh, and Sandra for putting up with Puccini and me.

The editor and publishers wish to thank the following for permission to reproduce material in this book:

1 **J. Hassard**: 'Images of Time in Work and Organization' in S. Clegg, C. Hardy and W. R. Nord (eds): *Handbook of Organization Studies* (Sage, 1996), reprinted by permission of the author and publisher.

2 **Bruno Latour**: 'Technology is Society Made Durable' in J. Law (ed.): *A Sociology of Monsters* (Routledge 1991), copyright © The Sociological Review 1991, reprinted by permission of the author and The Sociological Review, Keele University.

3 **Christian Grootaert** and **Ravi Kanbur**: 'Child Labour: An Economic Perspective' from *International Labour Review*, Geneva, vol. 134, no. 2 (1995), reprinted by permission of International Labour Review.

4 **P. du Gay** and **J. Salman**:'The Cult(ure) of the Customer' from *Journal of Management Studies*, vol. 29, no. 4 (1992), reprinted by permission of the authors and Blackwell Publishers Ltd.

5 **S. Newell**: 'The Superwoman Syndrome: Gender Differences in Attitudes towards Equal Opportunities at Work and Towards Domestic Responsibilities

at Home' from *Work, Employment and Society*, vol. 7, no. 2 (1993), copyright © BSA Publications Ltd, reprinted by permission of the publishers, Cambridge University Press.

6 **M. Rowlinson** and **J. Hassard**: 'The Invention of Corporate Culture: A History of the Histories of Cadbury' from *Human Relations*, vol. 46, no. 3 (1993), reprinted by permission of the authors and Kluwer Academic/Plenum Publishers.

7 **D. Deetz**: 'Disciplinary Power in the Modern Corporation' in M. Alvesson and H. Wilmott (eds): *Critical Management Studies* (Sage, 1992), reprinted by permission of the author and publisher.

8 **D. Collinson**: 'Strategies of Resistance: Power, Knowledge and Subjectivity in the Workplace' in J. Jermier, D. Knights and W. R. Nord (eds): *Resistance and Power in Organizations* (ITBP, 1994), reprinted by permission of the author and publishers.

9 **T. Modood**: 'Employment' from T. Modood, R. Berthoud, J. Lakey, J. Nazroo, P. Smith, S. Virdee and S. Beishon: *Ethnic Minorities in Britain* (Policy Studies Institute, London, 1997), reprinted by permission of the author and the Policy Studies Institute.

10 **Judy Wajcman**: 'It's Hard to be Soft' from J. Wajcman: *Managing Like a Man* (Polity, 1998), earlier version published as 'Desperately Seeking Differences: Is Management Style Gendered?' in *British Journal of Industrial Relations*, vol. 34, no. 3 (1996), copyright © Blackwell Publishers and the London School of Economics, reprinted by permission of the author and publishers.

11 **F. Belussi** and **F. Garibaldo**: 'Variety of Pattern of the Post-Fordist Economy: Why are the "Old Times" still with us and the "New Times" still to come?' from *Futures*, vol. 28, no. 2 (1996), reprinted by permission of Elsevier Science Ltd.

12 **Stephen R. Barley** and **Gideon Kunda**: 'Design and Devotion: Surges of Rational and Normative Ideologies of Control' from *Administrative Science Quarterly*, vol. 37, no. 3, (September 1992), reprinted by permission of Administrative Science Quarterly.

Editor's Note

An ellipsis within square brackets indicates an omission from the original publication, thus: [. . .]. Where more than a paragraph has been excluded, a line space
appears above and below such ellipses. Apart from minor amendments (e.g.
capitalization, British rather than American spellings and the presentation of
reference material), the few editorial interventions necessitated by publishing
these extracts in a single volume also appear in square brackets. Books referred
to in the Introduction and in editorial introductions to each of the book's five
sections are listed in the Editor's Bibliography on page 343. The authors' opinions
are, of course, those held at the time of writing; dates of original publication are
given in the Notes to each reading.

Abbreviations

AA VV	various authors
ASME	American Association for Mechanical Engineers
ATM	automated teller machine
BPI	*Business Periodicals Index*
CBI	Confederation of British Industry
CEO	Cheif Executive Officer
CNRS	Centre National de la Recherche Scientifique
CPM	critical path method
CRE	Commission for Racial Equality
EC	European Community
EU	European Union
FTSE 100	Financial Times Stock Exchange 100 Index
HMSO	Her Majesty's Stationery Office
HND	Higher National Diploma
ICC	Interstate Commerce Commission
ILO	International Labour Organization
JIT	just in time
LFS	Labour Force Survey
LSE	London School of Economics
MBA	Master of Business Administration
MBO	management by objectives
NCR	National Cash Register
OECD	Organization for Economic Co-operation and Development
OPCS	Office of Population Censuses and Surveys
OR	operations research
ORSA	Operations Research Society of America
PERT	programme evaluation and review technique
PSI	Policy Studies Institute
R&D	research and development
SAS	Special Air Service

TQM	total quality management
UCL	University College, London
UK	United Kingdom
UKACIA	United Kingdom Action Committee on Islamic Affairs
UNICEF	United Nations Children's Fund (formerly United Nations International Children's Emergency Fund)
USA	United States of America
YMCA	Young Men's Christian Association

Editor's Introduction

The sociology of work is a potentially enormous topic covering what many would consider a large proportion of all human activity right across the globe and throughout time. In my publication *The Sociology of Work* (2nd edition 1998) I provided a detailed overview of some of the elements of work that I consider to be most significant, but even an encyclopaedia could not hope to do more than scratch the surface of the available material. Not only do the empirical data change continuously, but the theoretical accounts and explanations of the data are constantly rewritten, disputed, defended and returned to. This volume provides a complement to my previous one, though it is not directly tied into the same structure. That is to say the two have what Weber might call an 'elective affinity' for each other but they are not systematically related; they are colleagues rather than partners.

In an age when it appears that technology is displacing jobs, when ecommerce appears to be displacing industry, when the late 1990s global financial crisis appeared to bring the world close to economic collapse, and when many people work exhausting hours while some have no paid work at all, it is by no means clear whether the world of work will continue in the manner that evolved and to which we became accustomed during the last two centuries. For some people – represented most effectively by André Gorz (1997) and Jeremy Rifkin (1996) – work is on the brink of a terminal decline, at least in the West, either because technology and global competition have made Western labour so expensive, or because there is no longer any practical need to devote ourselves to 'a job' for life. Yet the evidence for the 'end of work' is difficult to discern – after all, there are now more people in work, that is paid employment, in Britain than at any other time in history. In short, to misquote Mark Twain, the report of the death of work has been much exaggerated. This collection is not therefore concerned with any brave new post-work world but with the tough current world of work in all its shame and glory.

In this edited volume I have selected a wide diversity of material, some of which would probably not fit within the remit of some rather more traditional approaches to the sociology of work. Within these covers, then, the reader will find works by economists, psychologists and historians as well as by sociologists. This, in part, reflects the breadth of the material: I have often tried to establish boundaries for the sociology of work, either in terms of time or method or focus or space, but it always proved a fruitless exercise. This is not because the 'sociology of work' equates with the 'sociology of everything' – though it sometimes feels as if it does – but rather because its boundaries with related areas are so blurred. For example, for some people digging is work; for others it is a release from work; for yet others it is a punishment. Ultimately we might all disagree on what counts as work – but we do not all have the same power to establish and support the definitions of work that seem to matter.

The power of definition also operates inside academic subjects such as sociology and can effectively deter us from stepping outside conventional boundaries, even though many theoretical advances are made by just such boundary-breaking activities. This collection is not intended to break new theoretical ground but it is intended to encourage readers to go beyond subject conventions. To encourage this I have looked for readings that provide contemporary reviews of the state of play or that generate new ways of looking at work or that look at activities that have hitherto been regarded as the province of other disciplines.* For example, Christiaan Grootaert and Ravi Kanbur are economists rather than sociologists, but their review of child labour fills a considerable gap in our general understanding of work. On the other hand Bruno Latour is a sociologist of science and technology but his account of the way power is constructed and reproduced has provided a foundation for others to consider a radically different way of looking at work processes. Thus the novelty in these 'redirections in work' does not necessarily lie in the contemporary nature of the data, nor even of the article's publication, rather it rests in the ways that the articles ask questions that make us think again, think in different ways about the world of work, and think differently about the future of work.

The book is structured around five separate themes, each of which attempts to take the reader beyond the boundaries and conventions of the study of work. The structure does not require readers to begin at the beginning and follow the order but facilitates any amount of 'dipping' in and out of the parts and the readings. Each part is prefaced by a short introduction and overview that contextualizes the material and provides a brief synopsis of the main points of the readings.

In Part I, 'Beyond the Conventions of Work' each of the three readings takes a perspective on work that questions the way we have tended to view it as a mirror of the human life-cycle. That is, as something restricted to adult humans who face – and resolve – novel problems. In effect all three, in their different ways, question the general denigration of history, technology and age by focusing upon time, theories of 'human' power and the significance of child labour. In each case my intention is not to suggest that none of these issues has been considered before but instead to refocus attention in a radically different way. For instance, it is the case

---

* A good example of this can be seen in Thomas's (1999) collection which amasses a wealth of short pieces on 'Work' from a wide variety of literary sources.

that our perceptions of time have great import for our understanding of change –
and this is an important lesson for those who appear to be constantly faced with
novel changes – many of which have already been faced in previous generations.
And while we lock this approach into an evolutionary model that sees work as
decreasingly reliant on child labour, in fact child labour is a mainstay of many
economies and, in some respects, never really disappeared from some of the more
'advanced' economies. It is also true that we seem guilty of sins of omission and
commission with regard to technology, for we regularly argue about work either
as if the technology was irrelevant or as if we can take its 'effects' for granted.

Part II, 'Outside the Factory Gate', takes a vigorous swing at the representation
of work *qua* male factory workers, for although such people have never comprised
more than a minority of the working population, they have come to be seen as the
icons of the industrial age, the norm, the template against which all other experiences should be measured. However, as Sue Newell's analysis of domestic work,
and Paul du Gay's and Graeme Salaman's review of the utility of the customer
suggests, the study of work should be radically stretched to include these and
many other activities previously confined to oblivion or restricted to specialized
texts.

Part III, 'Configuring Consensus at Work' provides three more readings that
undermine whatever myths have emerged on the terminal decline of workers'
resistance and the permanent victory of consensus. For Michael Rowlinson and
John Hassard that consensus, as it appears in Cadbury's, is itself the product of
considerable work – at least in rewriting history to fit the demands of the present,
and to eliminate contending reports of the past. In contrast, Stanley Deetz and
David Collinson review opposite sides of the coin, with the former concentrating
upon the measures by which managers hope to produce and reproduce consensus
through new methods of disciplinary power, while the latter unearths evidence
that such a suggestion can never be assured given the relative influence of employees at work.

But if class power remains alive – if transformed by the 1980s and 1990s – this
does not mean that the study of work is still besotted with trade unions and
workers. Far from it, as Part IV, 'After Class', suggests, the very identity of
employees is now the subject of vigorous attempts by management to reconstruct
the worker into a more compliant and management-friendly creature. For women
seeking to progress through the management career ladders, such reconstruction
may mean rebuilding themselves in the image of men. For, as Judy Wajcman
implies, although women have achieved some success at work, the notion that
women have gendered competences that are more suitable for the twenty-first
century than the twentieth is not supported by the data. Nor have ethnic minorities made the radical progress that they may have hoped for. But, as Tariq
Modood's reading suggests, although some groups remain steadfastly stuck at
the bottom of the employment league, those with educational qualifications have,
at last, begun to move towards, and occasionally beyond, the rewards and
authority levels achieved by the white population.

Finally, Part V of the book, 'The Future of Work', looks 'back' at the future, in
particular with Fiorenza Belussi's and Francesco Garibaldo's reading on what

economic patterns we can expect over the twenty-first century. Lastly, we turn to Stephen Barley's and Gideon Kunda's overview of change to consider the extent to which the future of work can indeed be predicted and, if it can, what we might expect. One thing is certain, the world of work is constantly changing but often looks familiar. If this collection helps you to understand this paradox then it will have achieved its purpose.

Part I

Beyond the Conventions of Work

Introduction

Part I sets the context for redirections in work by considering three aspects which are all too often subordinated to the traditional icons of work: the present, the people and the adults. That is not to say that time, technology and children are missing from conventional treatments of the sociology of work but rather that the way they are represented leaves many other approaches untouched. For example, time is always 'present' but seldom the focus of research in itself. Similarly, there are many accounts of technology at work but all too often technology is treated as either beyond the sociologist's remit, a given, or its 'effects' are taken for granted. And while child labour forms a prominent part of many histories of the industrial revolution its contemporary presence seems remarkably neglected.

In the case of time, it seems, we tend to focus on the apparent uniqueness of the present and thereby miss out on the critical outlook provided by a comparative historical viewpoint. For example, almost every report on educational standards seems to suggest that they are not as high as they used to be – but this depressing conclusion ought to be situated against the very earliest reports in the late nineteenth century – when education first became compulsory in England for example – which seemed to say exactly the same thing. Similarly, an ahistorical approach to work can rapidly seduce us into assuming that before the mind-numbing repetitive labour of car factories or call centres – the early twenty-first-century white-collar equivalent – all labour was essentially skilled, involving independent thought and action on the part of the common labourer. But a glance through the archives of labourers in previous times suggests that for most people, most of the time, work was anything but innovative or invigorating or satisfying.

A second aspect of time relates not to the passing of time and its implication for change or stasis but to the time spent working. In October 1998 the European Union Working Time Directive limited the working week to forty-eight hours,[*] unless employees signed away their rights. Working time in Britain has been gradually declining since the first limits placed on working hours by the various

---

[*] This figure is inclusive of overtime and averaged out over a seventeen-week period.

Factory Acts of the nineteenth century but the British still work longer hours than most other members of the EU, with 47 per cent working over forty hours in Britain, while only 10 per cent of the French, 14 per cent of the Germans, 31 per cent of the Spanish and 41 per cent of the Italians do the same (*The Observer*, 27 September 1998).

In the first reading, 'Images of Time in Work and Organization', John Hassard concentrates on a third aspect of time – the way it has been perceived. Hassard begins by contrasting the two most conventional metaphors of time: the line and the cycle. Whereas we tend to associate contemporary life with the line, that is with progress, with evolution, with development, with life-spans and so on, we also often assume that pre-industrial societies were more concerned with time as a cycle. In the latter, the cycles of the seasons and of the day set the rhythms of work, and the passage of time was seldom regarded as 'going' somewhere different but rather in constantly returning to somewhere familiar. In effect, working hours and practices were determined by the season, by the weather and by the recurrent pattern of traditions. But the 'myth of the eternal return' came to be replaced by the 'idea of irreversibility' when the line of time displaced the cycle of time, and it became most evident when time became commodified through industrialization, when time became money. For this to occur, time also had to be measurable and Hassard follows Lewis Mumford in proposing that the clock, rather than the steam engine, was the critical machine of the industrial revolution since it facilitated the synchronization and control of activities across space. This also encouraged a switch from effort and skill to time, for the new machines could now produce equivalent production quicker – but only if the previously independent workers could be constrained within the walls of the factory to produce for a specified number of hours, rather than for a particular amount of production. In short, the clock regulated hitherto irregular working patterns, and that regulation reached its zenith under Taylorism where the 'stopwatch' literally sliced up the time for each work process and subsequently oversaw the detailed description and timing of the new 'rational' process. Seldom has this 'time and motion' process been more clearly expressed than in Harry Braverman's (1974: 321) description of 'Office time', in which an office manual of 1960 suggested standard times for a whole range of mundane procedures, for example:

File drawer, open and close, no selection	0.04 minutes
Desk drawer, open side drawer of standard desk	0.014 minutes
Get up from chair	0.33 minutes
Turn in swivel chair	0.09 minutes
Normal longhand, per letter	0.015 minutes

What the regulation of time also introduced was the marked division between work and non-work, between company time and free time, because before this period many activities would have been undertaken from home and the divisions between labour and leisure would have been much more difficult to discern. Yet, as Hassard's review of the ethnographic studies of time suggests, that division is itself as much a product of the researcher as the process researched. For example, in Donald Roy's 'banana time' – probably *the* classic ethnography in the sociology of work – much of the 'work' that occurs has only an indeterminate and indirect link to the 'work' for which the workers are paid. Perhaps more importantly, Roy suggests that the division of work into temporal periods is not the equivalent of 'clock watching', but more a means to structure the day. One might liken this to a walk on Christmas day after lunch with hordes of relatives: the walk is not just to 'walk off' lunch, nor just a way of 'killing time', but instead it becomes a symbolic dividing line between feasting (and drinking) sessions, a temporal and temporary gap between phases of indigestion certainly, but also a mechanism for marking and giving meaning to time, rather than just passing time.

Ditton's 'baking time' is written in the same mould and concentrates on the collective strategies for manipulating time at work, whereas Ruth Cavendish reveals a set of individual strategies that closely resemble those I experienced during my own years working in factories: inordinately tedious jobs like machine-minding or floor-cleaning could be massaged out of consciousness simply by day dreaming for most of the shift.

Clark's work is slightly different insofar as he considers the temporal link between an organization's culture and its structure. In effect, he suggests that structures and cultures vary with time and situation, particularly in the seasonal industries that he considers but also with regard to non-seasonal industries where variable conditions pose problems for organizations that are unable to respond by reproducing different, and often previously developed structures and cultures.

The second part of Hassard's reading focuses upon the way time is a critical element of organization and how work organizations have come to dominate so much of our time. Thus infants are socialized, usually by families, into accepting that their biological requirements have to be tempered by the social needs of others, a disciplining element that is more clearly visible in schools, where pupils rapidly learn that success involves the subordination of personal needs to school time. For many[*] there are strong connections between work, correctional and educational institutions and the relatively painless transfer for most people from an educational to a work institution is testament to the role the former have in accommodating people to the discipline of time.

In his final section Hassard moves on to identify the time problems faced by organizations, rather than individuals. Here he suggests that the temporal uncertainty faced by most is usually resolved by time scheduling while the co-ordination of functionally separate institutions is resolved not by equally bureaucratic routines but by the development of a system of interpersonal norms that provide the flexibility necessary to keep the organization going. We can probably see this most easily when groups of workers 'work to rule'. In theory this should mean maximum efficiency, as the procedures and rules have been designed to elicit maximum productivity; but in practice it usually means that little work gets done, as the procedures cannot cover the infinite complexity of events. Thus normative procedures act to synchronize the temporally differentiated elements of organizations.

---

[*]   Contrast, for example, Bowles and Gintis (1976) and Foucault (1977).

At the individual level such temporal synchronization also exists as people attempt to juggle the different demands on their time of family, job or hobby and so on. However, to return to the second element of time discussed above in the context of working hours, it should be clear that organizational attempts to resolve the problems of time may often be at the direct expense of the individuals employed, either through the elimination of 'wasted time', by paying employees only when they are actively involved in 'work' – as some fast-food restaurants currently do – or by demanding that employees' working hours are more closely matched to the demands of the organization, through, for example, annualized hours, in which employees' time is unevenly distributed across the year not by their choice but by the level of demand. We have then, ironically, returned to the dawn of the industrialization period when work was not set by the clock but by the custom(er).

The general aversion to considering time in any historical sense also lays us open to assuming that contemporary work issues are unique because the technology is novel. It might be thought, for example, that the modern pace of life, the speed with which we travel and at which we work, is in itself so radically different from all previous eras that we must be the first generation to experience concerns like work stress. Yet the development of the railways in the nineteenth century rapidly ensured that by 1854 speeds of 80 m.p.h. were common – a phenomenal increase on the previous speed of most transport – the horse. When such speeds were first reached the reaction was what we would now regard as little short of hysterical: Queen Victoria insisted on a maximum of 20 m.p.h. and the Shah of Persia, fearing suffocation, demanded an even lower maximum speed. The real danger, according to the orthodox medical opinion of the day, was 'railway spine' in which the nerves of the spinal column could be so disturbed that migraine, back pain, sleeplessness and even personality disorders were likely. In sum the speed itself induced stress that the human body could not cope with (Harrington 1998).

The assumption that stress is a disease restricted to the post-1980s is clearly dubious but the assumption that technology can be both distinguished from the social context, and that its effects can be scientifically determined, is still prevalent. Yet ironically much social science seems to insist that sociology cannot be extended to interrogate technology. Further, the consequence for management texts is often that aspiring managers are led to believe that the 'people issue' is hardly something that can be laid at the feet of most managers, and certainly not British ones, for whom people, employees, workers or 'them' have always seemed to be a 'cost' to be reduced or a 'problem' to be resolved, rather than a crucial source of ideas and competitive advantage. Yet the engineering vision of a people-less factory where mistakes are eliminated along with tea-breaks, trade unions and work-shy workers, is as unrealistic as the opposite – an industrial society without technology. Despite this, many accounts of work seem to generate a world where 'good people skills' are the sole criteria for assessing success. This is particularly prevalent in sociology, where the study of technology has often been limited to a concern either for the social background of the scientist or technologist or to the unambiguous 'effects' of machines.* In his discussion of technology Bruno Latour attacks this division between people and things with characteristic vigour, and insists that we retain the same conceptual approach to both.

Latour demonstrates the significance of this Actor–Network approach with an apparently simple example: hotel keys. In theory, since the keys are of no use to guests once they leave, one might expect keys to be left behind; indeed, this would be the 'rational' thing to do. However, for various reasons rationality is something about which we disagree and the consequence is that some hotel guests remove their keys, leaving the hotel with the expense and effort of replacing them. Where moral obligation fails, hotel managers have to ally themselves to a non-human in order to secure the key returns. In the first case this may be a large sign reminding people of their responsibilities or even a large key-fob which acts to deter guests from their forgetfulness. In either case the issue demonstrates that the reminder by the manager, either verbal or through the inscription or the key-fob, does not necessarily determine whether the guest will comply. In effect, power is not a causal but a consequential element of the relationship: *if* guests comply then the manager's power is increased; but if they do not then the manager's power is reduced. Latour terms these efforts by the manager and counter-efforts by the guests as programmes and anti-programmes, and the consequence of each additional change to the programme is a translation, not a transmission, of the order. In other words, what was once a polite verbal request becomes a rather different phenomenon – it becomes a huge key-fob that constantly reminds the guests that they are not trustworthy – thus transforming the hotel from a courteous and friendly institution to one where mutual suspicion reigns.

Beyond this example, Latour is keen to establish the difficulty of distinguishing between human and non-human, between verbal request, written statement and key-fob, because they are all interdependent and contextually situated. For Latour, the methodological consequences suggest that we should be tracing the way such 'statements' are 'translated' through the chain of moves, always accepting that the difference between humans and non-humans is not the critical issue. Instead it is the strength of the association that he is interested in, for it is these associations between the elements that explain the success or failure of a programme. Put another way, we can analyse organizational success by considering the extent to which the association between the elements in one organization is stronger than that between another. In the hotel case it is only those managers who maintain the associations between the oral, inscripted and weighted reminders about keys that will prove to be successful. Thus 'we are never faced with objects or social relations, we are faced with chains which are associations of human and non-humans [...] by "actants" not "actors".'

One consequence of adopting this approach is the construction of radically counter-intuitive analyses. For example, we might begin to talk of the interests of the key-fob in attaching itself to the manager's programme as a way of ensuring it does not get kidnapped by the guests. Even if we reject such an interpretation as nonsensical it should nevertheless alert us to a major problem in conventional

---

* See Grint and Woolgar (1997) for a critical review of some of these approaches.

social science, in short that we regularly attribute the actions of people on the basis of motivations and attitudes of which we can have little knowledge. For example, we may explain the actions of managers on the basis of greed or stupidity or deviousness when none of these may be appropriate. Within actor–network theory lies a significant lesson for us all – beware of explanations rooted in unexamined attributions when descriptions are probably all we can safely assume.

The final reading in Part I introduces a third dimension which, like the other two (time and technology) has always been significant but seems to have fallen out of view: age. In this case we consider child labour but a focus on older workers would also have been appropriate had space allowed. Child labour introduces two issues: morality and temporality. The two are often linked in linear assumptions of progress – child labour was prominent during the industrial revolution of Europe and North America but has since been all but eliminated as the civilizing mission of a few became the norm of the majority. In contrast, child labour still persists in many countries that are only now industrializing – but will presumably follow the pattern set by the so-called advanced industrial nations. Such is the traditional view. On the other hand, child labour still persists in many of the latter nations, either in terms of Saturday jobs or newspaper deliveries and so on, and recently appears to have been making something of a comeback, at least in Britain, as the minimum wage legislation is not applicable to children. Moreover, such labour is frequently justified in terms of the 'independence' it provides and the 'responsibility' it generates for the child. Thus we can contrast the value of child labour in the West, because it teaches our children useful social values, with the exploitative child labour of the East, because it merely serves the interests of hard-hearted capitalists or wicked parents or whatever. That the labour invoking the attitudes *may* be identical should alert us to the role of culture in constructing our viewpoints.

Christiaan Grootaert and Ravi Kanbur's reading combines the temporal and moral issues by setting out both what appears to be the various developments around the globe and then attempting to explain the persistence of child labour by issues that throw doubt on the utility of the moral case against child labour *per se*. In other words, although we may still perceive child labour as an exploitative system, running from small children sewing footballs together for the European market to child prostitutes in South-East Asia servicing the demand of European and American men, it is nevertheless the case that many families can stay together and survive only through the work of children.

Grootaert and Kanbur begin by raising the problem of defining childhood as a temporal or a social issue and suggest that one resolution of the confusion is to concentrate on whether the relationship between the employer and the 'child' is exploitative in the sense that it hinders 'normal' development. This might be considered as less than helpful since 'normal' is a culturally variable term and because 'exploitation' might better be regarded in unambiguous economic terms – and no employer will persist in employing anyone unless some degree of profit – that is exploitation – is derived from the relationship. On the other hand, an age-related definition provides a measure of the numbers without establishing the degree of exploitation that varies from marginal all the way to slave labour.

While it is difficult to establish reliable numbers, it seems clear from the reading that the precise nature of child labour varies considerably with space and time. That is, it depends on which country we are considering, when we are examining the issue, and what the prevailing culture and conditions are in the particular market. Generally speaking it would seem that girls are more likely to work than boys, and that poorer families are more likely to depend upon child labour than more wealthy families. Moreover, the likelihood of girls attending school rather than working is contingent upon their parents', and especially their mother's, education. Even labour market opportunities for women do not automatically result in a decrease in girls attending school, for the eldest daughter in particular may be required to undertake domestic responsibilities for the rest of her siblings. We should also be wary of the assumption that education is, in and of itself, perceived as a good, for where education has palpably failed to deliver benefits it can appear more economically rational to seek employment rather than education for children. Yet beyond these generalities a whole raft of variables can alter the extent of child labour, depending on the form and nature of state intervention, the wages paid to adults, the extent to which poor families are at risk of imminent economic disaster and, of course, the nature of the labour market itself.

The second part of the reading moves on to discuss ways of reducing child labour and these, in turn, are partly dependent on differentiating between the social benefits of reducing child labour and the private benefits. It is clear that where the latter is minimal, but the former significant, some form of state intervention in the operation of the 'free' labour market may be necessary, either by prohibiting child labour by law (and adequately policing this), or by taxation changes or reducing family size or subsidizing education and so on. It should also be clear that simply banning child labour may not remove the problem of family poverty but considerably increase it – and that such an argument may also be appropriated by the most exploitative employers merely to protect their heinous schemes. Furthermore, if child labour is illegal, but continues, then those children involved are even less likely to receive adequate protection by the state because no system for monitoring such work will exist; instead there will be a system that merely tries to eliminate it where it can be uncovered. Ultimately Grootaert and Kanbur suggest that gradualist solutions are the most viable and, given the complexity of the problem and the interdependence of education, work and family, perhaps the messy and unsatisfactory compromises that most of us live with are the best we can hope for.

1 Time

Images of Time in Work and Organization

JOHN HASSARD

[...]

Images of time

To develop a sociologically informed analysis of time, we will first construct a conceptual framework. To achieve this, we draw upon some of the main images of time in social philosophy and upon two of the main time metaphors in social theory. These concerns are then brought together in the main body of the reading, which analyses how these various temporal images are employed in studies of work and organization.

Social philosophy

In philosophy, there is a long and sophisticated tradition of temporal analysis. The concept of time has, as Jacques (1982: xi) notes, been of central concern to philosophers for over 2000 years. Debate is found at a number of abstract levels, ranging from ontological concerns with time and existence to epistemological concerns with time and understanding. It is a tradition which has yielded a wealth of abstract, complex, yet unresolved questions (see Gale 1968). Although a detailed analysis of such questions is beyond our scope, we can note some of the main issues which confront the philsopher of time. To achieve this, we turn to the excellent introduction to temporal philosophy presented by Heath (1956).

Heath introduces the philosophy of time by asking three questions central to discussions in the field. First, at the level of ontology, he asks whether we should regard time as an objective 'fact' located 'out there' in the external world, or as a subjective 'essence' which is constructed via a 'network of meanings'; that is, should we think of time as real and concrete or as essential and abstract? Second, he asks whether we should think of time as homogeneous (where time units are equivalent) or as heterogeneous (where time units are experienced differentially); is time atomistic and divisible or continuous and infinite? And third, he asks whether time can be measured, and if so, whether we can have more than one valid time: should time be regarded as a 'unitary quantitative commodity' or as a 'manifold qualitative experience?'

It can be argued that the ways in which we answer these questions will determine how we conceptualize time in relation to the analysis of work and organization. Heath's antinomies represent basic constructs for interpreting the nature of time in formal institutions. Moreover, they provide a set of tools for dissecting sociological concepts relating to temporal issues of organization, and lay analytical foundations for associated research perspectives.

Metaphor

Sociologists have argued that metaphor is another powerful tool for social analysis (Manning 1979; Pinder and Moore 1979; Tinker 1986). In particular, it has become popular to use metaphors, or other related tropes, when illustrating the imagery of sociological concepts (see Lakoff and Johnson 1980). Morgan (1986), for example, has shown the power of metaphor for interpreting work organizations as 'systems', 'machines', 'dramas', 'organisms' and even 'psychic prisons'.

Although the literature on the philosophy of time is replete with metaphoric images (see Gale 1968), thus far only a few generic metaphors have evolved to conceptualize what is, like organization, an abstract and elusive notion (see Jacques 1982). Of those that have evolved, the most sociologically illuminating have been the 'cycle' and the 'line'.

Cyclic time   For the metaphor of the cycle, one of the most sophisticated analyses has been that provided by Eliade (1959). Eliade describes how the cycle was the basic time metaphor of what he calls 'archaic man' (or 'pre-Christian man'). He suggests that for archaic man events unfolded in an ever recurring rhythm; his sense of time was developed out of his struggle with the seasons; his time horizon was defined by the 'myth of the eternal return'. In contrast, Eliade argues that when 'Christian man' abandoned this bounded world for a direct, linear progression to redemption and salvation, for the first time he found himself exposed to the dangers inherent in the historical process. Since then humankind has tried to master history and to bring it to a conclusion; as, for example, Marx and Hegel sought to do. In the modern world, we seek refuge in various forms of faith in order to rationalize a historical process that seems to have neither beginning nor end (Eliade 1959; see also Park 1980; Fabian 1983).

Linear time   A complementary analysis is developed by de Grazia (1972) in his assessment of the linear time metaphor. De Grazia suggests similarly that, whereas primitive concepts of time are dominated by the metaphor of the cycle, for modern societies Christian beliefs give the image of time as a straight line – as a testing pathway from sin on earth, through redemption, to eternal salvation in heaven. He argues that in the evolution of modern culture the idea of irreversibility has replaced that of eternal return. The distinguishing feature of ultimate progression has led the way to a new linear concept of time, and with it a sense of firm beginning. For example, in book II of his *Confessions*, Augustine broke the circle of Roman time. In contrast to Herodotus and his notion of the cycle of human events, Augustine dispelled 'false circles' and instead purported the straight line of human history. Although *anno Domini* chronology became widespread only during the eighteenth century, history began to be dated from the birth of Jesus Christ.

Time, industrialism and the workplace

For us, the linear metaphor is important because of its link with a further concept, time as a commodity of the industrial process. This link is central to the development of what we shall term the linear-quantitative tradition of temporal imagery in industrial sociology.

The linear-quantitative tradition

During the rise of industrial capitalism this sense of unilinearity was to find time equated with value (E.P. Thompson 1967; Nyland 1986; Thrift 1990). Time, like the individual, became a commodity of the production process, for in the crucial equation linking acceleration and accumulation, a human value could be placed upon time. Surplus value could be accrued through extracting more time from labourers than was required to produce goods having the value of their wages (Marx 1976). The emphasis was upon formality and scarcity. The images came from Newton and Descartes: time was real, uniform and all-embracing; it was a mathematical phenomenon; it could be plotted as an abscissa.

In this tradition, modern industrial cultures adopt predominantly linear time perspectives. Here, the past is unrepeatable, the present is transient, and the future is infinite and exploitable. Time is homogeneous: it is objective, measurable, and infinitely divisible; it is related to change in the sense of motion and development; it is quantitative. Whereas in modern theology linear time has as its conclusion the promise of eternity, in the mundane, secular activities of industrialism temporal units are seen as finite. Time is a resource that has the potential to be consumed by a plethora of activities. In advanced societies time scarcity makes events become more concentrated and segregated, with special 'times' being given over for various forms of activities. Time is experienced not only as a sequence but also as a boundary condition. As the functionalist sociologist Wilbert Moore stated, time becomes 'a way of locating human behaviour, a mode of fixing the action that is particularly appropriate to circumstances' (1963a: 7).

By uniting the ideas of linearity and value we begin to see time as a limited good: its scarcity enhances its worth. Lakoff and Johnson (1980) crystallize this idea by citing three further metaphors to illustrate the dominant conception of linear time: time is money; time is a limited resource; time is a valuable commodity. Graham (1981), likewise, suggests that time and money are increasingly exchangeable commodities: time is one means by which money can be appropriated, in the same way as money can be used to buy time; money increases in value over time, while time can be invested now to yield money later.

This quantitative, commodified image of time thus emerges as primarily a by-product of industrialism. Mumford (1934: 14) for instance has emphasized how 'the clock, not the steam engine [was] the key machine of the industrial age'. He argues that rapid developments in synchronization were responsible for organizations of the industrial revolution being able to display such high levels of functional specialization. Large production-based firms required considerable segmentation of both parts and processes in time and space. Such specialization set requirements for extensive time/space co-ordination at both intra- and inter-organizational levels. As high levels of co-ordination needed high levels of planning, so sophisticated temporal schedules were necessary to provide a satisfactory degree of predictability. The basis of fine prediction became that of sophisticated measurement, with efficient organization becoming synonymous with detailed temporal assessments of productivity. As the machine became the focal point of work, so time schedules became the central feature of planning. During industrialism the clock was *the* instrument of co-ordination and control. The time period replaced the task as the focal unit of production (Mumford 1934; see also Landes 1983).

In another landmark study, E.P. Thompson (1967) argues that industrialism sees a crucial change in the employment relation, as it is now time rather than skill or effort that becomes of paramount concern. In large-scale manufacturing, the worker becomes subject to extremely elaborate and detailed forms of time discipline (E.P. Thompson 1967; see also McKendrick 1962). Whereas prior to industrialism 'nearly all craftsmen were self employed, working in their own homes with their tools, to their own hours' (Wright 1968: 16), with the factory system came temporal rigidification. Before the industrial revolution the prime characteristic of work was its irregularity. Periods of intense working were followed by periods of relative inactivity. There was the tradition of 'St Monday', with Mondays often being taken as a casual day like Saturday and Sunday; most of the work was done in the middle of the week (Reid 1976). Similarly, the length of the working day was irregular and determined largely by the time of the year. E.P. Thompson's quote from Hardy complements his analysis well: 'Tess . . . started her way up the dark and crooked lane or street not made for hasty progress; a street laid out before inches of land had value, and when one-handed clocks sufficiently subdivided the day' (1967: 56).

The linear-quantitative tradition thus emphasizes how, in contrast to the task-oriented experience of most historical and developing economies, under industrial capitalism not only have the great majority of workers become subject to rigidly determined time schedules, but they have also become remunerated in terms of temporal units: that is, paid by the hour, day, week, month or year. The omnipresence of the factory clock brought with it the idea that one is exchanging time rather than skill: selling labour-time rather than labour. Under industrial capitalism, workers are forced to sell their time by the hour (see Gioscia 1972).

Out of this form of analysis industrial sociology came to view modern conceptions of time as hegemonic structures whose essences are precision, control and discipline. In industrial societies, the clock becomes the dominant machine of productive organization; it provides the signal for labour to commence or halt activity. Workers must consult the time-clock before they begin working. Although life in modern societies is structured around times allocated for many different activities, it is always production that takes preference: 'Man is synchronized to work, rather than technology being synchronized to man' (de Grazia 1972: 439). Time is given first to production; other times must be fitted around the margins of the production process. Ideal productive organizations are those having temporal assets which are highly precise in their structuring and distribution. As technological determinism dominates modern perceptions of time, so correct arithmetical equations are seen as the solutions to time problems: there are finite limits and optimal solutions to temporal structuring. The basic rule is that a modern productive society is effective only if its members follow a highly patterned series of temporal conventions; each society's productive day must be launched precisely on time. In this process, clock-time holds advantages for capital as it is both visible and standardized. It has two strengths in particular: it provides a common organizing framework to synchronize activities, and it commodifies labour as a factor of production (Clark 1982; Hassard 1990).

It is indeed from this scenario that, for industrial sociology, Frederick W. Taylor was to emerge as the heir to Adam Smith's pin factory, and thus to become the high priest of rational time use. It is in the manuals of industrial engineers following Taylor (1911) that were found the logical conclusions to the ideas of Smith, Ricardo and Babbage. Scientific management, and the time and motion techniques that were its legacy, established by direct administrative authority what the machine accomplished indirectly, namely fine control of human actions. In Taylorism we reach the highpoint in separating labour from the varied rhythms experienced in craft or agricultural work: clock rhythms replace fluctuating rhythms; machine-pacing replaces self-pacing; labour serves technology.

Thus, for modern industrial societies, the linear conception of time became 'commodified' due to a major change in economic development; that is, when time was discovered as a factor in production. Time was a value that could be translated into economic terms: 'it became the medium in which human activities, especially economic activities, could be stepped up to a previously unimagined rate of growth' (Nowotny 1976: 330). Time was a major symbol for the production of economic wealth. No longer was it merely given, and reproducible through cultural notions of the 'eternal return', but it represented instead an economic object whose production it symbolized. Under industrial capitalism, timekeepers were the new regulators and controllers of work; they quantified and transformed activity into monetary value. When time became a valuable commodity its users were obliged to display good stewardship; time was scarce and must be used rationally (see Julkunnen 1977; Thrift 1990).

The neglect of qualitative time-reckoning

The linear-quantitative thesis is powerful because it describes how, under industrial capitalism, time became an object for consumption. Time becomes reified and given commodity status so that relative surplus value can be extracted from the labour process. The emphasis is upon time as a boundary condition of the employment relation. Time is an objective parameter rather than an experiential state (Fabian 1983).

However, the standard linear-quantitative thesis is one needing qualification. When taken up by industrial sociologists, especially those concerned with labour process analysis, it is often used to overstate the quantitative rationality of production practices and to understate the qualitative construction of temporal meanings (Starkey 1988). There is a tendency, for example, to gloss over the fact that the industrial world is not simply composed of machine-paced work systems, but includes a wealth of work processes based on self-paced production.

Although temporal flexibility has [. . .] been associated with new structural forms of employment (see Atkinson 1984; Pollert 1988), in the more subtle sense of social construction it has long remained widespread in boundary spanning organizational functions, such as sales, marketing, R&D and corporate planning. Moreover, while professional roles retain flexible, event-based task trajectories, also many non-professional occupations operate within irregular, if not totally self-determined, temporal patterns. As Moore (1963b: 29ff) pointed out [. . .], examples here include the emergency services, police and maintenance crews. Further, event-based temporal trajectories have long been commonplace within Britain's large service economy, while new forms of employment systems have violated the tradition of selling labour-time in the homogeneous sense of eight hours a day, five days a week, fifty weeks a year. An example of this increasing heterogeneity in work-time arrangements is the 'no-hours' contract in retailing, where an employee can (in theory) decline to accept the work schedules offered by management.

We can begin to question, therefore, whether the linear-quantitative thesis should be applied so readily as the basis for explaining the nature of time at work. Whereas writers sympathetic to Braverman's (1974) structuralist thesis suggest that progressive temporal commodification accompanies increased de-skilling, other writers note that employers' time-structuring practices are far more complex and less deterministic than mainstream labour process theory implies (see Clark 1982; Clark et al. 1984; Starkey 1988; Hassard 1990).

Clark (1982: 18), for instance, suggests that 'the claim that commodified time has to be transposed into a highly fractionated division of labour through Taylorian recipes is naive'. Drawing upon socio-technical theory, he offers examples of 'rational' task designs that are not anticipated by the Marxian theory of the 'porous day' (see also Clark et al. 1984). For example, in socio-technical systems a major key to improving productivity, and also the quality of working life, is to permit temporal autonomy. Here, much time-structuring is taken away from the 'planners' and handed over to the 'executors', that is, to the semi-autonomous work group or work cell.

Indeed many of the scenarios that emerge from an unrestrained linear-quantitative thesis require scrutiny. The standard image is of homogeneous activities being measured in microseconds in order to form some optimal, aggregate, standardized production output. However, production line ethnographies (e.g. by Roy 1960; Cavendish 1982; Kamata 1982) have documented how this image ignores the power of work groups, on even the most externally determined task processes, to construct their own time-reckoning systems. While in comparison to other forms of organization the temporal inventories of manufacturing are exact, they remain of bounded rationality when we consider contingencies such as effort, technical failure, market demand and withdrawals of labour.

For contemporary market-based organizations, time inventories are by no means so finite and determined as the so-called 'rational' models would portray. Stability and the deployment of long-term time horizons are luxuries rarely available within the conditions of chaos and turbulence which characterize the 'post-modern' organizational world (see Clegg 1990; Hassard 1993). Despite the emergence of technologies designed to ensure temporal stability (e.g. robotics, flexible manufacturing systems, computer integrated manufacturing), most indus-trial time-structuring sees production processes subject to the fallible judgements of planners and supervisors. In everyday practice, time systems are rarely a set of optimal solutions to mechanical problems: temporal strategies are factors which seldom equate with ideal calculations. Bounded rationality still characterizes decision-making linked to production management. Firms which have sought to eliminate temporal porosity, through attempting to realize computer integrated manufacturing, have often reverted to less technologically sophisticated operating systems (e.g. cellular manufacturing) when faced with the difficulties experienced in achieving database integrity for their own operations and adequate electronic data interchange with suppliers and customers.

Towards cyclic-qualitative time analysis

It can be argued, therefore, that working time is a much richer phenomenon than is portrayed in mainstream industrial sociology. Dominant perspectives such as functionalism and structuralism mostly fail to capture the complexity of industrial temporality. Such paradigms concentrate either on delineating ideal types of temporal structuring, or on suggesting that working time reflects the social rela-tions of capitalist production.

However, in contrast to the wealth of sociological studies which reflect elements of the linear-quantitative tradition (see table 1.1), studies of temporal experience are few. The qualitative dimension of working time is understated, and research evidence is found only in occasional pieces of ethnography. To conduct research into working time, it can be argued that we need qualitative as well as quantitative approaches: we need methods which access intersubjective features as well as structural ones; methods which describe subjective as well as objective features of time-structuring.

In developing such a qualitative approach we are not, however, as ill-equipped as we might think. The identification of qualitative tools has been a major theme in both the French and the American traditions in the sociology of time (see Hassard 1990). In the French tradition, the writings of Hubert (1905), Hubert and Mauss (1909), Mauss (1966) and Durkheim (1976) all emphasize the 'rhythmical' nature of social life through developing a notion of 'qualitative' time; that is, an

Table 1.1 Two paradigms for working time

Linear-quantitative paradigm emphasizes:	Cyclic-qualitative paradigm emphasizes:
Realism	Nominalism
Determinism	Voluntarism
Linearity	Circularity
Homogeneity	Heterogeneity
Nomothesis	Ideography
Quantity	Quality

appreciation of time far removed from writers who present it as simply measurable duration. Hubert (1905), for example, defined time as a symbolic structure representing the organization of society through its temporal rhythms, this being a theme also developed by Durkheim who analysed the social nature of time (Isambert 1979). Durkheim focused on time as a collective phenomenon, as a product of collective consciousness (see Pronovost 1986). For Durkheim, all members of a society share a common temporal consciousness; time is a social category of thought, a product of society. In Durkheim we find a macro-level exposition of the concept of social rhythm. Collective time is the sum of temporal procedures which interlock to form the cultural rhythm of a given society. Durkheim argues that: 'The rhythm of collective life dominates and encompasses the varied rhythms of all the elementary lives from which it results; consequently, the time that is expressed dominates and encompasses all particular durations' (1976: 69). For Durkheim, time is derived from social life and becomes the subject of collective representations. It is fragmented into a plethora of temporal activities which are reconstituted into an overall cultural rhythm that gives it meaning (see Pronovost 1986).

In the American tradition, Sorokin and Merton (1937) also highlight this qualitative nature of social time. In so doing, they draw not only on Durkheim, but also, and significantly, on the works of early cultural anthropologists, such as Codrington (1891), Hodson (1908), Nilsonn (1920), Best (1922) and Kroeber (1923). This synthesis allows Sorokin and Merton to identify qualitative themes at both micro and macro levels. While, at the micro level, they emphasize the discontinuity, relativity and specificity of time – 'social time is qualitatively differentiated' – they also suggest, like Durkheim, that: 'units of time are often fixed by the rhythm of collective life' (1937: 615).

Indeed, they take this position a step further. Whereas Evans-Pritchard (1940) in his studies of the Nuer illustrated how certain activities give significance to social time, Sorokin and Merton adopt a position more characteristic of the sociology of knowledge. They argue that meaning comes to associate an event with its temporal setting, and that the recognition of specific periods is dependent on the degree of significance attributed to them. Drawing on Gurdon's (1914) anthropology, they argue that 'systems of time-reckoning reflect the social activities of the group' (1937: 620). They show that the concept of qualitative time is important not only for primitive societies, but also for modern industrial states. They suggest that: 'Social time is qualitative and not purely quantitative.... These qualities derive from the beliefs and customs common to the group.... They serve to reveal the rhythms, pulsations and beats of the societies in which they are found' (1937: 623).

Finally, perhaps the most ambitious attempt to outline the qualitative nature of social time has been made by Gurvitch (1964). In a sophisticated, if at times rather opaque, thesis, Gurvitch offers a typology of eight 'times' to illustrate the temporal complexity of modern, class-bound society (i.e. enduring, deceptive, erratic, cyclical, retarded, alternating, pushing forward, explosive). He illustrates how cultures are characterized by a *mélange* of conflicting times, and how social groups are constantly competing over a choice of 'appropriate' times. Like earlier writers, Gurvitch distinguishes between the micro-social times characteristic of groups and communities, and the macro-social times characteristic of, for example, systems and institutions. He makes constant reference to a plurality of social times, and notes how in different social classes we find differences of time scales and levels. He suggests that through analysing time at the societal level we can reveal a double time scale operating – with on the one hand the 'hierarchically ordered and unified' time of social structure, and on the other the 'more flexible time of the society itself' (1964: 391).

This literature suggests, then, that modern societies – as well as primitive ones – hold pluralities of qualitative time-reckoning systems, and that these are based on combinations of duration, sequence and meaning. Unlike with homogeneous time-reckoning, there is no uniformity of pace and no quantitative divisibility or cumulation of units. The emphasis is on cultural experience and sense-making, on creating temporal meanings rather than responding to temporal structures. The goal is to explain the cyclical and qualitative nature of social time.

Cyclic-qualitative studies in the workplace

Having introduced elements of a cyclic-qualitative paradigm for work-time *thought*, we will now overlay this with evidence from a cyclic-qualitative paradigm for work-time *research*. In this section, the tone of the analysis changes, from theoretical discussion to empirical description, as we present field studies which develop this approach, research which reflects cyclic and qualitative elements of time at work (see table 1.1).

Although the paradigm is at present a nascent one, and as such there are relatively few fieldwork studies to consult, we can nevertheless trace four clear examples. We review Roy's (1960) account of time-structuring among factory workers, Ditton's (1979) analysis of the time strategies of bakers, Cavendish's (1982) portrayal of time battles on the assembly line and Clark's (1978; 1982) attempts to link temporal experience with organization structure. Although these studies represent essentially isolated and unconscious attempts at paradigm building, they are important in that they move towards a nominalist ontology, produce explanations from ideographic data, and illustrate how time-structuring can be voluntarist as well as determinist. Above all, they describe how our everyday understanding of work is based on the experience and construction of recurrent 'event-times' (Clark 1982). As such, these cases offer examples on which to build an ethnographic, cyclic-qualitative paradigm for work-time research.

Roy: banana time   Of the above accounts, Roy's is probably the best known. In what has become a classic paper in industrial sociology, he outlines how workers who are subject to monotonous tasks make their experiences bearable by putting meaning into their (largely meaningless) days. In Roy's machine shop, the work was both long (twelve-hour day, six-day week) and tedious (simple machine operation). He describes how he nearly quit the work immediately when first confronted with the combination of the 'extra-long work-day, the infinitesimal cerebral excitement, and the extreme limitation of physical movement' (1960: 207). It was only on discovering the 'game of work' which existed within the shop that the job became bearable. The group in which he worked had established its own event-based, time-reckoning system for structuring the day, although it was one which took some time to understand. As the working day stretched out infinitely, the group punctuated it with several 'times', each of which was the signal for a particular form of social interaction. The regularity of 'peach time', 'banana time', 'window time', 'pick up time', 'fish time' and 'coke time', together with the specific themes (variations on 'kidding' themes and 'serious' themes) which accompanied each time, meant that instead of the day being endless *durée* it was transformed into a series of regular social activities. In place of one long time horizon, the day contained several short horizons. Roy explains that after his initial discouragement with the meagreness of the situation, he gradually began to appreciate how

> interaction was there, in constant flow. It captured attention and held interest to make the long day pass. The twelve hours of 'click, – move die, – click, – move die' became as easy to endure as eight hours of varied activity in the oil fields or eight hours of playing the piece work game in a machine shop. The 'beast of boredom' was gentled to the harmlessness of a kitten. (1960: 215)

Ditton: baking time   Ditton's (1979) analysis of the time perceptions of bakery workers is in the same tradition. Like Roy, he describes the social construction of time, and how workers develop 'consummatory acts to manage the monotony of time ... breaking endless time down into digestible fragments to make it psychologically manageable' (1979: 160). He illustrates how time is both handled differently and experienced differently according to the type of work being done. For example, in the bakery there were two main production lines – the 'big (loaf) plant' and the 'small (roll) plant' – each with a range of tasks. Whereas in the big plant the work was physically more difficult ('hot, hard and heavy'), it was preferred because the number and speed of events made the day pass quickly. In contrast, life on the small plant was made bearable only because slower production meant there were more opportunities to 'manipulate' time.

In the bakery study, not only do we see (as in Roy's study) the use of event-based time-reckoning to give meaning to the day, but further how such time-reckoning is strategic. Ditton shows not only how management and workforce possess different time strategies but, furthermore, how these are linked, directly, to their differing time orientations. Ditton distinguishes between the linear time orientation of management and the cyclic time orientation of workers. Management is consumed by the linearity of clock-time: with the calculation and division of duration, and with the unending rhythm of the machinery. Workers, on the other hand, use their knowledge of event cycles in order to control time. The bakers possessed a whole repertoire of 'unofficial instrumental acts' for exercising control over the pace of the line. Ditton's work is aimed, specifically, at showing how these acts were appropriated in five main ways, that is, as strategies for 'making time', 'taking time twice', 'arresting time', 'negotiating time' and 'avoiding time'. In the bakery, individual work roles were evaluated according to their potential for manipulating time to a worker's advantage.

Cavendish: doing time   Cavendish (1982) is another to show the strategic importance of time in the workplace. In her account of women assembly workers 'doing time', she portrays time as fundamental to a global struggle between capital and labour. As time was what the assemblers were paid for, sharp distinctions were made between 'our time and their time'. Time obedience was the crucial discipline that management had to enforce, with skirmishes over clocking-off being more than just symbolic:

> they were real attempts by them to encroach on our time and, by us, to resist such encroachments...UMEC counted the minutes between 4.10 and 4.15 in lost UMO's, and every day the last few minutes before lunch and before the end of the afternoon were tense – each side tried to see what it could get away with. (1982: 117)

Like Roy and Ditton, Cavendish outlines how working time is not only an objective boundary condition, but also a subjective state; time was experienced differently according to the social situations the work group faced. Indeed working on the line 'changed the way you experienced time altogether...the minutes and hours went very slowly but the days passed very quickly once they were over, and the weeks rushed by' (1982: 117). There was a general consensus among the women as to the speed at which time was passing: 'Everyone agreed whether the morning was fast or slow, and whether the afternoon was faster or slower than the morning' (1982: 112). Similar to Roy's machine operatives, the women at UMEC developed time 'rituals', which served both to 'make the day go faster and divide up the week...all the days were the same, but we made them significant by their small dramas' (1982: 115).

However, while Cavendish, like Roy, shows how such events gave work days a sense of temporal structure, she delves deeper into the phenomenology of the situation and makes us aware of the personal time strategies within the network of meaning. In the interstices between rituals/events, or simply during periods when time seemed unusually burdensome, the women would devise personal strategies for 'getting through' the day. Cavendish explains how:

> Sometimes 7.30 to 9.10 seemed like several days itself, and I would redivide it up by starting on my sandwiches at 8 am. I would look at the clock when we'd already been

working for ages, and find it was still only 8.05, or, on very bad days 7.50.... Then I
redivided the time into half hours, and ten-minute periods to get through, and worked
out how many UMO's I'd have done in ten minutes, twenty minutes and half an hour.
(1982: 113)

Group members would adopt different strategies for getting through these
periods: 'Arlene was deep in memories, and Alice sang hymns to herself. Grace
always found something to laugh about, and Daphne watched everything that
went on' (1982: 115). In general, older workers were better at 'handling' time. In
particular, the older women were adept at 'going inside', or deciding to cut off
from chatting in order to pass the time by daydreaming.

In Cavendish's account organizational time was also reckoned differently
according to the day of the working week. She notes how Monday was a good
day time-wise, because it was the first day of the week and everyone was fresh ('it
seemed a long time since Friday'), and because the group could catch up on the
weekend's news. Tuesday, however, was a 'very bad day' because it wasn't special
in any sense. On Wednesday the supervisor came around with the bonus points
which would form part of the basis for Thursday's pay. This made Wednesday
bearable; first, because the bonus points gave the group a vehicle for ritual
discussion, and second because, as the points were related to the pay packet, it
gave the impression that it was 'almost Thursday', and thus near to the end of the
week: 'By Wednesday lunchtime, people would say half the week was over and we
could see our way to Friday afternoon'. Although Thursday was pay day, it could
be experienced as a long day. This was mainly because the pay slips arrived in the
first half of the morning. However, the pay slips often served as a vehicle to give
the group 'a few minutes interest', especially if one of the packets had been
calculated incorrectly. Friday, although being the last day of the week, was also
a slow day as there were few external incidents to supplement the group's own
daily rituals. Apart from the horizon of subsidized fish and chips at lunchtime, the
day was a long haul to finishing at 4.10. At the end of the afternoon the women
always tried to spin out the last break by an extra five minutes, so there was only
half an hour or so to finishing time.

Clark: the temporal repertoire   Finally, some of the most innovative of case
work in this area has been by Clark (1978; 1982), who in studies of two contrasting
industries – sugar beet processing and hosiery manufacture – illustrates how
temporal differentiation represents a crucial link between a firm's culture and its
structure. One of the few writers to make this link, Clark argues that in depicting
organizations in a static mode sociologists have failed to consider how structures
'vary rhythmically' (1978: 406). Following Kuznets (1933), Sorokin (1943) and
Etzioni (1961), he suggests that all large firms experience periodic differences in
the intensity of production or service, and that these changes bring differences to
the organization's character and culture.

In sugar beet production, Clark notes how the time frame 'contains two sharply
contrasting sets of recurring activities' (1978: 12). He notes the marked differences
in activities and attitudes between the period of sugar beet processing ('100–20
days after 26 September') and the rest of the year ('when the factory is dismantled

and rebuilt by the labour force') (1978: 12). Clark highlights the cultural rhythms that ebb and flow during these two periods: he illustrates the excitement at the commencement of the 'campaign' ('26 September onwards'); how 'start-up' is full of anticipation; and how processing seems to change the relationships between the men and their families. Clark also notes, however, that as the campaign 'matures' the workforce becomes somewhat alienated from the work, the corollary being open expressions of control by management. Indeed, by January the workforce comes to welcome the second major transitional period, when, after the processing is completed, the men are dispersed to relatively self-regulating groups with distinct tasks.

In seeking a concept with which to analyse this 'structural and cultural flexibility' Clark (1982) draws upon the anthropology of Gearing (1958) and the notion of the 'structural pose'. The structural pose is a concept which denotes: the set of rules for categorizing a recurring situation; the type of social actors required for the situation; and the forms of action that should be employed. Gearing located four main structural poses in the organization of the Cherokee Indian village of the eighteenth century. He gave the example of the cue of the red flag which, although ostensibly representing the signal for conducting warfare against another village, also acted as the signal for organizing the village on a clan basis under the council of elders, and for allocating specific roles among the village community. He insists, however, that the concept does not simply imply a set of organizing procedures, for the same pose can be evoked for situations which, although of a qualitatively different nature, are deemed to require similar structural responses (for example, playing ball against another village).

For organizations, Clark uses the concept to denote how similar sequences fit several occasions. Structural poses are the tacit rules of conduct shared by those familiar with relationships between the organization's structure and culture; they are keys to anticipation and intersubjectivity, and are founded on experience; they are blueprints which suggest the actions to take in response to certain sets of circumstances.

This is well demonstrated in Clark's second study, concerning a marketing group within a large hosiery firm, and how it drew on its structural poses to account for, and react to, a major seasonal shift in fashion and demand. The case involved a comparison between two of the firm's marketing departments and how each handled this major shift. The two groups were from different divisions and located in different parts of the country. With regard to personnel, while one division (Acorn) was composed mainly of experienced staff, the other (Harp) comprised marketing managers new to the industry. Clark shows how, of these groups, only the Acorn team were able to anticipate and handle the change satisfactorily. They were able to respond to the situation by 'activat[ing] a structural arrangement by which employees in various parts of the firm were redesignated as members of an innovation group' (1982: 31). In contrast the Harp team who in the short four-year history of the site had only experienced seasons of expanded production, interpreted the poor sales figures as being merely the result of a bad season:

It was some time before they realized that a major shift in style was unfolding. When they did realize, they had neither the credibility nor the capability to achieve the appropriate collateral structure for innovation. It was not in the structural repertoire of Harp Mill. (1982: 31)

Clark argues that organizations possess whole repertoires of structural poses based on the premise of temporal recursiveness. In developing such repertoires, employees are able to account for the recurrent, but varying, rhythms of the organization, and thus for its heterogeneous time-reckoning system. Clark's marketing study, in particular, illustrates the links between temporal experience, structural differentiation and strategic time-reckoning. It indicates how organizations, over time, develop mechanisms for activating new structures from their repertoires in order to deal with anticipated events in the environment. Instead of the case turning on the linear, clock-time metaphor, it highlights the importance of cyclic, event-based trajectories.

Organizations, careers and temporal structuring

Having examined images of time in work and industrialism, we now consider temporal aspects of organization. We describe how individuals learn time discipline through membership of formal organizations such as the family and the school, institutions which prepare them for the organization demanding the greatest time discipline of all, the workplace. We also note how on gaining entry into a workplace, individuals embark upon a 'career', a process which sees them constantly evaluated in time-related terms. The focus shifts, subsequently, to the study of 'organizations in themselves'. The ontological emphasis changes as organizations are portrayed as systems which have time problems of their own. We look specifically at the temporal resources of work organizations, and assess the difficulties such institutions face in controlling temporal assets. In so doing, we draw upon the works of Moore (1963b), Lauer (1980), and McGrath and Rotchford (1983) to describe the measures organizations take for resolving problems of scheduling, allocation and synchronization.

Coming to terms with organization

Time is an inherent quality of human life. The sheer nature of existence prompts awareness of temporal differences between, for example, hunger and satisfaction, comfort and pain, and waking and dreaming. We first place structure on existence by assimilating times which have a natural and physiological basis.

Despite the potency of such natural times, we must remember that many of our physiological times become linked, inextricably, to social times. As an infant is unable to sustain life unaided, its physical well-being becomes dependent not only on its capacity to demand, but also on the willingness of those responsible for it to meet such demands. Given the nature of this relationship, the infant has no other

27

choice than to allow the timing of demands to be regulated by social convention. Gradually needs become influenced by social constraints which dictate the 'correct' times for feeding, drinking, sleeping etc. As the process of physical development is joined by social development, so the infant begins to appreciate time as a vehicle which brings it within the orbit of human organization.

So that individuals may function adequately in society, they must, therefore, come to terms with the temporality which underlies social organization. Although physiological time needs persist throughout life, and while there are limits to the social ingenuity which can be placed upon their structuring, nevertheless social convention comes in time to regulate their satisfaction. The dominance of the physiological as the basis for action is seen to moderate and then to decline as the individual matures. Physiological demand gives way to social performance; biological decree succumbs to social negotiation. While our sense of temporality is founded on the biology of the human organism, it becomes refined and ordered by participation in society and culture. In maturation, individuals learn to organize temporal experience in accordance with particular social and cultural processes.

For the infant, the temporal parameters of its actions become modified from their basis in physiological need to a new locus in the normative structures of an organization, the family. The development of social relations with parents and siblings signals that experience has become increasingly controlled, and that the infant has grasped a sense of organization. The acceptance of normative constraints sees physiological needs – for multiple feeds, or for sleeping during the middle of the day – deferred in favour of alternative possibilities, such as play. Through time, the infant becomes aware of how its actions are organized into formal patterns by agents in its environment.

This familiarization with the temporal structures of the family in turn prepares the child for a further, more formal, encounter with organization, the school. It is at school that the child experiences a more rigid temporal discipline, from the fixed lengths of daily and weekly attendance, to the formal separation of activities. The school day is segmented into precise temporal units, with each unit devoted to a specific topic or task. The child learns that school has a primary claim on time. Children learn that the school's organization of time must be accepted as legitimate, even when the school extends its temporal influence beyond its physical boundaries, as for example in the assignment of homework.

Above all, the formal time-structuring of the school prepares the individual for the institution demanding the greatest time discipline of all, the work organization. Joining a formal work organization represents the final stage in conditioning the individual to an 'organized' time consciousness. While earlier we noted how in most primitive and developing economies work systems either are, or have been, primarily task-oriented, in modern economies they are time-oriented. In the factory or office employees are held to minimum temporal standards: their work day is characterized by known temporal parameters and constraints. Through the combination of minute specialization and fine measurement, employees become subject not merely to temporal cycles based on the week, day or hour, but to ones defined by minutes or even seconds.

Externality and specialization   Our analysis begins to suggest that while individuals experience time as natural and inherent, and while subjective awareness of time becomes expressed in the construction of intersubjective temporal meanings, nevertheless, in modern society pressures for synchronization force time sense to become objectified and constrained. In order to be organized, individuals must subscribe to times which are rational but external.

As societies have become increasingly complex, work organizations become primary claimants of social time. In modern societies the formal, external organization has replaced the family as the main locus of time-structuring. As the family has lost many of its functions to outside agencies, it has likewise relinquished claims on its members' time. Familial functions have been surrendered in line with greater specialization around distinct foreign agencies. Social functions have become the province of organizations such as the state, the factory, the shop and the school. Notable here has been the externalization of child education, and the removal from the home of the main forms of economic production. Despite a qualified return to homeworking, the only significant productive functions which remain in the home are those of cooking, cleaning, childcare, laundry and shopping.

In the wake of this specialization, family members devote their time, typically, to performing one particular role within a single place of work. Modern employment practice has demanded that we acquire expertise in one specific field. It demands that we develop skills relevant to a particular 'career'. As individuals have since long exchanged 'organic utility' for 'mechanistic specialization' (Laslett 1965), so their worth has become checked against a linear, external and generic social instrument, the career 'ladder'. Increasingly, success or failure is judged on one criterion, the timing of personal accomplishments.

The career   The career has become the dominant model for contemporary employment. As a concept it has become ingrained into everyday common sense and culture. When Western adults meet for the first time, the question they ask – 'What do you do?' – begs an answer that is singular, functional and career-oriented; it begs an answer that is status-loaded and linear; an answer that can be indexed directly to the wider social structure.

The notion of career is thus central to an assessment of the social position: it is the definer *par excellence* of the individual's progress in organized society; it is the central element in the list of social times which regulate biographies and determine personal worth. Society determines a normative time chart for its members, and it is according to this chart that we construct appropriate timetables and schedules for living. So important are these timetables that individuals construct their biographies no longer simply by passing through states determined by nature, but more importantly by reference to the sophisticated, normative structures of social life. An individual's biography is evaluated according to the rate and sequence with which he or she passes through what Glaser and Strauss (1965) term 'status passages': that is, though stages which relate the various positions and identities available in society.

The career thus charts how an individual has passed through a socially recognized and meaningful sequence of related events. As Hughes (1971: 137) puts it, the career is 'the moving perspective in which the person sees his life as a whole and interprets the meaning of his various attributes, actions, and the things which happen to him'. Through time, individuals develop a perspective in which their careers are endowed with particular meanings and values. As the person passes from one stage to another, this perspective serves as a basis for assessment. Careers give the individual an acute sense of social time, and we think of ourselves in terms of a career path which includes the states of past, present and future. As we move from status to status, from organization to organization, we become sensitive to our relative position on the ladder of social biography. We ask: are we living too rapidly or not rapidly enough? Is the pace of our biography concordant with the ideal? The career timetable is socially sanctioned and based on a normative assessment of achievement; it prescribes the normal time for a person to pass from position to position. Individuals who are seen to progress at a rate faster or slower than normal risk being identified as age deviates. Anyone who departs from age-related normalcy is likely to be attributed with extraordinary skills, qualities or characteristics.

In modern societies, then, the relationship between age and career has become highly structured and formalized. Many organizations, starting with the school, provide detailed inventories which compare age with skill in order to arrive at selection. In large work organizations careers become interpreted in terms of age–grade relationships. Qualifications notwithstanding, an individual may simply be deemed too young or too old for higher office.

Organizations and temporal structuring

We now turn to the time problems faced by organizations as entities in themselves. Given the dominant conception of time in Western culture as scarce, valuable, homogeneous, linear and divisible, and given the dominant characteristics of work organizations as functional, specialized, formalized and rational, organizations are confronted with three key time problems: the reduction of temporal uncertainty; the resolution of conflicts over temporal activities; and the allocation of scarce temporal resources (McGrath and Rotchford 1983). In attempting to solve these problems, three temporal needs emerge: the need for time schedules (for reliable predictions of the points in time at which specific actions will occur); the need for synchronization (for temporal coordination among functionally segmented parts and activities); and the need for time allocations (for distributing time so that activities will consume it in the most efficient and rational way) (Moore 1963b). In this section, we analyse the relationships between these various problems and needs.

Uncertainty and control   For a structural analysis of temporal uncertainty, J. D. Thompson's (1967) classic text on organizational design, *Organizations in Action*, represents a valuable first model (see Clark 1982; McGrath and Rotchford 1983). In this work, Thompson contrasts problems of temporal structuring with those of organizational structuring. In focusing upon the changing nature of organizational environments, he brings out the difficulties encountered when organizations seek to establish stable and efficient time-structures. Thompson illustrates not only problems which stem from temporal uncertainty, but also those which arise when we apply generic solutions such as scheduling, synchronization and allocation.

A main theme of Thompson's analysis is that organizations have a technical core that requires protection against uncertainty. To operate successfully, an organization must comprehend, and as far as possible control, the numerous environmental forces which impinge on its activities. Whereas this may seem a straightforward task for organizations operating in stable environments, Thompson notes that for those operating in dynamic ones there is a need to protect the technical core through: 'buffering to absorb the uncertainty'; 'smoothing and levelling to reduce the amount of uncertainty'; and 'anticipating and adapting the environmental uncertainty so that it can be treated as a constant constraint within the organization's functions'. It is these strategies which make the interaction of organization and environment more predictable, because they reduce the uncertainty over the availability and timing of resources. In particular, it is these processes which illustrate the importance of efficient scheduling; for they suggest ways of resolving temporal uncertainty by increasing the predictability of when some event will occur and/or when some product will be available.

In developing this argument, Thompson outlines three types of intra-organizational interdependence, each of which, he suggests, requires a different type of co-ordination (see figure 1.1). First, he talks of 'pooled interdependence', where all organization units contribute to and are supported by the organization as a whole, and where co-ordination is achieved by employing standardized units and regulations. Second, he discusses 'sequential interdependence', where the outputs of one unit form inputs to another, and where co-ordination is achieved through planning. And third, he talks of 'reciprocal interdependence', where the outputs of one unit are inputs to all other units, and where co-ordination is achieved through ongoing mutual adjustment among units. His argument is that for organizations to operate efficiently these interdependencies must be co-ordinated rationally. Organizations must group units by type of interdependence into layers and departments. The purpose of such grouping is to minimize the costs associated with communication and decision/effort times. Groupings must be made first on the basis of reciprocally interdependent units, because they involve the greatest communication and decision/effort time. The second most time-costly to co-ordinate are sequentially interdependent units, so they have the next priority in hierarchical and departmental grouping. And, finally, as the pooled interdependent units are the least time-costly to co-ordinate, they are grouped only after the reciprocal and sequentially interdependent positions have been arranged.

Thompson suggests, therefore, that the major imperative in organizational structuring is the desire to minimize communication and decision/effort times. He argues that co-ordination through the standardized rules of pooled interdependence requires 'less frequent decisions and a smaller volume of communication during a specific period of operations than does planning, and planning calls for less decision and communication than does mutual adjustment' (1967: 56). Through this analysis, we see that a major reason why decision and

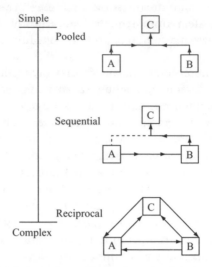

Figure 1.1 Types of task interdependence in organization design

communication activities incur costs is that they consume time: they use up scarce temporal resources.

Conflict over activities For our second problem – conflict over activities – we consider how functionally segmented actions can be co-ordinated through specialization and interpersonal norms.

In dealing with the co-ordination of segmented activities, we are concerned with questions of synchronization rather than with scheduling. We are concerned with: (a) the temporal patterning of an actor's multiple actions; (b) the temporal patterning of the actor's actions in relation to those of other actors; and (c) the temporal patterning of an actor's actions in relation to other objects or events (e.g. the timing of a machine, the activities of another unit). Such patterning is a problem in that it points to a need to operate within an elaborate set of procedures and norms.

As Weber (1947) described, the logic of organization is such that the larger and more complex an organization becomes, the greater functional specialization it will display. As functional specialization requires the synchronization of various parts and activities, the greater the need for temporal co-ordination of the various activities among the various parts. However, while the logic of specialization demands that each individual performs one function efficiently, this is at the cost of performing a number of functions overall. As activities become increasingly specialized, and in turn as their location in a temporal pattern becomes increasingly fixed, the greater the pressure to apply principles of formalization, or even to automate the whole activity. The irony here is that while the need for increased synchronization is a direct consequence of functional specialization, what is needed to accomplish this, the co-ordination of workers on individual tasks, violates one of the premises on which functional specialization is based, the interchangeability of parts.

Nevertheless, not all of an organization's activities are reducible to such tight specifications, nor is all temporal organizing so mechanical. There indeed remain many organizational activities which require the synchronizing of individuals – as subjective actors – as well as of processes. While these activities require temporal co-ordination, this is achieved not so much by mechanistic specialization, but by the organic process of developing implicit working norms.

Norms develop during interaction in order to synchronize the activities of participants. As failure to synchronize activities can be a major cost to both productive efficiency and group satisfaction, time norms emerge in order to reduce such costs. As we move from dyadic interaction to the activities of larger groups, synchronization of norms becomes all the more important, because the temporal and spatial needs of such large, complex systems become more demanding.

As norms take on an increasingly critical role, there is pressure to make them explicit. Eventually implicit regulatory norms become translated into explicit rules, regulations and standard operating procedures, with these formalized sets of expectations being associated with specific 'positions' or 'roles' in the organizational network. In the process of organizational growth, the norms by which actors regulate their actions become mere subsets of the role expectations extant in the formal organizational structure. No longer are behaviours indexed to particular individuals, groups and situations; instead they are objectified on to particular functions. It is the role which acts, not the actor. Positions which are formalized in the shape of recognized organizational procedures allow for expertise only within an established framework of regulations. Normative procedures become control devices which operate in the service of smooth temporal co-ordination; they effect explicit synchronization between the various activities of the organization's members (see Clark 1982: 22).

Scarcity   For the third problem, 'scarcity', we are concerned with matching productive activities to limited time allocations; that is, with 'the efficient assignment of temporal resources to tasks, hence the assignment of priorities or values to the tasks and assignment of responsibility for those tasks to staff' (McGrath and Rotchford 1983: 85). Our goals here are twofold: at the macro level, to balance temporal resources between units; and at the micro level, to obtain optimal matches between an employee's available time and the number of actions to be performed.

While in the next section we discuss scarcity issues at the macro level, we are concerned here with problems arising at the micro level. In particular we note how the matching of time and activities forms the basis for an employee's role/load problems, a form of stress which results from a perceived scarcity of time relative to the requirements of tasks to be performed. Role overload is an almost inevitable consequence of the interaction between Western time culture and modern forms of organization. This reflects the interaction of functional specialization, temporal and spatial segregation, synchronization and fine time measurement. In modern societies, adults are likely to divide their time between many spatially, functionally and temporally segregated organizations, in relation, for example, to work, the family, recreation and religion. These sophisticated time allocations, and the temporal precision that comes with them, can become double-edged. While on the one hand this makes synchronization within narrow time tolerances more feasible, on the other the ability to account for increasingly precise time allocations gives individuals scope to pack activities more tightly into their roles. This can have the effect of increasing: the perceived scarcity of time in each role; the precision required for synchronizing between roles; and the strains on the boundaries between roles.

Solving time problems in organizations

We finally describe some of the tactics which organizations use to cope with time scarcity. In particular we examine three ways of coping with tight temporal constraints: by adjusting the specific time locations of activities; by redistributing peak-time loads over other phases of time cycles; and by trying to recover time that would otherwise be lost (see McGrath and Rotchford 1983).

Altering time locations   For the first of the tactics, adjusting the specific time locations of activities, we refer to instances in which organizations need ways of freeing activities from their fixed locations in 'real' time. For example, the most pressing time problem for employees is the pressure to do two or more things simultaneously; or, in other words, the pressure imposed by multiple, conflicting demands either within one role or across two or more roles. The only solution to this problem is through time relocation: through having one or more of these events extracted from its location and rescheduled.

While some events are relatively amenable to temporal relocations, and can easily be extracted from context – processes which can be easily separated from related processes – others cannot be so readily extracted, and depend instead on being enacted at a specific place and time. While such temporal conflicts are not easily remedied, and while such problems must generally be solved by assigning priorities, nevertheless, technological developments have provided partial solutions. Video-taping, for example, has meant that we can record certain activities in real time and then react to them when convenient. This enables rescheduling, whereas previously the only viable solution would have been through prioritizing.

A related problem concerns the need for parts of activities to be accomplished in a fixed, temporally co-ordinated sequence. As work activities tend to be structured linearly, so that the sequence covers a substantial period of real time, this can be problematic in two ways: (a) because the total time required may not allow the task sequence to be accomplished quickly enough or (b) because the individual may not be able to commit sufficient time, at a given time, to the whole process. For these situations, methods are required for uncoupling the sequence linkages between substages of the task, so that constituent subtasks can be accomplished in temporal isolation.

For the first problem, large tasks are often subdivided into substages which are then executed in temporal parallel. Although this does not save time, in the sense of the hours used, it serves to get the whole task completed sooner in real time, even though a price may be paid in terms of the detailed co-ordination of the separately executed parts. Similarly, for the latter problem, a large task may be divided into several small segments that can be accomplished over a wide stretch of real time. For example, when prioritizing tasks, organizations often arrange for certain jobs to be accomplished only when no urgent work is at hand, such as maintenance, safety and renovation.

Distributing time loads   For the second coping strategy, redistributing peak-time loads, we are concerned with the reallocation of activities in order to make better use of the system capacity as a whole. In other words, we wish to operate more effectively by either increasing capacity during periods of low load or increasing capability during periods of high load.

In practice, the former often involves experiments in 'inverse pricing', or attempts to encourage demand during unfashionable or low-load periods. Common methods for accomplishing this are, for example, offering 'off-peak' rates for electricity, telephones, transport and advertising; 'off-season' rates for holidays and flights; and 'end-of-season' prices for clothes and sporting equipment.

During periods of high demand, organizations simply provide more capability, notably by getting more staff-hours devoted to peak-load activities. As markets have become more volatile, organizations have also started to balance loads by distinguishing between core and peripheral workforces, again so as to buffer against uncertainty. In order to balance staff demands with market demands, organizations have recruited a greater percentage of employees on short, fixed-term contracts, which offer little protection under employment law. Similarly, because firms wish to keep labour costs to a minimum, recent decades have seen a growth in agencies supplying temporary, predominantly female, labour for generic tasks at short notice, a practice commonly referred to as 'temping'.

Reclaiming time   The techniques above reflect strategies for avoiding time waste in work systems. However, despite our desire to eliminate temporal waste, the very logic of modern organization – functional specialization and temporal segregation – means that certain pieces of time are inevitably lost. As specialization and segregation encourage planning in ever more precise temporal divisions, so the very fact of slicing work into smaller intervals means that silvers of time are lost in the process.

Other arenas of 'wasted' time are those of travelling and waiting. While in one sense these sections of time are 'filled', in that they are dedicated to specific purposes, to most of us they represent intervals which are empty. As such, they are time spaces open to development. Many commuters for instance use up travelling time by writing reports, dictating letters or simply reading work-related literature. For others, travelling to work now represents an opportunity to conduct business with the office or with customers direct, through the use of car or other portable phones.

Finally, and related to the above, is the double use of time that is filled not with waiting, but with activity. Time can sometimes be 'saved' by the purposeful combining of activities which, while different in nature, are oriented towards the same functional end. Examples of these are the working lunch and the executive golf game. The aim of both is to enhance business dealings by making the interaction between the parties less formal.

Conclusions

In the early sections of the [reading], we outlined how industrial sociologists have portrayed the dominant image of time as objective, measurable, highly valued and scarce. The emphasis is upon rationality and homogeneity, and the view that time is quantifiable and evenly distributed. We accept that employment defines the pivotal time around which all other social times are structured. As economic performance is assessed by the number of hours it takes to produce certain goods, time is given a commodity image. A corollary of this is the portrayal of work organizations as marvels of synchronicity; contemporary production systems, with their fine arithmetic assembly operations, are held to be the most rational of technologies: they, more than anything, epitomize quantitative time-reckoning.

However, in concentrating upon quantitative time, industrial sociologists have overlooked the importance of qualitative time. Stress has been placed on time-structuring rather than experience. The focus has been upon how time is formally patterned in task systems rather than the way it is 'interpreted' in task execution. In concentrating upon temporal structuring, and thus in treating time as a hard, objective and homogeneous facility, we have neglected how it is experienced as a soft, subjective and heterogeneous abstraction.

Indeed, from the complex relationships linking production systems, labour and the environment, there emerge whole ranges of time patterns and rhythms. New employees learn these rhythms gradually, through experiencing how the character of work changes according to the particular time period being endured. While most work roles are structured according to a formal inventory of activities, new recruits discover the meaning of work by reference to an informal typology of events. Tasks are categorized not only in relation to explicit work schedules, but also according to the group's own personal and social constructs. As we noted in Ditton's study, time is one of the major criteria here. The experience of work is inextricably linked to the way time is socially constructed.

Thus, we have argued that industrial sociology needs research which accesses not only the concrete facts of time-structuring, but also the subjective essences of temporal meanings. While the discipline's conceptions of time are based, predominantly, on metaphors of linearity, rationality and quantification, we have illustrated how these images are overstated; they proffer a truncated awareness of time by ignoring the subjective and irrational features of time at work. By turning to the French and American traditions in the sociology of time, we have suggested that at the interface of sociology, philosophy and anthropology lies a position more sensitive to temporal heterogeneity – a position capable of illuminating the cyclical and qualitative features of working time.

In the third section of the [reading], we have analysed the complex relationship between time and organization. As we enter the world of affairs, we find that a major function of socialization is the structuring of our time sense within formal institutions. Notable here is the process whereby school and workplace teach us rigid time disciplines; they segment activities into precise temporal units and condition us to an 'organized' time consciousness. This conditioning sees us subscribe to times which are external and specialized, times which are technocratic. In the West, the external and highly specialized organization has become not only the main regulator of social time, but also its primary claimant.

In organized society, we structure our actions according to what we feel are 'proper' social times. We base our temporal understanding on practices we learn from the environment. In dealing with sophisticated social structures, we develop ways of expressing our needs for co-ordinated acts. To reproduce order, we create common definitions and assumptions in regard to the location of events in time. In particular, we form common understandings of synchronization, sequence and rate. Given the increasing scope of human communication – and thus the problem of dealing with a plurality of times – we seek means by which diverse groups can adjust their actions to meet the challenges of mutual dependence: we require general temporal agreements so that we can relate processes in ways which avoid activities becoming conflictual. This is especially necessary in situations where actions must be regulated in order to give scope for each to fulfil its potential.

Temporal structuring is thus at the heart of organization. When organizations are designed or changed, temporal factors are of primary concern. As the logic of organization is such that with increased size comes greater specialization, time emerges as a central feature of structuring. Time is basic to resolving problems of environmental uncertainty, conflicts over activities and the allocation of scarce resources. Synchronization, sequence and rate are critical factors when we seek predictions of when specific actions will occur relative to others; when we attempt to co-ordinate functionally segmented parts and activities; and when we want to distribute time so that activities consume it in the most efficient manner. In competitive markets, organizations are driven to find new ways of reducing communication and decision/effort times. They seek new techniques for reducing levels of conflict between activities, and in particular for effecting superior co-ordination, through meshing sophisticated specialization with appropriate cultural/normative values.

NOTE

From J. Hassard (1996), 'Images of Time in Work and Organization', in S. Clegg, C. Hardy and W. R. Nord, eds, *Handbook of Organization Studies* (London: Sage), pp. 581–98.

REFERENCES

Atkinson, J. (1984), 'Manpower strategies for flexible organizations', *Personnel Management*, August, pp. 28–31.

Best, E. (1922), 'The Maori division of time', *Dominion Museum Monograph*, vol. 4.

Braverman, H. (1974), *Labor and Monopoly Capital: The Degradation of Work in the Twentieth Century* (New York and London: Monthly Review Press).

Cavendish, R. (1982), *Women on the Line* (London: Routledge & Kegan Paul).

Clark, P.A. (1978), 'Temporal innovations and time structuring in large organizations', in J.T. Fraser, N. Lawrence and D. Park, eds, *The Study of Time*, vol. 3 (New York: Springer-Verlag).

Clark, P.A. (1982), 'A review of the theories of time and structure for organisational sociology', working paper no. 248, Management Centre, Aston University, UK.

Clark, P.A., L. Hantrais, J.S. Hassard, D. Linhart and K.P. Starkey (1984), 'The porous day and *temps choisi*', paper presented at the Third Annual Organization and Control of the Labour Process Conference, Aston University, UK.

Clegg, S. (1990), *Modern Organizations: Organization Studies in the Postmodern World* (London: Sage).

Codrington, R.H. (1891), *The Melanesians* (Oxford).

de Grazia, S. (1972), 'Time and work', in H. Yaker, H. Osmond and F. Cheek, eds, *The Future of Time* (New York: Anchor Books).

Ditton, J. (1979), 'Baking time', *Sociological Review*, vol. 27, pp. 157–67.

Durkheim, E. (1976), *The Elementary Forms of the Religious Life*, 2nd edn (London: George Allen & Unwin).

Eliade, M. (1959), *Cosmos and History: The Myth of the Eternal Return* (New York: Harper & Row).

Etzioni, A. (1961), *A Comparative Analysis of Complex Organizations*, (New York: Free Press).

Evans-Pritchard, E.E. (1940), *The Nuer* (Oxford: Oxford University Press).

Fabian, J. (1983), *Time and the Other: How Anthropology Makes its Object* (New York: Columbia University Press).

Gale, R., ed. (1968), *The Philosophy of Time: A Collection of Essays* (Sussex: Harvester).

Gearing, E. (1958), 'The structural poses of the 18th century Cherokee villages', *American Anthropologist*, vol. 60, pp. 1148–57.

Gioscia, V. (1972), 'On social time', in H. Yaker, H. Osmond and F. Cheek, eds, *The Future of Time* (New York: Anchor Books).

Glaser, B. G. and A. Strauss (1965), 'Temporal aspects of dying', *American Journal of Sociology*, vol. 71, pp. 48–59.

Graham, R.J. (1981), 'The perception of time in consumer research', *Journal of Consumer Research*, vol. 7, pp. 335–42.

Gurdon, P.T.R. (1914), *The Khasis* (London).

Gurvitch, G. (1964), *The Spectrum of Social Time* (Dordrecht: D. Reidel).

Hassard, J. (1990), 'Introduction', in J. Hassard, ed., *The Sociology of Time* (London: Macmillan).

Hassard, J. (1993), *Sociology and Organization Theory: Positivism, Paradigms and Post-modernity* (Cambridge: Cambridge University Press).

Heath, L.R. (1956), *The Concept of Time* (Chicago: University of Chicago Press).

Hodson, T.C. (1908), *The Meitheis* (London).

Hubert, H. (1905), 'Étude sommaire de la représentation du temps dans la religion et la magie', *Annuaire de l'École Pratique des Hautes Études*, pp. 1–39.

Hubert, H. and Mauss, M. (1909), *Mélanges d'histoire des religions* (Paris: Alcan).

Hughes, E.C. (1971), *The Sociological Eye* (New York: Aldine).

Isambert, F.-A. (1979), 'Henri Hubert et la sociologie du temps', *Revue française de sociologie*, vol. 20, pp. 183–204.

Jacques, E. (1982), *The Form of Time* (London: Heinemann).

Julkunnen, R.A. (1977), 'A contribution to the categories of social time and the economies of time', *Acta Sociologica*, vol. 20, pp. 5–24.

Kamata, S. (1982), *Life in the Passing Lane: An Insider's Account of Life in a Japanese Auto Factory* (London: Counterpoint).

Kroeber, A.L. (1923), *Anthropology* (New York: Harcourt Brace).

Kuznets, S. (1933), *Seasonal Variations in Industry and Trade* (New York: National Bureau of Economic Research).

Lakoff, G. and Johnson, M. (1980), *Metaphors We Live By* (Chicago: University of Chicago Press).

Landes, D.S. (1983), *Revolution in Time: Clocks and the Making of the Modern World* (Cambridge, MA: Belknap Press of Harvard University Press).

Laslett, P. (1965), *The World We Have Lost* (London: Methuen).

Lauer, R.H. (1980), *Temporal Man* (New York: Praeger).

McGrath, J.E. and N.L. Rotchford (1983), 'Time and behaviour in organizations', *Research in Organizational Behaviour*, vol. 5, pp. 57–101.

McKendrick, N. (1962), 'Josiah Wedgwood and the factory discipline', *The Historical Journal*, vol. 4, pp. 30–5.

Manning, P. (1979), 'Metaphors of the field', *Administrative Science Quarterly*, vol. 24, pp. 660–71.

Marx, K. (1976), *Capital* (1867), vol. 1 (Harmondsworth: Penguin).

Mauss, M. (1966), *Sociologie et anthropologie* (Paris: Presses Universitaires de France).

Moore, W.E. (1963a), *Man, Time and Society* (New York: Wiley).

Moore, W.E. (1963b), 'The temporal structure of organizations', in E.A. Tiryakian, ed., *Sociological Theory, Values and Sociocultural Change* (New York: Free Press).

Morgan, G. (1986), *Images of Organization* (New York: Sage).

Mumford, L. (1934), *Technics and Civilisation* (New York: Harcourt, Brace & World).

Nilsonn, P. (1920), *Primitive Time Reckoning* (London: Oxford University Press).

Nowotny, H. (1976), 'Time structuring and time measurement', in J.T. Fraser and N. Lawrence, eds, *The Study of Time*, vol. 2 (New York: Springer).

Nyland, C. (1986), 'Capitalism and the history of work-time thought', *British Journal of Sociology*, vol. 37, pp. 513–34; reprinted as chapter 8 in J. Hassard, ed., *The Sociology of Time* (London: Macmillan, 1990).

Park, D. (1980), *The Image of Eternity: Roots of Time in the Physical World* (Amherst, MA: University of Massachussetts Press).

Pinder, C. and L. Moore (1979), 'The resurrection of taxonomy to aid the development of middle range theories of organization behaviour', *Administrative Science Quarterly*, vol. 24, pp. 99–118.

Pollert, A. (1988), 'The flexible firm: fixation or fact?', *Work, Employment and Society*, vol. 2, pp. 281–316.

Pronovost, G. (1986), 'Time in a sociological and historical perspective', *International Social Science Journal*, vol. 107, pp. 5–18.

Reid, D.A. (1976), 'The decline of Saint Monday', *Past and Present*, vol. 71, pp. 76–101.

Roy, D.F. (1960), 'Banana time: job satisfaction and informal interaction', *Human Organization*, vol. 18, pp. 156–68; reprinted as chapter 9 in J. Hassard, ed., *The Sociology of Time* (London: Macmillan, 1990).

Sorokin, P.A. (1943), *Sociocultural Causality, Space and Time* (Durham, NC: Duke University Press).

Sorokin, P.A. and R.K. Merton (1937), 'Social time: a methodological and functional analysis', *American Journal of Sociology*, vol. 42, pp. 615–29.

Starkey, K.P. (1988), 'Time and the labour process: a theoretical and empirical analysis', paper presented at the Labour Process Conference, Aston University, UK.

Taylor, F.W. (1911), *Principles of Scientific Management* (New York: Harper).

Thompson, E.P. (1967), 'Time, work-discipline and industrial capitalism', *Past and Present*, vol. 38, pp. 56–97.

Thompson, J.D. (1967), *Organizations in Action* (New York: McGraw-Hill).

Thrift, N. (1990), 'Owners' time and own time: the making of a capitalist time consciousness 1300–1800', in J. Hassard, ed., *The Sociology of Time* (London: Macmillan).

Tinker, T. (1986), 'Metaphor or reification?', *Journal of Management Studies*, vol. 23, pp. 363–84.

Weber, M. (1947), *The Theory of Social and Economic Organization* (Glencoe, IL: Free Press).

Wright, L. (1968), *Clockwork Man* (London: Elek).

2 Technology

Technology is Society made Durable

BRUNO LATOUR

[...]

For a long time social theory has been concerned with defining power relations (Barnes 1988), but it has always found it difficult to see how domination is achieved. In this [reading] I argue that in order to understand domination we have to turn away from an exclusive concern with social relations and weave them into a fabric that includes non-human actants, actants that offer the possibility of holding society together as a durable whole. To be sure, the distinction between material infrastructure and symbolic superstructure has been useful to remind social theory of the importance of non-humans, but it is a very inaccurate portrayal of their mobilization and engagement inside the social links. This [reading] aims to explore another repertoire for studying this process of mobilization. [...] I will use a very simple example to illustrate what I believe to be the right focus for detecting the entry point of techniques into the human collective. [...] I [they] will try to explain how stability and domination may be accounted for once non-humans are woven into the social fabric.

From context and content to association and substitution

Consider a tiny innovation commonly found in European hotels: attaching large cumbersome weights to room keys in order to remind customers that they should leave their key at the front desk every time they leave the hotel instead of taking it along on a tour of the city. An imperative statement inscribed on a sign – 'Please leave your room key at the front desk before you go out' – appears to be not enough to make customers behave according to the speaker's wishes. Our fickle customers seemingly have other concerns, and room keys disappear into thin air. But if the innovator, called to the rescue, *displaces* the inscription by introducing a large metal weight, the hotel manager no longer has to rely on his customers' sense of moral obligation. Customers suddenly become only too happy to rid themselves of this annoying object which makes their pockets bulge and weighs down their handbags: they go to the front desk of their own accord to get rid of it. Where the sign, the inscription, the imperative, discipline or moral obligation all failed, the hotel manager, the innovator and the metal weight succeeded. And yet, obtaining such discipline has a price: the hotel manager had to ally himself with an innovator, and the innovator had to ally herself with various metal weights and their manufacturing processes.

This minor innovation clearly illustrates the fundamental principle underlying all studies of science and technology: the *force* with which a speaker makes a statement is never enough, *in the beginning*, to predict the path that the statement will follow. This path depends on what successive listeners do with the statement. If the listener – in this case the hotel customer – forgets the order inscribed on the sign, or if he doesn't speak the language, the statement is reduced to a bit of paint on the piece of board. If the scrupulous customer obeys the order, he has complied with the imperative, thereby adding reality to it. The strength of the statement thus depends in part on what is written on the sign, and in part on what each listener does with the inscription. A thousand different customers will follow a thousand different paths after reading the order. In order to be able to predict the path, the hotel manager has two choices. He can either make all the customers equal by ensuring that they will know how to read the language and that they will know that going to a hotel in Europe means that one has a private, locked room but that the key must be left at the desk upon exiting the hotel every day. Or he can *load* his statement in such a way that lots of different customers all behave in the same manner, regardless of their native language or their experience with hotels. The choice is between incorporation and excorporation.

The grammatical imperative acts as a first load – 'leave your keys'; the inscription on the sign is a second load; the polite word 'please', added to the imperative to win the good graces of the customer constitutes a third; the mass of the metal weight adds a fourth. The number of loads that one needs to attach to the statement depends on the customers' resistance, their carelessness, their savagery and their mood. It also depends on how badly the hotel manager wants to control his customers. And finally, it depends on the cleverness of the customers. The *programmes* of the speaker get more complicated as they respond to the *anti-programmes* of the listeners. If a weird client could break the ring connecting the light key to the heavy weight, the innovator would then have to add a soldered ring to prevent such breakage. This is an anti-anti-programme. If a paranoid hotel manager wanted to ensure zero key loss, he could place a guard at each door to search the customers – but then he would probably lose his customers instead. It is *only* once most of these anti-programmes are countered that the path taken by the statement becomes *predictable*. The customers obey the order, with only a few exceptions, and the hotel manager accepts the loss of a few keys.

But the order that is obeyed is *no longer the same* as the initial order. It has been *translated*, not *transmitted*. In following it, we are not following a sentence through the context of its application, nor are we moving from language to the praxis. The programme, 'leave your key at the front desk', which is now scrupulously executed by the majority of the customers, is simply not the one we started with. Its displacement has transformed it. Customers no longer leave their room keys: instead, they get rid of an unwieldy object that deforms their pockets. If they conform to the manager's wishes, it is not because they read the sign, nor because they are particularly well mannered. It is because they cannot do otherwise. They don't even think about it. The statement is no longer the same, the customers are no longer the same, the key is no longer the same – even the hotel is no longer quite exactly the same (Akrich 1987; Latour 1992; Law 1986a).

This little example illustrates the 'first principle' of any study of innovation in science and technology: the fate of a statement is in the hands of others (Latour 1987b). Any vocabulary we might adopt to follow the engagement of non-humans into the social link should consider both the succession of hands that *trans*port a statement and the succession of *trans*formations undergone by that statement. To take these successive transformations into account, the very meaning of the word 'statement' must be clarified. By statement we mean anything that is thrown, sent or delegated by an enunciator. The meaning of the statement can thus vary along the way, and it does so as a function of the load imposed by the enunciator. Sometimes it refers to a word, sometimes to a sentence, sometimes to an object, sometimes to an apparatus and sometimes to an institution. In our example, the statement can refer to a sentence uttered by the hotel manager – but it also refers to a material apparatus which forces customers to leave their keys at the front desk. The word 'statement' therefore refers not to linguistics, but to the *gradient* that carries us from words to things and from things to words.

Even with such a simple example, we can already understand that when studying science and technology, we are not to follow a given statement through a *context*. We are to follow the simultaneous production of a 'text' and a 'context'. In other words, any division we make between society on the one hand and scientific or technical content on the other is necessarily arbitrary. The only non-arbitrary division is the succession of distinctions between 'naked' and 'loaded' statements. These, and *only these*, are the distinctions and successions which make up our socio-technical world. These are the ones we must learn to document and to record.

We wish to be able to follow both the *chain* of speakers and their statements and the *transformation* of speakers and their statements. We thus define two dimensions: association (akin to the linguist's syntagm) and substitution (or paradigm for the linguists). To simplify even further, we can think of these as the AND dimension, which is like latitude, and the OR dimension, which plays the role of longitude. Any engagement of non-humans can be traced both by its position on the AND–OR axes and by the recording of the AND and OR positions which have successively defined it. The vertical dimension corresponds to the exploration of substitutions, and the horizontal dimension corresponds to the number of actors which have attached themselves to the innovation (see Latour, Mauguin and Teil [forth coming]).

To trace a diagram on the example of the key, we will pick the hotel manager's point of view as an origin (see figure 2.1). He is the speaker or the enunciator – that is, the one who emits the statement. The track that the manager wishes his customers – the listeners – to follow we will call the *programme of action*. We

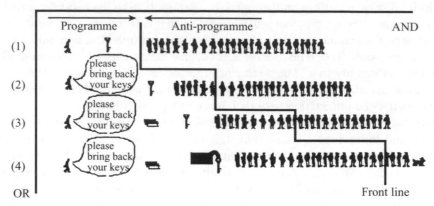

Figure 2.1 The key programme (1): the hotel manager successively adds keys, oral notices, written notices and finally metal weights; each time he modifies the attitude of some part of the 'hotel customers' group

shall use numbers in parentheses to enumerate the successive versions of a programme of action as seen from a single point of view. We will place all the programmes to the left of the chosen point of origin, and all the anti-programmes to the right. Let us also agree to enumerate the segments of the programmes of action with numbers in parentheses. Finally, let us agree to draw the dividing line between programmes and anti-programmes in bold face; this line corresponds to the front of the tiny controversy we are following here.

In version (4), the hotel manager and almost all of his customers are in agreement, while in version (1) the manager is the only one to wish for the return of his flighty keys. The syntagm or the association or the AND dimension have extended themselves in a lasting manner. But this extension to the right had a price: it became necessary to descend along the OR dimension by enriching the programme of action with a series of subtle translations. The manager's wishes are supplemented first by a sentence in the imperative [mood], then by a written sign and finally by metal weights. The customers were nibbled away at little by little: they finally abandoned their anti-programme and 'surrendered' to the programme. But the finances, the energy and the intelligence of the hotel manager have also been nibbled away at! In the beginning, the wish was naked; in the end – an end which can only be provisional, as other anti-programmes could always manifest themselves – it was clothed, or loaded. In the beginning it was unreal; in the end, it had gained some reality.

Such a diagram does not retrace the displacement of an immutable statement *within a context of use or application.* Nor does it retrace the displacement of a technical object – in this case a key weighed down by metal – within a context of use or application. Instead, it retraces a movement which is neither linguistic, nor social, nor technical, nor pragmatic. The diagram keeps track of successive changes undergone by customers, keys, hotels and hotel managers. It does this by recording the ways in which a (syntagmatic) displacement in the associations is 'paid for' by a (paradigmatic) displacement in the substitutions.

In such a diagram every move towards the right is to be paid by moving downward.

The degree of attachment of an actant to a programme of action varies from version to version. The terms 'actant' and 'degree of attachment' are symmetrical – that is, they apply indifferently to both humans and non-humans. The key is strongly attached to the weight by a ring, just as the manager is very attached to his keys. It does not matter here that the first link is called 'physical' and the second 'emotional' or 'financial' (Law 1986b; Bijker and Law 1992; Bijker, Hughes and Pinch 1986). The problem is precisely for the hotel manager to find a way to attach his keys to the front desk when his customers go out, and he does this by attaching his customers to the front desk in a stronger and more lasting manner than that with which the keys are attached to his customers' pockets or handbags!

We notice in the diagram that the social group of the hotel customers finds itself transformed little by little. The accumulation of elements – the will of the manager, the hardness of his words, the multiplicity of his signs, the weight of his keys – ends up trying the patience of some customers, who finally give up and agree to conspire with the manager, faithfully returning their keys. The group of customers which has not been enrolled at the (provisional) end is composed (according to the manager) either of folks of unmanageably bad faith or of exceptionally distracted professors. This gradual transformation, however, does not apply to the 'hotel customers' social group alone; it also applies to the keys. Suddenly, indifferent and undifferentiated keys have become 'European hotel keys' – very specific objects which we must now distinguish and isolate just as carefully as we did with clients. Herein lies the whole point of following innovations. Innovations show us that we never work in a world filled with actors to which fixed contours may be granted. It is not merely that their degree of attachment to a statement varies; their competence, and even their definition, can be transformed. These transformations undergone by actors are of crucial importance to us when we follow innovations, because they reveal that the unified actor – in this case, the hotel-customer-who-forgets-the-key – is itself an association made up of elements which can be redistributed. It is opening and closing these black boxes that, until now, have made understanding the entry points of innovations such a delicate process.

Note that in the case presented here the success of the innovation – that is, its extension toward the right from the manager's perspective – is only made possible by constantly *maintaining* the entire succession of accumulated elements. It is only because the hotel manager continues to want his keys back, reminds customers aloud, puts up signs and weights down the keys that he can finally manage to discipline his customers. It is this accumulation that gives the impression that we have gained some reality. But another scenario could be imagined (see figure 2.2).

The manager might ask his customers to leave their keys, but, after putting up a few signs, he feels that he's done enough and has nothing more to say. As a result, there are just as many customers who do not follow either the oral or the written instructions. A technicist at heart, our good man chooses a technical fix and proceeds to delegate all the work to the object. He weights down all his keys without bothering to put up signs or deliver oral instructions any more. He gets a

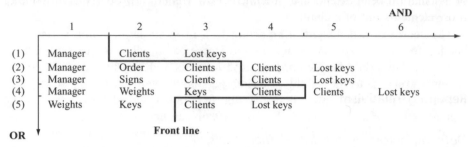

Figure 2.2 The key programme (2): variations of realization and de-realization of the socio-logics of the hotel key

few more customers to conspire with his wishes, but soon gets disgusted and abandons his programme. What is left in this case? A bunch of keys strongly attached to a bunch of metal weights by some beautiful metal rings, and customers who merrily carry the key-weight combination wherever they go. As for the hotel manager, no one knows what he wants any more. In this scenario the final version (5) would associate fewer elements from the point of view of the original enunciator and is thus, by our definition, less real. But for us, who wish to observe the mobilization of non-human into a human assembly, the only interesting reality is the *shape* of the front line. Whereas the asymmetry between the feasible and the unfeasible, the real and the imagined, or the realistic and the idealistic dominates most studies of innovation, our account only recognizes *variations of realization and de-realization*. The front line traced by the exploration of what holds and what does not hold together records the compatibilities and the incompatibilities of humans and non-humans – that is, the socio-logics of the worlds in which we live.

These two possible scenarios in our example show how difficult it is to avoid the twin pitfalls of sociologism and technologism. We are never faced with objects or social relations, we are faced with chains which are associations of humans (H) and non-humans (NH). No one has ever seen a social relation by itself – or else it is that of the hotel manager unable to discipline his customers – nor a technical relation – or else it is that of the keys and the weights forgotten by everyone.

Instead we are always faced by chains which look like this:

H-NH-H-NH-NH-NH-H-H-H-H-NH (where H stands for a human-like actant and NH for a non-human).

Of course, an H-H-H assembly looks like social relations while a NH-NH-NH portion looks like a mechanism or a machine, but the point is that they are always integrated into longer chains. It is the chain – the syntagm – we study or its transformation – the paradigm – but it is never some of its aggregates or lumps. So instead of asking 'is this social', 'is this technical or scientific', or asking 'are these techniques influenced by society' or is this 'social relation influenced by techniques' we simply ask: has a human replaced a non-human? has a non-human replaced a human? has the competence of this actor been modified? has this actor – human or non-human – been replaced by another one? has this chain of association been extended or modified? Power is not a property of any one of those elements but of a chain.

[...]

Repairing relativism

Defining actors by the list of their trials

We define an actor or an actant only by its actions in conformity with the etymology. If an innovation is defined by a diagram in which its essence is co-extensive to its existence – that is, the ever-provisional aggregate of its versions and their transformations – then these versions and transformations are in turn completely defined by the actants that constitute them. But where do we get these actants from? Where do the hotel customer, the manager, the key and the sign come from? What would be the use of displaying innovations without reduction-ism if we use a reductionist definition of actants? Luckily for us an actant is defined exactly like an innovation. All we have to do is shift our perspective: instead of using an innovation that passes from actor to actor as a starting-point, we must use one of these actors into whose 'hands' successive versions of the innovation pass. Here again, the linguistic metaphor can help us. A linguist can study either a syntagm – a group of associated elements in a meaningful sentence – or the element itself in the framework of all the meaningful sentences in which it appears, that is a paradigm. This would be like moving from:

The fisherman
The fisherman / fishes /
The fisherman / fishes / a shark/
The fisherman / fishes / a shark / with/ a gun
The painter /fishes / a trout / with / a knife

to

The painter/ paints/ pictures
The painter/paints/ houses
The painter/ is /a/ substantive
The painter/ is/ / hyper-realistic

What changes is the point we choose to hold fixed. In the first case, our object is the length of the syntagm as well as the group of paradigms that can be substituted in each articulation. In the second case, our object is a specific articulation, and we wish to reconstitute the group of syntagms in which it occurs. Defining the essence of innovations by the existence of their successive and simultaneous actants, and then turning around to define the actants by the successive innovations in which they appear, is no more circular or contradictory here than in linguistics.

How do we define an actant? An actant is a list of answers to trials – a list which, once stabilized, is hooked to a name of a thing and to a substance. This substance acts as a subject to all the predicates – in other words, it is made the origin of actions (Callon 1991). How do we define our hotel manager of the key story? He certainly 'is' the obstinate speaker who reminds customers to leave their keys, but he is also more than that. He 'is' also the one who makes up the bills, orders clean sheets, places ads in the phone book, summons painters, etc. The key also can be defined not merely by its appearance in our innovation story, but by the list of everything it must submit to in all the innovation stories in which it appears. Its sole purpose in life is not returning to the front desk; it also throws bolts, gets stuck when a drunken customer tries to force a lock, gets imitated by a master key, etc. And as for the metal weight, it does not merely intervene as a modest attachment to a hotel key. It undergoes many other tests, which define it much more completely: it melts at 1800° in a furnace, it is made up of iron or carbon, it contains up to 4 per cent silicon, it turns white or grey when it breaks, etc.

The longer the list, the more active the actor is. The more variations that exist among the actors to which it is linked, the more polymorphous our actor is. The more it appears as being composed of different elements from version to version, the less stable its essence. Conversely, the shorter the list, the less important the actor. The more diversity it encounters among the different actors it meets, or the more difficult it is to open its black box, the more coherent and firm it is. The list of tests undergone by a given actor defines its historicity, just as a socio-technical graph defines the historicity of an innovation or knowledge claim.

Just as an innovation can become increasingly predictable by black-boxing longer and longer chains of associations, an actor can become so coherent as to be almost predictable. If A is always associated with B or dissociated from D in the succession of stories, we can safely assume that when A relates to B in a new narrative, it will link itself with B and unlink itself from D. We can thus begin to deduce the *performance* of actors from their *competence*. We are then, but only then, allowed to be normative again, but these norms are not forced on to the data, they are extracted from the actor's own efforts at rendering each other's behaviour more predictable. Power and domination are the words given to those stabilizations and not an account of their coming into being. They are only one possible state of the associations. An essence emerges from the actor's very existence – an essence which could dissolve later. Its history becomes a nature, to use Sartre's expression, but perhaps we should add: to later become history again. The actor has gone from Name of Action to Name of Object (Latour 1987a). The lists constructed from the joint story of innovations and actors highlight the continual variation in an actor's isotopy, i.e., in its stability over time. Its behaviour becomes either more and more or less and less predictable. The list allows us to go from extremely shaky certainty to necessity, or from necessity to uncertainty. The force of habit, or of habits, will either exert itself *or not*; it will act or not as a function of the historical records of the actor.

Following the relativist variations of translation

In spite of this circular definition of actors and innovation we are still far from providing explanations: we can only predict how long an association will last if an innovation grabs an actor or if an actor grabs an innovation. To be more precise, we can only predict such reactions for those cases that interest us the least: those in which the innovation is already a black box, in which the actors have such a stable history that it has almost become second nature, in which the traditional notion of power and domination may be predictably used. How can we manage to antici- pate reactions in other cases when domination is not yet exerted? To do so, we must tame a third source of variation.

Since we are capable of mutually defining actants and innovations without any further essentialism we can therefore map the translation operation. This crucial operation engenders the establishment – albeit local and provisional – of social links. Thanks to translation, we do not have to begin our analysis by using actants with fixed borders and assigned interests. Instead, we can follow the way in which actant B attributes a fixed border to actant A, the way in which B assigns interests or goals to A, the definition of those borders and goals shared by A and B, and finally the distribution of responsibility between A and B for their joint action. In a universe of innovations solely defined by the associations and substitutions of actants, and of actants solely defined by the multiplicity of inventions in which they conspire, the translation operation becomes the essential principle of composi- tion, of linkage, of recruitment or of enrolment. But since there no longer exists any external point of view to which we could ascribe the degree of reality or of success of an innovation, we can only obtain an evaluation by triangulating the many points of view of the actors. It is thus crucial to be able to shift easily from one observer to another.

Consider a particularly elegant translation operation by Pasteur:

To the Minister of Public Education

Paris, 1 August 1864

Minister,

Wine constitutes one of the greatest agricultural riches of France. The value of this product of our soil is increased by the commercial treaty with England. Thus in all wine-growing countries, there is interest in improving methods with a view to increas- ing both the number and quality of those wines that can be profitably exported.

Unfortunately, our knowledge of this precious beverage leaves much to be desired. Studies of its composition are so incomplete that only in the past two years have two of its main components – glycerine and succinic acid – been identified. Despite the progress of modern chemistry, there is no more knowledgeable and precise treatise on wines than that of Chaptal, which came out more than sixty years ago. This is sufficient to indicate how much remains to be done.

For the past five years, I have been working on the problem of fermentation. I have taken particular interest in the fermentation of alcohol at the heart of the wine-making process. The very progress of my research has led me to want to continue it *in situ* and in countries known for the production of those wines that are most valued in France. I wish to study the fermentation processes there, and in particular to examine the microscopic vegetable matter that is the sole cause of this great and mysterious phenomenon.

I intend to carry out this work during my next leave. There will be about six weeks of travelling and of study, with one assistant and a few necessary items of equipment and chemical products. I estimate the outlay to be 2500 francs.

The aim of this letter is to put this project before your Excellency, and to ask for a grant to cover the cost of its execution. This will not be the end of my interest in the matter. I will follow it up with work in future years, at the same time of the year.

Further, I am the first to admit that there may be no immediate practical consequences of my studies. The application of the results of science to industry is always slow. My present goals are very modest. I should like to arrive at a better knowledge of the cryptogamic plant that is the sole cause of fermentation in grape juice.

Successive layers of actants – the Minister, chemistry, my research, my trip to the Arbois – get goals and borders attributed to them. Each of these layers is characterized by incompatible vocabulary: 2500F, the trade treaty with England, succinic acid, the cryptogamic plant. (Hence the word translation.) An anti-programme gets attributed to each of these programmes of action: it would be nice to sell wine to England, but these wines are diseased; it would be nice to know the origins of these diseases, but wine chemistry is sixty years old; I would like to pursue my research, but I lack money and assistants. On the one hand, the translation operation consists of defining successive layers of vocabulary, of attributing goals and of defining impossibilities; on the other hand, it consists of displacing – hence the other meaning of translation – one programme of action into another programme of action. The overall movement of the translation is defined by a *detour* and by a *return*. In the end, by giving Pasteur 2500F, the Minister is supposed to restore the balance of payments and Pasteur thereby attains his goals.

But the translation operation is always risky. Indeed, nothing guarantees that the detour will, in the end, be paid, rewarded by a return. In fact, Pasteur, always clever, gives a good indication of this in his last paragraph. The only goal that must be attained, he said, is that of pure knowledge of the cryptogamic plant: applying this knowledge – i.e., the return – is always problematic. One can imagine many other possible scenarios: the Minister might be uninterested in the wine trade, wine diseases might be due solely to chemical phenomena, the 2500F might never materialize, or Pasteur could change his research project. Those things composed and linked by the translation operation might disperse themselves like a flight of birds. This is precisely the possibility we must predict if we want to explain and produce some evaluations. And how else could we do this, since we no longer have an external referent, except by submitting Pasteur's version of the goals and desires of all the human and non-human actors to a *test* by *comparing* them with the goals and desires they give themselves or attribute to Pasteur? Indeed, nothing guarantees that the operation proposed by Pasteur corresponds to the version held by the actants named Minister, chemistry, cryptogamic plant, England or ferment. In order to measure the potential success or failure of the translation operations – relative, of course, to an enunciator and to an observer – we must verify whether or not they occupy the position expected by Pasteur. The durability of Pasteur's position is not to be explained by his power, but only by the convergence between what he expects others to do and what others expect him to do. It is this negotiation process that is always forgotten by those who use already acquired domination to explain a future one.

Suppose that we notice through further interviews and documents that as far as the Minister is concerned, the problem of balancing payments has nothing to do with wine and its diseases. His problem lies with silk, whose trade is hampered by Japan. As for the chemists, they certainly do not occupy the position predicted by Pasteur. Their tragedy has nothing to do with the fact that their discipline is out of date; on the contrary, they are concerned about the dramatic return to vitalism, which is slowing down progress in chemistry. In fact, Pasteur and his fermentations figure prominently in their anti-programmes! And finally, the ferments: they're beginning to die from lack of air, thereby annihilating Pasteur's efforts to cultivate them. By comparing what Pasteur says the others want and what the others say they want, we can easily imagine that Pasteur might have a few problems in getting his funds, because those mobilized in his version *do not occupy* the position he assigned them, at least, not yet. Such a comparison would show the actants' state of alignment or dispersion and would help predicting the complexity of future negotiations.

This example shows us that it is not merely statements which vary as a function of innovations. Both also vary *as a function of the perspective* of the observer or of the informant.

[...]

Conclusion

If we abandon the divide between material infrastructure on the one hand and social superstructure on the other, a much larger dose of relativism is possible. Unlike scholars who treat power and domination with special tools, we do not have to start from stable actors, from stable statements, from a stable repertoire of beliefs and interests, or even from a stable observer. And still, we regain the durability of social assemblage, but it is shared with the non-humans thus mobilized. When actors and points of view are aligned, then we enter a stable definition of society that looks like domination. When actors are unstable and the observers' points of view shift endlessly we are entering a highly unstable and negotiated situation in which domination is not yet exerted. The analyst's tools, however, do not have to be modified and the gradient that discriminates between more and less stable assemblages does not correspond in the least to the divide between technology and society. It is as if we might call technology the moment when social assemblages gain stability by aligning actors and observers. Society and technology are not two ontologically distinct entities but more like phases of the same essential action.

By replacing those two arbitrary divisions with syntagm and paradigm, we may draw a few more methodological conclusions. The *description* of socio-technical networks is often opposed to their *explanation*, which is supposed to come afterwards. Critics of the sociology of science and technology often suggest that even the most meticulous description of a case study would not suffice to give an explanation of its development. This kind of criticism borrows from epistemology the difference between the empirical and the theoretical, between 'how' and 'why', between stamp-collecting – a contemptible occupation – and the search for causality – the only activity worthy of attention. Yet nothing proves that this kind of distinction is necessary. If we display a socio-technical network – defining trajectories by actants' association and substitution, defining actants by all the trajectories in which they enter, by following translations and, finally, by varying the observer's point of view – we have no need to look for any additional causes. The explanation emerges once the description is saturated. We can certainly continue to follow actants, innovations and translation operations through *other networks*, but we will never find ourselves forced to abandon the task of description to take up that of explanation. The impression that one can sometimes offer in the social sciences an explanation similar to those of the exact sciences is due precisely to the stabilization of networks, a stabilization that the notion of explanation simply does not 'explain'! Explanation, as the name indicates, is to deploy, to explicate. There is no need to go searching for mysterious or global causes outside networks. If something is missing it is because the description is not complete. Period. Conversely, if one is capable of explaining effects of causes, it is because a stabilized network is already in place.

Our second conclusion relates to relativism and the heterogeneity of networks. Criticisms of studies of controversy insist on the local, soft and inconsistent nature of the results. They have the impression that network analysis re-creates 'that night when all the cows are grey' ridiculed by Hegel. Yet network analysis tends to lead us in exactly the opposite direction. To eliminate the great divides between science/society, technology/science, macro/micro, economics/research, humans/non-humans and rational/irrational is not to immerse ourselves in relativism and indifferentiation. Networks are not amorphous. They are highly differentiated, but their differences are fine, circumstantial and small, thus requiring new tools and concepts. Instead of 'sinking into relativism' it is relatively easy to float upon it.

Finally, we are left with the accusation of immorality, apoliticism or moral relativism. But this accusation makes no more sense than the first two. Refusing to explain the closure of a controversy by its consequences does not mean that we are indifferent to the possibility of judgement, but only that we refuse to accept judgements that transcend the situation. For network analysis does not prevent judgement any more than it prevents differentiation. Efficiency, truth, profitability and interest are simply properties of networks, not of statements. Domination is an effect not a cause. In order to make a diagnosis or a decision about the absurdity, the danger, the amorality or the unrealism of an innovation, one must first describe the network. If the capability of making judgements gives up its vain appeals to transcendence, it loses none of its acuity.

NOTE

From B. Latour (1991), 'Technology is Society Made Durable', in J. Law, ed., *A Sociology of Monsters* (London: Routledge), pp. 103–31.

REFERENCES

Akrich, M. (1987), 'Comment décrire les objects techniques', *Technique et culture*, vol. 5, pp. 49–63.

Barnes, B. (1988), *The Nature of Power* (Cambridge: Polity Press).

Bijker, W. and J. Law eds (1992), *Shaping Technology-Building Society: Studies in Sociotechnical Change* (Cambridge, MA: MIT Press).

Bijker, W. E., T. Hughes and T. Pinch, eds (1986), *New Developments in the Social Studies of Technology* (Cambridge, MA: MIT Press).

Callon, M. (1991), 'Techno-economic networks and irreversibility', in J. Law, ed., *A Sociology of Monsters* (London: Routledge), pp. 132–61.

Einstein, A. (1920), *Relativity: The Special and the General Theory* (London: Methuen).

Hughes, T. P. (1979), 'The electrification of America: the system builders', *Technology and Culture*, vol. 20, no. 1, pp. 124–62.

Hughes, T. P. (1983), *Networks of Power: Electric Supply Systems in the US, England and Germany, 1880–1930* (Baltimore: Johns Hopkins University Press).

Jenkins, R. V. (1975), 'Technology and the market: Georges Eastman and the origins of mass amateur photography', *Technology and Culture*, vol. 16, pp. 1–19.

Jenkins, R. V. (1976), *Images and Enterprises: Technology and the American Photographic Industry*, 1839–1925 (Baltimore: Johns Hopkins University Press).

Latour, B. (1987a), *Science in Action: How to Follow Scientists and Engineers through Society* (Cambridge, MA: Harvard University Press).

Latour, B. (1987b), *Science in Action: How to Follow Scientists and Engineers through Society* (Cambridge, MA: Harvard University Press).

Latour, B. (1992), 'Where are the missing masses: sociology of a few mundane artefacts', in W. Bijker and J. Law eds, *Shaping Technology-Building Society: Studies in Sociotechnical Change* (Cambridge, MA: MIT Press).

Latour, B., P. Mauguin and G. Teil (forthcoming), 'A note on sociotechnical graphs', *Social Studies of Science*.

Law, J. (1986a), 'On the methods of long-distance control: vessels, navigation, and the Portuguese route to India', in J. Law, ed., *Power Action and Belief: A New Sociology of Knowledge?* (London: Routledge & Kegan Paul, Sociological Review Monograph), pp. 234–63.

Law, J. ed. (1986b), *Power, Action and Belief: A New Sociology of Knowledge?*, (London: Routledge & Kegan Paul, Sociological Review Monograph).

Pavel, T. (1986), *Fictional Worlds* (Cambridge, MA: Harvard University Press).

Serres, M. (1987), *Statues* (Paris: François Bourin).

3 Age

Child Labour: An Economic Perspective

CHRISTIAAN GROOTAERT AND RAVI KANBUR

Child labour is upsetting. The popular images in the developed world are drawn from Dickens and the 'dark, satanic mills' of the industrial revolution on the one hand, and the sweatshops and street children of the cities of the developing world on the other. A common, and natural enough, reaction in developing countries has been to enact legislation to ban child labour as did the now-developed world when it emerged from its period of industrialization. Trade sanctions are being recommended in some developed countries against the exports of developing countries which use child labour. Many, including developing country governments, see this as a disguised protectionist device. Others, some economists among them, argue that legislation, even if it could be enforced, is not the only way, or necessarily the best way, of tackling the problem of child labour.

Against this background, this [reading] presents an overview of the recent literature on child labour with a view to determining consistent and feasible policies to deal with the problem. For this purpose it takes an economic perspective and focuses on demand and supply. A framework is set out for discussing the incentives that lead to child labour and that can be used as means of combating it. The first section considers conceptual and empirical problems in defining child labour and discusses some recent estimates of its magnitude. The second focuses on the determinants of child labour – first on supply, then on demand. The third sets out a welfare economics framework within which policy interventions can be analysed. In this light, the fourth assesses a range of policy interventions, including legislation.

There seems to be an emerging consensus that policies to deal with child labour will have to vary depending upon which types of child labour and accompanying arrangements are prevalent, and depending upon the institutional and administrative capacity of the country in question. While legislation is an important component of the policy package suggested here, by itself it is neither necessary nor sufficient for making a rapid and significant dent in the problem. It has to be accompanied by a range of incentives, for schooling, for example, and a range of targeted interventions. This, together with equitable economic growth, it is argued here, is what will eventually reduce child labour to levels that can be addressed satisfactorily by legislation.

The nature and magnitude of child labour

How much child labour is there in the world? The answer to this question depends, of course, on what one means by child labour. To begin with, it is not clear how to define 'child'. In Western countries it is customary to do so by chronological age, but in many societies cultural and social factors enter as well (Rodgers and Standing 1981). The evolution from childhood to adulthood passes through socially and biologically defined life phases, during which the degree of dependence and the need for protection of the child gradually decline. For example, in many societies an apprentice even if only eight or nine years old is often not considered a child – a determination based on social status rather than age (Morice 1981). In that sense too, many societies, especially poor rural ones, do not necessarily view child work as 'bad'. Rather, it is often part of the socialization process which gradually introduces a child to work activities and teaches survival skills. This view is present in many African countries (Bekombo 1981; Agiobu-Kemmer 1992).

The concept of 'work' is equally problematic to apply to many of the activities in which children are engaged. They can range from help with domestic work, to work in the household enterprise or farm, to wage work. It can be light artisanal work, trading, or heavy physical work.[1] For the purpose of defining a policy towards child labour, both the nature of the work and the nature of the relationship between the child and the employer must be considered. A key question is whether the arrangement is 'exploitative'. In the extreme, it can take the form of bonded labour, quasi-slavery or a feudal relationship. A debt incurred by the parents can be the 'bond' whereby a child is forced to work. It is estimated that in South Asia there are several million bonded child labourers (ILO 1992). It can also be considered exploitative when a child starts full-time work at too early an age, or works too many hours, or when the work imposes excessive physical, social and/or psychological strains which hamper his or her development (UNICEF 1986; ILO 1992).

The ILO recently produced statistics on child labour based on a uniform definition – economically active population under the age of fifteen (Ashagrie 1993). That attempt highlighted the difficulties that arise in terms of data availability; a number of sources had to be used, including a set of specially designed questionnaires sent to 200 countries and territories (with an uneven response rate across regions). On the basis of returns from 124 countries, the ILO obtained an acknowledged underestimate of 78.5 million economically active children under fifteen years of age in 1990; 70.9 million of them were aged ten to fourteen (a participation rate of 13.7 per cent).

UNICEF (1991) estimated that there were 80 million children aged ten to fourteen who undertook work so long or onerous that it interfered with their

Table 3.1 Incidence of child labour in selected countries

	Children	Labour force participation rate (%)
Rural Egypt, 1975 (Levy 1985)	Ages 6–11	17
	Ages 12–14	43
Two villages in rural Nigeria, 1992	Work on farm	42–50
(Okojie 1993)	Work at home	52–61
	Trading	24–27
	Craftwork	16–21
	Food processing	26–30
100 villages in Senegal River Valley, 1989	Apprentice:	
(Guèye et al. 1993)	Boys	15
	Girls	4
	Family aide:	
	Boys	22
	Girls	53
	Farm work:	
	Boys	32
	Girls	20
Bicol region in Philippines, 1983	Market work:	
(DeGraff et al. 1993)	Ages 7–12	22
	Ages 13–17	44
	Home production:	
	Ages 7–12	49
	Ages 13–17	68
Five villages in rural Pakistan, 1990	Boys	19–25
(Sathar 1993)	Girls	22–32
One district in rural Maharashtra, India	Household work:	
(Jejeebhoy 1993)	Boys	34
	Girls	65
	Family farm or business:	
	Boys	24
	Girls	16
	Wage work:	
	Boys	9
	Girls	6
Malaysia, 1980 (Jomo 1992)	Ages 10–14:	6
	Boys	7
	Girls	4
	Malays	5
	Chinese	7
	Indians	7
Pakistan, 1985	Ages 10–14:	
(Cochrane et al. 1990)	Boys	31
	Girls	7
Côte d'Ivoire, 1986	Ages 10–14	
(Cochrane et al. 1990)	Urban:	
	Boys	5
	Girls	6
	Rural:	
	Boys	55
	Girls	54
Peru, 1986 (Cochrane et al. 1990)	Ages 10–14:	
	Boys	41
	Girls	38

normal development. The differences in the estimates result from differing definitions and methodologies. Disparities can be illustrated by a discussion of estimates for India (Weiner 1991: 20, 21):

> How many of India's 82 million children not in school are in the work force? Given the uncertainties of definition and the complexities of remuneration, it is no wonder that estimates of child labour vary so greatly in India. India's 1981 census reports only 13.6 million in the work force . . . other studies put the number of child workers higher. The official National Sample Survey of 1983 reports 17.4 million child labourers, while a study by the Operations Research Group of Baroda, sponsored by the Labour Ministry, concluded that the child labour force was 44 million, including children paid in kind as well as in cash.

As a complement to aggregative global and national estimates, table 3.1 shows some selected estimates of child labour for Africa and Asia. These are based on micro-data collection, often of an anthropological nature, undertaken in order to study household behaviour. While such estimates can make no claim to representativeness, they show that participation rates for children may be in the 20–60 per cent range, depending upon age and type of work. These rates increase with age and tend to be higher for boys in the case of wage work or work in the household enterprise, with girls participating more in domestic activities. Such figures suggest that the incidence of child labour varies greatly from country to country and possibly within countries as well, but they confirm the impression that the numbers of working children are sufficiently high for the issue of child labour to be a matter of priority concern in many countries.

Determinants of child labour

The absence of systematic data collection on the incidence of child labour obviously affects the amount of research done on its determinants. Most research is based on case studies covering a subnational area, often one or a few villages, at best a province or region. Much of the analysis dates back to the period 1978–85, perhaps motivated by the United Nations' declaration of 1979 as the Year of the Child.[2] More recent case studies are reported by Bequele and Boyden (1988), Myers (1991), Jomo (1992), Goonesekere (1993) and Boyden and Myers (1995).

The following discussion of the determinants of child labour starts with the literature on fertility and time allocation with the household. Obviously, the number of children in the household determines the potential supply of child workers; hence fertility behaviour is a determinant of the supply of child labour. Also on the supply side, the role of risk management in the household is a factor influencing the extent of child labour. On the demand side, the two main determinants of child labour are the structure of the labour market and the prevailing production technology. These aspects are taken up in turn.

Household size and time allocation

In any household, a child's non-leisure time is available for schooling, home production or income-earning work in the market. The way the household allocates the child's time depends *inter alia* on household size and structure, the productive potential of the child and its parents (mainly its mother) in home and market work, and the degree of labour substitution possible between the child and its parents (again, mainly the mother). For a given labour market the allocation of time depends on the potential income from child labour; that potential in turn affects the desired household size (see, for example, Nakamura and Nakamura 1992; Hotz and Miller 1988; and Rivera-Batiz 1985). Expectations concern both their work as children and their potential support to parents in old age.[3]

A recent review of the evidence on this relationship from developing countries suggests that larger household size reduces children's educational participation and progress in school and reduces parents' investment in schooling (Lloyd 1994). This makes it likely that larger household size increases the probability that a child will work.[4] Lloyd's review finds that the magnitude of this effect is determined by at least four factors:

- the level of socio-economic development (the effect of household size is stronger in urban or more developed areas);
- the level of social expenditure by the state (the effect of household size is weaker if state expenditures are high);
- family culture (the effect of household size is weaker where extended family systems exist, e.g. through the practice of child fostering);
- the phase of demographic transition (the effect of household size is stronger in later phases).

One implication is that the empirically observed magnitude of the effect of household size on child labour varies enormously from place to place, depending upon the existing combination of factors (Cochrane et al. 1990).

A detailed econometric study of the Philippines found that the relationship between household size and child work is not the same for market as it is for domestic work, and that it depends on the sex and the birth order of the child (DeGraff et al. 1993). For example, the presence of older siblings decreases the likelihood of market work by a child, especially if it is of the same sex, suggesting substitution of older for younger siblings (perhaps because older children are likely to earn more). However, such a substitution effect was found to be absent for domestic work. This study as well as others (see Lloyd 1993) documents gender roles in child labour: in many settings boys are more likely to be engaged in market work and girls are more likely to be engaged in farm or domestic work.

The degree to which boys or girls, or all children equally, are affected by household size is also determined by cultural factors. In Malaysia, for example, Chinese girls appear disadvantaged in larger households but their brothers are not (Shreeniwas 1993). In India, families from urban slums in Tamil Nadu discriminate in order to provide a few children, mainly boys, with 'quality' private education. Families from Uttar Pradesh try to provide all children equally with less expensive public education (Basu 1993).

In rural areas, the relationship between fertility, household size and child labour depends also on land holdings. The evidence has indicated that children in landless and marginal farm households generally engage in wage labour while those in households with larger farms engage in agricultural work. The extent of child labour tends to increase with farm size because labour and land are complementary inputs (Sharif 1994).

Although school attendance cannot be considered the 'inverse' of child labour, the literature on the determinants of school enrolment has established two relevant effects. First, there is a substitution effect between schooling of girls and the labour force participation of mothers. When mothers go to work in the market, girls are more likely to stay at home. In this sense, the opportunity cost of girls' schooling is not their forgone wages, but those of their mothers. Second, the most important determinants of school enrolment are parents' education (especially mothers' education) and household income level. There is an income effect from mothers' earnings which will at some point establish a preference for 'quality' children. What this means for child labour is that in poor households, when mothers need to enter the labour force, child labour will increase because especially girls will be pulled out of school to take over domestic work or their entry into school will be delayed. As income increases, the income effect of the mother's work will outweigh the substitution effect and child labour will decrease. This process will likely be affected by the same societal factors identified above, namely the level of development, the level of social expenditure, cultural factors and the phase of demographic transition. Most case studies of child labour do indeed identify poverty of the household and a low level of parental education as important factors in determining child labour (ILO 1992).

It stands to reason that the overall condition of the education system can be a powerful influence on the supply of child labour. Bonnet (1993) argues that the failure of the education system in Africa has led many parents to view work as the preferred option for their children. Education is no longer a road towards obtaining a diploma assuring a modern sector job. In an economic environment where survival depends on work in the informal sector, many parents conclude that taking children out of school and putting them to work is the most sensible solution for survival and the education method which offers the best prospects for the future. As one African commentator put it: 'Education broadens your mind but it does not teach you how to survive' (Agiobu-Kemmer 1992: 7).

The extent to which the state can influence a household's behaviour with respect to child labour, in particular the effect of fertility and large household size, is highlighted in a study of Malaysia (Shreeniwas 1993). As part of its policy to reduce ethnic inequalities, the government of Malaysia systematically favours education of Malays through scholarships and other subsidies. As a result, no negative effects of household size emerged for these households in contrast to Chinese and Indian households, which did not benefit from government subsidies and among which a strong negative effect of household size on schooling was observed.

The final supply-side determinant of child labour considered here relates to the labour market itself: the wage level in the market – both the wages of children and those of adults. Evidence from Egypt (Levy 1985) and India (Rosenzweig 1981) suggests that the own-wage elasticity of child labour is positive and higher for younger children. For rural India, the own-wage elasticity was estimated at about 0.8. In the case of Egypt own-wage elasticity was estimated at 0.965 for children aged six to eleven and 0.379 for children aged twelve to fourteen. The cross-wage elasticity with the labour supply of the mother was found to be negative, i.e. an increase in wages for females is likely to reduce the supply of child labour, especially of female children. The effect is strongest for younger children. In Egypt, a 10 per cent increase in women's market wages would lead to a 15 per cent decline in the labour of children aged twelve to fourteen and a 27 per cent decline in the labour of children aged six to eleven. In India, a 10 per cent increase in women's wage rates would decrease girls' labour force participation by 9–10 per cent, but would have no effect on boys' participation. The opposite is true for men's wage rates, which have a cross-wage elasticity of about –1 with respect to boys' labour supply, but close to zero with respect to girls'. The question which remains unanswered is at which income level will the income effect of parents' labour force participation, especially that of the mother, outweigh the substitution effect mentioned earlier.

Household responses towards risk

Households send children to work in order to augment household income but also to manage better the income risk they face. Child labour can be part of a strategy to minimize the risk of interruption of a household's income stream, and hence to reduce the potential impact of job loss by a family member, of a failed harvest, etc. (Cain et al. 1980). The impact of such a loss is more severe for poor households. Where the level of income is very low any interruption can be life-threatening, particularly in the absence of savings, liquid assets or ability to borrow (Mende-lievich 1979). Therefore the risk argument provides a further explanation as to why child labour is more prevalent among poor households.[5]

Evidence from rural India confirms that child labour plays a significant role in the self-insurance strategy of poor households. It has been observed that when the variability of household income increased (measured by the difference in income from peak season to low season), children's school attendance declined. This was especially the case when a 'shock' occurred which was external to the village (which provides indirect evidence of some risk-sharing within the village). Small households suffer more from income shocks because they are less able to insure themselves (Jacoby and Skoufias 1994).

The policy implication is that in settings where household risk management is an important reason for child labour, attempts at its forced abolition (e.g. by legislation on child labour or compulsory schooling) are likely to fail since they could threaten the household's survival. Such attempts at abolition would need to be accompanied by mechanisms providing households with insurance against income fluctuations in other ways, e.g. by provision of short-term credit which does not require collateral.

The structure of the labour market

Cain et al. (1980) have argued that the economic value of children and its implications for reproductive behaviour cannot properly be assessed without reference to the structure of the labour market. The latter determines the level of wages, which in turn determines the contribution of child labour to household income. A key factor is the flexibility of wages. In competitive markets where wages are flexible, children can substitute for adults in the market place. Where wages are at a floor level, whether due to legislation, collective action or because they have reached an adult subsistence minimum, the employer will prefer adult workers (assuming their productivity is higher than that of children). Effective minimum wages can thus in principle deter child labour, although in practice one must ask whether minimum wage legislation is more likely to be effectively enforced than is legislation banning child labour.

There is little hard evidence on the level of remuneration of children, differentials in adult and child wage rates or the extent of wage discrimination against children. In a review of case studies, Bequele and Boyden (1988) concluded that children's earnings are consistently lower than those of adults, even where the two groups arc engaged in the same tasks. Jomo (1992) reached the same conclusion on the basis of several case studies on Malaysia. Monopsonistic demand conditions in the market will also depress children's wages. Monopsonistic conditions occur often in developing country labour markets and can be a result of concentrated ownership of land, credit and product monopolies, share-cropping arrangements, imposed or natural restrictions on labour mobility or a lack of alternative employment possibilities (Cain 1980).

The relative importance of the formal sector in the economy and the degree of segmentation between it and the informal sector are also determinants of the demand for child labour. In general, the evidence suggests that the extent of child labour in the formal economy is small, with the possible exception of plantations (e.g. Bonnet 1993, for Africa; Goonesekere 1993, for Sri Lanka). However, in many countries there is a tendency towards informalization of production methods, with formal enterprises either breaking up into smaller units or subcontracting to households or informal enterprises (mainly to try to escape social legislation and charges which add to the cost of labour). In such conditions the demand for child labour may well increase.

An important aspect of the issue of child labour and remuneration is an apprenticeship system which ties a child to a small enterprise, usually for many years, in principle to learn a trade. In practice, especially in the early years of the apprenticeship, the child often serves the master, and only later will there be any actual learning (Mendelievich 1979). Nevertheless, an apprenticeship can contribute to a process of socialization while transferring know-how, and some have argued that it would therefore be a mistake to view it as exploitation of child labour (Bonnet 1993).

The role of technology

Another major determinant of the demand for child labour is the technology of production, since it affects the extent to which children can be substitutes for adults. Many of the cases where this factor plays an extreme role are those that incite reports in the press and by voluntary agencies. Examples are the employment of boys in mines (because the tunnels are too small for adults to crawl through) or as chimney sweeps (for similar reasons); the employment of girls to weed and pick cotton; and the employment of children to weave carpets because they have more nimble fingers and can tie smaller knots than can adults.

By implication, changes in technology can have a profound impact on the incidence of child labour. In the industrial revolution, the mechanization of spinning and weaving led to a reduction in the demand for child labour (Galbi 1994). The green revolution in India led to reduced child labour and increased school attendance (Rosenzweig 1981). The mechanization of Egyptian agriculture, especially the expanded use of tractors and irrigation pumps, reduced the demand for child labour in tasks such as picking cotton or driving animals to power waterwheels or haul freight (Levy 1985). In some cases, the technological change in question can be fairly elementary: DeGraff et al. (1993) show that in the Philippines the introduction of electricity in the community reduces the amount of market labour for children and, similarly, that having electricity in the home reduces the amount of home production by children. In the quarries of Bogotá, the introduction of wheelbarrows displaced children who previously carried rocks piece by piece (Salazar 1988).

Today's technology can have ambivalent effects on the demand for child work. Miniaturization and assembly-line production in the electronics and electrical appliance industries has again led to some demand for 'nimble fingers'. Not everywhere are robots the ultimate suppliers of this skill. In garment production, the advent of fairly cheap multi-function sewing-machines has once again made possible home production, and much manufacturing relies on subcontracting arrangements, which can lead to girls' work at home. Empirical assessments of the implications of technological change are lacking and would be needed before the importance of technology relative to other demand factors can be assessed.

The welfare economics of child labour

Now that some key determinants have been discussed, the next task is to discuss policies to reduce child labour. However, a decision to seek to reduce or even ban child labour must be based on a conviction that there is too much of it relative to some social norm. Whether or not there is too much or too little of an activity in the short term can be examined systematically using the framework of conventional welfare economics, which may also provide insights into appropriate interventions. This section outlines a few of the issues and the ensuing interventions.

The basic analytical framework applied here is that of household decision-making in the allocation of children's time between labour and non-labour activities, together with an assessment of private and social returns to each activity. Each household will seek to allocate the time of its children to wherever the perceived gain to the household (the private return) is highest. The crucial question is whether the private return matches the social return, suitably defined. Conceptually, there are three sets of issues. First, there are those to do with pure efficiency, where no distributional questions are raised. Second, there are issues involving intra-household distributional considerations. Third, there are the issues involving inter-household distribution. Each of these is considered in turn.

Suppose, for example, that there is a failure in the market for education, whereby the social returns to primary education are higher than the private returns (e.g. primary education for girls leads to lower fertility and this is desirable from the social point of view). This means that in the social optimum more children would be at school than is the case on the basis of household decisions alone. What should be the nature of the intervention? Basic welfare economics teaches that it is best to attack market failures in the very markets in which they occur – it is always second best to intervene in related markets. Thus, in this situation it would be second best to attack the problem by taxing or banning child labour (thereby inducing the household to use that time in alternative ways). Rather, policy should focus on raising the private (household) rate of return to education to bring it closer to the social return. The same argument applies in cases where incomplete markets for risk-spreading lead to the use of child labour as a diversification device. The first best solution is to encourage the development of credit and risk markets.

In the case where there is discrimination against children within households then, even without market failure, child labour may be a problem. This refers to cases where the household's objective function gives a lower weight to the utility of children than does the social welfare function; the argument is perhaps most persuasive in the case of female children. The appropriate intervention will depend on the intra-household allocation process. In a unitary model of the household where the head of the household is the sole decision-maker, the issue is how to rearrange incentives for the head of household so that he (or she) does 'the right thing' from a social perspective. This can be done either by taxing (or banning) child labour or by subsidizing education. There is no longer a natural ranking of these two alternatives. If there is intra-household bargaining (perhaps between the father and the mother–child nexus), directly altering the bargaining power of the mother is a possible instrument. Increasing wages, even of the child, can then be seen as strengthening the mother–child nexus.

Households differ in their wealth and in their capabilities, such that an aggregation of households leads to a distribution of welfare outcomes. Child labour may well be associated with low-income households, in which case a reduction in household poverty would lead to a reduction in child labour. If so, child labour should be targeted. Interventions which transfer resources (nutrition, for example) to child labourers can be effective, since this is a way to transfer resources to poor households. Such interventions may lead to a temporary increase in child labour, but that should not necessarily be a cause for worry from this perspective and in the short term, if the objective is to help poor households and if the poverty alleviation effects dominate the incentive effects.

Within this framework, one can examine the consequences of a particularly attractive policy intervention: the banning of child labour. If the ban is enforced, it means that children will no longer be found in the labour market and their time will be shifted to family labour or to schooling. If there was previously an inefficiency in the education market so that there were too few children in school from the point of view of the social optimum, then an effective ban will move the outcome closer to that optimum. However, suppose that child welfare depends on the cash income of the child, e.g. because it strengthens the bargaining power of the mother–child nexus. Then, of course, banning child labour may leave the child worse off after the intra-household bargaining is completed. Likewise, where child labour is a manifestation of poverty, a ban on child labour makes the poor household worse off since it is a restriction of its opportunity set. If, as is quite likely, the ban is not enforced, it will create rents in the system. Quite simply, if employers are the ones who would be fined, they bribe policemen or others so that they can continue to employ children. Nevertheless, such payments are an extra cost to the employer, and thus have the effect of reducing the demand for child labour. To the extent that more children would then go to school this would move the system closer to efficiency if the market failure is in the market for education. But again, negative outcomes for the child are possible if mother–child bargaining power is reduced, or if poor households have fewer income opportunities.

The welfare economics of child labour thus leads to a complex and densely textured analysis which does not suggest a single, or even a dominant, way of approaching the issue. It implies that an array of policy instruments is likely to be required, addressing different aspects of failures arising from efficiency or distributional considerations. Legislation, even if it can be enforced, is at best only one instrument in the array that has to be deployed.

There is, however, a major counter-argument to the welfare economics perspective on child labour. This is the non-welfarist framework where certain rights are self-evident, natural and given. A good example is slavery. It is generally accepted that no one has the right even to sell himself or herself into slavery – irrespective of whether this would be welfare-improving from the standpoint of efficiency or even distribution. It can be argued that child labour falls into this category. The fact of child labour violates a basic human right, and it should be banned. It is also easy to see how a focus on international conventions and legislation emerges from the basic rights perspective. Not only is the signing of conventions and the passing of legislation symbolic – a clear expression of the acceptance of the right in question – but vigorous attempts at enforcing such legislation are seen as furthering a basic right. In this framework, the fact that attempts to enforce legislation may in some sense hurt the very group whose right is being protected diminishes in importance.

Policy intervention: the need for a diversified approach

It is now well understood that a major cause of child labour is the poverty of the household. General economic development, equitably distributed, is the best and most sustainable way of reducing child labour. Beyond this, the overview presented here has argued that special emphasis should be given to fertility reduction and to reducing the costs of school attendance, if the objective is to reduce child labour. A special watch also needs to be kept on the impact of technology in determining the demand for child labour. In terms of specific project interventions, programmes in Manila (Gunn and Ostos 1992) and elsewhere show the value of an integrated approach covering all of the above factors as well as the provision of alternative income sources for children and improved employment opportunities for their parents. While there is general agreement on such policy interventions, there is considerable debate on the role of legislation in addressing the issue of child labour.

Historically, the single most important and common approach to the problem of child labour has been the adoption of legislation. The ILO has sponsored many conventions and recommendations banning child labour and most countries now have some form of legislation or regulation prohibiting the employment of children below a certain age and specifying the conditions under which minors may work (Bequele and Boyden 1988). The age threshold and the scope of the legislation vary. In the majority of countries the minimum age for employment is fourteen or fifteen, but there are about thirty countries where it is only twelve or thirteen years (ILO 1992). In many countries higher minimum ages apply for hazardous work. Almost all legislation exempts work in household enterprises, but some limit the scope further by also excluding domestic service and agriculture.

One fundamental problem with enacting and enforcing legislation banning child labour is that there are few interest groups to support it: the government often considers it embarrassing to admit the existence of child labour, and the employers of children will be hostile to legislation as are likely to be the children themselves and their parents (Morice 1981). As discussed above, individual households may seek employment for their children in the pursuit of private returns. Legislation is therefore likely to be effective only where there is a capable administration determined to implement the laws, where there is considerable difficulty in hiding child labour, and where relatively little advantage is to be gained from child work (Rodgers and Standing 1981).

Documentation on effective enforcement of child labour legislation is spotty at best. Most information pertains to labour inspectors describing their degree of understaffing and their difficulties in visiting factories and enforcing penalties before the courts. There is little question that in many countries, labour inspectorates are seriously understaffed. In the Philippines, for example, there are fewer than 200 inspectors nationwide for almost 400,000 employers (Bequele and Boyden 1988).[6] The ongoing trend towards informalization in the labour market will make inspection even more difficult in the future.

In putting legislation in place, an argument can be made for using a graduated approach. As Rodgers and Standing pointed out, 'it is one of the ironies of child labour that, where it is prohibited by law, the law is likely to leave child workers unprotected, since legally they do not exist' (1981: 39). The law should thus also address working conditions (safety, working hours, etc.) and ensure that the relevant regulations apply to all workers, including children. It may be easier, in a first phase, to force employers to limit children's workdays and to provide adequate lighting or safety equipment rather than to force them to forgo child labour altogether. Compulsory schooling laws can be seen in this context. The record of enforcement seems better here than with legislation banning child labour (Weiner 1991). The possibility exists to allow, at least initially, the combination of school attendance with part-time work. Potentially, the community has a crucial role in this, since community-based monitoring of school enrolment and attendance is likely to be more effective than occasional visits from an inspector of the Ministry of Education.[7]

Ultimately then, child labour is best addressed through a combination of legislation and economic incentives (Myers 1991; Goonesekere 1993). This is now well accepted by international agencies addressing the problem of child labour, such as UNICEF and ILO (e.g. UNICEF 1986; ILO 1992). It is indeed unlikely that any one approach will succeed everywhere and the balance between legal and economic measures needs to be adapted to the incidence of child labour, the type of prevalent work and work arrangements, and market conditions.

To illustrate, Brazil and India have both followed approaches which combine legal action with economic incentives. In India, the legal framework is provided by the 1986 Child Labour Act, prohibiting the employment of children below fourteen in hazardous occupations. The economic framework is set by the National Policy on Child Labour, which targets education for all children up to fourteen and proposes an extensive system of non-formal education combined with employment and income-generating schemes in areas with a high incidence of child labour. A series of pilot projects has been set up (Narayan 1988). In Brazil, the focus is on street children. The government has recognized that its customary bureaucratic procedures would fail to address this problem effectively. Instead, a community-based strategy was set up whereby the government's role was limited to providing technical support. By 1986, local volunteer 'commissions' existed in most major urban areas which were able to mobilize community resources (Myers 1988).[8]

If economic incentives and legislation are the two pillars on which efforts to help working children need to be based, the effectiveness of each will be greatly enhanced by simultaneous efforts at advocacy and mobilization and by empowerment of the children and their families. Because many of the most exploited and endangered working children go unnoticed, their situation must be brought forcefully to the attention of government and the public, in an effort to mobilize a constituency to defend them. Advocacy entails combating ignorance but also prejudice, fear and the denigration of working children. There is irony in such negative views, because working children often assume great responsibility for helping themselves and their families (Myers 1991). Many working children and their families operate within very limited economic and social options. Effective empowerment can expand those options and give the children a larger share of society's possibilities and benefits. Myers (1991) discusses ways to achieve this, most of which are characterized by the strong involvement of local communities, aided and supported by national or international organizations.

As said earlier, child labour has stigma attached to it, certainly among government officials. Sometimes a more positive view can open a road to helping working children more effectively, especially by targeting working children and extending certain benefits to them. As the previous section indicated, this is especially appropriate where child labour is a manifestation of poverty. Many working children are inadequately fed and do not go to school. The government could provide factory meals to working children, just as it sometimes provides school meals to children in school. Similarly, primary healthcare workers could be mandated to visit and provide free care to child workers and employers to restrict children's workday to five or six hours so that they can attend school at least part time. Such measures would benefit children who are confronted by an economic situation which is not likely to change in the short run. The added benefits may be perceived by families as an increase in the children's real wage and thus have the effect of increasing the supply of child labour.

Such programmes, of course, would require rather profound shifts in many governments' current attitude of denial and/or 'all-or-nothing' bans. The argument presented in this [reading] is in favour of such gradual solutions which recognize an economic reality and utilize it to help those in an unfortunate situation, with the belief that this will contribute to the elimination of child labour in the longer term.

NOTES

From C. Grootaert and R. Kanbur (1995), 'Child Labour: An Economic Perspective', *International Labour Review*, vol. 134, no. 2, pp. 187–203; article is a condensed and edited version of a background paper, 'Child labour: a review', prepared for the World Bank's [...] *World Development Report 1995*. The views expressed in this article are those of the authors only and should not be attributed to the World Bank or its affiliated organizations.

1 See Rodgers and Standing (1981) for a useful typology of children's activities.

2   The ILO has put together a very useful bibliography which covers the literature of this period (ILO 1986).
3   Formal presentations of the model of the household economy which explicitly take into account the economic contributions of children can be found, *inter alia*, in Levy (1985), Rivera-Batiz (1985) and Sharif (1994). Much of that work is based on Rosenzweig and Evenson (1977).
4   Education and work are not the only factors which affect child welfare. There exists a vast literature which has demonstrated that large family size adversely affects many aspects of child welfare: health, intelligence, physical development, etc. (see the review in King 1987).
5   Notice that this income-insurance argument is not the same as that of old-age insurance (where parents want to have children so that they will take care of them in their old age). That argument explains a high demand for children, but not child labour. In fact, it should induce parents to send children to school since that would increase their earnings and hence the potential transfers they can provide for their parents in old age.
6   A detailed and interesting description of enforcement problems and issues in the case of Sri Lanka is given in Goonesekere (1993).
7   Weiner (1991) illustrates these points in the case of Europe and North America.
8   For more recent information on these cases, see Boyden and Myers (1995); and on street children, see UNICEF (1986) and Taçon (1991).

REFERENCES

Agiobu-Kemmer, I. S. (1992), *Child Survival and Child Development in Africa* (The Hague: Bernard van Leer Foundation Studies and Evaluation Papers, no. 6).
Ashagrie, K. (1993), 'Statistics on child labour: a brief report', in *Bulletin of Labour Statistics 1993* (Geneva), no. 3.
Basu, A. M. (1993), 'Family size and child welfare in an urban slum: some disadvantages of being poor but modern', in C. B. Lloyd, ed., op. cit.
Bekombo, M. (1981), 'The child in Africa: socialization, education and work', in G. Rodgers and G. Standing, eds, op. cit.
Bequele, A. and J. Boyden, eds (1988), *Combating Child Labour* (Geneva: ILO).
Bonnet, M. (1993), 'Child labour in Africa', in *International Labour Review* (Geneva), vol. 132, no. 3.
Boyden, J. and W. Myers, (1995), *Exploring Alternative Approaches to Combating Child Labour: Case Studies from Developing Countries*, Innocenti Occasional Papers, Child Rights Series, no. 8 (Florence: UNICEF).
Cain, M., A. B. M. Mozumder and A. Khorshed (1980), *Labour Market Structure, Child Employment, and Reproductive Behaviour in Rural South Asia*, World Employment Programme Research Working Paper, Population and Labour Policies Programme, no. 89 (Geneva: ILO).
Cochrane, S., V. Kozel, and H. Alderman (1990), *Household Consequences of High Fertility in Pakistan*, World Bank Discussion Paper no. 111 (Washington, DC: World Bank).
DeGraff, D. S., R. E. Bilsborrow, and A. N. Herrin (1993), 'The implications of high fertility for children's time use in the Philippines', in C. B. Lloyd, ed., op. cit.
Galbi, D. (1994), *Child Labour and the Division of Labour*, mimeo (Cambridge: Centre for History and Economics, King's College).
Goonesekere, S. W. E. (1993), *Child Labour in Sri Lanka: Learning from the Past* (Geneva: ILO).

Guèye, M., S. Pacqué-Margolis, M. Kanthiébo and M. Konaté (1993), 'Family structure, education, child fostering, and children's work in the Kayes and Yelimane Circles of Mali: results of focus-groups', in C. B. Lloyd, ed., op. cit.

Gunn, S. E. and Z. Ostos (1992), 'Dilemmas in tackling child labour: the case of scavenger children in the Philippines', in *International Labour Review* (Geneva), vol. 131, no. 6.

Hotz, V. J. and R. A. Miller (1988), 'An empirical analysis of life cycle fertility and female labour supply', in *Econometrica* (Oxford), vol. 56, January.

ILO (1992), *World Labour Report 1992* (Geneva: ILO).

ILO (1986), *Annotated Bibliography on Child Labour* (Geneva: ILO).

Jacoby, H. and E. Skoufias (1994), *Risk, Financial Markets and Human Capital in a Developing Country*, mimeo, World Bank Policy Research Department (Washington, DC: World Bank).

Jejeebhoy, S. J. (1993), 'Family size, outcomes for children, and gender disparities: the case of rural Maharashtra', in C. B. Lloyd, ed., op. cit.

Jomo, K. S., ed. (1992), *Child Labour in Malaysia* (Kuala Lumpur: Varlin Press).

King, E. M. (1987), 'The effect of family size on family welfare: what do we know?', in D. G. Johnson and R. D. Lee, eds, *Population Growth and Economic Development: Issues and Evidence* (Madison: University of Wisconsin Press).

Levy, V. (1985), 'Cropping pattern, mechanization, child labour, and fertility behavior in a farming economy: rural Egypt', in *Economic Development and Cultural Change* (Chicago), vol. 33, no. 4, July.

Lloyd, C. B. (1994), *Investing in the Next Generation: The Implication of High Fertility at the Level of the Family*, Research Division Working Paper no. 63 (New York: The Population Council).

Lloyd, C. B., ed. (1993), *Fertility, Family Size and Structure: Consequences for Families and Children*, Proceedings of a Population Council Seminar, New York, 9–10 June 1992 (New York, The Population Council).

Mendelievich, E. ed. (1979), *Children at Work* (Geneva: ILO).

Morice, A. (1981), 'The exploitation of children in the "informal sector": proposals for research', in G. Rodgers and G. Standing, eds, op. cit.

Myers, W. ed. (1991), *Protecting Working Children* (London: Zed Books).

Myers, W. (1988), 'Alternative services for street children: the Brazilian approach', in A. Bequele and J. Boyden, eds, op. cit.

Nakamura, A. and M. Nakamura (1992), 'The econometrics of female labour supply and children', in *Econometric Review* (New York), vol. 11, no. 1.

Narayan, A. (1988), 'Child labour policies and programmes: the Indian experience', in A. Bequele and J. Boyden, eds, op. cit.

Okojie, C. (1993), 'Micro-consequences of high fertility in Nigeria', in C. B. Lloyd, ed., op. cit.

Rivera-Batiz, F. L. (1985), *Child Labour Patterns and Legislation in Relation to Fertility*, mimeo (Bloomington: Department of Economics, Indiana University).

Rodgers, G. and G. Standing, eds (1981), *Child Work, Poverty and Underdevelopment* (Geneva: ILO).

Rosenzweig, M. R. (1981), 'Household and non-household activities of youths: issues of modelling, data and estimation strategies', in G. Rodgers and G. Standing, eds, op. cit.

Rosenzweig, M. R. and R. Evenson (1977), 'Fertility, schooling, and the economic contribution of children in rural India: an econometric analysis', in *Econometrica* (Oxford), vol. 45, no. 5, July.

Salazar, M. C. (1988), 'Child labour in Colombia: Bogotá's quarries and brickyards', in A. Bequele and J. Boyden, eds, op. cit.

Sathar, Z. A. (1993), 'Micro-consequences of high fertility: the case of child schooling in rural Pakistan', in C. B. Lloyd, ed., op. cit.

Sharif, M. (1994), 'Child participation, nature of work, and fertility demand: a theoretical analysis', in *Indian Economic Journal* (Allahabad), vol. 40, no. 4.

Shreeniwas, S. (1993), 'Family size, structure, and children's education: ethnic differentials over time in peninsular Malaysia', in C. B. Lloyd, ed., op. cit.

Taçon, P. (1991), 'A global overview of social mobilization on behalf of street children', in W. Myers, ed., op. cit.

UNICEF (1991), *The State of the World's Children 1991* (Oxford: Oxford University Press).

UNICEF (1986), *Exploitation of Working Children and Street Children*, UNICEF Executive Board, Report E/ICEF/1986/CRP.3 (New York: UNICEF).

Weiner, M. (1991), *The Child and the State in India: Child labour and Education Policy in Comparative Perspective* (Princeton: Princeton University Press).

Part II

Outside the Factory Gate

Introduction

While Part I concentrates on exploring popular themes in ways that have been generally under-represented in much of the sociology of work, Part II is concerned with going beyond the boundaries of so much of the history of work sociology: the factory and the factory proletarian. Although such work groups have always formed a politically and economically important part of the workforce, they have seldom if ever formed a majority of the people engaged in 'work' of one form or another. Thus, for example, the largest single occupational group in the early twentieth century in Britain was not the miners or factory operatives but domestic workers, most of whom were relatively young women. Indeed, there were probably few families at this time that either did not have a domestic servant or did not supply one. This part seeks to open up the factory gates and go beyond them to seek out three quite different aspects of work: domestic work; the 'work' of the customer; and war work.

Ruth Schwartz Cowan's (1989) analysis of domestic labour in nineteenth-century America suggests that men's domestic work tended to be externalized to the market while women's remained internal; whatever else happened, there was little attempt by men to share the duties then undertaken wholly by women. A century later little seems to have changed. As the review by Suzanne Franks (1998) suggests, when women in the 1960s and after sought equality in the workplace they ended up juggling extra responsibilities rather than sharing the domestic work with their male partners. The experience of Soviet women in the Russian revolution was an earlier version of this irony, for while the state often encouraged women to undertake work hitherto restricted to men (for example, road-building, medicine and the armed forces) there was little attempt by men to shoulder any of the domestic responsibilities of these 'liberated' women.

Sue Newell's 'The Superwoman Syndrome' reviews the contemporary evidence for transformation of the gendered division of domestic labour and its links to equal opportunities at work. However, while enormous changes in the gendered composition of the workforce have occurred since the end of the Second World War, those changes have not really been transformed into a proportionate increase in managerial jobs, neither has the domestic division of labour altered radically. Instead, employment for most women remains something which has to be achieved in addition to whatever domestic responsibilities they hold. And while younger women are now less likely to hold traditional views on the gendered divisions of work than older women, men remain remarkably consistent in their conservatism. The result is that women are all too often faced with the 'super-woman syndrome': the corpus of beliefs that suggests women can – and should – be able to hold down a job and a family simultaneously. That the most successful role models for this appear to be women who can purchase considerable domestic help in the guise of nannies and other women domestic workers does not seem to lessen the social pressure on those who have to undertake both activities on their own.

Newell's own survey-based research supports the wealth of anecdotes that already exist: men believed in patriarchy and enacted it; women believed in equality and embodied the results of inequality. Moreover, the persistence of gendered inequality at home persisted, irrespective of whether women were employed and once children arrived: the burden of domestic responsibility increased for women and decreased for men. And, just to ensure that such responsibilities were rationalized as freely made choices, men tended to assume that women subordinated their career to their family in an act of volition that simply did not exist for men. Thus whatever employing organizations did to promote equal opportunities at work was consistently undermined by the prevailing division of labour in the home. In short, employment and domestic work are two sides of the same coin, they are not independent of each other.

If domestic work is the precondition for paid work (the all too often invisible support) then the customer or consumer is an equivalently transparent participant at the other end of work. And while a focus on consumption may not necessarily fit easily with the traditional focus on work as the act of production, it is the case that the cult(ure) of the customer, as Paul du Gay and Graeme Salaman suggest, can have critical implications for the way work is organized and constituted.[*] What particularly interests them is the way the market imperatives of the customer-oriented approach supplant the bureaucratic processes that pre-existed, and do so through the conduit provided by the language of 'excellence'. The authors begin by noting the changing environmental pressures on producers throughout the last two decades, most notably in the striving for a high quality differentiated product but – more importantly for them – the way in which the idea of the customer has been incorporated into the work organization. In effect, organizations have restructured themselves on the assumption that relationships between different individuals and groups within them operate *as if* they are customers. That they are not real customers, since the internal market seldom exists, does not undermine the significance of assuming that organizations should be reorganized as if they were. At an organizational level this often involves their decentralization into

* This is different from the usual connection between customers and producers, perhaps best represented by what happened when Delia Smith, a popular British TV chef, recommended a particular omelette pan to her viewers on BBC: sales of the pan increased by 44,000 per cent from 200 in 1997 to 90,000 in just four months of 1998 (Wainwright 1998).

business units that are independent profit centres in an attempt to mimic the market imperative and drive out bureaucratic inefficiencies and inflexibilities – though in the case of the British National Health Service reforms of the Conservative administration many such reforms were reversed in the late 1990s. And one of the reasons for this reversal is the paradox noted by du Gay and Salaman – quality controls to support customer-oriented production and remove bureaucratic impediments are essentially bureaucratic in nature.

In practical terms the consequences of operating in this way have been to encourage managers to adopt unitarist philosophies that stress partnerships with all organizational members, including trade unions. These philosophies also demand that each and every individual in the newly empowered units adopts an enterprising attitude to their work and their colleagues. This is what Foucault describes as 'governing through the soul', that is securing managerial control by sponsoring self-control as freedom. In short, employee commitment becomes the precondition for organizational success – though, given the increased insecurity of employment that has accompanied most organizations recently, perhaps managers should consider whether commitment can ever be an asymmetric relationship.

Du Gay and Salaman end by considering how the language or discourse of enterprise draws strength from the global developments that underpin it. This is particularly in the way that enterprise now seems to have been accepted as a social norm for all, rather than a pattern of thought and action appropriate only to those engaged in free market relationships. In other words, the discourse of enterprise has now spread from business to colonize all social life. Here lies the most influential lesson, for, rather than the activities of producers determining those of consumers (as has been the convention in the study of work), it is the philosophy of the customer that has reversed the causal relationship and then spread beyond work itself to society at large. If 'enterprise' seems the 'normal' way to relate to others in or out of work we surely have succumbed to a new reality.

4   The Customer

The Cult[ure] of the Customer

PAUL DU GAY AND GRAEME SALAMAN

[. . .]

Introduction

In this [reading] we explore the nature, origins and consequences of a major aspect of current managerial thinking and theorizing about the structure and direction of work organization and the employment and governance of staff. Our subject matter is the managerial attempt to reconstruct work organizations in ways which are defined as characteristically commercial and customer focused. A fundamental aspect of managerial attempts to achieve this reconstruction involves the reimagination of the organization. Frequently this means the supplanting of bureaucratic principles by market relations.

In this first section we describe some of the major initiatives in work and organizational redesign which explicitly or covertly centre the managerial attempt to restructure organizational systems and relationships in terms of market relations. These restructuring programmes are located in the context of key environmental developments, also outlined in this first section.

However we do not argue that the supplanting of bureaucratic structures and relationships by market relations ('the sovereign consumer') is causally *determined* by environmental developments. The restructuring of work and work relations is as much supported by the discourse of enterprise (within and without the employing organization) as it is determined by environmental pressures. What we find currently is the coming together of environmental challenges, many of which are defined in terms of the imperative of fundamental organizational restructuring and the dominance of a discourse of enterprise. The most obvious location for the conjuncture of these two elements is in the 'excellence' literature.

Section two thus moves beyond developments in and at work to an analysis of the language which informs and supports these developments: the language of enterprise. In this section this discourse is addressed at the level of the corporation, and the corporation's customers, with particular attention being paid to the construction and redefinition of employees. In the third section we examine the role this discourse plays in reimagining the 'social' and the 'political' in contemporary Britain. One of the key arguments is the importance of mapping the resonances between the levels and spheres represented by the three constituent sections of the [reading]. The [reading] moves progressively through these three levels and offers an attempt to trace these connections.

'Close to the customer'

Current emphasis on the customer as a means of analysing and defining work performance and work relations represents a highly significant addition to management attempts to understand and explain the nature of the enterprise. We shall argue that the notion of the customer is fundamental to current management paradigms. Recent emphasis on a clearly defined notion of the customer as representing the key dynamic of market relations has become a central feature of work reorganization, and critically, of attempts by managers and their advisers to delineate and intervene in the organization of paid work.

We must start with a brief overview of the environmental developments which supply the justification for enormous emphasis on the consumer, whereby 'meeting the demands of the "sovereign" consumer becomes the new and overriding institutional imperative' (Keat 1991: 3). We shall find that one of many advantages of the emphasis on the customer as a method of understanding and directing organizational change is that it allows a conflation of external developments and pressures (the market) and internal relationships and strategies whereby both can be conceptualized in the same terms as if they were the same phenomenon, that is, in terms of a discourse of enterprise.

Many researchers have identified a cluster of related environmental developments which put pressure upon organizations to find new ways of enhancing their competitiveness and their market share: 'increased competition from foreign industry, a more quality-conscious consumer population, rapidly changing product markets, deregulation and new technologies' (Fuller and Smith 1991: 1). Most important of these developments is the increasing differentiation of demand.

The fragmentation and differentiation of demand for goods and services is a conspicuous and widely accepted feature of modern Western economic life. 'The changing nature of product markets is a significant determinant of contemporary economic restructuring' (Hill 1991: 397), 'Neo-Fordism arose out of "new constraints on the realization of value" stemming from the growth of product market variability' (Smith 1989: 209).

The differentiation of markets as a consequence of a change in consumer values and behaviour is frequently seen as a result of the successes of Fordism itself:

> To the extent that consumers demand a particular good in order to distinguish themselves from those who do not have it, the good becomes less appealing as more of it is sold. Consumers will be increasingly willing to pay a premium for a variant of the good whose possession sets it off from the mass; and as the number of variants competing for attention and encouraging further differentiation of tastes increases, it becomes harder and harder to consolidate production of a standard product. (Sabel 1982: 199)

Sabel, like many other writers, argues that if firms are to meet this challenge they must develop new ways of working which encourage innovation, flexibility and customer responsiveness.

This view of shifts in the nature of consumer demand is supported by analyses of consumption which stress its insatiability and striving for novelty. Consumption occurs in anticipation of actual use or consumption, for reality brings anti-climax: 'consumption is dynamic, for disillusionment (and moving on) is the necessary concomitant of the acquisition of goods that have been longed for in fantasy' (Abercrombie 1991: 178).

Furthermore, as Abercrombie notes, the current consumer/customer is also active, enterprising: searching, innovating, forcing change and movement upon producers in marked contrast to the passive, easily pleased customer of Fordism.

These pressures, particularly the differentiation of demand, have forced change on work organizations. Radical organizational change in response to these pressures is becoming the norm. Recent surveys in the UK by Thompson et al. (1985) and in the USA by Severance and Passino (1986) chart the frequency and scope of organizational change. Thompson et al. surveyed 1000 middle and senior managers in 190 organizations, and explored changes since 1979. Thirty-three per cent of respondents reported radical change; 56 per cent acknowledged some change. Key factors influencing these changes were recession and changing markets. Sisson identifies two common strategies used to cope with these pressures. The first is the more productive and profitable use of the organization's assets through more thorough knowledge of costs and margins – asset management: 'shifting the firm's capital away from the high-cost/low-profit businesses to those that are more profitable' (Sisson 1989: 23). The alternative approach, more important here, is the attempt to improve the value added by each employee. The study by Severance and Passino (1986: 1) concludes that the dominant strategy has been one of dramatic quality improvements allied to cost reduction achieved through reduced inventories, and Hendry et al. (1988) describe a set of generic strategic responses to environmental change: competitive restructuring coupled with quality improvement and new concepts of service and quality provision.

Central to these quality-focused strategies is an explicit emphasis on the customer, and on establishing a close and direct relationship between organization and customer, and between elements of the organization *as if* these were customer/supplier relations. The value placed on the customer in current programmes of organizational change represents an attempt to re-create within the organization types of relationship which normally occur on the interface of the organization with its customers.

References to the customer and uses of the customer in management analysis offer ways of understanding the organization and, based on these understadings, ways of reconstructing it. This emphasis is usually closely related to changes in market – i.e. customer – behaviour. And these changes are frequently conceptualized in terms of the differentiation of markets.

That demand is now highly differentiated, with consumers being both knowledgeable and *demanding*, is not simply an important *fact* of modern economic life, it is, more significantly, an important *idea* in modern economic life which plays a critical role in attempts to restructure organizations. Smith remarks that the new, radical consumers, by their good 'taste' are restructuring workers' lives in capitalist labour processes. 'Sabel warns us of the purchasing power of yuppie shoppers: "do not forget all those fashion, health and quality conscious consumers who, quite independently of foreign competition, are unsettling the manufacture of everything, from shirts to bread"' (Smith 1989: 213).

Current restructuring within organizations involves considerable emphasis on enterprise within the organization, and this emphasis is closely related to achieving customer focus. The expression 'customer' has displaced other ways of describing those who are served by the organization. Those who travel by British Rail are no longer passengers; they are customers. The term has become paradigmatic, and represents a major shift in the ways in which the purpose and structure of work organizations are defined. However, the idea of the paradigmatic customer depends upon, and closely relates to, other arguments and developments.

First, it assumes 'an actual or at least achievable relationship between the conduct of commercial enterprises in a free market economy and the display of enterprising characteristics by those involved in the process of production' (Keat 1991: 6). That is, it is possible and desirable to reproduce, within the organization, relationships which resemble those between the organization and its clients. In this way, current emphasis on customer-focused behaviour and relationships relates directly to attempts to restructure work.

Secondly, managerial emphasis on the significance of the customer assumes 'a high degree of control over what is produced being exercised by the freely made choices of "sovereign" consumers' (Keat 1991: 7). This overlooks the extent to which consumers' preferences are generated and structured by the producers themselves.

Nevertheless, although there is evidence that this emphasis on customer sovereignty is exaggerated, there is no doubt that managerial representations of the customer as a means of restructuring organizations, and of influencing employees' behaviour and attitudes, are of real importance.

The importance of managerial discussions of the paradigmatic sovereign consumer lies in the ways in which this idea and its associated language and assumptions relate to current programmes of organizational change. These programmes focus on the redesign of organizational structures, work structures and practices. The common element of these programmes is that they argue the need to impose the model of the customer–supplier relationship on internal organizational relations, so departments now behave as if they were actors in a market, workers treat each other as if they were customers, and customers are treated as if they were managers.

Chandler (1977) and Williamson (1975) have both argued that the large corporation developed because the

> co-ordination of collective action can be conducted more efficiently and cheaply by means of an administrative hierarchy than by transactions in the market place. Thus under pressure of competition many firms have engaged in vertical integration. Moreover, at least according to Chandler, the larger the throughput of business down the vertically integrated chain the greater does the advantage of hierarchy over the market show up. (Francis 1983: 105)

This traditional view of the merits of bureaucratic structures is entirely opposed by the current language of the sovereign consumer; for this asserts that in order to compete successfully against competitor suppliers, and to achieve adequate profit margins, organizations must be able to satisfy customers. And in order to do this, internal organizational relations must resemble – indeed even become market relations. Thus, in a curious inversion of what was for many years the received wisdom, that the inadequacies of the market should be ameliorated by the bureaucratic method of controlling transactions, market co-ordination is imposed on administrative co-ordination. 'A central feature of current attempts to construct "an enterprise culture" in Britain has been a series of institutional reforms designed to introduce market principles and commercially modelled forms of organization into a wide range of activities previously conducted upon different principles' (Keat and Abercrombie 1991: 216).

Thus a major thrust of current programmes of organizational change is to replace management hierarchical control with simulated market control: divisions, regions, become quasi-firms, and transactions between them become those of customer or supplier or even competitor. Corporations are decentralized into a number of semi-autonomous business units or profit centres, each of which is required to achieve a given level of financial contribution to head office. This policy is seen to remove obstructive and expensive bureaucratic controls; to liberate innate entrepreneurship and to make local management 'more sensitive to the satisfaction of product market requirements in order to meet ... performance targets' (Hill 1991: 402). It is argued that by this means, sub-unit goals will necessarily become clearer, as each sub-unit pursues its own self-interest within the context of head office policy and financial constraints.

This form of organizational restructuring is not confined to those organizations which literally operate within a clearly defined market; it is also apparent within the public sector – the National Health Service and local authorities – where the notion of a market, and of customers exercising choice is not an obvious one. In these cases the imposition (or creation) of customer sovereignty is forced through central government legislation requiring competitive tendering of services previously supplied by hierarchies, not markets; by service-level agreements between separate functional specialities or by patients' charters. The interesting point here is the way in which the emphasis on the sovereign consumer as a method of restructuring organizations gains a further level of reality and conviction by becoming enshrined in legislation covering those organizations which are furthest removed from market and consumer pressures. Paradoxically, we thus find that the adaptation of market relations and structures in organizations is frequently a result of formal, centralized and bureaucratic compulsion.

Another important area where management conceptions of the value of customer-type relations have been pervasively applied is in the sphere of work restructuring. Many writers have argued the connection between the emergence of differentiated markets and post-Fordist forms of work organization, with greater choice and variety of consumption being related to flexible work forms, and classic Fordist economic structures (mass production) being inherently tied to mass consumption. 'The changing nature of product markets is a significant determinant of contemporary economics restructuring' (Hill 1991: 397). While it remains true that the link between market developments and changes in work organization requires empirical examination (Smith 1989: 212), it is possible to trace more direct and detailed connections between new work forms and management emphasis on the customer as a paradigm of internal organizational relationships. Two key mechanisms of work restructuring both frequently associated with work (functional) flexibility programmes, total quality management (TQM) and just-in-time (JIT) systems, both require the redefinition of the relationship between workers in terms of the customer model: workers become each others' customers.

In the case of TQM, quality is defined initially in terms of conformance to the requirements of the customer, but more significantly, relations between workers and departments are also defined in these terms – as internal customers: 'An organizational unit receives inputs from the previous process and transforms these to produce outputs for the next.... As a "customer", a unit should expect conformance to its own requirements, while as a supplier it has an obligation to conform to the requirements of others' (Hill 1991: 400). Quality management theory argues that exposure to customer pressure (even when this is simulated within the organization) is a powerful and necessary pressure for enhanced quality – i.e. the pressure to satisfy the customer.

JIT systems encapsulate three forms of flexibility (Sayer 1986): flexibility of skills, flexibility of response to cope with variations in the quantity of output, and flexibility to respond to technological and product changes (Dawson and Webb 1989: 222). All three forms of flexibility are necessary to cope with the basic principle of JIT: that stocks are reduced to such an extent that each worker (or team or department) in a sequence of interdependent operations receives the necessary assembly just in time, and to acceptable quality standards. He or she then passes the assembly on to the next operator, and so on. The 'essence of the JIT system is that work is done only when needed' (Sayer 1986: 233). The system is inherently customer-dependent. First, production is now determined not by an established pace of work but by customer demand, and customer quality requirements; secondly, relations between operators in a JIT system are defined as essentially analogous to relations between a series of internal customers. Work control is achieved through workers controlling each other in the guise of customers (Fuller and Smith 1991).

The third way in which the language of the paradigmatic customer is focused and applied in work restructuring occurs when customers – as constructed by management through customer survey technologies – are made to exert control over employees. We have seen that organizational departments may be defined *as if* customers, and work colleagues relate to each other as customers. Now, in the case of service industries with significant employee/customer interaction, customers are made to function in the role of management. In this sector, customer satisfaction is now defined as critical to competitive success, because of its importance in achieving high levels of customer retention. Quality is thus defined as usual, in terms of giving customers what they want, yet at the same time traditional methods of control (i.e. bureaucratic control) are too overtly oppressive, too alienating and too inflexible to encourage employees to behave in the subtle ways which customers define as indicating quality service, many of which – subtleties of facial expression, nuances of verbal tone or type of eye-contact – are difficult to enforce through rules, particularly when the employee is out of sight of any supervisor.

This is not to argue that these forms of employee control are any less oppressive. They are simply oppressive in new ways: by stipulating behavioural standards, installing new technologies of surveillance (such as consumer reports, 'professional' customers and random staff visits) associated with attempts to define and structure employees' subjective meanings and identities.

Furthermore, bureaucratic control may achieve compliance with the letter of the regulation but may also allow the minimal performance standard to become the norm, and to stifle individual spontaneity and responsiveness. The 'solution' is to seek to change behaviour, values and attitudes through culture change rather than structural change, and to measure the success of these programmes through customer feedback. It is of course possible to see the use of elaborate and sophisticated customer feedback data as a method of measuring, monitoring and ultimately managing service employees as a new solution to a traditional managerial dilemma: achieving sufficient control and direction without destroying the very behaviour that is required. (Fuller and Smith (1991) document this aspect of the managerial use of customer feedback very thoroughly.) But our interest in this is less in the development of new managerial forms of control, and more in the ways in which the language of the sovereign customer is increasingly embedded in a wide-ranging series of organizational structures, practices and technologies.

In the following section we describe and analyse this language in terms of a consideration of the discourse of enterprise. This discourse both sustains and is supported by the restructuring initiatives described earlier. The discourse of enterprise allows a timely and elegant mode of understanding and responding to the pressures of environmental challenge and market differentiation on the one hand and the accepted need for organizational restructuring on the other.

The enterprising cult[ure] of the customer

If bureaucratic and Taylorist forms of administration are intimately linked to the process of differentiation, then governing organizational life in an enterprising manner is intricately bound up with the process of de-differentiation: with a pronounced blurring between the spheres of 'production' and 'consumption', the 'corporate' and 'culture' (Jameson 1990; Lash 1988). As the language of 'the market' becomes the only valid vocabulary of moral and social calculation, 'civic culture' gradually becomes 'consumer culture', with citizens reconceptualized as enterprising 'sovereign consumers'.

In the public sector, for example, as a number of commentators have argued (Edgar 1991; Hall 1991), there can hardly be a school, hospital, social services department, university or college in the UK that has not in some way become permeated by the language of enterprise. Enterprise has remorselessly reconceptualized and remodelled almost everything in its path. Ostensibly different 'spheres of existence' have fallen prey to its 'totalizing' and 'individualizing' economic rationality (Foucault 1988b; Gorz 1989) – from the hospital to the railway station, from the classroom to the museum, the nation finds itself translated. 'Patients', 'parents', 'passengers' and 'pupils' are reimaged as 'customers'.

While this process of relabelling may appear as a totalitarian attack on diversity and difference it is never conceived of or represented as such. Rather, the enterprising customer–consumer is imagined as an empowered human being – the moral centre of the enterprising universe. Within the discourse of enterprise customers–consumers are constituted as autonomous, self-regulating and self-actualizing individual actors, seeking to maximize the worth of their existence to themselves through personalized acts of choice in a world of goods and services.

As a wide range of public institutions and services are remodelled along the lines of the private business enterprise their survival and future success becomes increasingly dependent upon their ability to be 'market driven' and 'customer led'. For example, in a 1985 speech entitled 'Towards a Consumer Oriented V&A', Sir Roy Strong, then Director of the Victoria and Albert Museum in London, argued that if the V&A were to survive and prosper it would have to learn some lessons from the private sector and tune itself more to the logic of the market. If the museum were able to reorient itself accordingly, Sir Roy had no doubt that 'it could become the Laura Ashley of the 1990s'.

While the enterprising language of the customer structures political debate, providing the rationale for programmes of intervention and rectification in the public domain – such as the delivery of healthcare, the provision of local government services and the delivery of education – it is also linked to a transformation in programmes and technologies for regulating the internal world of the business enterprise. In other words, although private enterprise provides the model for the reconstruction of social relations in the public domain, this does not mean that there are not varying degrees of enterprising enterprise.

Enterprising enterprises

Within the discourse of enterprise, private sector corporations are not considered to be inherently enterprising. Certainly the free market system provides the inherently virtuous model through which all forms of social relation should be structured, but in order to guarantee that maximum benefits accrue from the workings of this intrinsically virtuous system it is the moral obligation of each and every commercial organization, and each and every member of such an organization, to become obsessed with 'staying close to the customer' and thus with achieving 'continuous business improvement'. To put it simply: commercial organizations must continually struggle to become ever more enterprising. Thus the discourse of enterprise also envisages a new type of rule and imagines new ways for people to conduct themselves within the private business enterprise, as well as in public sector institutions.

The notion of 'Total Customer Responsiveness' (Peters 1987), in this sense, appears as both symptom of, and answer to, the problems thrown up by the increasingly dislocated ground upon which globalized capitalism operates. The more dislocated the ground upon which business organizations must operate, the less they are able to rely upon a framework of stable social and political relations and the more they are forced to engage in a project of 'hegemonic construction' (Laclau 1990: 56). In other words, the effects of dislocation require constant 'creativity' and the continuous construction of collective operational spaces that rest less and less on inherited objective forms (bureaucracy) and more frequently on cultural reconstruction. The only way to 'run a tight ship' in the inherently 'chaotic' global economy, it is argued, is through 're-enchanting' the work organization around the figure of the 'customer':

> the focus on the outside, the external perspective, the attention to the customers, is one of the tightest properties of all...it is perhaps the most stringent means of self-discipline. If one really is paying attention to what the customer is saying, being blown in the wind by the customer's demands, one may be sure he (*sic*) is sailing a tight ship. (Peters and Waterman 1982: 32)

Reimagining the corporation through the culture of the customer means encouraging organizations and their participants to become more enterprising. In this sense enterprise refers to a series of techniques for restructuring the internal world of the organization along 'market' lines in order to anticipate and satisfy the needs and desires of the enterprising sovereign consumer, and thus ensure business success. Through the medium of various technologies and practices inscribed with the presuppositions of the 'enterprising self' – techniques for reducing dependency by reorganizing management structures ('de-layering'); for cutting across internal organizational boundaries (the creation of 'special project teams', for example); for encouraging internal competitiveness through small group working; and for eliciting individual accountability and responsibility through peer-review and appraisal schemes – the internal world of the business organization is reconceptualized as one in which customers' demands and desires are satisfied, productivity enhanced, quality assured, innovation fostered, and flexibility guaranteed through the active engagement of the self-fulfilling impulses of all the organization's members.

Through the discourse of enterprise, the relations between 'production' and 'consumption', between the 'inside' and 'outside' of the corporation, and crucially between work-and non-work-based identities, are progressively blurred (Sabel 1990). Operating with a unitary frame of reference, enterprise projects the vision of a cohesive but inherently flexible organization where an organic complementarity is established between the 'greatest possible realization of the intrinsic abilities of individuals at work' and the 'optimum productivity and profitability of the corporation'. In this vision the 'no win' scenario associated with a mechanistic, bureaucratic lack of enterprise is transformed into a permanent 'win/win' situation through the active development of a flexible, creative and organic entrepreneurialism (Kanter 1990; Pascale 1991; Pinchot 1985). Enterprising corporations are those in which 'customer relations' mirror 'employee relations', where 'staying close to the customer' means gaining 'productivity through people' (Peters and Waterman 1982: 166).

As the Confederation of British Industry argues, enterprising enterprises are those which increasingly turn:

> to the people who work for them to develop . . . competitive advantage. The winners are those who can organise and motivate their people at all levels so that they give willingly their ideas, their initiative and their commitment to the continuous improvement that winning requires. . . . And it is up to those people as individuals to make the difference. They can no longer be treated as part of the collective mass . . . people want to do a good job, to have opportunities for self development, to contribute their thoughts as well as their physical skills to the teams and firms for which they work, and to be recognised and rewarded for their whole contribution. (CBI 1988: 5)

Governing the business organization in an enterprising manner is therefore said to involve 'empowering', 'responsibilizing' and 'enabling' all members of that organization to 'add value' – both to the company for which they work and to themselves. 'Total customer responsiveness' inaugurates a 'new form of control – self control born of the involvement and ownership that follows from, among other things, training people . . . to take on many traditionally supervisory roles. Being fully responsible for results will concentrate the mind more effectively than any out of touch cop' (Peters 1987: 363).

In this way the government of the enterprising firm can be seen to operate through the 'soul' (Foucault 1988a) of the individual employee. These firms get the most out of their employees by harnessing 'the psychological strivings of individuals for autonomy and creativity and channelling them into the search for 'total customer responsiveness', 'excellence' and success. Enterprising companies 'make meaning for people' by encouraging them to believe that they have control over their own lives; that no matter what position they may hold within an organization their contribution is vital, not only to the success of the company but to the enterprise of their own lives. Peters and Waterman (1982: 76, 81), for example, quote approvingly Nietzche's axiom that 'he who has a why to live for can bear almost any how'. They argue that 'the fact . . . that we think we have a bit more discretion leads to much greater commitment'. The enterprising firm is therefore one that engages in controlled de-control. To govern the corporation in an enterprising fashion is to 'totalize' and 'individualize' (Foucault 1988b) at one and the same time; or, to deploy Peters and Waterman's (1982: 318) terminology, to be 'simultaneously loose and tight' – 'organizations that live by the loose/tight principle are on the one hand rigidly controlled, yet at the same time allow, indeed, insist on, autonomy, entrepreneurship, and innovation from the rank and file'.

The key to 'loose/tight' is culture. According to Peters and Waterman, the effective management of meanings, beliefs and values (which accompanies the increasing 'capitalization' of all areas of human activity) can transform an apparent contradiction – between increasing central control while extending individual autonomy and responsibility – into 'no contradiction at all'. If an organization has an appropriate 'culture' of enterprise, if all its members adopt an enterprising relation to self, then efficiency, economy, autonomy, quality and innovation all 'become words that belong on the same side of the coin' (Peters and Waterman 1982: 321).

At truly enterprising companies:

> cost and efficiency, over the long run, follow on from the emphasis on quality, service, innovativeness, result-sharing, participation, excitement and an external problem-solving focus that is tailored to the customer.... Quite simply these companies are simultaneously externally focused and internally focused – externally in that they are driven by the desire to provide service, quality and innovative problem-solving in support of their customers, internally in that quality control, for example, is put on the back of the individual line worker, not primarily in the lap of the quality control department. Service standards are likewise largely self-monitored.... This constitutes the crucial internal focus: the focus on people.... By offering meaning as well as money, they give their employees a mission as well as a sense of feeling great. Every man (*sic*) becomes a pioneer, an experimenter, a leader. The institution provides the guiding belief and creates a sense of excitement, a sense of being part of the best. (Peters and Waterman 1982: 321–3)

Although the resource to 'culture' by Peters and Waterman and other proponents of enterprise is often criticized within the social sciences for its 'remarkable vagueness' (Howard 1985), these 'cultural intermediaries' of enterprise are quite adamant that 'the aesthetic and moral vision' driving the enterprising organization from above only finds life 'in details, not broad strokes' (Peters 1987: 404). In other words, the 'culture' of the business enterprise is only operationalized through particular practices and technologies – through 'specific measures' (Hunter 1987) – which are linked together in a relatively systematic way.

Rather than being some vague, incalculable 'spirit', the culture of enterprise is inscribed into a variety of mechanisms, such as application forms, recruitment 'auditions' and communication groups, through which senior management in enterprising companies seek to delineate, normalize and instrumentalize the conduct of persons in order to achieve the ends they postulate as desirable. Thus governing the business organization in an enterprising manner involves cultivating enterprising subjects – autonomous, self-regulating, productive, responsible individuals – through the development of simultaneous loose/tight 'enabling and empowering vision' articulated in the everyday practices of the organization.

The discourse of enterprise brooks no opposition between the mode of self-presentation required of managers and employees, and the ethics of the personal self. Becoming a better worker is represented as the same thing as becoming a more virtuous person, a better self. In other words, under the regime of enterprise, technologies of power – 'Which determine the conduct of individuals and submit them to certain ends or domination, an objectivizing of the subject' – and tech-nologies of the self – 'which permit individuals to effect by their own means or with the help of others, a certain number of operations over their own bodies and souls, thoughts, conduct, and way of being, so as to transform themselves in order to attain a certain state of happiness, purity, wisdom, perfection or immortality' – are imperceptibly merged (Foucault 1988a: 18). The values of self-realization, of personal responsibility, of 'ownership', accountability and self-management are both personally attractive and economically desirable (Hollway 1991; Miller and Rose 1990).

This 'autonomization' and 'responsibilization' of the self, the instilling of a reflexive self-monitoring which will afford self-knowledge and therefore self-mastery, makes paid work, no matter how ostensibly 'deskilled' or 'degraded' it may appear to social scientists, an essential element in the path to self-fulfilment, and provides the reasoning that links together work and non-work life. The employee, just as much as the sovereign consumer, is represented as an individual in search of meaning and fulfilment, looking to 'add value' in every sphere of existence. Paid work and consumption are just different playing grounds for the same activity; different terrains upon which the enterprising self seeks to master, fulfil and better itself. In making oneself a better sovereign consumer, or a better employee, one becomes a more virtuous and empowered human being.

Through 'capitalizing' the meaning of life, enterprise allows different 'spheres of existence' to be brought into alignment and achieve translatability. The 'rap-prochement' of the self-actualization of the individual employee with the com-petitive advancement of the business organization for which he or she works, for example,

> enables an alignment to take place between the technologies of work and the techno-logies of subjectivity. For the entrepreneurial self, work is no longer necessarily a constraint upon the freedom of the individual to fulfil his or her potential through striving for autonomy, creativity, and responsibility. Work is an essential element in the path to self-realization. There is no longer any barrier between the economic, the psychological and the social. The government of work now passes through the psychological strivings of each and every individual for fulfilment. (Miller and Rose 1990: 27)

The discourse of 'enterprise'

Although the discourse of enterprise, and contemporary attempts to create an 'enterprise culture' in the UK, are virtually synonymous with the politico-ethical project of 'Thatcherism' they are not reducible to this phenomenon. Rather, as Robins (1991: 25) has indicated, the development of an 'enterprise culture' must be located within the context of increasing globalization. In other words, the project of reconstruction that the notion of an 'enterprise culture' signifies and encapsulates may be seen as one that has its roots in developments outside the will and control of any one national government (Held 1991). At the same time, this also suggests that the decline of Margaret Thatcher herself in no way heralds an end to the project of enterprise and the cult of the customer. Indeed it can be persuasively argued that the 'enterpreneurial revolution' to which Thatcherism contributed with such passionate brutality is 'still working its way through the system' (Hall 1991: 10).

In Britain attempts to construct a culture of enterprise have proceeded through the progressive enlargement of the territory of the market – of the realm of private enterprise and economic rationality – by a series of redefinitions of its object. Thus the task of creating an 'enterprise culture' has involved the reconstruction of a wide range of institutions and activities along the lines of the commercial business organization, with attention focused, in particular, on their orientation towards the customer. At the same time, however, the market has also come to define the sort of relation that an individual should have with him/herself and the 'habits of action' he or she should acquire and exhibit. Enterprise refers here to the 'kind of action, or project' that exhibits 'enterprising' qualities or characteristics on the part of individuals or groups. In this latter sense, an 'enterprise culture' is one in which certain enterprising qualities – such as self-reliance, personal responsibility, boldness and a willingness to take risks in the pursuit of goals – are regarded as human virtues and promoted as such. As Keat has indicated, in the contemporary discourse of enterprise these two strands, the 'structural' and the 'ethical', are intricately interwoven:

> On the one hand, the conduct of commercial enterprises is presented as a (indeed the) primary field of activity in which enterprising qualities are displayed. And given that these qualities are themselves regarded as intrinsically desirable... this serves to valorize engagement in such activities and hence, more generally, the workings of a free market economy. On the other hand, however, it is also claimed that in order to maximize the benefits of this economic system, commercial enterprises must themselves be encouraged to be enterprising, i.e. to act in ways that fully express these qualities. In other words, it seems to be acknowledged that 'enterprises are not inherently enterprising', and enterprising qualities are thus given an instrumental value in relation to the optimal performance of a market economy. (Keat 1991: 3–4)

According to Gordon (1991: 43), enterprise has become an approach capable, in principle, 'of addressing the totality of human behaviour, and, thus, of envisaging a coherent, purely economic method of programming the totality of governmental action'. In other words, enterprise can be understood to constitute a particular form of 'governmental rationality' (Foucault 1979). It invents and attempts to exercise a form of rule through the production of certain sorts of human subject.

In the work of neo-liberals such as Friedman and Hayek, for example, the well-being of social and political existence is to be established not through the practice of bureaucratic administration but rather through the 'enterprising' activities and choices of autonomous entities – organizations, groups and individuals – operating in the market place, each attempting to maximize their 'competitive advantage'. Thus, in an 'enterprise culture' freedom and independence emanate not from civil rights but from choices exercised in the market: 'the sovereignty that matters is not that of the king or the queen, the lord or the white man, but the sovereignty of the consumer in the market place' (Corner and Harvey 1991: 11).

No longer simply implying the creation of an independent business venture, enterprise now refers to the application of 'market forces' and 'entrepreneurial principles' to every sphere of human existence. A basic indicator of the way in which the language of enterprise has traversed its traditional limits is provided by the cultural theorist Judith Williamson in her weekly column in the Guardian newspaper. 'What intrigued me', she writes, 'is not only that enterprise now means business, but the fact that . . . it can be seen as . . . a personal attribute in its own right. The language has colonized our interiors; if you can't speak it you haven't got it!' (the Guardian, 4 July 1991: 28).

According to Gordon (1987: 300), rather than being a travesty of genuine value, as Williamson implies, the pervasive presence of the language of enterprise is indicative of a profound mutation in governmental rationality whereby 'a certain idea of the enterprise of government promotes and capitalizes on a widely disseminated conception of individuality as an enterprise, of the person as an entrepreneur of the self'.

This idea of an individual human life as an 'enterprise of the self' suggests that there is a sense in which, no matter what hand circumstance may have dealt a person, he or she remains always continuously engaged (even if technically 'unemployed', for example) in that one enterprise, and that it is 'part of the continuous business of living to make adequate provision for the preservation, reproduction and reconstruction of one's own human capital' (Gordon 1991: 44). The power of enterprise lies in its apparent universality and in its simplicity, in its ability to offer a standard benchmark by which all of life can be judged. By living one's life as an 'enterprise of the self', modes of existence that often appear to be philosophically opposed – business success and personal growth, for example – can be 'brought into alignment and achieve translatability'. Hence the discourse of enterprise establishes links between the 'ways we are governed by others, and the ways we should govern ourselves' (Rose 1989: 7–8).

Here, enterprise refers to the plethora of 'rules of conduct' for everyday life mentioned earlier: energy, initiative, calculation, self-reliance and personal responsibility. This 'enterprising self' is a calculating self, a self that 'calculates about itself, and that works upon itself in order to better itself'. In other words, enterprise designates a form of rule that is intrinsically ethical – 'good government is to be grounded in the ways in which persons govern themselves' (Rose 1989: 7–8) – and inherently economic; enterprising self-regulation accords well with Jeremy Bentham's rallying cry of 'Cheap Government!'. Thus enterprise is the contemporary 'care of the self' which government commends as the corrective to collective greed (Foucault 1988c; Gordon 1991).

For Miller and Rose (1990: 24), the significance of enterprise as a discourse resides in its ability to act as translation device, a cypher 'between the most general *a priori* of political thought', and a range of specific programmes for managing aspects of economic and social existence. Thus, enterprise can be seen to be more than a political rationality, it also takes a technological form: it is inscribed into a variety of often simple mechanisms – contemporary organizational examples could include quality circles, assessment centres, appraisal systems and personality profiling – through which various authorities seek to shape, normalize and instrumentalize the conduct of persons in order to achieve the ends they postulate as desirable. Inscribed with the presuppositions of the 'enterprising self', these technologies accord a priority to the self-steering and self-actualizing capacities of individuals. In other words, enterprise serves not only to articulate a diversity of programmes for making the world 'work better', but, in addition, it also enables these programmes 'to be translated into a range of technologies to administer individuals and groups in a way ... consonant with prevailing ethical systems and political mentalities' (Miller and Rose: 1990: 24; Rose 1990).

The discourse of enterprise can be understood, therefore, in terms of the linkages it forges between the 'political', the 'technological' and the 'ethical'. Enterprise acts as a 'nodal point' connecting a powerful critique of contemporary institutional reality, a seemingly coherent design for the radical transformation of social, cultural and economic arrangements, and a 'seductive' ethics of the self (Rose 1990).

Although the removal of Margaret Thatcher from office quickly spawned talk of a 'post-enterprise culture' and even of a return to 'business as usual', our argument is an attempt to indicate that such views severely underestimate the power and pervasiveness of the discourse of enterprise and the cult of the customer. Certainly, the political atmosphere in the UK has changed very noticably since Thatcher's departure, but this does not in any way signal the decline and fall of the whole entrepreneurial edifice. Enterprise was always bigger than Thatcherism alone, and has entered people's daily lives in a number of ways not directly related to the policy initiatives of successive Conservative administrations. Enterprise has operated on many fronts at the same time, changing the world by rewriting the language, redefining the relation between the public and the private, the corporate and culture. Rather than viewing this process of translation as in some sense a side-show to, or 'ideological distortion' of, the realities of restructuring, it is important to recognize that if an activity or institution is redefined, reimagined or reconceptualized it does not maintain some 'real', 'essential' or 'originary' identity outside its dominant discursive articulation, but assumes a new identity.

Similarly, it is useful to note that in order for an ideology/discourse to be considered hegemonic it is not necessary for it to be loved. Rather, 'it is merely necessary that it have no serious rival' (Leys 1990: 127). Certainly the discourse of enterprise appears to have no serious rivals today. While critics of enterprise (Jessop et al. 1990) point to people's continued attachment to the welfare state, and to equality rather than 'excellence', in order to highlight their lack of conscious identification with the aims and objectives of enterprise, they tend to forget that the dominance of that discourse is not so much inscribed in people's consciousness as in the practices and technologies to which they are subjected. As Zizek (1989: 32; 1991) has argued, people 'know very well how things really are, but still they are doing it as if they did not know'. In other words, even if people do not take enterprise seriously, even if they keep a certain cynical distance from its claims, they are still reproducing it through their involvement in the everyday practices within which enterprise is inscribed.

Thus enterprise should not be viewed as a 'pure' discourse as that term is often (mis)understood – i.e. as a combination of speech and writing – but always and only as a dimension of material practices, with material conditions of emergence and effectiveness. While the success of enterprise indicates that 'articulation is constitutive of all social practice' (Laclau 1990), it is not the case that 'just anything can be articulated with everything else'. All discourses have conditions of possibility and emergence which put 'limits or constraints on the process of articulation itself' (Hall 1988: 10–11).

By focusing upon the context within which enterprise emerged, rather than dismissing it out of hand as 'evil', 'philistine' or 'wicked' – in other words, as part of the old capitalist conspiracy – it becomes possible to reveal its contingent nature, and thus the possibility of its transformation. It must be remembered, for example, that the current 'triumph of the entrepreneur' within the public sector is directly related to the crisis of the Keynesian state and its attempts at the social management of the economy. Enterprise may well be the colonization of the public sphere by the market but its ascendance is certainly predicated upon the visible failure of the welfare state's own utopia (Wright 1987).

The discourse of enterprise deserves much more serious attention than it has tended to receive within the social sciences, especially when reports of its death are so exaggerated. Rather than being a travesty of genuine value, or on its last legs, the continued triumph of the entrepreneur is symptomatic of a 'profound mutation in governmental rationality'. As Rose (1989: 14) has argued, the success of neo-liberalism in the UK with its flagship image of an enterprise culture, 'operates within a much more general transformation in "mentalities of government", in which the autonomous, free, choosing self...has become central to the moral bases of political arguments from all parts of the political spectrum'. The language of enterprise has established an affinity between the politico-ethical objectives of neo-liberal government in the UK, the economic objectives of contemporary business, and the self-actualizing, self-regulating capacities of human subjects.

NOTE

From P. du Gay and G. Salaman, 1992 'The Cult[ure] of the Customer', *Journal of Management Studies*, vol. 29, no. 5, pp. 615–33.

REFERENCES

Abercrombie, N. (1991), 'The privilege of the producer', in R Keat and N. Abercrombie, eds, *Enterprise Culture* (London: Routledge), pp. 171–85.

Chandler, A. D. (1977), *The Visible Hand: The Managerial Revolution in American Business* (Harvard: Belknap Press).

Confederation of British Industry (1988), *People: The Cutting Edge* (London: CBI).

Corner, J. and S. Harvey, eds (1991), *Enterprise and Heritage* (London: Routledge).

PAUL DU GAY AND GRAEME SALAMAN

Dawson, P. and J. Webb (1989), 'New production arrangements: the totally flexible cage?', *Work, Employment and Society*, vol. 3, no. 2, pp. 221–38.
Edgar, D. (1991), 'Are you being served?', *Marxism Today*, May, p. 28.
Foucault, M. (1979), 'On governmentality', *Ideology and Consciousness* (Harmondsworth: Penguin) pp. 5–21.
Foucault, M. (1988a), 'Technologies of the self', in L. H. Martin, H. Gutman and P. H. Hutton, eds, *Technologies of the Self* (London: Tavistock).
Foucault, M. (1988b), 'The political technology of individuals', in L. H. Martin, H. Gutman and P. H. Hutton, eds., *Technologies of the Self* (London: Tavistock).
Foucault, M. (1988c), *The Care of the Self: The History of Sexuality*, vol. 3 (Harmondsworth: Penguin).
Francis, A. (1983), 'Markets and hierarchies: efficiency or domination?' in A. Francis, J. Turk and P. Willman, eds, *Power, Efficiency and Institutions* (London: Heinemann), pp. 105–17.
Fuller, L. and V. Smith (1991), 'Consumers' report: management by customers in a changing economy, *Work, Employment and Society*, vol. 5, pp. 1–16.
Gordon, C. (1987), 'The soul of the citizen: Max Weber and Michael Foucault on rationality and government', in S. Whimster and S. Lash, eds, *Max Weber: Rationality and Modernity* (London: Allen & Unwin).
Gordon, C. (1991), 'Governmental rationality: an introduction', in G. Burchell, C. Gordon and P. Miller, eds, *The Foucault Effect* (London: Harvester Wheatsheaf).
Gorz, A. (1989), *Critique of Economic Reason* (London: Verso).
Hall, S. (1988), *The Hard Road to Renewal* (London: Verso).
Hall, S. (1991), 'And not a shot fired', *Marxism Today*, December, pp. 10–15.
Held, D. (1991), 'Democracy, the nation-state and the global system', *Economy and Society*, vol. 20, no. 2, pp. 138–72.
Hendry, C., A. M. Pettigrew and P. Sparrow (1988), 'Changing patterns of human resource management', *Personnel Management*, November, vol. 20, pp. 37–41.
Hill, S. (1991), 'How do you manage a flexible firm?', *Work, Employment and Society*, vol. 5, no. 3, pp. 397–416.
Hollway, W. (1991), *Work Psychology and Organizational Behaviour* (London: Sage).
Howard, R. (1985), *Brave New Workplace* (New York: Viking Penguin).
Hunter, I. (1987), 'Setting limits to culture', *New Formations*, vol. 4, pp. 103–23.
Jameson, F. (1990), 'Clinging to the wreckage: a conversation with Stuart Hall', *Marxism Today*, September, p. 29.
Jessop, B., K. Bonnett and S. Bromley (1990), 'Farewell to Thatcherism?: neo-liberalism and "new times"', *New Left Review*, vol. 179, pp. 81–102.
Kanter, R. M. (1990), *When Giants Learn to Dance* (London: Unwin Hyman).
Keat, R. (1991), 'Introduction', in R. Keat and N. Abercrombie, eds, *Enterprise Culture*, (London: Routledge), pp. 3–10.
Laclau, E. (1990), *New Reflections on the Revolution of Our Time* (London: Verso).
Lash, S. (1988), 'Discourse or figure?: postmodernism as a regime of signification', *Theory, Culture and Society*, vol. 5, pp. 311–36.
Leys, C. (1990), 'Still a question of hegemony', *New Left Review*, vol. 180, pp. 119–28.
Miller, P. and N. Rose (1990), 'Governing economic life', *Economy and Society*, vol. 19, pp. 1–31.
Pascale, R. (1991), *Managing on the Edge* (Harmondsworth: Penguin).
Peters, T. (1987), *Thriving on Chaos* (Basingstoke: Macmillan).
Peters, T. and R. H. Waterman (1982), *In Search of Excellence* (New York: Harper & Row).

92

Pinchot, G. (1985), *Intrapreneuring: Why You Don't Have to Leave the Corporation to Become an Entrepreneur* (New York: Harper & Row).

Robins, K. (1991), 'Tradition or translation: national culture in its global context', in J. Corner and S. Harvey, eds, *Enterprise and Heritage* (London: Routledge).

Rose, N. (1989), 'Governing the enterprising self', paper presented to a conference on 'The Values of the Enterprise Culture', University of Lancaster, September.

Rose, N. (1990), *Governing the Soul* (London: Routledge).

Sabel, C. (1982), *Work and Politics* (Cambridge: Cambridge University Press).

Sabel, C. (1990), 'Skills without a place: the reorganization of the corporation and the experience of work', paper presented to the British Sociological Association Annual Conference, University of Surrey, Guildford, April.

Sayer, A. (1986), 'New developments in manufacturing: the JIT system', *Capital and Class*, vol. 30, no. 3, pp. 43–72.

Severance, D. G. and J. H. Passino (1986), *Senior Management Attitudes towards Strategic Change in US Manufacturing Companies* (Ann Arbor: University of Michigan Press).

Sisson, K. (1989), 'Personnel management in transition', in K. Sisson, ed., *Personnel Management in Britain* (Oxford: Blackwell), pp. 23–54.

Smith, C. (1989), 'Flexible specialization, automation and mass production', *Work, Employment and Society*, vol. 3, no. 2, pp. 203–20.

Thomson, A., A. M. Pettigrew and N. Rubashow (1985), 'British management: strategic change', *European Management Journal*, vol. 3, no. 3, pp. 165–73.

Williamson, O. E. (1975), *Markets and Hierarchies: Analysis and Antitrust Implications* (New York: Free Press).

Wright, P. (1987), 'Excellence', *London Review of Books*, May.

Zizek, S. (1989), *The Sublime Object of Ideology* (London: Verso).

Zizek, S. (1991), *For They Know Not What They Do: Enjoyment as a Political Factor* (London: Verso).

5 Domestic Work

The Superwoman Syndrome: Gender Differences in Attitudes towards Equal Opportunities at Work and towards Domestic Responsibilities at Home

SUE NEWELL

Introduction

The greatest social change [since the 1970s] has been the increase of women in the labour force. The 1951 Census showed that only 22 per cent of married women were economically active (Hakim 1979) but by 1987, 68 per cent of married women were active (Office of Population Censuses and Surveys 1987). The total labour force has grown by nearly 3 million since 1971, and most of this increase (approximately 90 per cent) has been among women (Department of Employment 1990). This has been achieved in conjunction with a change in attitudes towards working women. Jowell et al. (1988) compare data from a 1965 study of working age women (Hunt 1968) with their 1987 data on British social attitudes. Even in 1965 only a small minority of married women felt that being married disqualified a woman from working. So these attitudes have changed little. However, there has been a fairly radical change in beliefs about women with children. In 1965, 78 per cent of women felt that mothers with children under five should stay at home. By 1980 that proportion had fallen to 62 per cent and by 1987 it had dropped to only 45 per cent. A closer examination of the results of such surveys does highlight some potential anomalies in the attitudes measured. For example, Martin and Roberts (1984), analysing data from the 1980 Women and Employment survey, found that only 25 per cent of women held the view that a woman's place is in the home, yet 46 per cent agreed that a husband's job is to earn money, a wife's job is to care for the home and family. Clearly, the view must be that work for a woman must be accommodated alongside domestic demands and responsibilities. Younger full-time working women and students were found to hold less traditional attitudes, but husbands were repeatedly found to be more traditional than their wives with regard to gender roles at home and work.

Forecasters have used such evidence to predict that the rate of participation of women in the labour force will continue to increase. Britain has one of the highest levels of female participation in the EC (Dale and Glover 1990). However, it also has one of the highest rates of part-time work, with 45 per cent of all women in the UK working part-time (Beechey and Perkins 1987).

Another feature of women's employment, especially in the UK, is that there are clear trends in the rate according to family responsibilities. Only about 37 per cent of mothers with children aged [up to four] years old work, compared with 63 per cent of mothers with children between five and nine years (Franzetti 1991). Thus, although becoming a mother rarely leads today to a permanent departure from the labour force (Sharpe 1984), a woman's employment is typically characterized by one or more career breaks, coinciding with the birth and pre-school development of her child(ren) (Larwood and Gutek 1989). In Britain there is virtually no state-funded childcare for the under threes and even when children start school, after-school care is very problematic (Cohen 1988).

It is clear that childcare facilities do have a direct bearing on women's employment (Berry -Lound 1990). The costs of childcare can take up much of a woman's earnings. Joshi (1987) has shown that many women in the UK spend up to 30 per cent of their pay on childcare costs. Dex and Shaw (1986) conclude that part of the explanation for American women's preference for full-time work, as opposed to British women's preference for part-time work, is that there are tax provisions which help to offset the costs of childcare in the USA. The fact that childcare in Britain is not subsidized thus makes it uneconomic for many women to work, especially with women so dominant in low-paid jobs (Joshi and Newell 1985).

Women in Britain also fare poorly in comparison to their European peers in the provision of maternity rights. The actual length of leave is comparable, but while in Britain women receive 90 per cent of their full pay for only six weeks, in Italy or Spain women receive eighteen weeks leave on 80 per cent of their rate of full pay. Furthermore, in Britain it is harder to qualify for the statutory maternity leave than in other European countries because of the qualifying length of service requirement (Davidson and Cooper 1983). The Policy Studies Unit has estimated that about 40 per cent of women are excluded because of this (Whitfield 1991).

The result of all this is that the average British woman experiences motherhood as a negative influence on both earnings and job status. The more breaks from employment a woman has, the more likely it is that she returns to a lower occupational category than before the periods of leave (Stewart and Greenhalgh 1984; Martin and Roberts 1984). Thus, despite the increasing numerical equality of women in the workforce, the segregation of women's work remains pervasive (Hakim 1981). Women remain concentrated in a narrow range of occupations, most of which can be seen as an extension of their role within the family, and at the lower echelons of organizational structures (Dex 1987; Shipley 1990).

Despite this clear segregation of women's work, the traditional family with a female housewife and a male breadwinner is no longer typical, with women also increasingly being breadwinners. So what has become of the traditional domestic role of the housewife? Despite the popular myth that there is an increasingly equal sharing of domestic responsibilities (Young and Wilmott 1973), research shows that the segregation of household chores is still very clear. The reality is that millions of women go home at the end of the working day to several hours of additional work, a so-called 'second shift' (Hochshild 1989). Nash (1990) reports that on average, working women have only twenty-two hours of leisure per week, compared with forty-nine hours for men. Men may be participating more, but the sharing of home roles is far from egalitarian (Oakley 1990; Kiernan and Wicks 1990), even in households where the woman works full-time (Jowell et al. 1988).

Brannen and Moss (1988) found that a large majority of women believed domestic chores should be shared equally, but that in reality this was not the case. What is more interesting is that the women expressed little overt dissatisfaction with the situation. They believed that their husbands were domestically incapable and saw the problem of juggling full-time employment with motherhood as essentially theirs. Many of the men in the study were said to accept the return to work of their wives as inevitable because of the need for two incomes, but, at the same time, they failed to grasp the difficulties of running a home as well as working.

Llewelyn and Osbourne (1990) suggest that this is a reflection of women trying to apply themselves to a 'superwoman' ideal, often inspired by well-known successful working mothers who appear to 'do it all'. However, as Nash (1990) points out, such role models are unrealistic for the majority of mothers, as in most cases these 'superwomen' have a lot of external help from nannies or housekeepers. The media paragon of the superwoman exists more in fantasy than reality, with much research now testifying to the stresses on women of trying to balance family, domestic and work demands (for example Davidson and Cooper 1984; Scase et al. 1987). Nash (1990) cites evidence of people in the USA 'beginning to turn their backs on careers because running a home and a job is too much like hard work'. For many women, however, such a choice in itself would appear to be a luxury, many being forced to work out of financial necessity, irrespective of the double burden placed on them (Carter 1988).

Thus, despite the difficulties of combining a family and work, this is a choice that more and more women are making (Polakoff 1991). Yet there are many hurdles that a woman must overcome if she is to return to work with a family. The Equal Pay Act of 1970 and the Sex Discrimination Act of 1975 were designed to help remove inequalities between men and women at work (Beechey 1987) but while direct forms of discrimination have been abated, the extent to which these laws have reduced indirect discrimination is minimal (Coyle 1989). What many organizations fail to recognize is the extent to which personnel policies indirectly discriminate against a female labour force which increasingly consists of women with young children.

The gendered division of domestic and parental responsibilities restricts the time many women are able to give towards their careers. Colgan and Tomlinson (1991) reflect on the factors influencing an individual's career progression. Two main ones are having a full-time uninterrupted working life and being seen as promotable through having the ability and commitment to appear as a viable long-term prospect. Part of that commitment involves working long hours. It is therefore not surprising to find that women who are in demanding executive jobs are more likely to be single compared with their male colleagues (Valdez and Gutek 1989).

High status, well-paid jobs are organized as full-time and therefore are generally incompatible with the successful managing of a woman's home and family responsibilities. In response to this double burden the compromise that many women are adopting is to combine both roles through working part-time (Newell 1992). Unfortunately, this option will generally sacrifice long-term career prospects (Hunt 1988). On top of these structural problems, prejudices and stereotyping still appear to linger in Britain (Carter and Kirkup 1990; Jameson and Raine 1990).

All the evidence suggests that women's attitudes are changing and in consequence they are expanding their roles. However, there is little evidence that men are expanding their roles to encompass the domestic and childcare responsibilities traditionally undertaken by women. Women are thus left to occupy two roles, which to some extent are incompatible, unless the woman compromises by taking part-time employment. The survey reported in this paper set out to look at how far these problems, very clear in the literature, were recognized by a group of men and women working full-time, in two major blue-chip companies. Specifically, the study compares male and female attitudes and beliefs about the traditional gender roles within the home/family and work domains.

Methodology

Access to two major British companies was negotiated, the headquarters of an oil company based in the south-east of England and the administrative offices of an engineering company based in the north of England. A questionnaire was designed and extensively piloted in the two companies. The questionnaire was distributed to the sample populations in January 1992. The questionnaires were given out through department heads who were first briefed individually about the purpose of the research. The questionnaires were accompanied by a covering letter explaining the research, ensuring confidentiality and describing what was required of the respondent. An envelope was included with the researcher's name on it and respondents were asked to return the completed questionnaire in this envelope through the internal mail. They were asked to do this within one week, and to try and increase the response rate the researcher circulated around the departments encouraging people to complete the questionnaire. The sample chosen consisted of male and female full-time employees. It was decided that a comparison of full-time male and female employees would be more appropriate as it was not possible to find a comparative sample of part-time males had part-time females been included. Also, had part-time females been included, any differences found in the division of domestic responsibilities between males and females could have been accounted for by the extra time available if only working part-time, rather than to differences arising from gender *per se*.

97

SUE NEWELL

In the oil company the whole headquarters was sampled, which consisted of 235 males and 153 females, totalling 388 employees. The response rate from this organization was 67 per cent (102 females and 157 males). As the engineering company was larger a one in three sample was used, excluding all employees in the manufacturing department. This made the job profiles of the two groups comparable, as both samples consisted of non-manual, office-based employees. Two hundred and twenty-nine employees in the engineering company were sent questionnaires and the response rate was 72 per cent (41 females and 125 males). The total sample thus consists of 143 females and 282 males, reflecting the proportions of males and females in the two companies.

The questionnaire was designed to provide biographical data on the respondents plus information on a variety of attitudes, beliefs and behaviours in relation to gender roles. Not all questions are covered in this paper, and those which are will be described fully as the results are reported.

Results

A three-way analysis of variance has been used to look at differences in attitudes and behaviours by sex (males and females), age (under forty and over forty) and whether the individual has a family (children and no children). These variables were chosen as the independent variables because of the focus of the study. Marital status was not used in the analyses as the literature reviewed suggests that it is the presence of a child which most significantly affects family roles, bringing with it increased domestic responsibility. Geographical location was also initially considered to be a potentially discriminating factor, but preliminary analyses of the data found very few differences between subjects from the two companies, despite the fact that one company was based in the north and one in the south. Similarly, a comparison of responses according to job grade found few differences among subjects.

Of the total sample, 34 per cent (143) were female and 66 per cent (282) were male. Ages ranged from seventeen to over sixty, with 20 per cent (87) being under 24, 45 per cent (193) aged between 24 and 40, 34 per cent (142) aged between forty-one and sixty and 1 per cent (3) aged over sixty. For the analysis those under forty (65 per cent) are compared with those over forty (35 per cent). Forty-three per cent (182) of the respondents had children and 57 per cent (242) did not. The females in the sample were slightly younger than the males (t = 3.01, <0.003) and were less likely to have children (Chi = 27.99, df = 1, <0.0001). This is because those participating in the survey were working full-time. From the literature review it is clear that married women with children are more likely to be working part-time, if they are working at all. Thus the comparison of males and females takes into consideration age and family commitments through factor analyses.

98

Gender differences in attitudes towards equal opportunities

The questionnaire [included] a number of questions [intended] to gauge a person's attitude to the concept of equal opportunities in the workplace. For all these questions [the respondent] had to reply using a five-point scale from strongly agree (1) to strongly disagree (5). The first question simply asked respondents to agree or disagree with the statement 'men and women do not have equal opportunities in the workplace'. Women were significantly more likely to agree with this statement than their male colleagues ($F = 16.41$, < 0.0001). Similarly, the women were more likely to agree that 'women are less likely to be promoted to high-ranking positions within an organization, because employers fear they will leave to have children' ($F = 19.61$, < 0.0001), indicating that the males are less likely to recognize that there is a problem of equal opportunities in work. At the same time men were more likely to disagree that 'a woman can effectively combine the dual role of mother and worker' ($F = 30.96$, < 0.0001) to agree that 'a woman's place is in the home' ($F = 27.31$, < 0.0001), and to agree that 'women's maternal instincts make them more suited to look after the children than men' ($F = 28.02$, < 0.0001). Both men and women agreed that 'it is necessary for the father to participate as strongly as possible in a child's upbringing', but the men saw less need for a period of statutory paternity leave, disagreeing more with the statement 'all firms should provide men with statutory paternity leave' ($F = 12.82$, < 0.0001).

The men were therefore more likely to endorse the traditional role model for women, and were less likely to recognize that women might suffer in the workplace because of their domestic responsibilities. They were more likely to believe that equal opportunities already exist in the workplace, in spite of the fact that they also assumed that the woman was the person to look after the children, justifying this because of a woman's supposed 'maternal instincts'. They wanted to be involved with the children, as long as this did not impinge on their career, not recognizing a need for paternity leave, although admitting that they might take such leave if it were available: 'who wouldn't accept two weeks' extra holiday?'

The research referred to in the introduction suggests that attitudes to women and employment are changing over time. To look at this within the context of this research, analysis was undertaken to compare younger (under forty) and older (over forty) respondents. Younger respondents were less likely to agree that a woman's place is in the home ($F = 22.02$, < 0.0001) and that a woman's maternal instincts make them more suited to looking after the children ($F = 16.77$, < 0.0001). Younger respondents were also more likely to believe that firms should provide paternity leave ($F = 45.6$, < 0.0001) and to agree that, if offered, the majority of men would take such leave ($F = 4.2$, < 0.04).

The individual's sex was the strongest determinant of these attitudes, with age having a significant but lesser effect. However, the effects of having children were minimal, once age and sex were also taken into account in the analyses. The only

Table 5.1 Mean scores on attitude questions relating to equal opportunities issues

Attitude statements	Gender		Age		Family	
	Male	Female	-40	+40	Child	No child
1	2.93	2.41**	2.83	2.72	2.86	2.69
2	3.05	2.40**	2.82	2.85	2.89	2.78
3	1.49	1.39	1.42	1.52	1.45	1.47
4	2.81	2.23**	2.26	3.30**	2.97	2.36
5	2.78	2.82	2.71	2.96*	2.85	2.75
6	2.61	2.84	2.86	2.35**	2.56	2.78
7	3.85	4.47**	4.25	3.67**	3.89	4.17
8	2.83	2.24**	2.51	2.75	2.86	2.46**
9	2.35	3.05**	2.81	2.15**	2.29	2.79
10	2.32	1.90**	2.0	2.53**	2.22	2.15

* significant at the 0.05 level; ** significant at the 0.01 level

Key to Attitude statements:
1 Men and women do not have equal opportunities within the workplace.
2 A woman can effectively combine the 'dual role' of mother and worker.
3 It is necessary for the father to participate as strongly as possible in a child's upbringing.
4 All firms should provide men with statutory paternity leave of up to twenty-two weeks.
5 The majority of men would make use of paternity leave, if it were offered by their employers.
6 Statutory maternity benefits which are offered to women are of a fair nature.
7 A woman's place is in the home.
8 Women are less likely to be promoted to high-ranking positions within an organization, because employers fear they will leave to have children.
9 Women's maternal instinct makes them more suited to look after children than men.
10 The government should be responsible for providing more day-care facilities for pre-school children.

(Subjects responded to the questions on a 5-point scale from: 1 = strongly agree to 5 = strongly disagree.)

significant difference was that those without children agreed more with the statement that a woman is more likely not to be promoted because of employer's fears that she will leave to have a baby (F = 5.14, < 0.024).

The Factor Analyses showed no significant interaction effects. This indicates that females were significantly different from males irrespective of age or the presence of a family. This was further supported by a comparison of younger males and older females. These results showed fewer significant differences than when the total population of males and females was compared, but the results were in the same direction, with younger males maintaining more traditional attitudes than older females about the women's role in the home and in work.

Indeed, younger males were significantly less likely than older females to agree with the statements that men and women do not have equal opportunities at work (t = 2.02, < 0.049), that women can combine the dual role of mother and worker (t = 4.07, < 0.0001) and that women often do not get promoted because employers fear that they will leave to have children (t = 2.37, < 0.021). Clearly, the emancipation of men lags more than a generation behind the changing attitudes of females, as can be seen in table 5.1.

The domestic division of labour

Respondents were given a list of common household tasks and asked who *should* be responsible for these – mainly the woman (1), the woman more than the man (2), shared equally (3), the man more than the woman (4) or mainly the man (5). They were asked the same question, but in terms of the *current reality*.

There were significant differences between males and females in their replies. Male respondents were more likely to believe that males should be more respons-ible than females for providing financially for the family (t = 5.07, < 0.0001), mowing the lawn (F = 11.41, < 0.0001), painting and decorating (F = 4.87, < 0.028), household maintenance (F = 6.51, < 0.01) and washing the car (F = 10.9, < 0.0001). They were also more likely to believe that females should be more responsible than males for washing and ironing (F = 17.96, < 0.0001), washing dishes (F = 7.59, < 0.006) and food shopping (F = 5.79, < 0.017). In other words, males had a much clearer view of how household tasks should be divided up which had a well-defined gender base to it. The females believed less in the traditional gendered division of household labour and more in the equal sharing of all tasks. However, it was the males' gendered vision that had more relation to reality than the female vision of equality. Thus there was a significant correlation for the males between their vision of how tasks should be divided up and how they were divided up in reality for all the tasks in the question. For the females, the only significant correlation was between their view of who should be and who was responsible for household maintenance, which women continued to see as principally a male task. On all the other tasks, while women endorsed a much more equal sharing of the tasks, in reality they remained highly gendered. Thus responses indicated that the female member of the household was more likely to do more of the washing and ironing, dish washing and food shopping, while the male member was more likely to do more of the painting and decorating, household maintenance, car washing and lawn mowing. The only 'ungendered' activity appeared to be cleaning the windows, which females were just as likely to do as males.

The analyses of these questions by age showed that this was also an important variable influencing the division of household labour. Younger employees had a significantly reduced gendered belief about how household tasks should be divided up between males and females, as can be seen in table 5.2, which also shows differences between male and female respondents. Furthermore, younger

Table 5.2 Mean scores for gendered responses on: (a) who SHOULD be responsible for various household chores and (b) who is in REALITY responsible

(a)			SHOULD			
	Male	Female	Younger	Older	Child	No child
Washing/ironing	2.06	2.54**	2.42	1.85**	1.95	2.43
Washing dishes	2.75	2.95**	2.87	2.71*	2.76	2.86
Food shopping	2.47	2.73**	2.63	2.43*	2.34	2.69*
Windows	3.38	3.36	3.28	3.55**	3.46	3.32
Lawn	3.94	3.55**	3.68	4.06**	4.00	3.66
Paint/decorating	3.72	3.45*	3.47	3.94**	3.8	3.49
Maintenance	4.03	3.69**	3.75	4.22**	4.17	3.7*
Washing car	3.71	3.36**	3.45	3.86**	3.73	3.49

(b)			REALITY			
	Male	Female	Younger	Older	Child	No child
Washing/ironing	1.73	2.0	2.1	1.37**	1.54	2.18*
Washing dishes	2.88	2.77	3.08	2.53**	2.72	3.03
Food shopping	2.14	2.57**	2.42	2.03**	1.98	2.66*
Windows	3.05	2.94	2.95	3.09	3.0	2.03
Lawn	4.23	3.77*	3.86	4.43**	4.31	3.79
Paint/decorating	3.80	3.54	3.51	4.04**	3.91	3.47
Maintenance	4.31	3.90**	3.96	4.53**	4.44	3.84*
Washing car	4.23	3.90**	3.95	4.39**	4.31	3.89

* significant at the 0.05 level; ** significant at the 0.001 level
(Higher scores (4, 5) indicate the male is considered to be more responsible, lower scores (1, 2) the female, with 3 denoting equal sharing.)

employees operated in households where there was a much greater degree of egalitarianism in household tasks. Age appeared to have more effect on the actual division of these tasks than did sex. Thus, apart from on cleaning windows, there were main effects for both age and sex on perceived views about how household tasks *should* be divided up, males and older respondents believing in a much clearer gendered division. But in terms of *reality* age had a significant effect on all the tasks considered, while sex had a significant impact on only half the tasks. Interestingly, there was one significant interaction effect between age and sex on the perception of who should be responsible for household maintenance. Older females saw this as a more masculine task than did younger males, against the basic trend of females being less traditional than males (F = 6.527, < 0.0011).

Again the effects of having a family were less significant, although there was a trend towards a more equal sharing of household duties between partners when there were *no* children in the family. Once children were present there was a reversal to a more traditional gendered distribution of tasks. Significant differences between those with and without children were found on the division of washing and ironing (F = 6.59, < 0.01), food shopping (F = 17.45, < 0.0001) and household maintenance (F = 8.085, < 0.005). A separate analysis (using t-tests) of males and females with and without children revealed the source of these differences. For males there was a significant difference between those with and without children on the division of all of the household tasks, except cleaning windows, with males without a family sharing tasks more equally with their partner than those with a family. This may be because the female partners of the males with a family have either stopped working or reduced their hours in order to look after the family home and so have taken over even more of the general household management from the male partner. For females, however, there were no significant differences between those with and without children on any of the variables related to the division of household tasks.

Childcare

A question asked respondents to indicate how adequate they believed a range of childcare options to be. They were asked to choose on a five-point scale from very adequate (1) to very inadequate (5). On every single alternative except one the males perceived the care as less adequate than did the females (see table 5.3). This difference was significant on the ratings of the adequacy of nannies and friends as childcarers (F = 7.56, < 0.006; F = 12.19, < 0.001 respectively), and in the same direction on the ratings for au-pairs, nurseries and childminders. The one exception was the male rating of the adequacy of the mother, where males rated the mother as more adequate than did the females. Thus, while males and females saw the mother as the best person to look after the children (followed by the father), males saw the adequacy of alternative arrangements in a more negative light.

Age and the presence of children did not affect perceptions of the adequacy of different childcare arrangements, except that older respondents rated the father as a less adequate childcarer (F = 13.15, < 0.0001). Analysis of variance identified no significant interactions between age and sex and presence of children in the ratings of childcare adequacy.

Organizational initiatives

Many organizations that are introducing equal opportunities policies are including structural arrangements that are seen to help women combine their work and domestic roles. Respondents were asked to indicate how effective they saw three of the most popular initiatives to be in encouraging more women back into the workplace after having a child. They were asked to rate the three initiatives on a five-point scale from very effective (1) to very ineffective (5). Men in the sample saw all three initiatives as significantly less effective. Flexible working hours (F = 9.69, < 0.002), job sharing (F = 32.64, < 0.0001) and career breaks of up to five years (F = 12.15, < 0.001) were all seen as more effective by women than men. It

Table 5.3 Mean scores for rating the adequacy of various childcare arrangements

| | Gender | | Age | | Family | |
	Male	Female	-40	+40	Child	No Child
Mother	1.09	1.14	1.10	1.11	1.10	1.10
Father	1.71	1.54	1.54	1.88**	1.71	1.61
Relatives	2.57	2.35	2.49	2.51	2.55	2.45
Friends	3.21	2.82*	2.93	3.0	3.14	3.03
Nursery	2.52	2.35	2.38	2.62	2.55	2.40
Childminder	2.88	2.69	2.71	3.01	2.96	2.71
Au-pair	3.13	2.91	2.98	3.20	3.19	2.95
Nanny	2.55	2.22**	2.44	2.44	2.53	2.37

* significant at the 0.05 level; ** significant at the 0.01 level
(Subjects responded on a 5-point scale from: 1 = very adequate to 5 = very inadequate.)

appears that men are less aware of the difficulties which women face in combining career and family commitments and so do not appreciate the benefits that changed organizational arrangements can provide.

Age had a less significant impact on the perception of the efficacy of these organizational arrangements, although younger respondents did perceive career breaks as significantly more useful than older workers (F $= 6.72, < 0.01$). The comparison of those with and without children showed no significant effects. Analysis of variance showed that there were no significant age/sex/children interactions on these perceptions.

Discussions and conclusions

Clearly attitudes to women and work are changing as women increasingly enter the labour market. However, what is clear from these data is that the men in the sample maintain significantly more traditional ideas about women's role in work and in the home than do the women. For example, males in the sample were much more likely to agree that a woman is more suited to looking after children because of her 'maternal instincts' and to rate alternatives to the mother as childcarer significantly less favourably compared with the women. The men also retained a significantly more traditional view about how household tasks should be divided up, making the day-to-day management of the home the responsibility of the women. The data also make it clear that this traditional division of responsibility in the home remains dominant, even in households where women work full-time.

What is perhaps more revealing is that for the males, having a family resulted in a reduced household management burden and a return to a more traditional gendered division. This is presumably because their female partner had reduced or given up her commitment to paid employment and devoted more time to domestic employment. For the females, having children did not reduce their domestic burden and probably increased it. There were no significant differences between females with and without children in how they shared domestic roles with their partners. However, the results showed that the women in general took on a greater responsibility for the day-to-day household management. Therefore working women with children, and so increased domestic commitment, are likely to have a particularly high home workload, which they must try to accommodate alongside their full-time employment.

The data also revealed something of a contradiction as the males were less likely to acknowledge that women do not have equal opportunities in the workplace despite the fact that they expected women to undertake the general household management. Either they assume that women can be 'superwomen' and effectively manage both a career and the home, or they simply do not expect women to have, or indeed to want to have, progressive careers. The latter interpretation is more likely to be correct, given that the men in the sample were less likely to believe that women can combine the dual role of mother and worker. This would explain why men saw less need for organizational arrangements that might facilitate the ability to cope with home and job demands, such as flexible working, career breaks and job sharing. Yet it could be argued that the encouragement of such organizational arrangements by women might, in the long term, not be in the best interests of women themselves. As Cockburn (1991) points out, such 'mother's privileges' are a mixed blessing as they enable women to sustain a career after motherhood, but confirm them as the domestic sex. Men, then, do not perceive the need to change their own career schedules when they become fathers as the organizational arrangements are already well established for their wives. This extends to the men in this sample not even believing that paternity leave is important – their wives already have a statutory maternity right.

Friedan (1981) recognized that, while women have been pulled into the public domain, men have not been enticed into the private realm. The resulting lop-sided division of familial responsibilities led to the condition Friedan termed 'super-woman syndrome'. While women attempt to excel at both the traditional female sex roles and the role of paid labourer, men avoid women's traditional role of housekeeper/homemaker/hostess. The results reported in this paper suggest that while women would like to divest themselves of the household management, in reality the domestic division of labour remains gender specific. And this must be associated with the fact that male attitudes revealed a much less positive inclination to change traditional domestic roles. Men want, and indeed expect, their wives/partners to carry the domestic burden. Yet, when it comes to work, the fact that their female colleague is leaving work at 5.00 p.m. to pick up the children is her *choice* and because she is letting her domestic life affect her work it is her fault that she is hitting the glass ceiling (Kelly 1991). She is simply seen as not being prepared to make sacrifices for her career. This construction of reality shifts the blame for women's difficulties in the workplace to the women themselves, rather than recognizing the socially institutionalized and individually internalized stereotypes that underpin these 'choices'. Men continue to expect the women to run the home and look after their children, to take time off when the children are sick and arrange childcare in school holidays and on teacher training days. Yet, when she is not devoting herself 100 per cent to her job precisely because of this, she is to blame.

In the light of this, equal opportunities policies introduced by organizations are going to have a limited effect for the majority of women. Generally such policies have as their goal opening access to all jobs within an organization by the introduction of fair recruitment, appraisal and promotion practices, supplemented by training courses for women that will enable them to compete with men on an equal basis. In 'progressive' organizations this is also combined with organizational arrangements such as extended maternity leave, flexible working and job sharing. Yet none of this confronts the issue of the difference between men and women (and especially mothers and fathers) in their domestic roles. And, as argued above, in some ways the organizational arrangements help to reconfirm the woman as the primary manager of the home. What needs to be confronted is the gendered domestic economy as, without change here, equal opportunities policies are, for the majority of women, simply enabling them to be exploited in dead-end jobs which are low paid and with few, if any, promotion prospects.

NOTE

From S. Newell (1993), 'The Superwoman Syndrome: Gender Differences in Attitudes towards Equal Opportunities at Work and Towards Domestic Responsibilities at Home', *Work, Employment and Society*, vol. 7, no. 2, pp. 275–80.

REFERENCES

Beechey, V. (1987), *Unequal Work* (London: Verso).

Beechey, V. and T. Perkins (1987), *A Matter of Hours: Women, Part-time Work and the Labour Market* (Cambridge: Polity Press).

Berry-Lound, D. (1990), *Work and the Family: Carer-friendly Employment Practices* (London: Institute of Personnel Management).

Brannen, J. and P. Moss (1988), *New Mothers at Work: Employment and Childcare* (London: Unwin Paperbacks).

Carter, A. (1988), *The Politics of Women's Rights* (London: Longman).

Carter, R. and G. Kirkup (1990), *Women in Engineering: A Good Place to Be?* (London: Macmillan Education).

Cockburn, C. (1991), *In the Way of Women: Men's Resistance to Sex Equality in Organisations* (London: Macmillan).

Cohen, B. (1988), *Caring for Children: Services and Policies for Childcare and Equal Opportunities in the UK*, Report for the European Commission's Childcare Network (London: Family Policy Studies Centre).

Colgan, F. and F. Tomlinson (1991), 'Women in publishing: jobs or careers?', *Personnel Review*, vol. 20, no. 5, pp. 16–26.

Coyle, A. (1989), 'The limits of change: local government and equal opportunities', *Public Administration*, Spring.

Dale, A. and J. Glover (1990), *An Analysis of Women's Employment Patterns in the UK, France and the USA*, Research Paper no. 75 (London: Department of Employment Group).

Davidson, M. and C. Cooper (1983), 'Working women in the European Community: the future prospect', *Long Range Planning*, vol. 16, no. 4, pp. 49–54.

Davidson, M. and C. Cooper (1984), 'Occupational stress in female managers: a comparative study', *Journal of Management Studies*, vol. 21, no. 2, pp. 185–205.

Department of Employment (1990), 'Labour force outlook to 2001', *Employment Gazette*, April, pp. 186–195.

Dex, S. (1987), *Women's Occupational Mobility: A Lifetime Perspective* (London: Macmillan).

Dex, S. and L. Shaw (1986), *British and American Women at Work: Do Equal Opportunities Policies Matter?* (London: Macmillan).

Franzetti, V. (1991), *Women and Socio-economic Indices in the EC and UN*, unpublished MA dissertation (York: Centre for Women's Studies).

Friedan, B. (1981), *The Second Stage* (New York: Summit).

Hakim, C. (1979), 'Occupational segregation', *Department of Employment Research Paper*, no. 9.

Hakim, C. (1981), 'Job segregation: trends in the 1970s', *Department of Employment Gazette*, December, pp. 521–9.

Hochshild, A. (1989), *The Second Shift* (New York: Viking).

Hunt, A. (1968), *A Survey of Women's Employment* (London: Government Social Survey).

Hunt, A. (1988), *Women and Paid Work: Issues of Inequality* (London: Macmillan).

Jameson, B. J. and R. L. Raine (1990), 'A woman's perspective of a man's perspective of a woman's place in work: a personal opinion', *Management Services*, vol. 34, no. 5, pp. 12–14.

Joshi, H. (1987), 'The cost of caring', in C. Glendinning and J. Millar, eds, *Women and Poverty in Britain* (London: Wheatsheaf Books).

Joshi, H. and M. Newell (1985), *Parenthood and Pay Differences: Evidence from the MRC National Survey of Health and Development of the 1946 Birth Cohort*, Report to the Department of Employment, February.

Jowell, R., S. Witherspoon and L. Brook, (1988), *British Social Attitudes: The 5th Report* (Aldershot: Gower).

Kelly, R. M. (1991), *The Gendered Economy: Women, Careers and Success* (London: Sage).

Kiernan, K. and M. Wicks (1990), *Family Change and Future Policy* (London: Family Policy Studies Centre and Joseph Rowntree Foundation).

Larwood, L. and B. Gutek (1989), 'Working towards a theory of women's career development', in B. Gutek and L. Larwood, eds, *Women's Career Development* (London: Sage).

Llewelyn, S. and K. Osbourne (1990), *Women's Lives* (London: Routledge).

Martin, J. and C. Roberts (1984), *Women and Employment: A Lifetime Perspective* (London: HMSO).

Nash, T. (1990), 'The great no-win situation', *Director*, vol. 43, no. 4, pp. 46–50.

Newell, S. (1992), 'The myth and destructiveness of equal opportunities: the continued dominance of the mothering role', *Personnel Review*, vol. 21, no. 4, pp. 37–47.

Oakley, A. (1990), *Housewife* (London: Penguin).

Office of Population Censuses and Surveys (1987), *General Household Survey* (London: HMSO).

Polakoff, P. (1991), 'Business taking a much closer look at working women', *Occupational Health and Safety*, vol. 60, pp. 58–9.

Scase, R., R. Goffee and A. Mann (1987), 'Women managers: room at the top: destroying the myths', *Management Today*, March, pp. 64–7.

Sharpe, S. (1984), *Double Identity: The Lives of Working Mothers* (Harmondsworth: Penguin).

Shipley, P. (1990), 'Personnel management and working women in the 1990s: beyond paternalism', *Personnel Review*, vol. 19, pp. 3–12.

Stewart, M. and C. Greenhalgh, (1984), 'Work history patterns and occupational attainment of women', *Economic Journal*, vol. 94, pp. 493–519.

Valdez, R. and B. Gutek (1989), 'Family roles: a help or a hindrance for working women', in B. Gutek and L. Larwood, eds, *Women's Career Development* (London: Sage).

Whitfield, M. (1991), 'Pregnancy still costs women jobs', *The Independent*, 21 November.

Young, M. and P. Wilmott (1973), *The Symmetrical Family* (London: Routledge & Kegan Paul).

Part III

Constraints and Consensus at Work

Introduction

Part III moves us beyond a concern for under-researched areas, or the frailties of received wisdom, to one about the apparent decline of conflict. If the study of work until the 1980s often seemed obsessed by the action of shop stewards and trade unions, the post-1990s seem to be going in the opposite direction – assuming that the decline of industrial action and trade union membership is the equivalent of consensus – a correlation most effectively demolished by Steven Lukes (1974) in his *Power: A Radical View*.

The 1980s and 1990s were replete with enquiries into and recommendations for 'corporate culture'. Indeed, if often seemed that culture became a default category: if something could not be explained by any other means it must be to do with culture. The parallel movement was the sharp rise in Human Resource Management and a consequential decline in 'Industrial Relations' such that the familial urge of unitarism rapidly displaced the disunity inherent in pluralism. At least that was the theory, and a quick glance at the strike figures in any form usually implies that industrial conflict is now all but dead and the new partnerships between management and employees prevail over the brave new world – a vision effectively demolished by Willmott (1993). However the construction of a management vision that is sharply at odds with views from below or outside is hardly novel. One version of that vision is incorporated in the company's annual reports, and one might be forgiven for assuming that such publications are truthful reflections on the company's situation. Yet of the eleven most profitable companies in the UK between 1979 and 1990 four had collapsed by 1998.[*] Either something quite extraordinary and unforeseeable occurred or the figures were 'economical with the truth.' Such active constructions of the truth are not restricted to the controversies of the present but frequently erupt among the graves of the long dead and buried. For example, Michael Rowlinson's and John Hassard's reading digs into the past corporate culture of Cadbury's to suggest that history is anything but dead.

[*] Centre for Tomorrow's Company (1998), *Shorter, Sharper, Simpler* (London: Centre for Tomorrow's Company).

Rowlinson and Hassard begin by noting that the demand by sociologists to understand behaviour through the sets of meanings adopted by the actors involved poses a critical problem for those interested in sociologically informed historical analyses: dead people tell few tales.* The result is that historical archives tend to be seen either as a resource of marginal value or merely of value to those interested in recording the 'true' past or, in postmodernist vein, the past simply cannot be agreed and therefore should be avoided. Yet this is to leave the past to the powerful voices, and to imply agreement by acquiescence. Thus Rowlinson and Hassard set out to investigate Cadbury's corporate culture, wary of the way that founding business leaders do not so much establish a corporate culture in their image but ensure that their version of that history prevails.

Cadbury, now part of Cadbury Schweppes, was originally started in 1824 in Birmingham and specialized in the coffee and tea trade. The second generation of Cadbury brothers moved the company into the cocoa and chocolate trade in 1879 to Bournville – a greenfield site where the company provided housing and working facilities that were the envy of all and the consequence of religion, or so we are led to believe. In 1931 the company, having taken over the Fry chocolate company, celebrated its centenary with a couple of publications which linked the paternalistic labour-management policies to the Quaker beliefs of both the Cadbury and Fry founders. Yet Rowlinson and Hassard claim that the model village built at Bournville owed more to the fashion for early town planning and the Garden-City idea rather than Quakerism. Similarly, the provision of good working facilities and 'progressive' management were derived from turn-of-the-century changes to Cadbury's forced on them by competition rather than something inherent from the beginning. Likewise, the Works Council, a forum for discussing work-related issues (but not pay), was the foster child of the British government's own Whitley Committee in 1916–17 and not the consequence of any Quaker idealism. Indeed, the foundational assumption that Quakerism was somehow morally superior to any other ideological framework is radically undermined by the knowledge that Quakers were significant supporters of slavery in the eighteenth century and were prominent opponents of the Factory Acts in the nineteenth century – which attempted to restrict the exploitation of factory labour. Hence rather than Cadbury claiming a long lineage of Quaker philanthropy at the heart of its corporate culture it almost seems as though Quaker history was rewritten through the 'constructed' accounts of Cadbury's history.

A final point is to note the utility of corporate cultures that emphasize the continuity of the firm, for in a world where change is the only apparent constant, some method of hanging on to the past, to traditions and to the reassurance of familiarity seems valuable to management. In effect, a recognizable past in the present and future is held to provide the cultural cement that keeps organizations together.

Another way of keeping organizations coherent is by suppressing contemporary conflict, rather than conflicts about the past, and Stanley Deetz provides a sophis-

---

* I had originally written 'tell no tales' but, as one of my anonymous referees rightly points out, this is to ignore the records left by such people.

ticated overview of the role of corporations in decisions that affect public life and the way that such decision-making is achieved. Fundamentally, Deetz suggests that tracing the operation of power should not be restricted to economic exploitation and recognizable inequalities but should also include the ways that patterns of thought can restrict our outlook. This involves casting doubt on the freedom of sovereign individuals to think and act autonomously, and on a sceptical account of language as a neutral carrier of information. Foucault plays a prominent role in this approach, in particular in his conceptions of power as intimately related to knowledge as a creative rather than a negative force, and in the associated way in which power should be seen as a relationship that inveigles all involved, rather than as something which the powerful have and the powerless do not have. That said, Deetz maintains that management's superior position *vis-à-vis* its workforce is rooted in both economic-based structures and what he calls 'systems of discursive monopoly'. Hence what work could be – a site for the explicit discussion of legitimately contending interests – is transformed into an arena of 'invisible politics'. But Deetz is careful to insist that such managerial control cannot be obtained through ideological developments alone. In other words, he is not saying that workers are falsely conscious of their own needs and are easily fooled into supporting the system by the persuasive siren calls of capitalist consumerism. Rather, it is because the system encourages workers to seek their own interests in ways that simultaneously render support to the system itself and in which value-conflicts are suppressed.

At the heart of the modern corporation, according to this view, is a triple positioning of the individual:

- The individual freely chooses to subordinate himself or herself to the corporation on the basis of self-interest;
- The individual operates within a social world where the modern corporation is in sympathy with and not antagonistic to the rest of society's institutions;
- The individual is free to choose meanings and social relations for herself or himself.

But, suggests Deetz, individuals are not the sites for the construction of meaning or decision-making because the world is socially not individually constituted through discursive practices. That is to say, we can understand the world only through language and practices that are inherently social and which predate us, thus constraining and channelling the way we think and act. For example, we may think we are free to choose an identity but we are also subject to the identification process by others, such that we are identified as men or women or managers or the unemployed and so on. The consequence is an unequal struggle between what we want to be and what we are regarded as, and even if we deny the veracity of some identities – say for example those based on 'race' – this does not stop such identities playing significant roles in the distribution of power and reward at work and beyond. That all these identities are arbitrary does not diminish their importance, nor that those operating within such identities may believe themselves free and rational agents in the choice and deployment of action. For example, those individuals who find themselves unemployed may soon acquire a raft of attributes of which they were previously unaware (lazy, scrounger and so on) and which they may vehemently deny – but it may be extremely difficult to separate their personal and private accounts of themselves from those allocated through the identity 'unemployed' – which of course operates in clear distinction from the socially valued attributes assumed to exist in all those 'employed'. Or, in the example used by Deetz, as the banking world changes, so the configuration of the bank's customers changes from an individual account holder at a large central site to a numbered consumer of cash at an ATM (automated teller machine). For instance, I cannot remember the last time I went into my bank and spoke to a human and while I used to know my bank manager by name I have no idea who it now is nor even whether there is one behind the row of ATMs. Moreover, in Deetz's view, the complexity of the relationships we now have with multiple institutions renders our relative powerlessness and passivity invisible and provides a normalizing gloss on the world that makes the status quo uncontestable because it appears so normal, so inevitable, so necessary. Here it becomes impossible to question the inequalities of organizational life because no alternative form seems viable. Moreover, the everyday actions of those who may be the least powerful are fundamental to the continuation of inequalities while simultaneously appearing to be beyond the control of anyone. For example, it is only because employees regularly carry out their duties and responsibilities that corporate power is reproduced, yet it often seems to the employees that they are obliged to carry out their duties and responsibilities because the corporation can enforce its will upon them. At one level there is, then, a manifest consensus, but the consensus is not necessarily rooted in a voluntary appreciation of the benefits of management, it may simply be an inability to conceive of any alternative and an unwitting compliance in the construction of self-disciplinary systems. In particular, it is the way that control is institutionalized into a myriad of routines and practices that enables managerial control to persist, for the relationship between manager and employee is transformed from one grounded in personal exploitation to one where the system intervenes between them and appears both necessary and rational. Being told to go and do something unpleasant by a manager is one thing that many employees may object to, but being persuaded that routines are inevitable and must inevitably be followed (including the unpleasant ones) reduces that objection to arguing with a book of procedures – and whoever wins that kind of disembodied argument?

Well some people do, according to David Collinson's reading, for the abstract and theoretical accounts provided by the likes of Deetz do not always predict the actions of those subject to the arbitrary nature of organizations at the sharp end. For Collinson, the decline in overt and collective resistance, manifest in strike action, for example, is by no means the equivalent of an outbreak of industrial peace, nor should we take Foucault's theoretical perspectives on self-discipline to imply that recalcitrant employees can now be relegated to the dustbin of history. Collinson suggests that at least two forms of resistance persist in contemporary work: one he calls 'resistance through distance', in which employees literally or symbolically disengage from management's requirements and avoid compliance;

the second he calls 'resistance through persistence', in which employees seek to negate managerial authority by forcing them to act more transparently and make them more accountable.

Collinson begins by noting a common theme – the active consent of the subordinates to their subordination – but insists that such subordination is overdrawn and often based on a misunderstanding of the way knowledge is appropriated by management and employees. In short, while the former have greater access to knowledge this does not automatically deny the utility of knowledge control to employees. Nor does simple control over or access to knowledge necessarily ensure success for either side, because it is how such knowledge is *deployed* that crucially distinguishes between success and failure. However, Collinson is also keen to assert that his review does not displace a model of compliance and consensus with an alternative model of resistance and conflict, for all too often resistance simultaneously embodies elements of compliance and vice versa. Thus the complexity of the moves at work here cannot be distilled to a clinically discrete form of employee action called resistance. Resistance may not be dead, but neither is it a coherent nor consistent strategy deployed by employees against the ranks of management.

In Collinson's first case study of an engineering factory, we once again meet 'corporate culture', though this time it is summarily dismissed by many of the workers as propaganda – and the more the management try to sell it, the more the workers resist. The counter-culture that prevailed in the factory is clearly dominated by a strong class and masculine bias in which the 'real' work of engineering is something that manual workers do despite, rather than because of, managerial interventions. Furthermore, the expertise developed by those producing the goods enables them to outwit management – and especially the rate-fixer – in the operation of the bonus scheme and the level of production. But, as Collinson makes clear, such resistance does little to challenge the system itself and merely results in management retaining overall control of the plant with little proactive effort by employees or trade unions to alter the way the plant was run or where it was going. In effect, the strategy of 'resistance through distance' effectively legitimized managerial control and left the employees open to virtually unopposed mass redundancy and radical restructuring later on; it may have provided short-term relief from the symptoms of employee weakness but it did little to address the long-term causes because management was also deemed to be solely responsible for running the factory.

The second case relates to the attempts by a single woman to protest at what she regarded as the unfair promotion system at work in one area of the British insurance industry. Rather than choose not to co-operate with management, as the predominantly male workforce in the first case study, this employee demanded a transparent account of the reasoning behind her failure to secure promotion. Then, with the help of her trade union representative, she gradually pushed management into a self-contradictory corner that they had painted through their own incompetence and bias. In this case the woman won her promotion case but again Collinson suggests that the 'victory' made no radical difference to the status quo. Nevertheless, we should be clear that these two examples throw a different light on the claim to consensus in the post-1970s: insurrection we certainly do not have, insubordination we have in plenty. But it is insubordination within the confines of managerial legitimacy and it is this confusing contradiction that so bedevils attempts to explain the nature of workers' behaviour in any clear or discrete manner as radical *or* conservative, as complaint *or* resistant – for it is all of these things simultaneously.

6 Culture

The Invention of Corporate Culture: A History of the Histories of Cadbury

MICHAEL ROWLINSON AND JOHN HASSARD

[...]

> Everyone remembers things that never happened. And it is common knowledge that
> people often forget things which did. Either we are all fantasists and liars or the past
> has nothing definite in it.
>
> Jeanette Winterson 1990: 92

Introduction

The continuing interest in the concept of culture suggests a change in emphasis in
the study of organizations. The focus on culture is associated with a stress on the
subjective realm, and a turn to interpretative and qualitative approaches in sociology, and organization sociology in particular (Hofstede 1986: 254). The rise of
organizational symbolism should involve the introduction into organization theory of formerly remote disciplines, including history, anthropology and literary
criticism (Turner 1990: 83). The field of organizational behaviour is 'notoriously
ahistorical', and the concept of culture has been welcomed in the hope that it might
induce 'a historical perspective' (Nord 1985: 191). A 'historically informed' emphasis on culture should make organizational behaviour 'relatively less reliant on the
empirical analytical sciences and more dependent on the historical-hermeneutic
sciences' (ibid.). 'History as a mode of inquiry in organizational life' has even been
claimed as 'a liberating activity', dereifying social structures and revealing choices
to organization members (Barrett and Srivastva 1991: 248).

   Since most definitions of culture in organizations have a 'temporal dimension',
this should have opened up opportunities for historians to contribute a long-term
perspective to organization studies (Dellheim 1986: 11). However, these promises
have not been fulfilled; history, hermeneutically inclined or otherwise, and organization studies have not been drawn together significantly through the concept of
culture.

This paper suggests possible reasons for the lack of integration between corporate culture and business history, and then attempts to rectify this by offering a case study of the history of the invention of a culture by Cadbury, the British chocolate confectionery manufacturer. Although mostly published sources are cited, the study is based on extensive research in the historical collection held by the company. In the absence of extensive historical research, corporate culture writers have usually imposed upon the histories of companies a story about the founder creating a culture. The data for this case study were approached with great scepticism about such a narrative.

Corporate culture and business history

Organization studies and history

Several reasons can be suggested for the failure of organization studies to incorporate history into the concept of culture. They are similar to the problems encountered by sociologists in their efforts to erode the distinction between sociology and history. First:

> Sociologists had become sensitized to the problems of meaning and understanding, to the view that explaining behaviour had to be embedded in the sets of meanings and orientations which actors brought to their actions. If these could best be explored by in-depth, qualitative interviewing, then dead people told no tales. (Kendrick, Straw and McCrone 1990: 3)

This methodological problem of meaning is exacerbated because corporate culture writers tend to focus on the interpersonal level and rarely accept 'the need for a macro-sociological analysis' (Thompson and McHugh 1990: 230). From an interpersonal perspective 'the reality of an organization is very much influenced by values, norms, and assumptions that cannot be traced to its history' (Berg 1985: 288).

Schein (1985) is a good example of a corporate culture writer, inclined toward psychological analysis at the interpersonal level, who accepts that 'historical data' are vital for the study of organizational culture because culture is 'to be found only where there is a definable group with a significant history' (pp. 7–8), and so, 'one must be able to reconstruct the history of the group' (p. 167). However, he believes history to be methodologically more or less inaccessible because of the problem of meaning: 'Real history is fantastically complex, difficult to unravel, and itself culture bound . . . cultures simplify and reinterpret the events to fit into themes that make cultural sense' (p. 303).

It is worth noting the Schein relies wholly on interviews 'to discover key historical events and the manner in which they were handled' (p. 119). Like most corporate culture writers he does not seriously consider the use of documentary sources to research the history of an organization. In most organization studies, archives are not seen as part of an organization's memory, and business historians are dismissed as being just one among many actors in an organization's external environment trying to record its 'past performance' (Walsh and Ungson 1991: 66–7). This overlooks the important role that business historians play within organizations. Business historians themselves argue that history matters to managers because one important use of history is, 'simply getting things, events, and facts into shared memory' (Tedlow 1986: 82). It is almost as if, because the 'culture concept has been borrowed from anthropology' (Smircich 1983: 339), corporate culture has been researched as if modern business organizations were illiterate tribes (cf. Smircich 1985: 62) which did not possess written histories. However, there is no obvious reason why the 'objective culture' that is 'written into the subjectivity of corporate members' (Fitzgerald 1988: 11) should not also be written into the archives and histories of a corporation. Similar problems of meaning apply both to interviews and historical documents; the subjectivity of archivists and historians is reflected in company archives and histories. In a popular novel very much concerned with time and history, Jeanette Winterson writes: 'I will have to assume that I had a childhood, but I cannot assume to have had the one I remember' (1990: 92). Just as a child's school reports make an interesting comparison with the school days remembered, so an organization's recorded history should provide a revealing insight into the past remembered by its members.

The second problem for sociology in relation to history is epistemological; there is a strand of thinking within sociology that is sceptical about 'the solidity of historical "events"' (Kendrick et al. 1990: 3). Many organizational analysts (e.g., Turner 1990: 87) have succumbed to the 'fatal distraction' of 'postmodernism' (Thompson 1991), and postmodernism is vulnerable to the 'impositionalist claim ... that recounting the past in the form of a story inevitably imposes a false narrative structure upon it' (Norman 1991: 122). From this perspective 'History cannot be rescued from deconstruction – nor should it be', and postmodern history 'may dissolve into endlessly circulating present discourses – it can, apparently, be anything one cares to make it' (Widdowson 1990). Such a claim for the 'legitimacy of fiction as history' is guaranteed to incur the wrath of 'professional historians' (Marwick 1990) because: 'The emphasis on the role of the historian in the making of history tends, if pressed to its logical conclusion, to rule out any objective history at all: history is what the historian makes' (Carr 1964: 26).

It is this position of scepticism and subjectivism which has prevailed in the more critical approaches to culture in organizations:

Events in an organization's history are raw material that members of a culture can mold into a form that both reflects and reconstitutes the culture itself. Underlying this view is the recognition that both cultures and organizational histories are socially constructed. Far from being objective descriptions, accounts of key events in an organization's history reflect differential attention, selective perception, and incomplete recall. As organizational members arrive at mutually acceptable interpretations of events, distortions and omissions multiply. By the time accounts have ossified in the form of organizational stories, legends and sagas, a new reality has been socially constructed. (Martin et al. 1985: 103)

However, the reality of a past need not be abandoned simply because it has undergone a process of social construction – to do so would result in abandoning historical research. Instead, the production of history itself, the process of social construction, can be incorporated into the historian's account. It should be accepted that there is not a clear separation between 'events' and their selection: 'Like a dike covered with ice floes at the end of the winter, the past has been covered by a thick crust of narrative interpretations; and historical debate is as much a debate about the components of this crust as about the past hidden beneath it' (Ankersmit 1986: 26). The social construction of business archives, histories and biographies can be incorporated into historians' competing narratives. Historians have long recognized some simple guidelines; a useful starting-point is to remember, 'that when we take up a work of history, our first concern should be not with the facts which it contains but with the historian who wrote it' (Carr 1964: 22). With company-sponsored business histories this calls for research into the conditions which called for a history to be commissioned and written, as well as the relationship between the company and the hired historian. With Cadbury, changing conditions and different authors produced alternative histories.

Business history and the concept of culture

For business history, the 'boom in the study of corporate culture and the concern with the role of rituals, symbols, beliefs and myths within the corporation . . . suggested new lines of inquiry' (Dellheim 1987: 13; 1986). Unfortunately, business history is not well placed to take up such opportunities. Because business historians tend to avoid much theoretical and methodological reflection, they are unlikely to be able to give an adequate response to the scepticism of organization studies concerning history and culture. British business historians have been castigated by one of their own leading lights for being 'inveterate empiricists', obsessed with simply getting the story right (Hannah, quoted in Coleman 1987: 141).

British business historians have complained of the absence of appropriate theoretical models for them to use (Coleman 1987: 151), but to some extent it is their own ideological distaste for theoretical issues, such as those raised by Marxist historians (p. 149), which has effectively cut them off from wider concerns. Engagement in such debate might have led business historians to a closer understanding of the reflexive, interpretative, hermeneutic and subjective approaches expected from historians in the organizational analysis of the concept of culture. But 'objectivity' is seen as essential for the credibility of business history. Without it, 'there is the risk that the historian may become little better than an archival hired-gun fighting a rearguard action armed with index cards . . . such behavior would incur the outrage of professional colleagues who would, with reason, call into question the integrity of the offender' (Dellheim 1986: 16).

Even when business history has been more theoretical, the preference has been for 'institutional' rather than 'psychological' history (Chandler 1988: 302). Strategy and structure have been considered rather than 'beliefs and symbols' (Dellheim 1986: 10). This tends to privilege certain kinds of data; the evidence for formal organizational structures exists, first and foremost, in the form of official organization charts (Chandler 1962).

A problem for business historians is that the usual way to gain access to the records of a company is through being commissioned to write a history of the company, and: 'the fact remains that however scholarly, accurate, fair, objective and serious that company history, its content is necessarily shaped by the need for the author to give his client something approaching what he wants' (Coleman 1987: 142). In other words, the subjective, cultural requirements of companies to have written histories produced are best served by business historians professing a self-effacing 'objectivity', which does not allow for the problems of meaning and subjectivity raised by the concept of culture to be addressed. The apparently contradictory advice given to organizations commissioning a history is that the best way to make their 'constructive accomplishments known . . . encourage investor interest and, not insignificantly, spark employee pride', is to 'strive for . . . objectivity'. Apparently, the 'old-style company history, long on self-laudation but short on objectivity is no longer acceptable' because of the general scepticism about 'the objectivity and balance in "management sanctioned" corporate histories' (Campion 1987: 31; cf. Hannah 1986).

Paradoxically, the strength of the Cadbury culture and the interest in the company's history, especially on the part of its former chairman Sir Adrian Cadbury, has meant that the firm has kept its archives intact and allowed relatively free access to them. This has allowed the present account to be constructed contesting the basis of the corporate culture in a company where the culture might appear all but incontestable. It might be suspected that cultures that do not allow access or criticism are not so strong.

In their efforts to prove their credibility and objectivity, business historians have been keen to distance themselves from vital cultural artefacts, the old in-house histories and hagiographies. These are seen as an embarrassing legacy from the time when 'the writing of company histories was seen as a form of inferior journalistic hack-work' (Coleman 1984; 1987: 145; Campion 1987: 32).

Consequences of the ahistorical approach to corporate culture

Two consequences of the failure to integrate history and organization studies in the analysis of the concept of culture can be identified. First, instead of delving into history as such, organizational analysts of culture have tended to invoke their own culture construction, namely the 'founder'. Numerous studies offer variations on a theme, 'descriptively portraying founders as the prime movers behind historical events or prescriptively urging leaders to articulate a vision and create a culture' (Martin et al. 1985: 100).

Schein (1985), again, draws on 'group and leadership theory' from psychology (p. 50), instead of history itself, to explain the 'historical factors' concerning the origins of culture (p. 148). He makes the cultural assumption that 'culture and leadership are really two sides of the same coin' (p. 4), and uses 'studies of the psychodynamic make-up of leaders' (p. 172) to paint an idealized picture of 'how organization founders shape culture' (chapter 9): 'Firms are created by entrepreneurs who have a vision of how the concerted effort of the right group of people can create a new product or service in the marketplace' (p. 209); and 'Organizations begin to create cultures through the actions of founders' (p. 221).

All too conveniently, as the interests of 'academics' and 'practitioners' in the area of culture have converged (Barley 1988), 'organizational studies of the culture creation process' have offered 'a seductive promise to entrepreneurs':

> namely that a founder can create a culture, cast in the founder's own image and reflecting the founder's own values, priorities, and vision of the future. Thus a founder's own perspective can be transformed into a shared legacy that will survive death or departure from the institution – a personal form of organizational immortality. (Martin et al. 1985: 99)

In other words corporate culture writers have imposed their own socially constructed narrative on history, the story of the founder. For the most part, this conforms to the rhetoric of organization studies in which social psychological theories and interview data rather than historical evidence are seen as persuasive. However, even when 'documentary sources' have been consulted, it is the 'founder' narrative which has been imposed upon them (Pettigrew 1979: 570).

A second consequence is that history is taken up for the study of culture by less methodologically scrupulous researchers. Two of the best-known books of the aeroplane-reading corporate culture genre can be used for illustration. Peters and Waterman (1982) accept a neat conceptual split between history and myth. They attribute far more power to myth: 'History doesn't move us as much as does a good current anecdote (or presumably, a juicy bit of gossip)' (p. 62). This is because whereas 'stories, myths and legends' can be constructed to 'convey the organization's shared values, or culture' (p. 75), history is fixed and taken as given. Peters and Waterman use histories and accounts by prominent members of firms uncritically. Their material on 'IBM's philosophy', for example, is taken almost wholly from *A Business and its Beliefs: The Ideas that Helped Build IBM*, by Thomas Watson, Jr., the founder's son.

In *Corporate Cultures* (1982), Deal and Kennedy placed great emphasis on historical sources. They wanted to find out 'what had made America's great companies not merely organizations, but successful human institutions', and in their search they:

> stumbled into a goldmine of evidence. Biographies, speeches, and documents from such giants of business as Thomas Watson of IBM, John Patterson (the founder of NCR), Will Durant of General Motors, William Kellogg of Kelloggs, and a host of others show a remarkable intuitive understanding of the importance of a strong culture in the affairs of their companies. (Deal and Kennedy 1982: 7–8)

As critics of the corporate culture writings have commented, 'what executives and managers say in words or on paper is taken as proof. There is little critical reflection on this' (Thompson and McHugh 1990: 231–2).

The status of historical evidence

At issue therefore is the status of historical evidence for culture. The view taken in this [reading] is that it is not necessary to choose between either discounting company-sponsored histories out of hand, or accepting them more or less uncritically. Instead of treating the company-sponsored history as a faithful record of events, as the popular corporate writers do, it can be used as a valuable cultural artefact in its own right. The narratives constructed in such histories reveal much about the cultural concerns of companies at the time they were commissioned and written; a hagiography may reveal little about the life of a saint, but it gives a valuable insight into the hagiographer's view of saintly qualities. So in this [reading], the histories of Cadbury written to commemorate a centenary in 1931 are used as the starting-point in tracing the construction of a distinctive culture in the late 1920s and early 1930s, rather than the creation of a culture in 1831.

One objection to the corporate culture literature is that it fails to acknowledge that people are subject to more cultures than the organization, such as their social class or profession. There are many 'traditions' which might be 'a good deal older than most of our organizations', and by implication more influential. Corporate culture writers have overlooked the wider concept of 'tradition', which is 'not far removed, after all, from "culture"' (Thomas 1985: 25).

It turns out that many ' "traditions" which appear or claim to be old are often quite recent in origin and sometimes invented' (Hobsbawm 1983a: 2). Historians have coined the term 'invented tradition'. The concept of corporate culture is similar to the definition of an invented tradition, which is:

> a set of practices, normally governed by overtly or tacitly accepted rules and of a ritual or symbolic nature, which seek to inculcate certain values and norms of behaviour by repetition, which automatically implies continuity with the past. Insofar as there is such reference to a historic past, the peculiarity of 'invented' traditions is that the continuity with it is largely factitious. In short, they are responses to novel situations which establish their own past by quasi-obligatory repetition. (Hobsbawm 1983a: 2)

If the ostensibly ancient traditions of nations, such as the rituals of the British monarchy (Cannadine 1983), turn out to have been invented in order to reinforce a cohesive national identity, then the same might well apply to many corporate cultures. In the same way that historians have turned their attention to the history of the invention of traditions by nations, this [reading] attempts to construct a history of the invention of the Cadbury corporate culture (cf. Hobsbawm 1983b: 307).

Cadbury is significant because as well as having a strong cultural identity, up until now it has generally been accepted that its culture is as old as some of the company's sponsored histories have claimed it is. The aim of the [reading] is not to demythify Cadbury, or to try to reduce its history to myth. To do so would be to claim a superior objectivity, or to deny the importance of history in the Cadbury culture, and both claims would be untenable. Instead, a competing narrative is

constructed which incorporates and explains rather than refutes previous narrative histories of the company. The competing narrative is of an 'invented tradition', instead of a story of a 'founder'. The test of the narrative will be whether the
reader is persuaded that it is convincing even in the case of a culture as strong as
Cadbury's, and in the confines of a journal in which the weight of historical
evidence, the usual measure of historical argument, cannot be judged by counting
the number of footnotes.

The Cadbury culture

The Cadbury centenary

Cadbury, now part of Cadbury Schweppes, is a large chocolate confectionary
manufacturing company based in Britain. Until 1962 it was a private limited
company, largely owned and continuously managed by members of the Cadbury
family. The company's history is easily identified with the prominent members of
the Cadbury family who founded and ran the business (Dellheim 1986: 13). It was
started by John Cadbury (1801–89) in 1824, in the centre of Birmingham. It
became Cadbury Brothers in 1847 when John was joined by his older brother,
Benjamin Head Cadbury (1798–1880), as a partner. Initially, the business was
mainly concerned with the tea and coffee trade. In 1861, when John Cadbury
handed over the business to his sons Richard (1835–99) and George (1839–1922),
cocoa still accounted for only about a quarter of the firm's trade. Richard and
George revived the firm's flagging fortunes and started to shape the business along
the lines on which it has developed since, concentrating on cocoa and chocolate
production. In 1879 Cadbury moved out of Birmingham city centre, Bridge Street,
to a purpose-built cocoa and chocolate factory at Bournville, a greenfield site
about 4 miles south of Birmingham.

The Cadbury corporate culture can be summarized as the identification of the
company's distinctive labour-management policies with the Cadbury family's
Quaker beliefs. This was clearly expressed in 1931 when the firm celebrated a
centenary. Two publications marked the centenary. The major one was *The Firm
of Cadbury 1831–1931*, nearly 300 pages, published by Constable. The firm paid
the author, Iolo A. Williams, £350 for his work, and a Centenary Celebration
Committee allocated £200–£300 to advertise it; 4450 copies were given to employees with at least ten years' service, and 450 were distributed to pensioners. The
firm was pleased with the press reviews of the books, which were quoted with
approval in the *Bournville Works Magazine*. *The Times* reviewer praised Williams
for making 'a contribution of value to industrial history'. Williams was a journal-
ist and writer, a botanist, bibliographer and an authority on early English water-
colours: 'Among the great interests of his life were British flora and the minor
poets of the 18th century' (*Bournville Works Magazine*, February 1962). From
1905 T. B. Rogers was the full-time editor of the *Bournville Works Magazine*
(*Bournville Magazine*, March 1970). His more modest work, *A Century of Progress
1831–1931*, was published by Cadbury, and the Advertising Department spent

over £7500 to produce 180,000 copies. Cadbury's customers in Britain received a copy, and it was also used by associated companies in Australia, New Zealand and Canada.

These two histories constructed a continuity between the firm's past and present policies. Both drew heavily on an unpublished book of Personal Reminiscences of Bridge Street and Bournville 1929. This volume itself appears to have been edited, because any accounts that were less than deferential in tone were excluded from it. Some of the recollections had appeared earlier in the *Bournville Works Magazine* (September and October 1909) and others were collected in preparation for the centenary. The vocabulary used by the long-serving Cadbury workers gives a flavour of paternalism. They referred to the Cadbury brothers as 'Mr. George' and 'Mr. Richard'. One of them remembered, 'During the struggles of the [1860s] I never knew men work harder than our masters, who were indeed more like fathers to us' (Rogers 1931: 27). Rogers described the reminiscences as an 'intimate history' of the firm:

> These records tell of the unflagging energy of Richard and George Cadbury to make their business succeed, and of their cheerfulness even in times when disaster faced them, but first and foremost they tell of the close human relations between master and man, who together were 'like a family'. (1931: 27)

In their search for a unity between past and present, these histories presented precedents that are so tenuous as to almost belie the very continuity they are supposed to demonstrate. In his account of the old city centre site Williams wrote: 'though the organization of physical training and athletics, as we understand it to-day in a factory, was a thing undreamed of then, the men were encouraged to play cricket and football' (1931: 47). Williams's 'postscript' concluded:

> throughout the century of progress and change, there has been unity – a unity brought about because during the whole period the business has been the daily personal concern of a family that has steadily tried to apply, as an employer of labour, the principles of Quaker faith. (1931: 259)

It is worth noting that it is not clear why the firm decided to celebrate a centenary in 1931. According to Williams, it was in 1931 that John Cadbury 'began the actual manufacture of cocoa and chocolate. In 1831, then, the firm of Cadbury may be said to have been born' (1931: 6). However, in an earlier biography of Richard Cadbury, by his daughter Helen Cadbury Alexander (1906), the date for the start of cocoa manufacturing is unclear, although she believed John Cadbury started experimenting with a pestle and mortar to make cocoa and chocolate around 1835 (1906: 36). George Cadbury's biographer (Gardiner 1923) and other publications make no mention of 1831 as significant.

Nor is it clear when the firm decided to celebrate a centenary. There was an anniversary of the move to Bournville in 1879, and the *Bournville Works Magazine* (1929) explained that:

The way in which the Jubilee should be celebrated was very carefully considered more than a year ago ... the firm had to bear in mind two facts of historical importance to them, namely, that while they would complete fifty years at Bournville in 1929, they would two years later complete their hundredth year as cocoa and chocolate manufacturers.

Possibly the success of the Fry bicentenary in 1928 gave the Cadburys the idea to have a centenary of their own. Fry of Bristol was another cocoa and confectionery firm. It was also owned and managed by a prominent Quaker family, the Frys. In 1919 Fry merged with, but was in effect taken over by Cadbury. Soon after the merger Fry moved out of [central] Bristol to a greenfield site modelled on Bournville, and its labour-management policies were directed by Cadbury.

A special issue of the *Fry Works Magazine* was produced for the bicentenary. The opening address by Lord Riddell, 'The Chocolate Age', outlined Fry's claims to distinction:

For generations they have taken the keenest interest in the welfare of their workpeople. In furtherance of this policy they decided to transfer their factories from the heart of Bristol to Somerdale, a few miles out of the City on the banks of the Avon. (p. 13)

A brief history of Fry told of the 'honest God-fearing Quaker founder' who would have been alarmed by the lawlessness of the eighteenth century (p. 14). 'In the England of 1728, therefore, where excess both in language and behaviour was the rule, the restrained and precise lives led by the Quakers must have made them almost a race apart' (p. 19).

According to a memory of Fry in 1866:

The personal touch was always in evidence ... This attitude was part and parcel – in fact the very essence – of the Fry psychology, since it was ingrained in the Frys not to look upon their employees as so many cogs in a machine for producing dividends but as human creatures possessed of immortal souls, for whom they were largely responsible. (p. 28)

Then there was 'The Fry Spirit':

Candour, freedom of speech and humour are the dominant notes in our social life both at Bristol and Somerdale ... This spirit of toleration and liberty is one of the finest things at J. S. Fry and Sons Ltd., where one may think like an Anarchist so long as one does one's job like a decent citizen. (p. 29)

Readers were assured that, 'the Frys of bygone years always felt a certain responsibility for the welfare – spiritual, mental and physical – of their employees' (p. 81).

In a contribution on 'The Growth of Trade Unionism' at the firm, the General Secretary of the Transport and General Workers' Union, Ernest Bevin, wrote:

It is almost impossible to believe that an institution such as Fry's could be 200 years old and yet be so youthful and vigorous. It has associated with it a great tradition, and if the record of the firm could be produced it would make very interesting reading. (*Fry Works Magazine*, Bicentenary Number, p. 36)

That Cadbury selected the year to mark its centenary, and Fry celebrated the labour-management policies recently imposed by the merger with Cadbury for its bicentenary, demonstrates clearly how the firms themselves decided how and when to mark certain dates with celebratory events. Organizations impose the timing and significance of historical events such as centenaries upon history, history does not impose these events upon organizations.

The Cadbury institutions

The generally accepted view of Cadbury's labour-management policies is that they were inspired by the Cadbury family's Quaker religious beliefs (Jeremy 1990; Corley 1988), which created the Cadbury 'company culture' (Dellheim 1987). Cadbury is seen as providing 'An opportunity for analysing the relationship between religious beliefs and economic action' (p. 14) because:

> The Quaker beliefs of the Cadbury family shaped the ethic of the firm. The Cadbury family's social and industrial experiments were, on one level, an attempt to reconcile religious convictions and business practices.... Three main influences formed George and Richard Cadbury's beliefs: the Quaker ethic, which shaped their views of the nature and purpose of business; the experience of turning around a failing firm; and an exposure to the social problems of the industrial city.... The Quaker ethic was the cornerstone of Cadburys. (Dellheim 1987: 14–15).

Notice how the role of founder is taken by George and Richard Cadbury, even though they did not actually found the business, but took over the running of it in 1861 (Dellheim 1986: 12). Founder type narratives achieve this by associating those identified with the founder role with the turn-around of a company. This gets over the problem that in the Cadbury case associating the culture with the original founders of the business would be too tenuous. It also illustrates how founders are selected by historians retrospectively, they are not fixed by history.

An alternative account of Cadbury is that five specific labour-management institutions can be identified, and each of them was developed by the firm in response to contemporary social movements rather than Quaker inspiration. First, there is the Bournville village. In 1893, some time after the move to Bournville, 120 acres adjacent to the factory were purchased, and the next year house-building began. The houses were sold at cost price, with mortgages available from Cadbury. Some of the purchasers were too thrifty and sold up, making a hefty profit. George Cadbury then decided to turn the Bournville Building Estate into a Charitable Trust and on 14 December 1900 the Bournville Village Trust was formed. In the view of a BVT Community and Information Officer: 'It is difficult to say precisely when the concept of a Building Estate developed into that of a Garden Village, but all evidence points to the period just before the Trust was founded in December 1900' (Henselowe 1984: 5).

Bournville represented a departure from the earlier nineteenth-century paternalist community builders (Jeremy 1990: 143; Jeremy 1991). The Village Trust was nominally independent and imbued with a democratic vision (Gardiner 1923: 145, 152). For this, it owed much to the nascent Garden City movement. Ebenezer Howard's book setting out a blueprint for a 'Garden City' was first published in October 1898. During 1899 the Garden City Association was started, and its first conference was held at Bournville in September 1901 (Howard 1946). The character of the Bournville village owed more to the influence of the early town planning movement than to the inspiration of Quakerism.

The second institution to be considered is the welfare provided by the firm. The move to Bournville more or less necessitated the provision of dining-rooms for workers, although these were substantially improved around the turn of the century after members of the firm visited other companies and saw their superior facilities (Marks n.d.: 11; Meakin 1905: 184, 422; Williams 1931: 73, 88). The personnel measures undertaken in the 1900s were more substantive than anything which preceded them, and cannot be seen as *ad hoc* additions within a continuous policy or philosophy. There was a definite break in the history of the firm and in the development of its personnel management. This was acknowledged by George Cadbury's biographer (Gardiner 1923). He divided the history of 'the experiments' at Bournville into two phases. The two brothers George and Richard Cadbury were responsible for the measures taken in the earlier phase, which were appropriate for a 'smaller enterprise'. This 'was a highly personal and in some ways a paternal effort to humanize the conditions of labour' (p. 113). When Richard Cadbury died in 1899 the business was converted into a private limited company. George Cadbury was joined on the Board of Directors by his own sons Edward (1873–1948) and George Jr. (1878–1954) and Richard's sons Barrow (1862–1958) and William Adlington (1867–1957). This marked the beginning of the second, more complicated phase, which:

> developed with the great expansion of the business, and the emergence of the new ideas in the industrial movement. . . . It was under this new government, later enlarged by the admission of other members of the family that the larger organized schemes of insurance, education, and so on, were developed. (Gardiner 1923: 114)

The 1900s were years of expansion for Cadbury. Trade increased from £977,010 in 1899 to £1,607,417 in 1909, and the Cadbury workforce rose from 2883 to 4991. It was also a period in which the Cadbury Board became increasingly aware of pressure from competitors, both at home and abroad. This was the context in which substantial welfare and personnel policies were started. These were largely derived from similar schemes which the Cadburys saw in operation at other firms. Continental firms were visited in order to study production techniques, but in 1901 George Cadbury, Jr. visited America specifically to study industrial organization. According to a short biography, he 'saw in a few enlightened firms there schemes by which employees could make known to the management their ideas and suggestions about improving products and working conditions' (Marks n.d.: 18). He went to the National Cash Register company (NCR), where the flamboyant and unorthodox president, John H. Patterson, had introduced a 'sweeping welfare program' which was already well known among American manufacturers by 1900. The welfare plan at NCR 'had a marked impact on the development of systematic welfare work [and] foreshadowed the future course of welfare activity, notably the shift in emphasis from housing and community work to factory working conditions' (Nelson 1975: 106–7; see also Crowther 1923; Gilman 1899; Nelson 1974).

Several initiatives were undertaken at Bournville after George Cadbury, Jr. reported back to the Board on his US visit, including the introduction of a Suggestion Scheme and the publication of the *Bournville Works Magazine*. The first issue announced that, 'above all, the aim of the paper is to promote what for lack of a better word we may describe as the Bournville "spirit"' (*Bournville Works Magazine*, vol. 1, no. 1, November 1902). It became 'one of the great Bournville institutions', and appeared in much the same format for sixty-seven years (*Bournville Works Magazine*, January 1969, the last issue, p. 51). NCR was noted for its 'unique and highly decentralized committee system' (Gilman 1899: 228; Nelson 1975: 107–9); and in the 1900s Cadbury also developed a committee system which was gradually extended subsequently (Cadbury 1979; *Industrial Record 1919–1939*, 1945; Williams 1931).

A third institution within the Bournville factory was the rigid sexual division of labour. In common with many of the American firms which introduced extensive welfare programmes before the First World War, Cadbury employed large numbers of women (Nelson 1975). In 1899 the newly formed Board made the 'marriage bar' a strict policy; it had operated loosely before. Cadbury was neither alone nor anachronistic in this (Lewenhak 1977: 91–6), and it continued to operate, as it did in the Civil Service, until the 1940s (Boston 1980: 240).

Those emphasizing the role of the Cadbury family's Quaker beliefs (Dellheim 1987: 27; Jeremy 1990: 143) have found it difficult to accept that the firm applied scientific management. However, it was introduced to such an extent that it can be considered as a fourth Bournville institution (Smith et al. 1990: 3, 65). While Edward Cadbury may have viewed Taylorism 'with caution and distrust' (Littler 1982: 95) his response to scientific management is best seen as an assertion that its essential elements, work measurement in particular, could be implemented without Taylor's hostility to trade unions (Cadbury 1915; 1979). In fact, as early as 1913, Cadbury hired an American 'efficiency man' to extend and revise the piecework system, which was a long-standing feature of labour-management at Bournville (Rowlinson 1988: 388).

Finally, there was the Works Council scheme. Reflecting the sexual division of labour in the factory, separate councils were set up for men and women. The Bournville Works Men's Council first met on 21 November 1918. The Works Councils were introduced in response to the Whitley Reports produced by the Ministry of Labour, which advocated the setting up of Industrial Councils and Works Committees. The Cadburys wanted to pre-empt any government intervention in industry by setting up their own scheme. Although the company secured trade union support for the Works Councils, the latter were not a forum for pay negotiations or other union matters. The Works Councils became enmeshed in the administration of welfare and educational provisions which gave them an appearance of importance. It was management which finally withdrew from the Factory Council in 1978 (Smith et al. 1990: 326).

This outline of the institutional framework of Cadbury's labour management should be sufficient to indicate the context of each development, and to question the adequacy of invoking Quakerism as the source of inspiration. The cultural phenomenon which needs to be explained is not the influence of Quakerism on Cadbury's labour management, but how the narrative that privileged the role of Quakerism came to be constructed and accepted.

Quaker employers

Before this question is addressed, however, the wider issue of Quakers as employers should be considered. Several accounts more or less accept the idea that Quakerism itself made Quakers better employers (Bradley 1987; Child 1964; Corley 1972, 1988; Emden 1939; Jeremy 1990; Windsor 1980). Child's influential study focuses on the attitudes of British Quaker employers toward industrial relations and labour management during the interwar period. Although he situates their interest in labour management in the context of industrial and social unrest in the first quarter of [the twentieth] century, Child contends that the Society of Friends provided the main impetus for the formulation of 'new conceptions of industrial management' by Quaker employers (1964: 293). The impression given is one of continuity, 'Quakerism has always stressed the need for democratic human inter-relationships' (p. 304).

An earlier history of *Quakers in Commerce* (Emden 1939) describes the Quakers' 'burning passion for social justice ... rooted in the Quaker tenets' (p. 88). The 'middle-class respectability' of the nineteenth-century Quaker merchants is praised on the grounds that 'the English middle class was once described as the natural representatives of the human race, the most outstanding figure of which was the independent shopkeeper.... Quakerism bred men who did business like saints, and saints who were most efficient businessmen'. The Quakers 'helped make England what it is: a manufacturing country', as well as being 'the most enlightened employers that ever existed', never losing 'sight of the human factor' (p. 22).

In its [...] publicity material the Society is keen to dispel the view that it is a group of 'wealthy philanthropists' (Gorman 1981: 3). A history of *The Quaker Enterprise* by a member of the Society (Windsor 1980) reflects the way in which the image of the respectable middle-class shopkeeper has lost its appeal for the Quakers of today:

> The great Quaker entrepreneurs of the [nineteenth] century were true Victorians. They stand out as members of the new, large, self-satisfied, self-righteous middle-class, who regarded themselves as the arbiters of a civilised society and administrators to a less educated world.... Benevolent they may have been, charitable and anxious to improve the lot of mankind, but it tended to be a fatherly benevolence predicated on a view that they knew what was right and good for people. Their image was inseparable from the ideal self-image of their time. (p. 3)

Against this, he stresses that although *Friends in Business* 'attained enormous power as individuals [they] chose to use that power for the benefit of their employees, their local community, or their industry' (Windsor 1980: 27). These histories show how the requirements from history can change. For Emden (1939), the virtue of the Quakers was that they were typical of the middle class. Very much in response to the effect of histories such as Emden's, Windsor (1980) tries to show that, middle class though they were, Quaker employers were different.

To sustain the notion of a continuity in the approach to labour management by Quaker employers in general, and Cadbury in particular, an indication of a similar continuity in Quaker thinking is needed. This view is contradicted by several histories.

The eighteenth-century capitalist and Quietist Friend closely resembled Weber's description of the 'ideal type of the capitalistic entrepreneur' who avoids ostentation and social recognition and has a tendency to asceticism (Weber 1930: 71; cf. Raistrick 1953: 272, 1968: 43). Whether or not, in an earlier period, Quakerism had been, as Marxists might see it, an important element in the dissimulatory ideological superstructure, or else, from a Weberian viewpoint, a vital component in the ethical basis of capitalism (cf. Birnbaum 1965; Jeremy 1988: 18; Jeremy 1990: 5), by the end of the eighteenth century Quakerism was losing its particular significance; Quaker industrialists 'had to conform to the new world which their own industry was creating' (Raistrick 1968: 344; cf. Nevaskar 1971: 39; Weber 1930: 17).

Isichei's valuable history of *Victorian Quakers* (1970) traces the changes within the Society of Friends. For the first half of the nineteenth century, the Society was in decline, the number of Friends went down from an estimated 19,800 in 1800 to 13,859 in 1861 (pp. 111–12). Revival came when the Society became more outward looking and allowed Friends to marry outside the Society. Between the 1830s and the 1850s 'Quaker attitudes to politics were transformed'. Previously, although they had been an effective pressure group, they officially deplored and had a deep distrust for elections and party politics. That distrust was almost completely abandoned, however, in what 'was one of the most rapid and complete reversals of attitude in Quaker history', particularly over the abolition of slavery. It was a manifestation of the important change which took place within Victorian Quakerism, 'by which friends grew closer to the society in which they lived', this 'reflected changes in dissent in general' (p. 193).

In two important respects, there was continuity in the Society. First, its solidly middle-class composition: apart from 'a glittering superstructure of great industrialists and financiers', the average Quaker was a prosperous tradesman (Isichei 1970: 187). Second, money-making by members of the Society: 'Victorian Quakerism sanctioned and indeed encouraged the pursuit of wealth' (p. 183). The Quakers' stance on various social issues reflected their class position, as did the attitudes of others toward the Quakers.

Although Quakers were later identified with the emancipation of slaves (Aykroyd 1967; Bebbington 1982; 110), in the mid-eighteenth century 'Quaker nonconformity did not extend to the slave trade. . . . Slave dealing was one of the most lucrative investments of English as of American Quakers'. The name of a slave ship, *The Willing Quaker*, 'symbolizes the approval with which the slave trade was regarded in Quaker circles' (Williams 1964: 43). The nineteenth-century view that the anti-slavery movement represented the English middle class at its best was the creation of British historians who 'wrote almost as if Britain had introduced Negro slavery solely for the satisfaction of abolishing it' (Williams 1964; quoted in Aykroyd 1967: 62). In *The Wealth of Nations*, Adam Smith remarked that 'the late resolution of the Quakers in Pennsylvania to set at liberty all their Negro slaves, may satisfy us that their number cannot be very great' (quoted in Galbraith 1987; 62). William Cobbett 'hated Quaker speculators' (Thompson 1980: 833) and throughout his *Rural Rides*, he 'heaped violent and vulgar abuse on Quakers and Jews alike'. For him, the Friends were a 'pestiferous sect of non-labouring, sleek and fat hypocrites' (Isichei 1970: 284).

In the 1900s the Cadburys supported campaigns for old age pensions, minimum wages and an end to homeworking. They sponsored, carried out and published research on *Sweating* (Cadbury and Shann 1907; Mudie-Smith 1906) and *Women's Work and Wages* (Cadbury et al. 1906), and defended, against feminist criticism, the inclusion of women in the nineteenth-century protective legislation restricting the hours of work for women and children (Cadbury et al. 1906: 24–5; cf. Morris 1986).

In contrast, earlier Quaker employers took a free trade view, and opposed the Factory Acts: 'No Quaker played a prominent part in the agitation for the limitation of factory hours. Where they appear in its history at all, it is almost always as its inveterate opponents' (Isichei 1970: 247). Marx had nothing but contempt for the Quaker beliefs of the manufacturers who were fined for violating the Factory Act in 1836. They had kept five boys, aged between twelve and fifteen years, at work for almost thirty hours 'in the "shoddy-hole", the name for the hole where the woollen rags are pulled to pieces, and where a dense atmosphere of dust, shreds, etc. forces even the adult worker to cover his mouth continually with handkerchiefs for the protection of his lungs!' (Marx 1976: 351–2, n. 22). He also denounced the 'pro-slavery rebellion' by manufacturers against the Ten Hours Act of 1847, which restricted the hours of work for women and young children. The manufacturers told the factory inspectors that 'they would set themselves above the letter of the law, and reintroduce the old system on their own account.... Thus, among others, the philanthropist Ashworth, in a letter to Leonard Horner [a factory inspector] which is repulsive in its Quaker manner' (Marx 1976: 400–1; cf. Cadbury et al. 1906: 22–3).

At times the Quakers themselves acknowledged the discontinuity in their history. In 1908 the Society of Friends held its Yearly Meeting in central Birmingham. A substantial *Handbook* was produced for those attending. Noticeable by its absence is any discussion of Bournville, or of an organized visit to the village or the factory, even though the publication was the responsibility of William A. Cadbury and another senior member of the firm, and the organizing committee of fifty-six included five Cadburys (*Handbook* 1908). Two members of the Society in Birmingham wrote a 'Local history of the Society of Friends during the last fifty years'. They identified three fairly clear-cut periods: 1861–75, 'Passing of the old order'; 1875–95, 'Period of revival and expansion'; and 1895–1908, 'Incoming of the modern spirit' (*Handbook* 1908: 66).

Given this clear discontinuity, the problem becomes one of explaining how the image of continuity has emerged in relation to both Cadbury and the Quakers as employers. Child gives a useful clue: 'The principle of democratic relationships in the workplace has long been held by Quakers, as Raistrick has indicated in this study of Quaker industry in the seventeenth and eighteenth centuries' (1964: 295).

Arthur Raistrick wrote three books on Quakers and industry (1953, 1968, 1977). He was a member of the Society of Friends himself, and a student of Friends' literature (Raistrick 1968). For most of his life he was a lecturer in civil and mining engineering at the University of Durham, but he also carried out research into a wide range of subjects, including archaeology and industrial history (Manby and Turnbull 1986: 1). He wrote the book cited by Child (Raistrick 1968) while on a Fellowship at Woodbrooke College near Bournville, which was founded by George Cadbury. Working almost near enough to the Bournville factory founded by his co-religionists to enjoy the sweet scent of chocolate that emanates from it, Raistrick was possibly looking for evidence to confirm the image the Cadburys had of themselves in the 1930s and 1940s. The title of his later book suggests a similar theme: *Two Centuries of Industrial Welfare: The London (Quaker) Lead Company 1692–1905* (1977).

The first of Raistrick's three books about the Quakers was on *The Darbys of Coalbrookdale* (1953), the ironmasters at the heart of the industrial revolution in Britain. It is unlikely that they could have had a similar commitment to industrial democracy in the eighteenth century as the Cadburys had in the mid-twentieth. T. S. Ashton, [an] eminent historian of the industrial revolution (1948), gave an account of the predominantly Quaker eighteenth-century ironmasters. Writing before Raistrick, he appears to have been oblivious to any reputation the Quakers had for industrial democracy (Ashton 1963). Ashton's portrait leaves something to be desired for those looking for precedents for the enlightened Quaker employers of the twentieth century:

> The austerity of the ironmasters, whether cause or effect of their sectarianism, affected every side of their lives. Successful themselves, they were intolerant of what might appear weakness or inefficiency in others; and though their charities were numerous there was little of the milk of human kindness in their constitutions. At that time, more than any other, industrial leadership demanded men of an autocratic mould; and, individualists as they were both by nature and circumstance, they resented any attempt on the part of the workers to determine, in any measure, the conditions of their working life. In more than one, indeed, there was developed something approaching contempt for the aspirations of labour... most of the ironmasters had little time or inclination for political speculation and their main concern was that industry should be left alone: although there were among them philanthropists, and demagogues... most of them were, apparently, content to accept social conditions as they found them. (1963: 225–6)

So the construction of a history of Quaker employers characterized by continuity and a commitment to welfare is of fairly recent origin, and in part it can be attributed to the firm of Cadbury.

The histories of Cadbury

The first 'history' of Cadbury to come from the firm itself was *Cocoa: All About It*, a short book written by Richard Cadbury, probably for advertising purposes, and published under the pseudonym 'Historicus' (1892). He made the most of Bournville in terms of the standards of the time, stressing the separation of men and women, as well as the fact that it was a purpose-built plant. Richard Cadbury hardly mentioned welfare at the works, and neither did his daughter, Helen Cadbury Alexander, in her biography of him, although she dealt at length with his philanthropic works (1906).

A. G. Gardiner was the editor of the Liberal newspaper, the *Daily News*, from 1902 to 1921. He had been appointed after George Cadbury took over the ownership of the paper (Wagner 1987: 74–5, 84–5). Gardiner wrote the *Life of George Cadbury* (1923) after George's death in 1922. He discussed George Cadbury's reasons for introducing welfare at Bournville, specifically privileging a worldly, rational explanation and discounting a religious, Quaker motive:

> He did not inherit a business previously well-established. He created it, and it was his deliberate conviction that the welfare policy so far from hindering the development of the firm assisted it. He based this belief, not upon the inner light or the sanctions of religion, but upon plain reasoning from cause to effect. (1923: 98)

For the most part, during the period in which the Cadbury institutions were being developed, the firm identified itself with wider progressive social movements. Bournville was among the outstanding *Model Factories and Villages* in a survey sponsored by the firm (Meakin 1905; Harvey 1906). As the focus of interest shifted from the old kind of welfare, which was 'extraneous to the actual process of managing' (Child 1969: 36), so Cadbury projected itself as at the forefront of factory management. Edward Cadbury's *Experiments in Industrial Organization* (1979) gives a 'description of Bournville practice' before the First World War, which reads 'much like a modern personnel manual' of the 1960s (Child 1969: 36).

By the 1920s the New Liberal political views adhered to by the Cadburys in the 1900s had lost their distinctiveness, 'Liberalism had become Englishness' (Smith 1986: 255). As the trees grew and the suburbs of the City of Birmingham expanded to surround it, Bournville probably seemed less a symbol of the 'industrial spirit' and more a reminder of a mythical rural idyll (Weiner 1985), less ahead of than out of its time and place. This changing temporal and spatial location of the firm facilitated and called for the construction of a new identity, one which stressed its uniqueness and separation from the upheavals of the 1920s and 1930s: labour unrest and mass unemployment.

Cadbury itself was stung by the response of its workforce to the General Strike in May 1926. Nearly every union responded to the strike call and approximately 50 per cent of the male workforce, but only 12 per cent of the women came out (Birmingham Public Libraries 1976: 31). The strike was shortlived at Cadbury, most of the strikers stayed out for only four of the nine days of the General Strike.

At no time did Bournville have to close. After the strike the unions lost many of their members (Birmingham Public Libraries 1976: 40). Unlike other Birmingham employers, Cadbury did not victimize strikers (Branson 1976), but the Board did insist on the removal of restrictions on non-trades unionists holding office under the Works Council Scheme. These events were later rationalized in the firm's centenary history:

> Cadbury Brothers Ltd. has never had a strike of its workpeople, directed against the firm itself; and, though many men and women were called out by their Unions in May 1926, it was generally felt that there was no personal animus against the Company. Those who were then called upon to strike felt, indeed, a very difficult opposition between two loyalties – that to their firm and that to their Trade Union. (Williams 1931: 125–6)

The Directors' Annual Report for 1927 summarized the previous three years, in which sales had remained practically static, as:

> the first comparatively long period in the history of the firm during which we have failed to go forward...it is unfortunate that a failure to increase our sales has coincided with a period when other factors have been working against the fullest employment of personnel. Improvements in processes and machinery, and the shifting of the incidence of demand from products requiring a large proportion of human labour to those needing but little, have aggravated the employment position.

With some fluctuations, employment at Bournville continued to decrease, especially for women, from a high point in 1925 through to the mid-1930s. Payments were made from the firm's Short Time and Unemployment Schemes to ameliorate the effects on the workforce.

The stability, continuity and enduring values identified with Cadbury by the centenary publications must have been reassuring. The 'successful Centenary Year' came during a difficult period for the firm and against a background of 'national upheaval' (Directors' Annual Report 1931). Both prices and wages fell in Britain during the year, but the Directors at Bournville noted that: 'No such general movement has taken place here in the standard rates of wages with the exception of Building Trades in February 1931' (p. 13). If they read it, Bournville workers would have been reassured to learn from their copy of Rogers's *A Century of Progress* that even before the firm moved out to Bournville, wages were paid above the normal in Birmingham even when the business was in a precarious state, because it was recognized that standard wages were inadequate (1931: 36).

Conclusion

The specific historical situation of 1931 produced a historically specific history of Cadbury, but one which has proved enduring and largely uncontested. Social psychological concepts of 'social cognition biases' may satisfactorily explain the prevalence of 'founders', both in corporate culture and business history writings: 'Salience causes leaders to figure prominently in people's memories of events', and 'attribution research suggests that people may have only minimal awareness of the situational determinants of a leader's behavior' (Martin et al. 1985: 101). However, history can complement this by explaining why the identities of founders with particular idiosyncrasies (Pettigrew 1979: 570) are selected at specific times in history; for example, why the Quaker beliefs of George and Richard Cadbury were given prominence in the late 1920s and 1930s, as opposed to, say, George's strong Liberal political views.

The history of Cadbury based on Quakerism served the purpose of corporate cultures (Pettigrew 1985: 44) and 'all invented traditions' (Hobsbawm 1983a: 12), by providing legitimacy. In a period of 'change, crisis and dislocation' a constructed history can represent a reassuring 'preservation of anachronism' (Cannadine 1983: 122). In an increasingly secular society the apparent conformity of Cadbury to a religious ideal gave the firm an identity which made it special, imbued with a morality probably perceived as lacking elsewhere. By 1931 the idea of an employer motivated by religious convictions must have appeared anachronistic, and, as it does today, more than a little quaint. The usefulness of 'invented practices' is that they tend 'to be quite unspecific and vague as to the nature of the values, rights and obligations of the group membership they inculcate ... objects or practices are liberated for full symbolic and ritual use when no longer fettered by practical use ... the wigs of lawyers could hardly acquire their modern significance until other people stopped wearing wigs' (Hobsbawm 1983a: 4, 10). Similarly, for Cadbury, the religious affiliation of its 'founders' could be invoked with convenient significance only once secularity had ensured that few people would have had any idea about the history of the Society of Friends and what it stood for, apart from the version presented to them by the firm itself. It also ensured that there was less likelihood of sectarian hostility being aroused. Possibly this explains the apparent willingness of British businessmen to appear 'closer to the churches' than might be expected [...] (Jeremy 1990: 5), why successful corporate cultures are thought to capture a 'religious tone' (Deal and Kennedy 1982: 195), and why, after the restructuring and layoffs of the 1980s, many companies today wish they could 'persuade workers to get religion again' (Dumaine 1990: 58).

If, in Selznick's readily quotable (Peters and Waterman 1982: 85) phrase, ' "to institutionalize" is to *infuse with value* beyond the technical requirements of the task at hand' (1957: 17), then the emphasis on Quakerism in the histories of the firm produced in its centenary year was a vital part of the institutionalization of Cadbury's labour-management practices. The Quaker beliefs of the Cadbury family were used to give meaning to the boundary between the firm and the troubled world outside. It should be remembered that 'the test of infusion with value is *expendability*' and 'when value-infusion takes place ... there is a resistance to change' (Selznick 1957: 18). Cadbury's labour-management practices proved to be enduring, and the firm's management found it difficult to abandon these practices when they conflicted with changes in the firm's strategy in the 1960s and 1970s (Smith et al. 1990; Rowlinson 1995).

History is therefore part of the process of institutionalization (Hobsbawm 1983a: 2). Founders themselves, and the act of founding, are institutionalized by history. The founders of cultures are selected retrospectively by historians, among others, including corporate culture writers, who adhere to the widespread cultural belief in the importance of founders. It may be thought that the position of the 'cultural pragmatists', those who 'see culture as a key to commitment, productivity, and profitability' and believe that culture can and should be managed (Martin 1985: 95), has already been largely undermined, but it may not be amiss to strike one more blow. The historical approach to the concept of culture in this [reading] suggests that culture cannot be managed unless a relatively uncontested history can be invented.

From the Cadbury case, two points can be made. First, the company had made substantial investments in material labour-management practices well before the Cadbury culture was invented to give a firm-specific meaning to those practices. Second, in constructing a history the firm was able to draw on appropriate and uncontested events in its past to differentiate itself from other companies. The success of the company's invented culture is indicated by the continued acceptance of its constructed history by business historians and corporate culture writers alike. This represents a considerable achievement. Those attempting to effect cultural change in the present without regard for the past want a culture on the cheap; by mere exhortation they hope to create a firm-specific identity, without having invested in any material practices that could be given a firm-specific meaning. They may well find to their cost that, 'a company with the wrong history and myths can get itself in big trouble' (Dumaine 1990: 56).

NOTE

From M. Rowlinson and J. Hassard (1993), 'The Invention of Corporate Culture: A History of the Histories of Cadbury', *Human Relations*, vol. 46, no. 3, pp. 299–326, which acknowledges Sir Adrian Cadbury for granting permission to consult the Cadbury archives and the library staff at Bournville for their assistance; also Peter Clark, Dawn Lyon, Graham Crow and the Keele History Society for their comments.

REFERENCES

Alexander, H. C. (1906), *Richard Cadbury of Birmingham* (London: Hodder & Stoughton).
Ankersmit, F. R. (1986), 'The dilemma of contemporary Anglo-Saxon philosophy of history', *History and Theory*, vol. 25, pp. 1–27.
Ashton, T. S. (1948), *Industrial Revolution, 1760–1830* (Oxford: Oxford University Press).
Ashton, T. S. (1963), *Iron and Steel in the Industrial Revolution*, 3rd edn (Manchester: Manchester University Press; first published 1924).
Aykroyd, W. R. (1967), *Sweet Malefactor: Sugar, Slavery and Human Society* (London: Heinemann).
Barley, S. R., G. Meyer and D. C. Gash (1988), 'Cultures of commitment: academics, practitioners and the pragmatics of normative control', *Administrative Science Quarterly*, vol. 33, pp. 24–60.

Barrett, F. J. and S. Srivastva (1991), 'History as a mode of inquiry in organizational life: a role for human cosmogeny', *Human Relations* vol. 44, pp. 231–54.

Bebbington, D. W. (1982), *The Nonconformist Conscience: Chapel and Politics. 1870–1914* (London: Allen & Unwin).

Berg, P.-O. (1985), 'Organizational change as a symbolic transformation process', in P. J. Frost, L. F. Moore, M. R. Louis, C. C. Lundberg and J. Martin, eds, *Organizational Culture* (London: Sage).

Birmingham Public Libraries (1976), *The Nine Days in Birmingham: The General Strike 4–12 May, 1926* (Birmingham: BPL).

Birnbaum, N. (1965), 'The rise of capitalism: Marx and Weber', in N. J. Smelser, ed., *Readings on Economic Sociology* (London: Prentice Hall).

Boston, S. (1980), *Women Workers and the Trade Union Movement* (London: Davis-Poynter, 1980).

Bradley, I. C. (1987), *Enlightened Entrepreneurs* (London: Weidenfield & Nicolson).

Branson, J. (1976), *The General Strike at Cadburys 1926*, unpublished BA dissertation, Birmingham University School of History.

Cadbury, E. (1915), 'The case against scientific management', in *Scientific Management in Industry*; reprinted from *Sociological Review*, 1914.

Cadbury, E. (1979), *Experiments in Industrial Organization* (New York: Arno Press; first published 1912).

Cadbury, E. and Shann, G. (1907), *Sweating* (London: Headley Brothers).

Cadbury, E., M. C. Matheson and G. Shann (1906), *Women's Work and Wages* (London: T. Fisher Unwin).

Campion, F. D. (1987), 'How to handle the corporate history', *Public Relations Journal*, vol. 43, pp. 31–2.

Cannadine, D. (1983), 'The context, performance and meaning of ritual: the British monarchy and the "invention of tradition" ', in E. Hobsbawm and T. Ranger, eds, *The Invention of Tradition* (Cambridge: Cambridge University Press).

Carr, E. H. (1964), *What is History?* (Harmondsworth: Penguin Books).

Chandler, A. D., Jr. (1962), *Strategy and Structure: Chapters in the History of the American Industrial Enterprise* (Cambridge, MA: MIT Press).

Chandler, A. D., Jr. (1988), 'Business history as institutional history', in T. K. McCraw, ed., *The Essential Alfred Chandler: Essays towards a Historical Theory of Big Business* (Cambridge, MA: Harvard Business School Press).

Child, J. (1964), 'Quaker employers and industrial relations', *Sociological Review*, vol. 12, pp. 293–315.

Child, J. (1969), *British Management Thought: A Critical Analysis* (London: Allen & Unwin).

Coleman, D. C. (1984), 'Historians and businessmen', in D. C. Coleman and P. Mathias, eds, *Enterprise and History: Essays in Honour of Charles Wilson* (Cambridge: Cambridge University Press).

Coleman, D. C. (1987), 'The uses and abuses of business history', *Business History*, vol. 29, pp. 141–56.

Corley, T. A. B. (1972), *Quaker Enterprise in Biscuits: Huntley and Palmers of Reading 1822–1972* (London: Hutchinson & Co.).

Corley, T. A. B. (1988), 'How Quakers coped with business success: Quaker industrialists, 1860–1914', in D. J. Jeremy, ed., *Business and Religion in Britain* (Aldershot: Gower).

Crowther, S. (1923), *John H. Patterson: Pioneer in Industrial Welfare* (Garden City, NY: Doubleday, Page & Co.).

Deal, T. E. and Kennedy, A. A. (1982), *Corporate Cultures: The Rites and Rituals of Corporate Life* (Reading, MA: Addison-Wesley).

Dellheim, C. (1986), 'Business in time: the historian and corporate culture', *The Public Historian*, vol. 8, pp. 9–22.

Dellheim, C. (1987), 'The creation of a company culture: Cadburys, 1861–1931', *The American Historical Review*, vol. 92, pp. 13–44.

Dumaine, B. (1990), 'Creating a new company culture', *Fortune*, 15 January, pp. 55–8.

Emden, P. H. (1939), *Quakers in Commerce: A Record of Business Achievement* (London: Sampson Low).

Fitzgerald, T. H. (1988), 'Can change in organizational culture really be managed?', *Organizational Dynamics*, Autumn, pp. 5–15.

Frost, P. J., L. F. Moore, M. R. Louis, C. C. Lundberg and J. Martin, *Organizational Culture* (London: Sage).

Gardiner, A. G. (1923), *Life of George Cadbury* (London: Cassell & Co.).

Galbraith, J. K. (1987), *A History of Economics: The Past as the Present* (London: Hamish Hamilton).

Gilman, N. P. (1899), *A Dividend to Labor: A Study of Employers' Welfare Institutions* (New York: Houghton Mifflin & Co.).

Gorman, G. H. (1981), *Introducing Quakers* (London: Quaker Home Service). *Handbook of the Yearly Meeting of the Society of Friends* (Birmingham, 1908).

Hannah, L. (1983), 'New issues in British business history', *Business History Review*, vol. 57, pp. 165–74.

Hannah, L. (1986), 'Corporate histories: limited liability offers a 1980s boom', *Financial Times*, 19 November.

Harvey, A. (1906), *The Model Village and its Cottages: Bournville* (London: B. T. Batsford).

Henselowe, P. (1984), *Ninety Years On: An Account of the Bournville Village Trust* (Birmingham: Bournville Village Trust).

'Historicus' [Cadbury, R.], (1892), *Cocoa: All About It* (London: Sampson, Low, Marston & Co.).

Hobsbawm, E. (1983a), 'Introduction: inventing traditions', in E. Hobsbawm and T. Ranger, eds, *The Invention of Tradition* (Cambridge: Cambridge University Press).

Hobsbawm, E. (1983b), 'Mass-producing traditions: Europe, 1870–1914', in E. Hobsbawm and T. Ranger, eds, *The Invention of Tradition* (Cambridge: Cambridge University Press).

Hofstede, G. (1986), 'Editorial: the usefulness of the "organizational culture" concept', *Journal of Management Studies*, vol. 23.

Howard, E. (1946), *Garden Cities of To-morrow* (London: Faber & Faber; first published in 1898, reissued with slight revisions in 1902).

Industrial Record 1919–1939 (Bournville: Cadbury Brothers, 1945).

Isichei, E. (1970), *Victorian Quakers* (Oxford: Oxford University Press).

Jeremy, D. J. ed. (1988), *Business and Religion in Britain* (Aldershot: Gower).

Jeremy, D. J. (1990), *Capitalists and Christians: Business Leaders and the Churches in Britain, 1990–1960* (Oxford: Clarendon Press).

Jeremy, D. J. (1991), 'The enlightened paternalist in action: William Hesketh Lever at Port Sunlight', *Business History*, vol. 33, pp. 58–81.

Kendrick, S., P. Straw and McCrone, D. (1990), *Interpreting the Past, Understanding the Present* (London: Macmillan).

Lewenhak, S. (1977), *Women and Trade Unions* (London: Ernest Benn).

Littler, C. R. (1982), *The Development of the Labour Process in Capitalist Societies* (London: Heinemann).

Manby, T. G. and P. Turnbull, eds (1986), 'Archeaology in the Pennines: essays in honour of Arthur Raistrick', *British Archaeological Reports*, British series 158.

Marks, W. in collaboration with C. Cadbury (n.d.), *George Cadbury Junior 1878–1954* (private publication).

Martin, J. (1985), 'Can organizational culture be managed?' in P. J. Frost, L. F. Moore, M. R. Louis, C. C. Lundberg and J. Martin, eds, *Organizational Culture* (London: Sage).

Martin, J., S. B. Sitkin and M. Boehm, (1985), 'Founders and the elusiveness of a cultural legacy', in P. J. Frost, L. F. Moore, M. R. Louis, C. C. Lundberg and J. Martin, eds, *Organizational Culture* (London: Sage).

Marwick, A. (1990), Letter to the editor, *The Times Higher Education*, December, suppl. 7.

Marx, K. (1976), *Capital*, vol. 1 (Harmondsworth: Penguin; first published 1867).

Meakin, B. (1905), *Model Factories and Villages* (London: T. Fisher Unwin).

Morris, J. (1986), *Women Workers and the Sweated Trades: The Origins of Minimum Wage Legislation* (Aldershot: Gower).

Mudie-Smith, R. (1906), *Sweated Industries: Being a Handbook of "The Daily News" Exhibition* (London).

Nelson, D. (1974), 'The new factory system and the unions: the National Cash Register Company dispute of 1901', *Labour History*, vol. 15, pp. 163–78.

Nelson, D. (1975), *Managers and Workers: Origins of the New Factory System in the United States 1880–1920* (Madison: University of Wisconsin Press).

Nevaskar, B. (1971), *Capitalists without Capitalism: The Jains of India and the Quakers of the West* (Connecticut: Greenwood Publishing).

Nord, W. R. (1985), 'Can organizational culture be managed?', in P. J. Frost, L. F. Moore, M. R. Louis, C. C. Lundberg and J. Martin, eds, *Organizational Culture* (London: Sage).

Norman, A. P. (1991), 'Telling it like it was: historical narratives on their own terms', *History and Theory*, vol. 30, pp. 119–35.

Peters, T. J. and R. H. Waterman (1982), *In Search of Excellence: Lessons from America's Best-run Companies* (New York: Harper & Row).

Pettigrew, A. M. (1979), 'On studying organizational cultures', *Administrative Science Quarterly*, vol. 24, pp. 570–81.

Pettigrew, A. M. (1985), *The Awakening Giant: Continuity and Change in Imperial Chemical Industries* (Oxford: Basil Blackwell).

Raistrick, A. (1953), *Dynasty of Iron Founders: The Darbys of Coalbrookdale* (London: Longmans Green & Co.).

Raistrick, A. (1968), *Quakers in Science and Industry: Quaker Contributions to Science and Industry during the Seventeenth and Eighteenth Centuries* (Newton Abbott: David & Charles Holdings; first published 1950).

Raistrick, A. (1977), *Two Centuries of Industrial Welfare: The London (Quaker) Lead Company 1692–1905* (London: Trowbridge & Esher).

Rogers, T. B. (1931), *A Century of Progress 1831–1931* (Bournville: Cadbury Brothers).

Rowlinson, M. (1988), 'The early application of scientific management by Cadbury', *Business History*, vol. 30, pp. 377–95.

Rowlinson, M. (1995), 'Strategy, Structure and Culture: Cadbury, Divisionalization and Merger in the 1960s', *Journal of Management Studies*, vol. 32, no. 2, pp. 121–40.

Schein, E. H. (1985), *Organizational Culture and Leadership: A Dynamic View* (San Francisco: Jossey-Bass).

Selznick, P. (1957), *Leadership in Administration: A Sociological Interpretation* (Evanston, IL: Row, Peterson & Co.).

Smircich, L. (1983), 'Concepts of culture and organizational analysis', *Administrative Science Quarterly*, vol. 28, pp. 339–58.

Smircich, L. (1985), 'Is the concept of culture a paradigm for understanding organizations and ourselves?', in P. J. Frost, L. F. Moore, M. R. Louis, C. C. Lundberg and J. Martin, eds, *Organizational Culture* (London: Sage).

Smith, C., J. Child and M. Rowlinson (1990), *Reshaping Work: The Cadbury Experience* (Cambridge: Cambridge University Press).

Smith, D. (1986), 'Englishness and the Liberal inheritance after 1886', in R. Colls and P. Dodd, eds, *Englishness: Politics and Culture 1880–1920* (London: Croom Helm).

Tedlow, R. S. (1986), participant in A. M. Kantrow, 'Why history matters to managers', *Harvard Business Review*, January–February.

Thomas, M. (1985), 'In search of culture: holy grail or gravy train?', *Personnel Management*, vol. 17, pp. 24–7.

Thompson, E. P. (1980), *The Making of the English Working Class* (Harmondsworth: Penguin).

Thompson, P. (1991), 'Fatal distraction: post-modernism and organisational analysis', paper for the conference 'Towards a New Theory of Organisations', University of Keele, April.

Turner, B. (1990), 'The rise of organizational symbolism', in J. Hassard and D. Pym, eds, *The Theory and Philosophy of Organizations: Critical Issues and New Perspectives* (London: Routledge).

Wagner, G. (1987), *The Chocolate Conscience* (London: Chatto & Windus).

Walsh, J. P. and G. R. Ungson (1991), 'Organizational memory', *Academy of Management Review*, vol. 16, pp. 57–91.

Weber, M. (1930), *The Protestant Ethic and the Spirit of Capitalism* (London: Unwin University Books).

Weiner, M. J. (1985), *English Culture and the Decline of the Industrial Spirit* (Harmondsworth: Penguin).

Widdowson, P. (1990), 'Perspective: the creation of a past', *The Times Higher Education Supplement*, 30 November.

Williams, E. (1964), *Capitalism and Slavery* (London: Andre Deutsch).

Williams, I. A. (1931), *The Firm of Cadbury 1831–1931* (London: Constable & Co.).

Windsor, P. B. (1980), *The Quaker Enterprise: Friends in Business* (London: Frederick Muller).

Winterson, J. (1990), *Sexing the Cherry* (London: Vintage).

7 Discipline

Disciplinary Power in the Modern Corporation

STANLEY DEETZ

Corporate organizations conceived as political systems is a common and productive image for organizational analysis (Morgan 1986). Conceptions developed from this root image have been useful in describing key processes of power and conflict and are likely to become more important as the social impact of large corporate units is more fully understood. Conceptualizing organizations as political systems draws attention to the ways large corporations serve as primary sites where different values, forms of knowledge and groups' interests are articulated and embodied in decisions, structures and practices. As political institutions, corporations are seen as providing meaning and personal identity to their various stakeholders as well as goods, services and income. But the political conception is more than an evocative metaphor.

Corporate organizations serve as a polity. In modern societies they make most public decisions on the use of resources, the development of technologies, the products available and the working relations among people. In many countries the corporate sector makes more public decisions than its governmental counterparts. Unfortunately, the common uncritical acceptance of corporations as naturally existing commercial entites, and concern with managerially conceived issues of efficiency and effectiveness, have led most analyses to be uninterested in the relation of organizational processes to the democratic interest in public participation (Burrell 1988). Even political conceptions of corporations are often reduced to concern with personal interests and internal strategies. The corporation is overlooked as an important site of *public* decision-making. Understanding corporations as political entities in relation to a democratic society calls for studies that investigate the significance of the exercise of power and control within corporations rather than studies that are concerned with the operation and enhancement of managerial control.

Several authors have [...] used concepts from Critical Theory to support studies of social arrangements and practices which foster wider and more open participation in the collective determination of the future (see Alvesson 1987a for a review). Much of this work has focused on power, ideology and symbolic/cultural practices (Clegg 1989; Mumby 1988; Alvesson 1987b). In order for these works to provide descriptions of more appropriate corporate practices, processes of communication and the issues of a modern democratic politics require greater elucidation. Central to such a project is an understanding of the relations between power, discursive practices and conflict suppression as they affect the production of individual identity and corporate knowledge.

Understanding these relations requires a conception of the political processes of everyday life. While the idea was hardly new and not always articulated clearly, during the 1960s significant segments of the general society, as well as scholars, began to develop a concern with these subtle political processes. Educational institutions, the workplace, the family and media were examined with regard to how they represented different group and individual interests in their decisions, and even more basically how they shaped the very meanings available for public thought and expression. In contrast to the traditional concern with the freedom of public expression and state political processes, the very concept of what was the 'public' became contestable (e.g. Donzelot 1979). From such a conception, the political battles, [since the mid-1960s] at least in the Western world, can be seen as waged over the content of the subjective world, and not just its expression, though such conflicts often remain obscured and misrecognized. Certain feminist groups popularized the sense of the issues in their slogan 'the personal is political'. Or as Baudrillard (1975) more completely argued, the issues cannot be attributed to economic distribution and speaking opportunities within the existing mode of representing interests; the fight must be against the monopoly of the 'code' itself. With such a view, concern shifts to examining alternative codes; and analysis often demonstrates that 'free' and autonomous expression suppresses alternative representations, and thus hides the monopoly of existing codes. The primary force of domination can no longer be seen as economic exploitation with false consciousness providing its excuse but can be conceptualized as the arbitrary, power-laden constitution of 'world', 'self' and 'other'. With such a conceptual shift, analysis focuses on systems that develop each subject's active role in producing and reproducing domination. Democratic communication in these terms must be about the formation of knowledge, experience and identity, not merely their expression. The development of the conceptual shift to a politics of meaning and identity construction is, however, often limited by linguistic and social forces, including the borrowing of most conceptions of power, domination, freedom and democracy from political theories concerned with the relation of the individual to the modern state. This can be seen in 'negotiated order' theories, for example. In most of these, the free agent, knowledge and decision-making are based on eighteenth-century conceptions of the individual and reason, views which both help sustain managerial domination in corporations and hamper the development of alternatives (see Laclau and Mouffe 1985: 115ff).

Modern Critical Theory's emancipatory project must claim some conception of reason and individual agency yet not be insensitive to issues raised by the politics of everyday life. The political analysis of organizations ultimately must be grounded in a conception of open participatory democracy, but this must be

143

informed by new concepts of the personal and of communication processes. The most common conceptions of the human character and the communication process are imaginary: that is, they are constructed as real within particular social/ historical systems of domination. If we understand this imaginary nature we can displace the constructed-as-presumed-free subject as the centre and origin of meaning and better understand how the subject is produced. And if discourse itself is understood as power-laden rather than neutral and transparent, we can better reveal the sites of power deployment and concealment. Studies like those of Alvesson (1987b) and Mumby (1988) have worked out new conceptions of power in organizations but can be seen as advancing a conception which Abercrombie et al. (1980) justifiably criticized as the 'dominant ideology thesis'. The presumption appears to be that ideology is produced by some dominant agents who are somehow outside it, that it is produced by identifiable material forces, and that it becomes fixed as a material sign located in some linguistic configuration or institution. Clegg (1989) has shown [...] how the limitations of these analyses can be corrected by using Foucault's (1977; 1980) conception of 'disciplinary' power. Power can be considered creative rather than limiting, it is inseparable from knowledge rather than directing it, and its productive force comes from below as well as above. An analysis using the conception of discipline allows a more sensitive description of the deployment and workings of power than ideology critique alone. The concern here will be with the workings of power in the formation of competing interests and representations, rather than with the possibility of false interests or distorted expression. This will include a reconception of power in regard to cultural formations, an analysis of possible hidden antagonisms in discourse and the manner of the suppression of conflict among them, and a description of the role of organizational analysis in the recovery of antagonism and member agency.

Corporations are the site of public political decisions

Concern with the representation of interests in corporations has provided useful initial conceptions for examining the politics of corporate practices. Critical Theory's concern with interest representation is an essential step toward a more basic conception made possible by recent works. From a Critical Theory perspective, organizational processes and products fulfil certain human needs. These needs have been described as the interests or 'stake' that various parties (managers, workers, consumers, suppliers and the wider society) have in the organization. Beyond these work-related distinctions, interest differences can often be demonstrated in groups divided by gender, ethnic and racial considerations.

Organizational structures, communication and decision systems, technologies and work design influence the representation and fulfilment of different human interests (Young 1989). While people produce organizations, all people are not equal in their ability to produce or reproduce organizations that fulfil their interests. From a Critical Theory perspective, organizations thus can never be considered politically neutral. In contemporary practice, managerial groups are clearly privileged in decision-making and most concepts of it. Other groups can be seen as exercising only occasional and usually reactive influences and are often represented as simply economic commodities or 'costs'. The advantages given to management are based on neither rational nor open consensual value foundations nor are they simply acquired through management's own (though often latent) strategic attempts. They are produced historically, and actively reproduced, through discursive practices in corporations themselves (Deetz and Mumby 1990). Managerial advantages and prerogative can be seen as taking place through economic-based structures *and* systems of discursive monopoly. In modern corporations such an advantage is not so much conceptualized as a right or as legitimate but is unproblematically reproduced in routines and discourses. As such this privilege is treated as natural and neutral. This presumed neutrality makes understanding the political nature of organizations more difficult. Order, efficiency and effectiveness as values aid the reproduction of advantages already vested in an organizational form. Concepts of organizational effectiveness tend to hide possible discussion of whose goals should be sought and how much each goal should count (Cameron and Whetten 1983).

Critical Theorists have shown that workers and the general society have interests in work that are only partially and indirectly shared by management and owners. These include the quality of the work experience and work environment, mental health and safety, the skill and intellectual development of the worker, the carry-over of thinking patterns and modes of action to social and political life, and the production of personal and social identity (Alvesson 1987a). Organizational life could be an explicit site of political struggle as different groups try to realize their own interests but the conflicts there are often routinized, evoke standard mechanisms for resolution, and reproduce presumed natural tensions (e.g. between workers and management). The essential politics thus become invisible. Even more basically, the work site could be considered a polysemic environment where the production of the individual or group interests could itself be seen as an end product (or temporary resting place) in a basically conflictual process defining personal and group identity and the development and articulation of interests. Such potential conflicts are even more completely suppressed in the normalization of conception, identity formation and non-decisional practice than is shown by Critical Theory's ideology critique. The production of the conflicts that exist, and the lack of other equally plausible ones, does not signify false consciousness so much as a type of discursive closure, a central conception for this analysis. The possible development of alternative interests and the subsequent tension between them is often suppressed in organizational practices and discourse through representational marginalization, reduction of alternative interests to economic costs, socialization of members, and the shift of responsibility to the individual.

Known power differences often lead to inequitable interest representation, but power differences are sometimes quite subtle. Different stakeholders are not always in a position to analyse their own interests owing to the lack of adequate undistorted information or insight into fundamental processes. Both stockholders and workers can be disadvantaged by particular accounting practices and the withholding of information. Further, the presence of ideology in the external social world or at the workplace, perpetuated through legitimation and socialization processes, can indicate the inability of certain or even all groups to carefully understand or assess the implicit values carried in their everyday practices, linguistic forms and perceptual experiences. And even more basically, even if they could be assessed, the individual assessing the ideology is a product of a social situation. As Lukes argued, the interior itself is contestable: 'Man's wants themselves may be a product of a system which works against their interests, and in such cases, relates the latter to what they would want and prefer, were they able to make the choice' (1974: 34). Under such conditions what might be accepted as legitimate power differences are best represented as a system of domination, since the empirical manifestation is that of free consent yet structures are reproduced that work against competitive practices and fulfilment of the variety of interests. With such a view, what are taken as legitimate consensual processes are more often evidence of domination and suppressed conflict than of free choice and agreement.

Ideological critique alone is not sufficient to account for the full nature of this domination. The presence of ideology and failure to understand self-interest fails to account for how compliance and consent may be a result of clear member understanding of the material conditions for their success. As Przeworski (1980) has argued, the desire to live well provides a pressure towards active participation in the corporate system. In many workers' minds, corporations have delivered the goods and workers have received a necessary and even desired standard of living for their participation. Who is to speak better than they of the quality of the trade-offs that they have made? The same interpretation could be made of Burawoy's (1979) description of the 'making-out' game. In his analysis the organization of 'making-the-rate' provides predictability, security and favourable relations even though the worker is co-opted. The worker is not living an illusion or failing to accomplish interests. The more deeply these systems are probed, the more clear it is that the individual is making a 'rational decision'. But in making rational, aware decisions, a structure of advantage is perpetuated, one of self *and* corporate advantage. The identities and decisions structured here, however, are not politically neutral or simply advantageous. They participate in the construction of a future in which there is a larger stake. The decisions lack an open democratic character not because the calculus or calculations are distorted, but because the human character and needs are specified in advance rather than responsive to the situational complexities. The lack of conflict in these self-referential systems precludes the discussion and open determination of the future (see Mingers 1989). A non-contentious decision has already been made (see Deetz 1992).

The concern expressed here is not just with managerial domination, but the corporate development of the obedient, normalized mind and body, which is held up against equally legitimate but unrealized alternatives. The interest is in describing the ways by which managers and workers both become obedient in their own structurally prescribed manner (Burrell 1988: 227). While managers and sometimes owners gain in these structures, the force which drives them is not simply or directly those gains. Rather it is a set of practices and routines which constitute identities and experiences and in doing so provide unproblematic asymmetries, privileged knowledge, and expertise located in some and not others, and in doing so instantiate inclusions and exclusions in decisional processes (Knights and Willmott 1985). The path I will begin here, and believe must be extended in research, is to reclaim conflicting experiences through describing the practices and routines by which alternatives are disregarded or rendered invisible. The understanding of the processes by which value conflict becomes suppressed and certain forms of reasoning and interests become privileged requires an investigation into the politics of meaning, language and personal identity.

The discursive politics of knowledge and identity

The most significant product of any corporation is its members. The very notions of free contract, social relations and agency as well as personal identity as a manager, secretary or worker are corporate productions and reproductions. Laclau and Mouffe summarized the three positions central to the corporate individual: 'the view of the subject as an agent both rational and transparent to itself; the supposed unity and homogeneity of the ensemble of its positions; and the conception of the subject as origin and basis of social relations' (1985: 115). The first is necessary for the illusion of freedom which allows the subject to be conceptualized as freely subordinating him/herself in the social contract of the corporation and having choices based on self-interests there. The second sets out the hope of a well-integrated society where the work relations fit without conflict into other institutions and coexist with the democratic processes and the basis for consensual decision-making and mutual understanding. And finally, the individual is conceptualized as the fundamental site of meaning production and chooser of relations with others; hence the personal itself is protected from the examination necessary if it were seen as an arbitrary historical social production resulting from certain social arrangements. Each of these conceptions is misleading and reproductive of forms of domination. Alternative conceptions, however, are difficult to come by.

The politics of identity and identity representation is the deepest and most suppressed struggle in the workplace and, hence, the 'site' where domination and responsive agency are most difficult to unravel. Conceptions which place experience within individuals present language as a neutral transparent representation, and treat communication as if it were simply a transmission process [thus making] it, difficult to describe these processes carefully. The position here differs greatly from this. As recent social theory has shown, conceptualizing the individual as the original site of meaning and decisional choices is misleading. Rather, each individual exists with produced identities placed in an already meaningful world. Both the subject and the presumed objective world arise out of a set of discursive and non-discursive practices which constitute the subject and produce a world of distinguished objects (Knights and Willmott 1989). Central to understanding the workplace is an understanding of these practices. Prior to any analysis focusing on managers, workers or women and their various interests and reasoning processes is a concern with how these classifications come to exist

147

at all. This leads further to questions regarding how they are reproduced as meaningful, how they are utilized in producing certain types of conflict and their resolutions, and how they preclude other interests and conflicts within and among the various groupings. With identities come interests and relations with other identities, but the first identities are not fixed but are themselves arbitrary social productions. Social groupings and their interests, types of rationality, and the concept of profit are social productions. Each is produced as distinguished from something else. The questions posed for Critical Theory are thus not how these things exist, have power, or explain organizational behaviour, but rather how they come to exist, coexist and interrelate in the production and reproduction of corporate organizations and work in the process of potential inner and outer colonization.

Several questions arise that are of concern. Which personal/relational identities are produced in the modern corporation? How are these identities specified with particular forms of interests and types of knowledge? How are these identities discursively and non-discursively inscribed, interrelated and reproduced? How do such identities become naturalized and reified so as to be taken for granted and suppress the conflict with potential competing identities? I will begin with a summary of what is known about these issues by initially exploring the linguistic constitution of identities through systems of distinctions and then move to consider the deployment of specific discursive practices.

Language as a system of distinction

The most common misleading conception of language is that it represents an absent, to be recalled, object. Instead, language is primarily constitutive rather than representational. The character of the object and expression arise together. As a system, language holds forth the historically developed dimensions of interests – the attributes of concern or the lines along which things of the world will be distinguished. Language holds the possible ways we will engage in the world and produce objects with particular characteristics. Thus when we consider language from a political point of view within organizations, the interest is not primarily in how different groups use language to accomplish goals, the rationality in language usage, nor how the profit motive influences language use. The concern is with the dimensions utilized to produce classifications and thus produce groups and their relations. And further, we must understand how representational conceptions of language themselves aid in making classification and identity production appear neutral and based in natural divisions rather than articulating choices with distinct political effect.

Saussure (1974) is most often given credit for the insight that language is primarily a system of distinctions rather than representational. This was accomplished in two arguments. First, signifiers (words or signs) and the signifieds (the potential constituted object to be referenced) are separate and arbitrarily related. This severed any assumption of natural, ahistorical or universal connections between specific words and constituted objects. Any particular language or set of distinctions is a social historical product, developed in social relations and subject to change. And secondly, the meaning of signs is neither intrinsic nor derived from the signified but derived from their difference from other signs in the language chain. Each word can reference only on the basis of its relation and contrasts with other words, a contrast which is reproduced in objects. For example, a term such as 'worker' has meaning only as it distinguishes from 'manager', 'unemployed' or 'lazy' within a particular socially produced linguistic chain. The word makes thematic a perspective against a hidden background of what it is not, which is simultaneously articulated. This part of Saussure's work is useful to the analysis here, though like others (Giddens 1979; Derrida 1976), I will reject Saussure's notion that the meanings of signs are fixed as conventions of a speech community. Every sign system contains the possibility of conflicting meanings; the fixing of signs against the plurality of meaning becomes the significant issue here.

Because it is a system of distinction, every linguistic system puts into place certain kinds of social relations and values – that is, certain things that are worthy of being distinguished from other things – and puts into play the attributes that will be utilized to make that distinction. For example, whenever we distinguish between men and women, in using a description that notes gender we claim that distinction along the line of gender is important and valuable to this society and that particular attributes can be used to make that distinction. Both the choice of distinction based on gender and the choice of attributes is arbitrary. It is chosen in choosing the signifying system. The word 'man' or 'woman' does not simply represent something real out there. It puts into play a way of paying attention to the 'out there'. The employment is not neutral. The distinction performs a production of identity for the subject as a woman or man and for the persons as objects with certain rights and characteristics. As the chain of signifiers fans out, the female can be upheld as a mother in a kinship system, a wife in a marital relation, and so forth. In each case, each individual so constituted is both advantaged and disadvantaged in the way that institutional arrangements specify opportunities and constraints. But the distinction remains arbitrary. The signifiers are arbitrary in the sense that, at the next moment, distinction on the basis of gender can be overlooked, rendered irrelevant, or difficult – in the sense that the system of relations between signifiers could be different.

To many it appears self-evident that men and women are different and that therefore the distinction is important. But such 'self-evidence' guides attention away from the political consequences of making the distinction and the choice of sites where it is deployed. The distinction enters into the play of power in the organization in important and conflicting ways. On the one hand, many would wish that the gender distinction would become irrelevant in the place of work so that the identity of people constituted as women, as well as pay and routine treatment practices, would be based on other dimensions of distinction and other constituted identities. Yet rendering gender invisible would exclude the possibility of women organizing and working towards distinct group interests which arise in a gendered society. Thus the distinction socially separates women, marginalizes female experience and provides a unitary identity which denies personal complexity and internal identity conflict. Yet it also provides a ground for resistance and retains a place for conflict of a different sort. The same type of analysis can be applied to each identity produced in the corporation. The double effect of representational practices is a key issue in any emancipatory project in corporations. First we must understand the ideological nature of distinction and then move on to develop the complexities of alternative practices within the discursive system.

Gender distinction is only one of many critical distinctions in the workplace, e.g. worker/manager, data/not data, private/public information, rational/irrational and expert/non-expert. Understanding the importance of the gender issue reminds us of the multitude of classificatory activities that have political implications and that are protected by seeming to be self-evident and empirical. Further, each of these becomes interwoven in a complex of signifiers, e.g. gender becomes tied to forms of understanding and knowledge, private and public becomes critical to various forms of expertise and proprietary information. Occupational classification is only one of many signifying practices that have significance for gender politics, e.g. stories, jokes and dress codes each implement distinctions and an associated chain of signifiers. Far less has been done about these things than about gender and occupational classification. If people could work back through the systems of distinctions they implement, they would often find a gap between what they reflectively think and feel and what they unwittingly express. The point is not to determine what they 'really' or freely think. But recalling the arbitrariness of such constructions is a step in understanding the plurality of equally plausible subject articulations momentarily out of the reach of proclaimed 'naturalness and self-evidence'. It is this self-evidence and presumed transparency of language that must be given up to understand power and the politics of experience. It is this that ideological criticism has accomplished well. This can easily be seen in the work on the linguistic production of subject identity.

The linguistic production of subject identity

Althusser (1971) has given the most commanding treatment of the relation of language to the production of the human subject. In Althusser's analysis language is the most general ideological mediation. Language to Althusser, building on Saussure, is not a system of signs that represent. Rather, language appears as discourse, a material practice which systematically forms that of which it speaks. Language as an ideological practice mediates between individuals and the conditions of their existence. This mediation is not between preformed individuals and objective conditions but it is the means by which the individual becomes a subject, a process called *interpellation*. Quoting Althusser: 'I shall then suggest that ideology "acts" or "functions" in such a way that it "recruits" subjects among individuals (it recruits them all), or "transforms" the individual into subjects (it transforms them all) by that very precise operation which I have called *interpellation* or hailing' (1971: 162–3). The specific relationship between subject in a particular world and the individual is *imaginary*. That is, the 'subject' is always an image or a constructed self rather than an individual in a full set of relations to the world. A 'real' form of domination or control is unnecessary to the extent that the individual takes the imaginary construction as if it is real. Or as Weedon has suggested:

> The crucial point ... is that in taking on a subject position, the individual assumes that she is the author of the ideology or discourse which she is speaking. She speaks or thinks as if she were in control of meaning. She 'imagines' that she is the type of subject which humanism proposes – rational, unified, the source rather than the effect of language. It is the imaginary quality of the individual's identification with a subject position which gives it so much psychological and emotional force. (1987: 31)

It is of little surprise that the individual makes the mistake since the processes through which this misrecognition takes place are subtle and complex. Pêcheux (1982), following Althusser (1971), argued that ideology 'interpellates individuals into subjects' through many complex, 'forgotten' interdiscourses whereby each subject has a signified, self-evident reality which is 'perceived-accepted-submitted to'. As Thompson (1984: 236) has presented Pêcheux's analysis: the hidden-forgotten discursive formation

> creates the illusion that the subject precedes discourse and lies at the origin of meaning. Far from this being the case, it is the subject which is 'produced' or 'called forth' by the discursive sequence; or more precisely, the subject is 'always already produced' by that which is 'preconstructed' in the sequence.

But discursive sequences are never singular and closed. The issue of concern, however, is not that an illusion or image is produced but, rather, the politics of preferring one type of image over others, precluding the conflict and dialogue among them, and structuring self-referential relationships that have no outside.

The consideration of alternative meanings and alternative subjectivities poses a threat to the individual's claimed identity, thus the individual rejects the possibility of freedom. The individual will often protect the constructions as natural and as one's own even though they are not, and reject alternatives as mere constructions that are unnatural and, ironically, politically motivated (see Knights and Willmott 1985, 1989). The first political act is forgotten as attention is paid to the second. As such, the individual is not simply identifying with those in power; that power is the subject. The subject as mediated through language is always ideologically produced. There is no place beyond the formation to claim an independent subject. The individual experiences a particular world, one which is the product of socially inscribed values and distinctions like the subject itself. Only on the basis of this does the individual claim personal beliefs or values or come to share them with others. A particular ideology is a particular way of being in the world, a social sharing prior to any individual taking it on as his/her own.

Let me sum up here by suggesting that systems of thought, expression and communication media contain embedded values that constitute a particular experience through the making of distinctions and relations through perception. The very ordinariness of common sense hides the implicit valuational structure of perceptual experience. Each discourse and attendant technology constitutes ways of knowing the world, privileges certain notions of what is real, and posits personal identities. Both mediated and non-mediated discourses posit a subject, have an epistemology, and structure value choices. The development of technical knowledge and conceptions of expertise do not simply advantage those who have them, but their presumed existence enables the qualification and disqualification of members' ways of knowing and are thus a major element in conflict suppression and the production of identity and experience. But language and expression alone do not exhaust the production of the subject's identity.

Institutions as discursive practices

Everyday life is filled with institutional artefacts, routines and standard practices. Each implements values and establishes a subject's point of view. Institutional practices are concretized (sometimes literally) in the construction of buildings, the laying of sidewalks, the writing of legal codes, the placement of postings and signs, the development and implementation of technologies, and the development of stories, jokes and vocabularies. Cultural researchers have long noted the presence of such features. Unfortunately, they are often treated as expressive of the individual or culture, and their role in the constitution of the subject and world is lost. Institutional forms are textual, they are human creations which, like language, position a subject and direct the construction of particular experiences with particular conflicts and opportunities for alternative perceptions.

For example, the change of banking facilities from an imposing, secure singular site to homely, dispersed branches and finally automated teller machines can be seen as expressive of changing images and needs, but more fundamentally produces and continually reproduces a different 'subject' with different social relations and a different object: 'money'. Such a reading recognizes that this happens against the backdrop of other possible relations and absences and possible subjects. The old 'subject' in the new configuration becomes absent and is difficult to produce even if the person wanted to. The modern person is produced as consumer, even of money. It is not simply the case that attitudes towards savings have changed; rather the institution, the very subject and routine of saving, is different. Interest rates, legal requirements and tax laws, for example, are among many institutional practices that both make possible these changes and are changed by them.

But the banking and monetary system itself is produced in a particular way of relating other social changes and practices and it alone does not produce the modern person even in relation to money. The person is a home owner, a product consumer, a parent and so forth. The relation between institutional arrangements produces a complex subject, a subject which is at once dispersed among many and competing institutions and unified as a common produced identity across inter-relatable institutions. The desire for, or expectation of, autonomy in certain institutions can create dependency in others. For example, to the extent that freedom and the pursuit of happiness are institutionally inscribed as a leisure activity, dependency and control become acceptable and even necessary characteristics of the place of work as a means of fulfilling the promise of leisure. The worker may demand greater work, presumably for his or her own interest. Not only across institutions: the modern workplace itself evidences such dispersion and provides a set of practices which unify, and thus suppress, the potential conflicts. The very complexity frequently hides the onesidedness of the matrix and stops exploration of possible identities that would be constituted in different institutional arrangements. The task of working out these relationships at any particular corporate site or for the more general corporate experience is great. And as the complexity increases, the descriptive and critical adequacy of economic and ideological explanations becomes increasingly limited.

The subject is subject to a range of discourses, some of which conflict. Meaning is not a singularity claimed by an individual text, or even an intersection of texts. It is pluralistic and 'deferred' in the sense that there can be no final determination. Unitary meaning is temporary and only held in place by force before it drifts away in a never-ending web of other texts. Only on the basis of the appearance of plurality could ideology be identified at all or could the subject be claimed as an agent. There is never one linguistic expression in one institutional arrangement, but many. And further, our interest does not end with the construction of the subject but extends to the realities in which subjects find themselves.

The notion of the psychological subject as an autonomous originator of meaning which phenomenology first showed to be an abstraction is now more precisely replaced by competing points of view arising in many simultaneous texts. People thus are not filled with independently existing thoughts, feelings, beliefs and plans that are brought to expression. As they move about the world, reading books, watching television or doing work, they take on the subjects of these texts as their own (Giddens 1984: 184). The self is not independent of texts but always finds itself in them. The unity of the reflected subject carries with it possibilities and problems and most importantly conceals its own social/cultural origin and an illusion of a certain presence and freedom: an illusion suggested at the outset as essential to domination in corporate functioning. The power given to the self to define its own meaning is an unwarranted privilege, conceals the process of construction, and leaves the subject unaware of multiple systems of control. Once texts are freed from the privilege of the subject or rational meaning, a new set of analyses of the organization of texts becomes possible.

Control of identity production

If the subject and the subject's world are an arbitrary production carefully (intentionally but without simple origin) integrated to appear necessary and unproblematic, we must account for their accomplishment, the complexity of the formation, and the political gains and losses in particular formations. Such an analysis, of course, parallels Gramsci's (1971) conception of hegemony. Gramsci argued that the willing assent of the mass was engineered through the production of the normality of everyday life beliefs and practices. Rather than visible control by elites, 'organic intellectuals' (e.g. teachers, writers, experts) produce a variety of cultural forms that express and shape values, actions and meanings, and reproduce hidden forms of domination. The site of hegemony is the myriad of everyday institutional activities and experiences that culminate in 'common sense', thus hiding the choices made and 'mystifying' the interests of dominant groups. Dominant group definitions of reality, norms and standards appear as normal rather than political and contestable. Bourdieu (1977) has extended this in his discussion of the role of 'symbolic elites' in defining the preferred representational systems in a society. And to some extent, this part of Gramsci's work is recalled in a new way when Foucault (1977) identifies psychiatrists, doctors and wardens as controllers of discourse. Their definitions of deviance and normality can be seen as expressions of power that often arbitrarily support certain ways of life as normal and others as pathological.

In a partial and overly simplistic conception, corporate managers, technical experts and consultants armed with their own social, economic and managerial science become the 'organic intellectuals' of our present formation. Their power, however, is not so simple. The modern corporate power is not a monolithic extension of class politics, but more like a web of arbitrary asymmetrical relations with specific means of decision and control. While certain groups benefit from these arrangements, they are in no simple way designed for these gains. The force of these arrangements is primarily in producing order, forgetfulness and dependency. Ideology critique is frequently limited by the assumption of hidden real interests or the possibility of new power-free rationality. Ideology as a concept is best seen as drawing attention to arbitrary representational practices rather than a false or class consciousness. Our opening to the future is better seen in the perpetual critique of each consensus and claim to rationality, but not for the sake of better reasoning and new consensus. The recovery of lost conflict and the retention of ongoing decision-making against presumption and closure can be developed as the central critical goal. This is best seen in reconsidering the nature of power. Understanding the deployment of power and the manner of its advantaging will require a number of reconceptions.

Power and discursive formations

The major problem ideological criticism faces rests in its conception of power. In many Critical Theory works, especially in Habermas, power differences *per se* are equated with domination and are held to be in opposition to reason. The Critical Theory ideal of a new public forum wherein competing claims and interests can be expressed and resolved requires a unitary rational subject, which has been shown as an illusion and itself part of a domination system. And further, the negative notion of power does not allow for the formation of perhaps arbitrary and distorted power blocs which may be essential to the development of alternative practices in actual power-laden contexts. The issue of power must be reconsidered within the Critical Theory project. The trick is to understand the power-laden nature of all human association and yet to retain some place and hope for democratic decision-making so that all is not reduced to arbitrary power advantages.

In Western societies few issues have commanded the discursive attention of the twin issues of freedom and the exercise of power. Foucault (1980), perhaps better than anyone else, has demonstrated that it is frequently because of these discussions rather than an inattention to power that we have failed to understand its presence and manner of deployment. So too in corporate organizations the attention to intergroup conflict, coalitions, regulations and rights has often led us further from understanding power and domination. As indicated, most conceptions and analyses of power in organizations have been derived from political scientists. Each of these conceptions was primarily designed to discuss power in relation to the influence different people or groups have in political processes or the rights of individuals in opposition to possible state domination. This I believe to be true in the Critical Theory tradition. Discussions of leadership, coalition formation, special interests and authority in corporations are often distinguished from similar 'public' process only by scale and the special applicable rights. Similarly, discussions of loyalty and collective priorities closely parallel conceptions developed for the relation to the state. Foucault has shown how each of these conceptions is tied to sovereign rights as expanded in a 'juridico' discourse. Since power is conceived as restrictive of individual freedom, the question 'by what right or necessity is the rule made' serves as a fundamental issue for the exercise of power.

Disciplinary power

Following Foucault (1980), disciplinary power rather than sovereign power is of utmost significance. The state or central administration still has much power but it is limited if only because, in its negative form, it is always felt as oppressive. This is merely the public extension of the same rational grounding for Critical Theory. Power is restriction and oppression. In corporations a kind of sovereign power exists and can be described as parallel in character to that of the state. But attention to this is misleading and often conceals the actual procedures of power and the operant sites of its deployment. Most significantly, in modern corporations control and influence are dispersed into norms and standard practices as products of moral, medical, sexual and psychological regulation – disciplinary power (see Burrell 1988). This is a conception of power that Habermas (1984; 1987) attempted to account for in his 'constitutive steering media' but he appears unable to sustain his critique of the power formations without appealing to a 'lifeworld' which is still laden with power, only of a different kind. Foucault's conception of disciplinary power allows a more complete description of the enabling as well as constraining constitutive capacity identified as power.

Disciplinary power resides in every perception, every judgement, every act. In its positive sense it enables, and negatively it excludes and marginalizes. Participatory democracy is itself a power-laden discipline, one which encourages certain practices (e.g. concept formation) and works against others (e.g. perceptual repetition and private interests). Rather than analysing power in the organization as if it were a sovereign state, the conception of power has to be reformed to account for this more massive and invisible structure of control. Administration has to be seen in relation to order and discipline if its power is to be understood. I believe that we gain in this conception over Edwards's (1979) discussion of the emergence of 'bureaucratic' control. It is not just the rule and routine which become internalized, but a complex set of practices which provide common sense, self-evident experience and personal identity. The question is not simply how to account for the presence of management defined as control rather than co-ordination, but also how control operates in 'organic' as well as 'bureaucratic' structured organizations.

Disciplinary power for Foucault is omnipresent as it is manifest and produced in each moment. Power is thus not dispersed in modern society to citizens who argue and vote, but spreads out through lines of conformity, commonsense observations, and determinations of propriety. Disciplinary power is evidenced in the production of a normalized body and response which is produced, reproduced and supported by arrangements of the material world which result in co-ordination and consent, not only regarding how the world is but how it should be. The focus on order with accompanying surveillance and education shifts control away from the explicit exercise of power through force and coercion and places it in the routine practices of everyday life. As Smart described his conception:

> Hegemony contributes to or constitutes a form of social cohesion not through force or coercion, nor necessarily through consent, but most effectively by way of practices, techniques, and methods which infiltrate minds and bodies, cultural practices which cultivate behaviours and beliefs, tastes, desires, and needs as seemingly naturally occurring qualities and properties embodied in the psychic and physical reality (or 'truth') of the subject. (1986: 160)

What is of interest then is not so much the powerlessness of the state, which presumably represents the will of the people, but the organization of these innumerable sites of power through other institutions and the complicity of the state in these hidden power relations.

Foucault (1977) defined the modern penal systems as the most extreme and purest exemplar of disciplinary power. The order, routine, rehabilitation, and constant surveillance, provide a vivid example of *formal* order. Giddens (1984) has objected that the model does not apply well to even the more formal organizations since individuals go home and relate to many competing institutions. I am inclined to go halfway with him. The model does not map well but this is because the modern corporation is the better exemplar of the full extent of disciplinary power. It goes home with its members, proposes electronic and self-surveillance, and colonizes competing institutions. The modern corporate form of work organization has become a new centre providing a modern co-ordination and relief of tension from competing institutional practices that the state arose to replace (suppress) in its time (Deetz 1992). Not only does the work experience structure a type of identity, but such identities are extended through corporate-sponsored media images in news, entertainment and advertising.

Disciplinary power has been present in corporations from their outset. Perhaps the clearest case is the development of the assembly line. The assembly line transformed an explicit authority relation between the worker and supervisor into a partially hidden one. Rather than the supervisor having to tell the worker how hard or fast to work and dealing with the question, 'by what right', the movement in the line already accomplished it. In the process the functional relation changed. This can be seen in Edwards's (1979) conception of the assembly line in terms of 'technical control'. The assembly line extended and enabled a particular worker capacity. Instead of being restrictive of the worker it facilitated an accomplishment. The assembly line, like the new organization, was a new tool extending collective bodies' capacity to produce. But it was also a new kind of tool. Rather than being subjugated to the body's rule, it subjugated the body into an extension of itself – a docile, useful body. Like any technology, it 'subjects' the individual in a particular way (Deetz 1990). While there was still no doubt that authority and explicit power kept the worker at the line and that it was the company's decision to implement work in this way, the relation to the supervisor could also change. Through training, the worker could keep up with the line with less effort, so the supervisor could be on the side of the worker in the worker's complicity with the systems that controlled him or her. The management interest in suppressing and routinizing conflict could be realized, often with the full involvement of the worker. While new forms of resistance are made possible, they are also made less likely by the complicity and new form of surveillance. Piece-rate payments on up through the various worker participation programmes merely extend this basic model (Burawoy 1979). Systems such as these do not lend themselves well to ideological criticism. They are not filled with false needs or hidden values. Rather it is the truth and naturalness of the domination, the *free* acceptance, that makes it so powerful.

In the modern context, disciplinary power exists largely in the new 'social technologies of control'. These include experts and specialists of various sorts who operate to create '*norm*alized' knowledge, operating procedures and methods of enquiry, and to suppress competitive practices. These are the accountants with standard (hardly known or contestable) accounting practices, efficiency experts and personnel officers. Like Gramsci's (1971) organic intellectuals, the outcome of their activities is a hegemonic social cohesion lacking the conflicts and differences that characterize an open world context. But unlike Gramsci's conception, the effect is neither simply coherent nor primarily accomplished through values and ideological consent. Foucault's conception of hegemony is a free-floating set of conflicts and incompatibilities which yet maintain asymmetrical relations. Power relations arise out of aims, objectives and strategies but there is no simple choice-making group or guidance to the network of power. In Foucault's words:

> the rationality of power is characterized by tactics that are often quite explicit at the restricted level where they are inscribed...tactics which, becoming connected to one another, attracting and propagating one another, but finding their base of support and their condition elsewhere, end by forming comprehensive systems: the logic is perfectly clear, the aims decipherable, and yet it is often the case that no one is there to have invented them, and few who can be said to have formulated them. (1980: 95)

For example, no management group can control the actions, let alone the thoughts, of other groups. The presence of fear (warranted or not), assumptions of knowledge differences, principles of least effort, wanting rewards and so forth must be provided by the controlled groups. However, these are not usually knowingly controlled and such things are not formed outside specific power relations which are often supported by other institutions. But rarely is explicit power displayed by management. The explicit and unilateral display of authority more often denotes the breakdown of power relations rather than the presence of them. It is the last resort of normal power relations.

Another key aspect of Foucault's conception of disciplinary power is the presence of new forms of surveillance. While the worker was always watched, disciplinary control allowed a new form of surveillance: self-surveillance. Self-surveillance uses norms backed by 'experts' for areas heretofore in the 'amateur' realm. Foucault (1977) developed Bentham's 'panoptic' prison design as the root vision of this new self-surveillance. In Bentham's design a single guardhouse stood with a view into each cell, but the prisoner could never tell when he was being watched. The surveillance, hence, could be more complete than from a number of guards walking the cell block; the prisoner imagined being watched constantly. Certainly this is a feeling enforced in the modern organization, particularly at the managerial levels. Whether or not it is true, the employee can never tell who might use what against him or her or when a statement will come back to cause one's own demise. And the wider the group participating in decision-making, the fewer people are safe confidants. Worker participation programmes, for example, can move the work group from interest solidarity to member self-surveillance. No cohort in resistance exists when everyone/anyone can be a member of the 'management team'. The implicit lawyer at the side censors discussion today as well as the fear of eternal damnation did in a past time. In such a configuration, managers are not simply controllers but are controlled as much as any other group.

But the surveillance is not just of words and actions. With the battery of psychological (and chemical) tests – experts in attitudes, culture and bodily fluids – the corporation assesses the purity of one's mind and soul (see Hollway 1984). But more importantly, employees self-assess on the corporation's behalf. The fear of someone seeing beneath the surface to detect a doubt or disloyalty or the fear that one's own gender or belief structure will be rejected, conspire to enforce the norms. The new-age self-manipulations are often far deeper and more extreme than Huxley could dream of or than any corporation could explicitly require.

In several ways the 1960s move of the 'backstage' (the hidden social order negotiation, professionalized by Goffman and the ethnomethodologists) into the open provided new areas of surveillance, particularly self-surveillance. For example, when common practices are totally taken for granted in traditional societies they discipline invisibly and completely, but they are also protected from manipulation by this same invisibility. As common practices are revealed as mere social conventions a measure of freedom is acquired since they can be enacted or not, or even openly negotiated. But as such they may be trained or manipulated. Goffman may have made visible the invisible disciplinary processes of culturally inscribed ways of managing appearances but in doing so he made a significant input to an industry of 'facial' surveillance and 'facial' production in the form of image management. Similarly in corporations, performance appraisals, designed to enable employee input into the formation of objectives, can open the personal to public appraisal. Not only is one's work being appraised, but also one's hopes, dreams and personal commitments. Most employees learn to bring these under prior assessment by their own private public eye. The failure of the 1960s' movements to promote an understanding of the politics of the personal enabled disclosure of a constructed psychological state as freedom rather than promoting more autonomous self-development. In doing so, the rightness of the insides became a matter of public appraisal rather than of the politics of that rightness.

The conception of the workplace as a game rather than a structure of life can create a cynical player who confidently hopes to both beat the game and remain untouched. But ultimately such a conception facilitates a game addict who is consumed by staying viable in the game, haunted by the prospect that he or she cannot control the self or others enough to win, yet unconcerned with the investment owing to an arrogance suggesting that it is merely a game and they could quit at any time. The impersonal and unlifelike quality of the workplace becomes reason enough not to critically investigate it.

The complicity of humanistic, cognitive and behavioural psychology in these processes should not be underestimated. Psychology has provided the study of the individual, especially the prediction and control of the individual. Fostered by the massive research support of the military and the professional drive of therapy, it has been the ideal provider of the tools of the new 'discipline' of corporations (see Driskell and Beckett 1989). As an academic discipline, psychology matches well what Scott (1985: 153) identified as the core beliefs of managerialism: 'People are Essentially Defective'; 'People are Totally Malleable'. The prospect of a well-integrated worker appropriately matched to the job, and the job to the individual, bespoke the harmony of managerial hope and the motives and confidence of self-manipulation. The centred self who knows who he or she is, and what he or she wants, provides the trustworthy person in control (well subject*ed*/sub*jected*). The testing/training programmes provide the mechanism of correction in a self-referential system oriented to control rather than autonomy. And significantly, the human self-understanding as malleable and values as subjective and learned, has discredited competing voices and glorified the secular and modern. The 'helping profession' could define healthiness based on social integration and lack of personal conflict, disqualifying radical voices and the fragmentation within and without. Adjustment and retooling could put problems, or at least the solutions to them, within the person. Both the individual and the corporation could be seen as gaining at once. The corporation is active in the production of a unitary personal identity armed with a science of the person. And all this is done in the realm of value-neutral social research, a discipline at its best.

Discipline is thus a configuration of power inserted as a way of thinking, acting and instituting. The disciplined member of the organization wants on his or her own what the corporation wants. The most powerful and powerless in traditional terms are equally subjected, though there is no doubt who is advantaged. But it is not as if either sees this advantage as 'rightful'. In fact its ideological rightfulness may well be contested. The struggle over sovereign rights can hide the discipline which situates the struggle (e.g. the existence of a labour union can create its opposite, a unified management). Contestation itself can follow practices which reposition the actors in terms of their difference and establish the resources of one as the preferred in the struggle. Concepts like ideology and interests are useful in enabling the identification of the difference and the manner of discursive moves, but the presence of specific identities and interests has to be situated in the disciplinary structure itself. They are produced there as well as playing a central role in its representation.

The political interpretation of organizational practices is to reproblematize the obvious. In some sense there is no surprise in showing power formations in discursive practices in organizations. Of course corporations are hierarchical, of course managers strategically deploy power. Control is the name of the game. But the self-evidence hides much. Why does management control rather than co-ordinate and how is that secured? Why isn't the co-ordination function seen as largely clerical and facilitative? To understand modern domination, we must take the routine, the commonsensical and the self-evident and subject them to reconsideration. The more distant dominations by the church and kings were not simply forced on subjects but were routine and ritualized, reproduced in innumerable practices; they were consented to but not chosen. Reproblematizing the obvious requires identifying conflicts which do not happen, pulling out latent experiences which are overlooked, and identifying discursive practices which block value discussion and close the exploration of differences. Ideological critique can be useful to define the conditions necessary for the articulation of conflicts regarding access to speaking forums and information (as equality of opportunity), social relations (a critique of historically derived asymmetries), personal experience (as conflictual rather than unitary), and the claim of the subject matter (a critique of the reduction of the otherness of the external world to any single description) (see Habermas 1984). But the politics of identity and knowledge construction requires a more complete understanding of discursive and non-discursive practices aided by the investigation of disciplinary power.

In sum, control of corporate institutions by democratic institutions is unlikely and less significant than the development of internal political democracy based on an understanding of micropolitics of disciplinary power and transformative communication practice at the corporate site. Meaningful democracy, which is positive in form and which invigorates the autonomy of citizens, can take place through corporate restructuring and the fostering of non-dependent rather than dependent and co-dependent participants within corporate practices. This becomes the leading political issue of the day. Such democracy would go well beyond simply more worker involvement in decision-making. It entails changes in the daily processes out of which identity, meaning and common sense are formed.

NOTE

From S. Deetz (1992), 'Disciplinary Power in the Modern Corporation', in M. Alvesson and H. Willmott, eds, *Critical Management Studies* (London: Sage), pp. 21–45.

REFERENCES

Abercrombie, N., S. Hill and B. Turner (1980), *The Dominant Ideology Thesis* (London: Allen & Unwin).
Althusser, L. (1971), 'Ideology and ideological state apparatuses', in *Lenin and Philosophy and Other Essays*, trans. Ben Brewster (London: New Left Books).
Alvesson, M. (1987a), *Organizational Theory and Technocratic Consciousness: Rationality, Ideology and Quality of Work* (New York: de Gruyter).
Alvesson, M. (1987b), 'Organizations, culture and ideology', *International Studies of Management and Organizations*, vol. 17, pp. 4–18.
Baudrillard, J. (1975), *The Mirror of Production*, trans. Michal Poster (St Louis: Telos Press).
Bourdieu, P. (1977), *Outline of a Theory of Practice* (Cambridge: Cambridge University Press).
Burawoy, M. (1979), *Manufacturing Consent* (Berkeley: University of California Press).
Burrell, G. (1988), 'Modernism, post modernism and organizational analysis 2: the contribution of Michel Foucault', *Organization Studies*, vol. 9, pp. 221–35.
Cameron, K. and D. Whetten eds (1983), *Organizational Effectiveness: A Comparison of Multiple Models* (New York: Academic Press).
Clegg, S. (1989), *Frameworks of Power* (Newbury Park, CA: Sage).
Deetz, S. (1990), 'Representation of interests and the new communication technologies', in M. Medicare, T. Peterson and A. Gonzalez, eds, *Communication and the Culture of Technology* (Pullman: Washington State University Press), pp. 43–62.
Deetz, S. (1992), *Democracy in an Age of Corporate Colonization: Developments in Communication and the Politics of Everyday Life* (Albany: State University of New York Press).
Deetz, S. and D. Mumby (1990), 'Power, discourse and the workplace: reclaiming the critical tradition in communication studies in organizations', in J. Anderson, ed., *Communication Yearbook 13* (Newbury Park, CA: Sage), pp. 18–47.
Derrida, J. (1976), *Of Grammatology* (Baltimore: Johns Hopkins University Press).
Donzelot, J. (1979), *The Policing of the Family* (London: Routledge).
Driskell, J. and O. Beckett (1989), 'Psychology and the military', *American psychologist*, vol. 44, pp. 43–54.
Edwards, R. (1979), *Contested Terrain: The Transformation of the Workplace in the Twentieth Century* (New York: Basic Books).
Foucault, M. (1972), *The Archaeology of Knowledge* (New York: Pantheon).
Foucault, M. (1977), *Discipline and Punish: The Birth of the Prison*, trans A. Sheridan (New York: Random House).
Foucault, M. (1980), *The History of Sexuality*, trans. R. Hurley (New York: Vintage).
Giddens, A. (1979), *Central Problems in Social Theory* (Berkeley: University of California Press).
Giddens, A. (1984), *The Constitution of Society* (Berkeley: Campus).

Gramsci, A. (1971), *Selections from the Prison Notebooks*, trans. Q. Hoare and G. Nowell-Smith (New York: International).

Habermas, J. (1984), *The Theory of Communicative Action*, vol. 1: *Reason and the Rationalization of Society*, trans. T. McCarthy (Boston: Beacon Press).

Habermas, J. (1987), *The Theory of Communicative Action*, vol. 2: *Lifeworld and System*, trans. T. McCarthy (Boston: Beacon Press).

Hollway, W. (1984), 'Fitting work: psychological assessment in organizations', in J. Henriques, W. Hollway, C. Urwin, C. Venn and V. Walkerdine, eds, *Changing the Subject* (New York: Methuen), pp. 26–59.

Knights, D. and H. Willmott (1985), 'Power and identity in theory and practice', *Sociological Review*, vol. 33, pp. 22–46.

Knights, D. and H. Willmott (1989), 'Power and subjectivity at work: from degredation to subjugation in social relations', *Sociology*, vol. 23, no. 4, pp. 535–58.

Laclau, E. and C. Mouffe (1985), *Hegemony and Socialist Strategy*, trans. W. Moore and P. Cammack (London: Verso).

Lukes, S. (1974), *Power: A Radical View* (London: Macmillan).

Mingers, J. (1989), 'An introduction to autopoiesis: implications and applications', *Systems Practice*, vol. 2, pp. 159–80.

Morgan, G. (1986), *Images of Organization* (Newbury Park, CA: Sage).

Mumby, D. K. (1987), 'The political function of narrative in organizations', *Communication Monographs*, no. 54, pp. 113–27.

Mumby, D. K. (1988), *Communication and Power in Organizations: Discourse, Ideology, and Domination* (Norwood, NJ: Ablex).

Pêcheux, M. (1982), *Language, Semantics and Ideology: Stating the Obvious*, trans. Harbans Nagpal (London: Macmillan).

Przeworski, A. (1980), 'Material bases of consent: economics and politics in a hegemonic system', *Political Power and Social Theory*, vol. 1, pp. 21–66.

Saussure, F. de (1974), *Course in General Linguistics* (London: Fontana).

Scott, W. G. (1985), 'Organizational revolution: an end to managerial orthodoxy', *Administration and Society*, vol. 17, pp. 149–70.

Smart, B. (1986), 'The politics of truth and the problem of hegemony', in D. C. Hoy, ed., *Foucault: A Critical Reader* (Oxford: Basil Blackwell), pp. 157–74.

Thompson, J. (1984), *Studies in the Theory of Ideology* (Berkeley: University of California Press).

Weedon, C. (1987), *Feminist Practice and Poststructuralist Theory* (Oxford: Basil Blackwell).

Young, E. (1989), 'On the naming of the rose: interests and multiple meanings as elements of organizational culture', *Organization Studies*, vol. 10, pp. 187–206.

8   Resistance

Strategies of Resistance: Power, Knowledge and Subjectivity in the Workplace

DAVID COLLINSON

Introduction

Throughout the twentieth century, employee resistance [was] a primary analytical concern of organizational scholars as well as a pervasive feature of labour process practices. Managerialist writers have explored various ways to eliminate or minimize employee recalcitrance and resistance (e.g. Taylor 1947; Kreitner 1986). Organizational psychologists have outlined different strategies designed to overcome resistance to change processes (e.g. Lewin 1951; Kotter and Schlesinger 1979; Plant 1987; Dunphy and Stace 1988). Industrial relations writers have examined strike patterns (Hyman 1989) while industrial sociologists have focused upon output restriction on the shopfloor (e.g. Mayo 1933; Roy 1952; Walker and Guest 1952; Goffman 1959; Lupton 1963; Klein 1964; Brown 1965; Ditton 1976; Emmett and Morgan 1982); workplace crime (Mars 1982); industrial sabotage (Taylor and Walton 1971; Brown 1977; Dubois 1979; Linstead 1985; Jermier 1988; Sprouse 1992) and the way that informal practices often contravene formalized policies (Gouldner 1954).

Labour process writers have made a distinctive contribution to this debate by highlighting the irreducible interrelationship between employee resistance and managerial control (e.g. Friedman 1977; Nicholas and Beynon 1977; R. Edwards 1979; Beynon 1980; Cressey and Maciness 1980; Littler 1982; Edwards and Scullion 1982; Storey 1985; Thompson and Bannon 1985; P. K. Edwards 1990). Emphasizing the extensive power asymmetries in contemporary organizations, these critical studies have explored the way that resistance is very much a *response* to practices of managerial control. In so doing, they have sought to overcome the neglect of labour resistance and subjectivity, for which Braverman (1974) has been heavily criticized. Yet despite this attention, important analytical questions about resistance remain underexplored. For example, why and how does resistance

DAVID COLLINSON

emerge? What discourses and practices constitute resistance? What resources and strategies are available to those who resist? How do we evaluate whether resistance is effective or ineffective? What are the consequences of resistance? Rather than address such questions, however, [late twentieth-century] critical analyses of worker behaviour tended to turn their attention to the manufacture of consent, the (self-)disciplining of subordinates and the outflanking of resistance (e.g. Burawoy 1979, 1985; Manwaring and Wood 1985; P. K. Edwards 1986; Clegg 1989; Rose 1989; Knights and Sturdy 1990; Sewell and Wilkinson 1992; Sturdy, Knights and Willmott 1992; Willmott 1993; Grey 1993). Although these studies are analytically important, some of them tend to neglect or underemphasize the significance and complexity of workplace resistance. This is illustrated by the [...] contribution of Clegg (1989), whose influential earlier work concentrated on control and resistance in the labour process (Clegg and Dunkerley 1980). Increasingly, however, he has been concerned with the way that workplace resistance is 'outflanked', a term he draws from Mann (1986).[1]

In seeking to explain 'why the dominated so frequently consent to their subordination and subordinators' (Clegg 1989: 220), Clegg draws upon both Foucault's (1977) arguments that knowledge and information are key aspects of power in organizations and on Burawoy's use of the game metaphor.[2] On the one hand, he contends that subordinates are often 'ignorant' (Clegg 1989: 221) of power in terms of strategy construction, the negotiation of routine procedures, rules, agenda setting, protocol and assessing the resources of the antagonist. Consequently, 'it is not that they do not know the rules of the game; they might not recognize the game, let alone the rules' (p. 221). Clegg argues that subordinates often have little knowledge of others who are equally powerless and with whom alliances could be constructed. On the other hand, he acknowledges that outflanking can also result from subordinates having extensive knowledge. Subordinates may know only too well that the associated costs of resistance are 'far in excess of the probability of either achieving the outcome, or if achieved, the benefits so obtained' (p. 222). Hence, Clegg concludes that outflanking is the result of two quite extreme and contrasting situations. Either subordinates have too little information and knowledge, or they possess highly accurate and predictive knowledge concerning the future outcomes of resistance.[3]

Yet, is it the case in this period of late modernism that subordinates are so easily outflanked? Are they so willing to consent to their subordination? Are they so lacking in knowledge and information that they are powerless or conversely so knowledgeable that they can always predict the detrimental consequences of their oppositional practices? To address these questions, this [reading] draws on Clegg's focus on knowledge and power but in a way that seeks to retrieve the analytical and empirical significance of workplace resistance. This is not to reject the importance of the manufacture of consent/compliance or the outflanking of resistance. Rather it is to question the analytical primacy increasingly ascribed to these practices and to argue for a much more detailed examination of the conditions, processes and consequences of workplace resistance.

The following [reading] is primarily concerned to highlight two different strategies of dissent and opposition. These are illustrated below by exploring two empirical case studies drawn from completed research projects, that are re-examined here in the light of a specific focus upon knowledge and resistance. First, I argue that specific forms of knowledge are a crucial resource and means through which resistance can be mobilized. Knowledge in organizations is multiple, contested and shifting.[4] Employees may not possess detailed understandings of certain bureaucratic/political processes, but they often do monopolize other technical, production-related knowledges that facilitate their oppositional practices.

Second, I argue that it is not in any simple sense merely the possession, or ownership of particular knowledges that determines consent, outflanking or resistance, as Clegg seems to imply. Rather, it is also the way that these knowledges are deployed in particular organizational conditions and practices. The data reveal two quite different *subjective* strategies of workplace resistance that are shaped by particular orientations to knowledge, information and to those in authority. In the first case, men workers' routine resistance practices concentrate on *restricting information* from managers. They seek to escape or to avoid the demands of authority. I term this strategy 'resistance through distance'. The second case explores a woman's resistance to a particular managerial promotion decision. The more formalized processes of her challenge to managerial decision-making are informed by the converse strategy of *extracting information* from management. This oppositional strategy I term 'resistance through persistence'. These examples are by no means exhaustive of possible resistance strategies. What they reveal are the limited possibilities available to those who engage in resistance through distance and the greater viability and effectiveness of oppositional practices designed to render management more accountable by extracting information, monitoring practices and challenging decision-making processes.

Third, it is suggested that these arguments raise important issues about the subjectivity of subordinates in relation to power, knowledge and resistance that have tended to be neglected (see also Knights 1990; Thompson 1990; Willmott 1990; Collinson 1992a). This [reading] seeks to demonstrate that oppositional practices are significantly shaped, not only by power, knowledge and specific organizational conditions, but also by the particular subjectivities of employees and of those in more senior hierarchical positions. These subjectivities are invariably creative and knowledgeable, but also multiple, shifting, sometimes fragmentary, often inconsistent and frequently contradictory (see also Kondo 1990).

Drawing on this analysis, the [reading] concludes by arguing that much of the critical literature on employee behaviour tends to overstate either consent or resistance and to separate one from the other. Within these polarized perspectives, employee resistance is frequently treated either as all but non-existent or alternatively as all-pervasive. Yet neither approach adequately accounts for the multiplicity of oppositional practices in various workplaces. Resistance and consent are rarely polarized extremes on a continuum of possible worker discursive practices. Rather, they are usually inextricably and simultaneously linked, often in contradictory ways within particular organizational cultures, discourses and practices. Resistance frequently contains elements of consent and consent often incorporates aspects of resistance.

Hence, in an effort to contribute to the critical analysis of resistance, compliance and consent in the labour process, this chapter highlights the significant interrelationship between power, knowledge/information[5] and subjectivity. In doing so, it follows a tradition of labour process thinking which has emphasized how the appropriation and monopolization of knowledge constitutes a key control strategy of scientific management (Taylor 1947; Braverman 1974). Much of the post-Braverman labour process debate has continued to examine this relationship between power and knowledge in terms of the politics of managerial control and de-skilling strategies (see e.g. Manwaring and Wood 1985; Zuboff 1988). Equally, feminist contributions have highlighted how job-related skills and knowledge are often 'saturated with sex' (Phillips and Taylor 1980) in ways that not only reflect but also reinforce men's power and the gendered division of labour both in paid work and in the domestic sphere (Cockburn 1983; Davies and Rosser 1986; Walby 1986, 1990). Yet, few studies have attended to the way that resistance is a condition and consequence of particular knowledges and subjectivities.

Strategies of resistance

The following sections re-examine two in-depth case studies on workplace resistance drawn from separate research projects conducted in UK organizations during the 1980s. The first study explored the shopfloor culture of an all-male engineering factory (see Collinson 1992a), while the second examined sex discrimination in the recruitment process (see Collinson et al. 1990). The class and gender issues arising in the first case of an all-male shopfloor are somewhat different from the second case study, which is drawn from the white-collar context of an insurance company. Here the workplace contained a gender mix and the oppositional practices examined below concentrate on resistance conducted by women.

Although quite distinct, the two cases also share certain commonalities. Both focus upon workplace resistance and both illustrate the importance of the strategic manipulation of knowledge and information in oppositional discursive practices. In each case, knowledge is contested and managers seek to retain and restrict information to enhance their control within the organization. Both companies had recently been taken over by US multinational corporations that in turn were beginning to have a significant influence on their respective corporate cultures. Moreover, strong trade unions with high membership levels were present in each company.

More detailed descriptions of the research objectives and methods that informed these projects are outlined in the appendices of the respective texts from which they are drawn. Suffice it to say here, that both projects used semi-structured in-depth interviews in order to explore the accounts of the research respondents. A distinctive methodological feature was the use of return interviews which facilitated the development both of trust relations and of a longitudinal analysis of events in the organizations. Extensive return interviews were conducted with certain respondents in both studies, who became key informants of 'insider' information (see Collinson 1992b: 105). Interviews were supplemented by the observation of work relations, social interactions and of particular practices (e.g.

production in the first case and selection interviewing in the second). In addition to these qualitative methods, company documents were examined and quantitative measures were collected (e.g. workforce profiles). The following discussion seeks to re-examine some of the research findings in a way that highlights both the consistent and distinctive patterns of resistance in each case and the interrelationships between workplace resistance, power, knowledge and subjectivity.

Resistance through distance

The first research project was conducted between 1979 and 1983 within the components division of a private heavy vehicle manufacturing company located in a predominantly working-class Lancashire town in the north-west of England. During this period, 64 of the 229 manual workers in this division were interviewed, all at least twice and some on innumerable occasions. Interviews were also conducted with four managers in the production and personnel departments. On the shopfloor, the social relations were particularly localized, familial and informal. The factory had always been a place where whole families of men had worked, one generation providing an engineering apprenticeship to the next. As a result, the all-male shopfloor was characterized by a strong class- and gender-based community spirit that had largely remained intact despite a merger in 1970 and a take-over by a US transnational corporation in 1974.

This community spirit, however, did not translate into a harmony of interests within the organization as a whole. The research revealed a great deal of mistrust, defensiveness and insecurity on the shopfloor. Initiatives by the new owners intended to generate employee confidence and consent merely exacerbated workers' suspicions and provided the resources for shopfloor resistance. The managerial initiatives of a corporate culture campaign and a collective bonus scheme failed to address and change the negative aspects of work that were most important to shopfloor workers. Their subjective experience of manual employment consisted of being treated, first as commodities that could be hired and fired according to managerial discretion, second as 'unthinking machines' who were excluded from all strategic discourses and decision-making and finally as 'second-class citizens' whose terms and conditions of employment were inferior to all other occupational groups within the company. Hence, for shopfloor workers, in particular, interrelated material and symbolic insecurities were built into the employment relationship. These insecurities covered many aspects of work such as pay, employment stability, job control and even personal status and identity. The workers experienced themselves as controlled, commodified and stratified labour.

The corporate culture campaign which emphasized teamwork and communication was widely dismissed on the shopfloor as 'yankee bullshit' and 'propaganda'. The more management tried to adopt a 'personal' approach, the more convinced were shopfloor workers that this was part of a 'yankee plot' simply designed to improve productivity. Equally, the bonus scheme had the effect of strengthening workers' purely economic orientation to work. As a consequence these new initiatives reinforced workers' practices of resistance through distance that took multiple forms on the shopfloor. Workers' determination to 'distance' (Goffman 1959) themselves as much as possible both symbolically and physically from managers, the organization and from shopfloor job requirements was the medium and outcome of a deeply embedded *counter-culture* on the shopfloor. Central to this counter-culture was a specific emphasis upon working-class masculinity that provided a primary sense of shopfloor identity and dignity for its members.

In response to the corporate culture campaign, shop stewards, for example, insisted that 'we don't have a relationship with management . . . they live in a different world from us, think differently and act differently'. Wary of being incorporated by a highly personal managerial approach, shop stewards refused to call managers by their first names as the latter requested, rejected their offers of lifts in cars and of cigarettes or cigars, and declined to have meetings with individual senior managers in the absence of other shop stewards who could witness the interaction. The shop steward in the axle department summarized the counter-cultural values of 'resistance through distance': 'We want to keep separate from them. We don't want to get personal. This "call me Barney"[6] bullshit. . . . The further away management are the better. We've nothing in common with them'. These formalized negotiation strategies with senior managers were mirrored by the informal discursive practices of the shopfloor culture where resistance and self-differentiation were simultaneously articulated. Indeed, workers' concern to redefine their identities in a more positive way than that formally ascribed by the organization was an important condition and consequence of their oppositional discursive practices. As I will suggest, however, these subjective attempts to secure culturally validated and differentiated identities significantly limited workers' otherwise radical-sounding oppositional practices of resistance through distance.

Workers' particular notions of what constitutes valuable knowledge played a key role in these dual processes of resistance through distance and identity construction. Most workers emphasized the social and organizational importance of production and engineering. They were quick to elevate the 'practical' and 'commonsense' knowledge that they believed was a condition and consequence of manual labour over the more abstract and theoretical forms of knowledge found in the middle-class world of white-collar work and management. For many, the latter was simply an unproductive 'paper chase' and 'pen pushing' that had little or no relevance to the important realities of manufacturing heavy vehicles. Equally, the whole idea of promotion was widely rejected because it would mean incorporation, compromise and conformity. The few manual workers who had been promoted were dismissed as 'yes men' for having sacrificed their independence, autonomy, even their manhood in hierarchical conformity. It was widely believed that 'Blokes are made to change' once they were promoted.

Hence the men symbolically inverted the class-based hierarchy of the organization (see also Stallybrass and White 1986). They redefined shopfloor work as a site of real, authentic and experiential knowledge, a belief that facilitated their resistance and self-differentiation. Part of this knowledge was derived from the workers' past experience of being treated as disposable commodities. This is illustrated by the following statement of one worker who rejected the corporate culture campaign: 'They give the impression we work together when it suits them, but when it gets rough, we're the ones who get it'. This class-based awareness of the ever-present possibility of disposability informed many workers' distancing from the incorporatist objectives of the corporate culture campaign. Providing a sense of power and identity for members of the counter-culture, these technical and social shopfloor knowledges emphasized manual workers' engineering skills and their 'real life' experience of organization.

These knowledges also facilitated a whole series of oppositional practices of resistance through distance in which shopfloor workers restricted the flow of technical and social information up the hierarchy by deploying their engineering and dramaturgical skills (Goffman 1959). In seeking greater control over job and self, workers sought to manipulate the commodity status of their labour by using their knowledge of the labour process to appropriate and privatize 'public' space, time and production on the shopfloor. Their oppositional practices were intended to 'exploit' the interrelated material and symbolic spaces that were available to them as commodified labourers. The bonus scheme, in particular, became an important 'weapon' of resistance (Scott 1985) through which workers could secure a degree of job control. Although management expected the bonus to generate employee flexibility and enhance productivity, it was actually reconverted by workers into a resource of inflexibility and output restriction.

The bonus scheme reinforced the widespread shopfloor view that 'management can't have what they don't pay for'. Having maximized the bonus, shopfloor workers frequently refused to produce further. When negotiating times with the rate-fixer, workers used their technical knowledge and engineering skills to mystify output potential. One fifty-seven-year-old turner in the machine shop illustrated workers' strategies of resistance using the bonus scheme. During his forty years' experience in engineering he had developed many 'tricks of the trade' and short-cuts on jobs. Proud of his engineering skills, he believed he could handle 'any job on a lathe'. In exercising some control over production and the 'effort bargain', he invariably mystified and concealed his technical knowledge and skills when nego-tiating a time with the rate-fixer, as he revealed:

> I do 400 of these a week. I always get them to do when they're needed. The time I got for this job from the rate-fixer was eight minutes. But I can do them in two. Why should I worry? It pays to know your job. . . . You can't tell them what you can do or else you'd be doing three men's jobs for one man's wages.

Behind the appearance of conformity that he constructed when negotiating with the rate-fixer, he maintained a deeper oppositional sense of self-determination. By manipulating the rate-fixer, he could accumulate what different writers have called a 'kitty' (Burawoy 1979), a 'bank' (Walker and Guest 1952) or a 'stash' (Goffman 1968). This comprised a private storage box concealed within his locker where he accumulated output in advance of it being required, which in turn enabled him to have some control over his production levels. This ability to mystify his potential output and to 'kid' the rate-fixer, was a real source of personal pride and self- validation. It confirmed his technical skills, knowledge and experience.

By restricting information, he was also able to exercise some control over his output and to avoid any intensification of his labour.

This example demonstrates how working the bonus system reinforced a very narrow, limited and defensive form of resistance that was concerned with the politics of controlling output, concealing information and producing false impressions of the individual for those in authority. Central to this resistance through distance was shopfloor workers' technical engineering skills and their social skills of appearance management which together enabled them to restrict the flow of knowledge and information back up the hierarchy. By controlling and managing production and information in this way, workers were able to appropriate both time and space. The toilets became an important 'back region' (Goffman 1968) through which these processes of subversive appropriation could be enacted. Axle department workers spent a considerable amount of time in the toilet each afternoon. They too had negotiated favourable times for their work with the rate-fixer. Since their bonus was calculated on a collective basis (i.e. the number of axles daily assembled by the twelve men), they had agreed among themselves to work 'flat out' in the morning to create some free time in the afternoon. In their view, the success of this resistance confirmed their skills and knowledgeability in exercising control over working times. Accordingly, these oppositional practices had the effect of validating identity and differentiating self. The toilets constituted a free space in which time could be appropriated and surveillance could be escaped.

In addition to controlling output, workers' management of knowledge and information facilitated their production of 'foreigners'. These were products for personal consumption that had no connection with lorry manufacture. Here workers used their technical and social knowledge to intensify production for their personal use. One winter, for example, when heavy snow fell in the Lancashire area, workers elicited the help of colleagues to create sledges for their children. Collective sharing and pooling of engineering knowledge also included extensive car maintenance that was conducted during working hours using company tools and equipment. Several men owned caravans and a reciprocal support network had developed of caravan parts and maintenance that had saved some workers enormous sums of money when compared with commercial repair costs. Such practices overlapped with more covert forms of workplace theft which included stealing materials, tools, car/lorry batteries and petrol.

In contrast with Burawoy's (1979) findings, the bonus scheme at this company proved to be a central site of conflict and resistance in everyday shopfloor relations (see also Knights and Collinson 1985). Bonus payments were calculated by management who aggregated together the production figures of individual departments in order to measure productivity across the plant. Only managers had access to these aggregated factory-wide data that formed the basis of the weekly payout, and their control of this information was an equally important feature of conflict on the shopfloor. Unable to monitor bonus calculations, many workers believed that managers were withholding important information: they were, as one worker put it, 'managing by mushroom'.[7] Consensus and consent were rarely in evidence as shopfloor workers insisted that managers were 'fiddling the figures'. Shopfloor cynicism and suspicion was fuelled by an oscillating weekly bonus payout, the widespread failure to understand how the figure was calculated and the uneven flow of production. Often individual departments would reach their necessary production targets, but would rarely receive full bonus after the collective payment had been averaged out with the other sections of the plant (see Collinson 1992a, for elaboration). Paradoxically, the relaxation of controls in the guise of the bonus scheme rebounded on managers by reinforcing the workers' belief in managerial manipulation – the very perception and rumours that the corporate culture campaign was designed to eliminate. The managerial concern to generate flexibility and control over the production process through the manipulation of bonuses was merely reconverted by workers into a resource of inflexibility and resistance through distance.

Yet these diverse practices of resistance should neither be overstated nor romanticized. They were also shot through with unresolved contradictions, conflicts, ambiguities and unintended consequences. Resistance through distance and the concealment of information had only limited effectiveness as a means of dissent. This particular oppositional strategy simultaneously incorporated elements of compliance and consent that severely threatened the possibilities and effects of resistance. It failed to challenge and thus actually reinforced the commodification of labour and managerial control. By merely seeking to secure a degree of personal discretion and autonomy in and around the edges of their formally controlled and commodified position, these manual workers resisted in ways that simultaneously accommodated themselves to the sale of their own labour power. Their resistance failed to question and thereby remained confined within the commodity status of labour. Workers' contradictory search for security on the shopfloor actually reinforced the commodification of their labour and, paradoxically, reproduced their own material and symbolic insecurity. Hence, resistance, compliance and consent co-existed on the shopfloor, sometimes in the very same discursive practice.

In resistance through distance, workers sought to deny any involvement in or responsibility for the running of the organization. They often treated paid work in the 'public' sphere as a sacrifice for leisure and domesticity in the 'private' sphere, retaining a strong sense of separation between these two lifeworlds. Yet the illusory and precarious character of this public/private separation was frequently demonstrated when managers exercised their prerogative and discretion. In 1983 management announced extensive redundancies and a partial plant closure. Redundancies 'bring home' to workers the real interdependence between their 'private' and 'public' lives. Paradoxically, despite the ever-present shopfloor opposition and resistance to authority, when management announced large-scale redundancies, no actual resistance emerged. While some have argued that to 'take the money and run' was a 'rational surrender to inevitability' (Ackers and Black 1992: 192), this was certainly not the view of the shop stewards' committee, which had tried to encourage their members to resist the decision or at minimum to demand higher redundancy settlements.

The redundancy process confirmed workers' experience and awareness of their own disposability as manual workers. Equally, it was characterized by their uncritical acceptance of managers' technical financial expertise and knowledge.

Managers provided the shopfloor with extensive accounting information to justify the redundancies, releasing much more data than they had ever done in relation to the collective bonus. Shopfloor workers failed to question these figures despite some inherent inconsistencies in the data (see Knights and Collinson 1987, for further discussion). Interrelated with workers' assumptions about managers' technical knowledge as accountants was their widespread acceptance of managerial prerogative. Although many workers routinely insisted that 'it's management's right to manage', they did not see this as an expression of compliance or consent. Rather it was a central assumption of their resistance through distance. Most workers were convinced and regularly insisted that managers were entirely responsible for the organization. For many shopfloor workers, the problem was that managers refused to accept this responsibility for which they were handsomely rewarded. One of the most oppositional shop stewards insisted, 'Management manage, workers work. That's how it should be. You can't play both sides like the yanks try to'.

Paradoxically, the widespread shopfloor insistence on managerial prerogative was viewed as an expression of opposition, critique and dissent. Yet this resistance through distance also had the contradictory effect of creating compliance and consent. Hence, resistance through distance can also incorporate an explicit discourse of consent, not only to labour commodification but also to and elite control of the enterprise. In taking for granted labour commodification and elite managerial control, workers' resistance in this factory comprised a contradictory and ambiguous set of discursive practices that shifted over time and according to circumstances. Resistance, compliance and consent were simultaneously embedded in a shifting combination of contradictions, ambiguities and unresolved paradoxes and tensions on the shopfloor.

These contradictions and tensions sometimes collapsed into division, conflict and acrimony. Internal shopfloor conflicts occurred, for example, between workers who criticized colleagues for failing to work hard enough to maximize bonus. Conflict also resulted when workers sought to confirm their identity by differentiating themselves from colleagues as well as managers and white-collar workers. In such cases, the counter-cultural discourse of collectivism was revealed to be highly fragile and liable to collapse. This was particularly so since workers often looked to foremen, managers and even shop stewards to discipline recalcitrant workers and those believed to be 'not pulling their weight for the bonus'. Hence, the precariousness of shopfloor collectivism was a condition and consequence of a widespread worker belief in the need for managers to exercise discipline. In practice, it was shop stewards who usually found themselves having to exercise discipline over highly indifferent workers.

The union was committed to protecting jobs and maximizing wages. In seeking to achieve the latter, shop stewards often had to discipline recalcitrant workers.[8] This inevitably generated conflict and antagonism between stewards and some members. The ensuing internal divisions within the union were intensified by the stewards' policy of prioritizing the security of jobs over and above the maximization of pay. So, for example, when jobs were threatened, the shop stewards' committee successfully persuaded management to reduce or suspend the bonus instead of announcing redundancies. This, however, generated a great deal of criticism from some shopfloor workers who were antagonistic to the stewards for reducing their take-home pay. Hence, the contradictory nature of resistance through distance was reflected and reproduced in the practices of shop stewards and their sometimes acrimonious relations with union members. (In the second case study below the absence of such tensions or conflicts within the trade union was an important basis on which more effective resistance could be mobilized.)

This first case study has highlighted the importance of social and technical knowledge as a medium for the articulation of workplace resistance. It demonstrates how shopfloor workers sought to restrict information and knowledge as part of a consistent strategy of resistance through distance. Workers' counter-cultural practices were intended to appropriate time, space, knowledge and production on the shopfloor. Some of these practices had important effects in the organization, not least in influencing managerial strategies. They also provided workers with an albeit precarious sense of control over their working lives.

Yet although this oppositional culture was a routine and pervasive feature of shopfloor practices, it also contained significant ambiguities, ambivalences and paradoxes. Many of these oppositional practices of distancing are best seen as short-term 'escape attempts' (Cohen and Taylor 1992), providing only temporary relief from the incessant pressures and insecurities of shopfloor production and subordination (Collinson 1993). Resistance was confined within the commodity status of labour and was shaped, at least in part, by workers' pervasive concern to secure a positive sense of identity. Workers did not seek to obtain greater information about the company, to influence strategic decision-making or to make suggestions about production-related matters. In their eyes, this would have both contradicted their sense of 'independence' and identity as shopfloor workers and created the danger of co-option and incorporation. They steadfastly insisted that management had the full responsibility for managing the enterprise. Hence, within workers' discursive practices, resistance, compliance and even consent were simultaneously embedded. Paradoxically, workers' resistance through distance reinforced the legitimacy of hierarchical control, left managerial prerogative unchallenged, and increased their vulnerability to disciplinary practices. This in turn suggests that it is not merely the absolute quantity of knowledge and information that significantly shapes the possibility for and effectiveness of resistance. Rather, it is the way in which this knowledge is used within particular power relations. The next case study illustrates this argument further, where far from restricting information, subordinates sought to extract it from management – an approach that proved to be both more strategic and effective.

Resistance through persistence

The second case study is drawn from the white-collar setting of the UK insurance industry. It concentrates on issues of gender discrimination and is drawn from a larger research project on sex discrimination in the selection process funded by the

DAVID COLLINSON

UK Equal Opportunities Commission (see Collinson et al. 1990). This project examined selection practices in sixty-four workplaces. It revealed that resistance through distance was the most common response of many women who believed that they may have been victims of gender-based discrimination. Rather than formally challenge potentially unfair selection decisions, women candidates often denied any interest in working for the recruiting organization. They would simply look elsewhere for employment. In the external labour market, this response is hardly surprising given that candidates have not as yet made a career investment in the company. Moreover, external recruitment is a process shrouded in a veil of secrecy about which most candidates frequently have very little information and in which managerial prerogative is extensive.

The research found that where resistance to sex discrimination was relatively effective, it was more likely to be articulated in promotion practices and in organizations that had a strong trade union presence. In such cases, women often had more power, knowledge and commitment to challenge promotion decisions perceived to be unfair. Again, knowledge and information were vital. Unlike external candidates, internal applicants often either had or could easily obtain information concerning: who the other candidates were, and their background and skills; who the interviewers were and their selection criteria; the culture and history of the organization and the background to the particular vacancy. In order to develop these themes, I will now examine one specific promotion exercise which illustrates the dynamics of a more effective form of resistance. The detailed data presented below are based on two interviews with the job candidate herself, three with her local trade union representative and three with the general secretary of the trade union. The two union officials also provided extensive documentation related to this case, including, most importantly, copies of minutes of all the formal meetings that took place during this process (see also Collinson 1992b). This documentation proved to be an invaluable source of information from which to piece together the discourses and practices of control and resistance that comprised the case.

The company in which this internal vacancy arose had been taken over five years earlier by an American multinational corporation. The new corporate culture that was evolving out of this changed ownership structure included a strong public commitment to equal opportunities and an even stronger sensitivity to the possibility of bad publicity regarding gender or ethnicity. In consequence, the corporate personnel team had disseminated an equal opportunity policy statement throughout the company. Line managers had received guidelines on good equal opportunity practices, detailed forms to be completed during selection exercises and head office training courses in equal opportunity principles and procedures.

This particular promotion case took place in the motor department of a main branch situated in the north of England. In October 1986 Jane Bamber (a pseudonym to preserve confidentiality), was a grade-six motor clerk who applied for a grade-seven vacancy. Although Jane was interviewed and seriously considered, she was unsuccessful, but was told that she was 'next in line' for a grade-seven post. At the beginning of March 1987 Jane informed the company that she was pregnant. Soon afterwards two grade-seven vacancies were advertised. Jane applied but was not interviewed. Yet, she was totally mobile and the only person in the department who had received an 'A' for her work performance in her annual appraisal in both the previous years. Jane also knew that she was the applicant with the highest educational qualifications. A woman who was not mobile and who had been rejected outright for the October vacancy and a man who had received a warning after being criticized by clients were appointed. When Jane requested an explanation, the superintendent gave no reason for her outright rejection except that he could not support her application and refused to discuss the matter further.

At this point, Jane might have decided to resist by taking her full entitlement of statutory maternity leave and then resigning from the company. Alternatively, she could have decided to remain in employment but with a different, less committed orientation to her work and to the company. But rather than choose a strategy of resistance through distance,[9] Jane decided to challenge management's refusal to justify their promotion decision. She sought to extract further information from them concerning their criteria and decision-making processes. This form of resistance was facilitated by the fact that as an internal candidate, Jane was familiar with the company, its practices and its management. She was also a local union representative. Jane's willingness to pursue the case was significantly influenced by her knowledge and experience of local union practices and of representing other members. Indeed, her determination was also reinforced by the strength of the national union and its commitment to equal opportunity principles. Hence Jane contacted a senior national official of the trade union who was also based at this main branch when not performing union duties.

The national union official arranged a meeting between the employers' branch administration manager, Jane and herself at which she requested information about the formal rejection criteria in Jane's case. None had so far been provided. The manager could give no adequate explanation for the decision because he was unaware of the specific details of the case. He stated that selection decisions were largely the responsibility of the superintendent. The manager had great difficulty in trying to explain why, although the clerk had been a serious contender for the previous vacancy in October, she could not even be recommended or considered in the following March. After assuring Jane that her pregnancy had no impact on the decision, the administration manager adjourned the meeting to allow him to consult with the superintendent.

When the meeting was reconvened, the manager affirmed his complete support for the decision of the superintendent. He outlined the five formal reasons to justify Jane's rejection sent to him in writing by the motor superintendent. These were as follows:

1 Jane did 'not demonstrate the personality to take on the job'. She 'needed to display a greater desire to move beyond grade six' and 'needed to improve her communication with trainee inspectors'.

2 Jane had 'never been fully committed' and 'allowed personal issues to interfere with her work'.

3   She was reputed to have made a critical comment about the company to a colleague.
4   She had shown no commitment to work overtime.
5   She had not begun to sit for her professional insurance examinations.

Ostensibly, these justifications seemed plausible, logical and difficult to challenge. The manager had avoided any mention of Jane's pregnancy in his formalized account. However, the information that management had very reluctantly provided proved to be useful in resisting their decision. At this point, the union official adjourned the meeting to discuss the points raised with Jane.

In fact the women were able to use the managers' disciplinary discourses and rationalizations to undermine the validity of the promotion decision. Extracting further information from management was an essential part of this resistance strategy. When she requested the meeting to be reconvened, the union official asked the administration manager to arrange an afternoon appointment because of Jane's morning sickness. In fact, the meeting was arranged for 9 a.m., which was construed by both women as a deliberate attempt by the manager to secure a tactical advantage. Prior to the meeting, the union official gave Jane three pieces of advice based on her experience of negotiations and representing cases. First, she told Jane not to respond to the manager if he tried to talk to her directly and added that she would do all the talking. Second, they would not criticize either of the two successful candidates but would simply concentrate on the decision-making processes in order to discover the managers' thinking about Jane's application. Third, she said that if Jane should start to feel nauseous she should on no account leave the room and if necessary should be sick on the managers' new office carpet.

During the meeting, the union official argued that the criteria outlined by management at the previous meeting were vague, inconsistent and incorrect. In response the manager began to talk directly to Jane. Using a highly personalized and paternalistic discourse, the older man asked Jane, 'Now why has it come to this? Surely we can resolve this problem without these formalities?' Jane failed to respond except to become increasingly nauseous and seemingly about to throw up. At this point, it might be expected that the two women would have been forced to leave the room apologetically and defensively. Yet far from this, the union representative did not even acknowledge that the managers' carpet was in grave danger of being tarnished. Not surprisingly, the administration manager became disconcerted and called for another adjournment. No subsequent meetings were timetabled for this early in the morning. The union official had been able to draw upon and convert what appeared to be a managerial tactic of control and discipline into an effective tactic of resistance, thereby shifting power from the manager to the subordinates.

At the reconvened meeting, the union official challenged each of the five justifications provided by the superintendent. The first point about personality was contradicted by written reports received from insurance brokers concerning Jane's work performance and communication skills. Jane had received excellent assessment reports which commented on the supervisory qualities that she had shown in motivating and guiding young trainee inspectors. Second, the view that Jane was not fully committed was contradicted by her outstanding assessment reports. Third, regarding the reputed critical comments, the union representative argued that it was completely untenable to base promotion decisions on hearsay. Moreover, Jane totally denied making these particular remarks. Fourth, statements regarding Jane's overtime record were incorrect since she had actually worked an extra ten hours in both January and February 1987. In addition, the union representative argued that commitment to overtime was not a valid criterion for making promotion decisions. Finally, that Jane had not begun to sit her professional examinations (although she had always intended to do so) was completely irrelevant anyway, it was argued, since neither had the two appointees. The union representative concluded that clearly these five justifications were based on incorrect information and thus could not be the real reason for Jane's rejection: 'so if these are not the formal criteria, because they can't be the criteria, what are the criteria?' she asked.

So far, the union strategy had sought to extract more detailed information from management about the formal selection criteria. This was a necessary precondition for resistance. However, it was by no means sufficient to translate a grievance into a successful challenge. Other more strategic and political knowledges and practices were now needed. Despite the union's counter-arguments, the administration manager refused to revise or even reconsider the decision. He stated that legally binding offer letters had already been sent to the successful candidates, there were no other vacancies and the branch manager had ratified the superintendent's decision which he also continued to support.

As the local management still refused to reconsider their decision, the trade union representative referred the case to the company's corporate personnel department. She implied that strong grounds existed for the case to be taken to the Equal Opportunities Commission. In the changing corporate climate senior personnel managers were very concerned about these possible developments. As a result, the latter placed extensive 'discreet' pressure on the local managers to upgrade the clerk regardless of whether another vacancy actually existed. Local managers knew that any promotion for Jane would exceed their staffing levels agreed with head office. This new grade-seven salary would be an additional unbudgeted cost that local management would have to cover from other financial sources within their branch. In addition, a change in the decision would lead to a loss of face for the local managers. They were therefore extremely reluctant to reverse their decision. However, as a result of the knowledge and resilience of the clerk, the experience and persistence of the trade union representative and her ability to expose the contradictions of the managers' rationalizations, combined with the informal pressure by corporate personnel, the local managers eventually conceded that the clerk would be upgraded. Jane Bamber took statutory maternity leave and subsequently returned to work after the minimum period of absence.

This case study reveals how during the grievance procedure managers' strategies of control, particularly through their attempts to restrict information, had the effect of reinforcing the determination of both the clerk and the union representative to persist in their resistance against this promotion decision. The superintendent's initial failure to offer any explanation for the clerk's rejection alerted her to the possibility that she was probably being unfairly treated. Her suspicions were compounded by inconsistencies and inaccuracies in the managers' formal rationalizations. Once these contradictions were exposed, the managers' continued refusal to reverse their decision and their failure to offer an adequate explanation confirmed to the clerk that behind these formal discourses, the managers' hidden concern was her pregnancy (see also Martin 1990).

The decision to arrange a crucial meeting in the early morning appeared to both women to constitute a managerial control strategy. However, this practice had precisely the opposite effect, because it merely strengthened the clerk's resolve to resist. To be effective, the woman's resistance had to be informed, extremely persistent and determined. A central strategy was the securing of more detailed technical information from managers about their decision-making process. Using various local and strategic knowledges, the clerk and the trade union representative were then able to press for the decision eventually to be overturned. In the power struggles that ensued, specific overlapping knowledges were crucially important factors in strengthening this resistance, which in turn eventually resulted in local management being outflanked.

In addition to the information extracted from local management during the grievance process, Jane had the *technical and organizational* knowledge concerning much of this specific selection exercise which reinforced her critical appraisal of those events. She was aware of the promotion criteria, the credentials of the other candidates, her own past performance and the superintendents' assurances of her future promotion. She had also observed the managerial practices leading up to this specific selection decision. To Jane, therefore, management was relatively visible throughout the exercise. She was, of course, also familiar with past selection practices in the branch. Such detailed, localized and historical knowledge is usually unavailable to external candidates.

The trade union official had considerable knowledge, understanding and experience of the bureaucratic formalities of the grievance procedure, having represented union members throughout the country over several years. This was combined with strategic knowledge concerning the politics of resistance which enabled her to counter the intended effects of management's disciplinary practices. By requesting the formal criteria for Jane's rejection, the union representative rendered management's practices even more visible and accountable. She could therefore expose the contradictions and inconsistencies in the management's formal promotion decision and use the company hierarchy against the branch-level management by going 'over their heads' and taking the case direct to corporate personnel. This information would otherwise never have come to the attention of personnel specialists at corporate level.

Furthermore, the union official was able to suggest that the Equal Opportunities Commission might be interested in the details of the case. Her legal knowledge of sex discrimination cases made her confident about the relative merits of pursuing the grievance. This suggestion resonated with a growing sensitivity in the ranks of corporate managers regarding equal opportunities that reflected the 'culture change' being introduced by the new American multinational owners of the insurance company. Indeed, the anti-discrimination legislation itself was a precondition for and legitimation of the employees' attempts to monitor and challenge management's decision-making about promotion. Prior to this legislation, such scrutiny of internal selection decisions by subordinates would never have been accepted by management.

The Equal Opportunities Commission research project uncovered several similar examples of persistent resistance where national-level trade unionists were able to exploit divisions between different levels of the managerial hierarchy in order to challenge and overturn unfair decisions. Unlike employees working in a specific location, national union officials have access to and knowledge of corporate managers. In Jane's case, social knowledge was an important precondition for effective resistance through persistence. Both women had some knowledge of the personalities and preferences of managers at local level which facilitated their ability to identify discrepancies, gaps and inconsistencies in the selection practices. The union representative knew corporate managers who were willing to examine the formal documents of the case and to rectify the position. Relatedly, the two women trusted each other. They were long-standing work colleagues, both from the north of England. Discussions with both women revealed a close gender-based identification between them. The trade union representative had two children of her own and understood some of the difficulties of managing paid work and pregnancy. Equally, Jane had confidence in the ability and commitment of the union representative and was therefore willing to follow the advice and guidance given to her throughout the procedure. Hence, the case also reveals a gendered form of knowledge that facilitated the effectiveness of their resistance.

Finally, some knowledge of or about self also appeared to be critically important for withstanding the tremendous psychological pressure involved in resistance through persistence. Jane's case illustrates the intensification of power struggles and strategies that often occur as the grievance procedure progresses. Jane had to withstand the cumulative pressures of managerial strategies of control, discounting and personalism; the fear of subsequent victimization by different supervisory levels and the ongoing disciplinary discourses of both men and women work colleagues, many of whom insisted that Jane was 'going too far'. This required extensive determination, fortitude and conviction. Trade union support was very helpful, but this in itself was unlikely to have been enough. Crucially important here was Jane's belief in the legitimacy of her grievance and her determination to reject the pejorative definitions of identity ascribed to her by managers, supervisors and even colleagues.

Those seeking to discipline subordinates and colleagues frequently seek to dismiss their resistance by imputing negative motives. So, for example, derogatory labels or identities such as 'trouble-maker', 'whinger', 'chip on their shoulder', 'jealous' and 'looney feminist' frequently have significant symbolic and disciplinary impact on those considering resistance. Hence, in addition to issues of power, knowledge and information, definitions of identity and subjectivity are an important feature of workplace struggles. On the one hand, the anticipation of these negative identities might be a crucial limitation on explicit oppositional practices. Yet, on the other hand, disciplinary practices can actually reinforce resistance through persistence by intensifying the determination of the aggrieved. This is most likely where those who resist are not dependent on authority for identity confirmation. Rather, they are confident in the legitimacy of the specific case and refuse to reduce the negotiations to issues of personality. Jane's case illustrates some of the difficulties facing individual resisters who may experience much greater visibility than those involved in collective action. It also demonstrates how subordinates can outflank disciplinary processes by engaging in resistance through persistence.

Conclusion: resistance, knowledge, power and subjectivity

What are the implications of the foregoing analysis for a critical understanding of workplace resistance and employee behaviour? Certainly, the analysis suggests that subordinates have available a variety of options, knowledges, cultural resources and strategic agencies through which they can and do initiate oppositional practices. Workplace resistance may seek to challenge, disrupt or invert prevailing assumptions, discourses and power relations. It can take multiple material and symbolic forms, and its strength, influence and intensity are likely to be variable and to shift over time (Brown 1992). Resistance constitutes a form of power exercised by subordinates in the workplace.

Employees resist despite their subordinate and insecure organizational position and despite their never having full information or knowledge of future consequences. Dissatisfaction, disenchantment and frustration pervades the lives of many employees in contemporary organizations. Those at the lower levels of hierarchies often feel particularly vulnerable, unfairly treated and unacknowledged and most excluded from decision-making procedures. Their sense of grievance and insecurity frequently translates into oppositional discursive practices. While these practices may not always be revolutionary or even effective in the sense of securing significant organizational change, it is equally overly simplistic to suggest that resistance is 'so frequently outflanked'. Accordingly, the current analytical concentration on consent or outflanking is in danger of neglecting this crucially important feature of routine organizational practices.

Workplace resistance crucially draws upon various forms of knowledge. In practice subordinates have extensive knowledge which may not be shared with those in more senior positions, and which can be used as an important 'weapon of resistance' (Scott 1985). Like resistance, knowledge itself can take multiple forms in organizational life. Oppositional practices are usually informed by the strategic exercise of particular knowledges which may be, for example, technical, bureaucratic and procedural, social, regional, cultural and historical, legal, economic, strategic/political and/or about self. These knowledges should neither be understated nor overstated when examining the discursive practices of subordinates. They are likely to overlap, be somewhat indeterminate, partial and shifting and often be couched in ambiguity, uncertainty and insecurity. Equally they may be highly specialist and narrow or more tacit and difficult to objectify (Polanyi and

Prosch 1975; Kusterer 1978; Manwaring and Wood 1985; Davies and Rosser 1986; Lazega 1992). They might even be used in ways that express co-operation and consent rather than resistance (Manwaring and Wood 1985). Nevertheless, these various knowledges can be an important condition and consequence of resistance. Whether specific practices are best defined in terms of resistance or consent or both will be determined by the particular power relations and by employees' subjective orientation, commitments and indeed motivation and determination.

This focus on employee knowledge therefore raises issues about subjectivity. The foregoing case studies display two quite distinct subjective orientations to the acquisition and use of information and to authority in organizations. Resistance through distance involves a denial of involvement or interest in key organizational processes. It is very much an 'escape attempt' (Cohen and Taylor 1992). In the engineering factory, knowledge and information were concealed by subordinates who engaged in defensive practices that sought to minimize their involvement in the company, while embellishing an oppositional sense of gender and class-specific identity and maximizing their economic return from work. Resistance through persistence, by contrast, may involve the acquisition of further information and knowledge in order to develop a critical analysis of organizational practices. In the insurance case study, this critical analysis was presented in such a strategic and determined way that an, albeit small, amount of organizational change was generated. Both companies were experiencing cultural change initiated by new American owners. While the shopfloor workers totally rejected the new corporate culture in their organization, the women insurance workers used the culture change as a means of justifying their monitoring and challenging of managerial practices. Resistance through persistence proved to be a much more effective oppositional strategy to conventional power relations. (See also McBarnet et al. 1993 for a similar kind of analysis regarding the disclosure and strategic acquisition of financial information.)

Whatever form resistance takes, however, it is always inextricably linked to organizational discipline, control and power. Resistance is rarely equal to control, neither is it necessarily successful nor fundamentally subversive in its effects (Henriques et al. 1984). Yet resistance cannot be examined as if it were separate from workplace discipline and control. Oppositional practices often draw upon the very forms of control that generate resistance in the first place. Indeed, control and resistance can be so mutually reproducing that they actually constitute one another. This is particularly likely where subordinates engage in resistance through distance. Moreover, it should be remembered that resistance is not always the rationally organized result of strategic planning and instrumental calculation. Opposition might be expressed through humour using ambiguity, irony and satire. It may be a spontaneous reaction to a particular event, possibly expressed in anger and frustration. Alternatively, it might not be an entirely conscious act but instead could be expressed in what Giddens terms 'practical consciousness' (Giddens 1979: 148). Here even those who resist might not identify, explain or even recognize their actions as explicitly oppositional. Such practices are unlikely to be effective forms of resistance given the disciplinary processes that characterize contemporary organizations.

While control frequently generates resistance, as various labour process writers have demonstrated, resistance may also reinforce a managerial concern with further controls, as Taylor's (1947) work illustrates. Both control and resistance can therefore become intertwined within an organizational vicious circle in which power is exercised through mutually reproducing strategies and counter-strategies.[10] Hence an unintended and contradictory consequence of both resistance and control might be the reproduction of one another (Collinson 1992a). Having said that, resistance will not reproduce conventional power relations in any simple, mechanical and predetermined way but will have a variety of important organizational effects, many of which cannot be specified outside particular workplaces and industries. Indeed resistance through persistence has the potential to overcome these mutually reinforcing vicious circles by outflanking disciplinary practices.

An important feature of the oppositional strategies examined in the foregoing case studies is the overlapping and mutually embedded character of consent, compliance and resistance. In each case, resistance was circumscribed by elements of ambiguity, consent and compliance. Even the most critical and radical workers in the engineering factory supported managerial prerogative. Although in their view this was consistent with their oppositional discourses, it simultaneously expressed an ambivalence and acceptance of the prevailing power asymmetries of the company. Resistance through distance was contained *within*, rather than *against*, the idea of hierarchy and authority.

Ostensibly, resistance through persistence in the insurance company was relatively more effective, since an unfair decision was successfully challenged and overturned, which in turn had the effect of promoting equal opportunity issues throughout the company. Yet, here again, resistance was limited. It constituted a partial challenge to, but was also paradoxically confined within the principle of managerial prerogative. While it would be inaccurate to dismiss or reduce this resistance to some notion of 'outflanking', equally it would be inappropriate to overstate its radical intentions and/or effects. The employee's demand for merito-cratic treatment in promotion can be interpreted simultaneously as an expression of both resistance to patriarchical control practices and of consent to conventional career progression and to the legitimacy of hierarchical organization. The case displays the rationality, knowledgeability and determination of those who resisted. Yet underpinning these strategic practices was a set of coexistent and partly incompatible and unresolved views about hierarchy and management. As in the engineering factory, managers were heavily criticized and attacked, but a fundamental and collective challenge to the prevailing organization of production seemed highly unlikely.[11]

Few studies in the literature on resistance and consent adequately account for these shifting ambiguities, ambivalences, confusions, partial knowledges, inconsistencies, multiple motives and paradoxical effects that comprise the subjective reality of organizational power relations. Indeed, a common problem with a great deal of the current critical literature on employee behaviour is its failure to address adequately the way in which conventional power relations are *subjectively* experienced, reproduced, challenged and sometimes even reversed in workplace practices.[12] When exploring these subjective dimensions, it is important for organization theorists to recognize that, on the one hand, all those involved in the labour process at all hierarchical levels are likely to be skilled, knowledgeable and creative actors in both a social and technical sense (Giddens 1979). Subjectivity should therefore not be neglected. On the other hand, subjectivity is also simultaneously a specific, historical product embedded within particular conditions and power relations. It is ambiguous, fragmentary and multiple, sometimes non-rational, often contradictory (Henriques et al. 1984) and frequently characterized by anxiety and uncertainty. Hence subjectivity should neither be subordinated to, nor treated as sovereign and privileged above, the analysis of power. Subjectivity and power are inextricably interwoven in all organizational practices [...].

Yet, in the literature, either employee subjectivity and knowledgeability are downgraded and treated as the determined outcome of the particular workplace 'rules of the game' (e.g. Burawoy 1979, 1985; Clegg 1989; Mills and Murgatroyd 1991) or else workers are seen as highly rational, knowledgeable and strategic in their subversive discursive practices (e.g. Willis 1977, 1980; Scott 1985). Both perspectives provide at best a partial analysis of workplace practices that is limited by a tendency to overstate either consent and compliance or dissent and resistance and to separate the latter from the former. I will briefly explore examples of each approach in turn.

Clegg's (1987) empirical analysis of the behaviour of joiners on a building site illustrates the tendency to overstate consent and to separate it from resistance. He described how joiners regularly stopped work on the pretext that the weather was 'inclement'. Drawing on Burawoy's game metaphor, Clegg argued that the joiners played these 'games' of work stoppage in order to 'put pressure on the management to increase control and thus more efficiently exploit them' (Clegg 1987: 65). According to Clegg, this was because the workers were unable to maximize their bonus since management failed to provide material and supplies in a timely manner. The 'inclemency rule' was the joiners' way of putting pressure on to management. He concluded that these workers 'happily collude in intensifying their own subjection' (p. 65). Yet this analysis fails to explore the accounts of the joiners themselves.[13] The author's own interpretation tends to be somewhat derogatory of the joiners in emphasizing their deliberate willingness to collude in their own subjection. No mention is made of resistance, even though the workers' strategies were consistent with an oppositional economic instrumentalism that sought to maximize bonus by improving the flow of supplies. In short, an alternative reading of Clegg's example would be that it illustrates the complex, contradictory and simultaneous expression of workplace resistance and consent.[14]

By contrast with this analysis, several of the most valuable qualitative studies of resistance tend to overstate and/or romanticize oppositional practices. These analyses are informed by overly rationalist and essentialist assumptions regarding agency, subjectivity and human action. For example, in his study of Malaysian peasant resistance, Scott (1985) argued that although the peasants are forced to conform in their actions, they still resist in their discourses, thoughts and ideas. Mitchell (1990) rejects Scott's emphasis on the internal mental autonomy of peasants because it presupposes that there is a social sphere 'where the play of power does not penetrate, where discourse becomes authentic' (Mitchell 1990: 564). Such analyses according to Mitchell seek to uncover 'a collective self that is the author of its own cultural constructions and actions... a site of "essential truth"' (p. 564). Overly rationalist and essentialist assumptions about subjectivity and resistance take for granted the notion of a pre-existing selfhood that is authentic, self-produced and sustained against an objective, oppressive and material world (see also Scott 1990). Accordingly, the identities and counter-culture of the subordinated are left unquestioned and an exaggerated radicalism is imputed to their class-cultural practices.

Overly rationalist assumptions regarding subjectivity and resistance are also found in Willis's (1977, 1980) examination of the counter-cultural practices of a group of English working-class kids known as 'the lads'. Willis argues that they see through the dominant ideology of equal opportunity, its claim to evaluate individuals objectively and its legitimization of prevailing hierarchical relations. Although their 'penetrations' currently remain partial, Willis sees in the counter-culture the 'potential here for a not merely partial and cultural but a total social transformation' (Willis 1977: 137). Willis's study highlights the agency and creativity of highly subordinated individuals in a class-ridden society and also displays some of the contradictory outcomes of their creative discursive practices of resistance.

However, Willis seems to overstate the knowledgeability of the lads and to exaggerate the extent of their partial 'penetrations' of class inequality. Like Scott, he assumes that subordinates' counter-culture contains an authenticity or existential truth that differentiates it from the objective, oppressive and material world of class inequality and capitalist domination. In the absence of any critical analysis of the lads' subjectivity, their motivations and proud boastings, Willis fails to recognize that their oppositional practices could simultaneously constitute acts of conformity to the expectations of the counter-cultural group. Class society reinforces identity problems or status anxieties particularly for those in subordinated positions (Sennett and Cobb 1977). A great deal of the lads' behaviour can be interpreted not so much as an entirely rational critique of class inequality, as Willis suggests, but rather as a defensive/aggressive means of constructing a more positive sense of self or group identity than that provided by the school.

Hence those who engage in collective forms of resistance are likely to do so for a multiplicity of different, often individualistic reasons. Some radical writers, however, have neglected this complexity and the defensiveness, fragility and precariousness that frequently characterizes collective practices. In searching for 'pure' and 'authentic' forms of resistance, they have also tended to deny or understate the possible organizational significance and effects of individual forms of resistance. Yet, in certain cases, individual opposition might be more significant than collective resistance. For example, Jane Bamber's face-to-face and highly visible resistance with management was not only more tenacious, traumatic and dangerous than the concealed, escapist and patriarchal strategies of shopfloor workers, but was also more effective in generating organizational change. For Jane, this sustained challenge to her superiors was indeed a radical act of defiance. Not only was Jane's approach important in enhancing her working life, but it may also have been the most appropriate strategy for establishing and sustaining further organizational change. Such oppositional practices should therefore not be ignored or underestimated by critical organization theorists. Neither, of course, should they be romanticized nor treated as the existential expression of a rational resisting subject.

The assumptions about human agency and subjectivity underpinning the work of Scott, Willis and other writers on resistance have been critiqued by Kondo (1990: 218–25). She argues that current notions of resistance and accommodation are inadequate particularly because they assume a wholly rational subject whose views would be consistent and uncontradictory were it not for the influence of dominant ideologies. Kondo highlights a failure in the literature to recognize that opposition is usually mitigated by elements of collusion and compromise, and that compliance can contain unanticipated subversive effects.[15] Rejecting the notion of a 'pristine space of authentic resistance' (p. 224), a realm of meaning beyond power relations, discourse or law, Kondo argues that actors should be seen as 'multiple selves whose lives are shot through with contradictions and creative tensions' (p. 224). She therefore rejects conventional notions of a fixed, static and singular identity and the simplistic assumption in the work of Scott and Willis that their respondents are 'true resisters' (pp. 220, 323). The subjective dimension cannot be reduced to an exclusive focus on labour resistance (Knights 1990).

Challenging the dominant views of subjectivity and power found in analyses of resistance, Kondo outlines her ethnographic study of a family-owned Japanese factory to reveal the embedded character of consent, compliance and resistance. She describes how the subversive discourses of men and women shopfloor workers, which often highlight managerial inconsistencies, can themselves be caught in contradictions and ironies, simultaneously legitimizing as they challenge dominant organizational and gendered discourses. In these workplace practices, characterized by ambiguity, paradox and shifting power relations, individuals construct multiple selves that are gendered, ambiguous and fragmented. Kondo's account reveals many of the ironies and ambiguities that are a condition and consequence of the crafting of selves within shifting fields of power. It therefore makes an important contribution to the critical analysis of workplace power, knowledge and subjectivity with its emphasis on the overlapping character of consent, compliance and resistance.[16]

What is missing from her analysis is any examination of the anxieties and insecurities that are frequently the medium and outcome of the subjective search to craft one or more selves through interwoven practices of control, resistance, compliance or consent. While technical and strategic knowledge is an important precondition for effective resistance, the subjective ability to deal with the disciplinary pressures and ensuing anxieties, ambiguities and uncertainties of conflict are equally crucial. A capacity to handle the pressures is at least in part derived from a recognition that the paradoxical search to secure particular social identities is likely to intensify rather than eliminate insecurity and anxiety (Knights 1990; Collinson 1992a). Hence identity concerns may not only facilitate but also constrain oppositional practices. Nonetheless, issues of identity are always likely to be one feature of the multiple motives that invariably inform human action. Where oppositional practices are shaped *predominantly* by identity-seeking motives, how-ever, they are likely to be characterized by greater self-consciousness, anxiety and defensiveness which in turn will lead to less effective forms of resistance. Two propositions follow. First, the more concerned individuals are with crafting selves, the less effective will be their oppositional practices. This is illustrated by the shopfloor workers' resistance through distance. Conversely, resistance is likely to be more effective when those involved are less concerned with the construction and protection of identity and more committed to the issues on which their opposition is based. This seemed to be the case in the second example of resistance through persistence. Hence, oppositional strategies that seek to increase employee involvement in organizational processes and to render managerial practices more visible and accountable have greater effectiveness than those primarily concerned with distancing.

To conclude, this [reading] has been concerned to highlight the analytical importance of workplace resistance and to explore some of its interconnections with knowledge, power and subjectivity. Workplace resistance remains a persis-tent, significant and remarkable feature of modern organizations. Subordinates do continue to resist and articulate their dissatisfaction in innumerable ways despite considerable disciplinary barriers and insecurities. As we have seen, the commod-ification of labour not only reflects and reinforces managerial and hierarchical control, but also intensifies extensive material and symbolic insecurity for those in subordinate positions. The ever-present possibility of losing one's job is a signific-ant discipline and disincentive to resist or challenge managerial practices (see also Littler 1990). Job insecurity has intensified in many countries over the past decade as market processes have increasingly impacted on occupations and industries and unemployment rates have grown.

These insecurities and barriers to resistance are reinforced by the organizational structures of multi-divisional and multinational companies. In these large and powerful corporations primary decision-making processes are usually undertaken far away from operating units, and often in another country (see Ramsay and Howarth 1989). Consequently, within these conglomerates, it is not merely labour, but operating units and even whole companies that are disposable. When com-bined with the additional pressures of domestic responsibilities and the need to provide for children and to finance a mortgage, dissatisfied employees may well decide to just 'grin and bear it' and to accommodate the status quo in order to guarantee a wage or salary.

Where employment or income are so precarious, career advancement is often perceived to be both an escape from the most vulnerable jobs at the bottom of the organization and a means of securing greater pay and status. Career structures invariably characterize contemporary organizations. Yet these structures consti-tute another significant barrier to the mobilization of any form of dissent because aspiring individuals will frequently perceive extensive career damage arising from opposing those who also make decisions regarding their hierarchical progress or who would be asked to provide references and testimonies regarding their work performance. Resistance can generate reprisals.[17] In addition, because the major-ity of work colleagues are unwilling to oppose management, those who would resist are aware that their actions have even less chance of being effective. The conformity or compliance of the many thus frequently disciplines the oppositional practices of the few.

As the second case study demonstrated, the marginalization of those who resist is further reinforced by the likely managerial response which typically will seek to negate the legitimacy of the particular grievance being articulated and to empha-size the so-called 'personality problems' of those who dissent. Negative motives may be imputed to the dissenters in order to discredit their legitimacy. While current systems and practices of control and discipline are deemed to be normal and legitimate, oppositional behaviour is thereby treated as aberrant, deviant and unjustifiable. In such discursive struggles, managers are in an advantaged position because they often have the material and symbolic resources and information to facilitate the widest dissemination of their definition of reality. Practices of resist-ance through distance are especially likely to reinforce subordinates' vulnerability to these disciplinary processes.

In what appear to be increasingly disciplinary and insecure employment condi-tions, it is remarkable indeed that strategies of workplace resistance continue to characterize organizational practices. This [reading] has examined some of the organizational conditions, processes and consequences of resistance. It has identi-fied two consistent and distinctive patterns of resistance that, while not being exhaustive of possible oppositional practices, might well have a broader applic-ability.[18] Highlighting how these different oppositional practices are shaped by specific power relations, knowledges and subjectivities, the foregoing analysis suggests that it is resistance through persistence in particular that has the potential to counter and even outflank disciplinary practices within contemporary organ-izations. Although workplace resistance does not always constitute a fundamental challenge to conventional power relations, it is a crucially important feature of organizational life which therefore requires further detailed conceptual and empirical examination by critical scholars of organizations.

NOTES

From D. Collinson (1994), 'Strategies of resistance: power, knowledge and subjectivity in the workplace', in J. Jermier, D. Knights and W. R. Nord, eds, *Resistance and Power in Organizations* (ITBP), pp. 25–68.

1   In Clegg's [. . .] *Modern Organisations* (1990), workplace resistance is rarely mentioned. The relationship between power and resistance is addressed in more detail in *Frame-works of Power* (1989). However, much more attention is paid here to the way that resistance is outflanked than to oppositional practices themselves.
2   Burawoy's (1979, 1985) emphasis on the way that consent is manufactured and repro-duced within the labour process has been enormously influential. His study of workers' involvement in the game of 'making out' has significantly shaped assumptions within the labour process literature regarding not only resistance but also employee behaviour, their discursive practices, counter-cultures and subjectivities more broadly. The result has been

DAVID COLLINSON

a tendency to assume that in late modern organizations conflict and oppositional practices are being replaced by forms of organization that are effective in generating employee consent, compliance and/or subordination. If shopfloor workers can so easily be absorbed into game playing and believe that their immersion in making out is 'freely chosen' (1979: 29) then, as writers on the labour process, we need not spend precious time researching resistance because the data will simply not be there. In what follows, I argue that this approach overstates employee consent in the labour process to the neglect of compliance and resistance. (For other critiques, see Clawson and Fantasia 1983; Knights and Collinson 1985; Knights 1990; Davies 1990; Collinson 1992a; see also n. 14 below.)

3   Clegg's approach to outflanking appears simultaneously to understate and overstate the knowledgeability of subordinates. The latter viewpoint rests on a set of highly rationalistic assumptions regarding subjectivity in which subordinates are seen as totally rational, calculative and instrumental with extensive skills of prediction. Yet those who resist are rarely, if ever fully aware of the consequences of their actions. While they may fear intensified discipline, material and symbolic reprisals and victimization, these anxieties are merely expectations or anticipations of possible consequences. They might or might not be accurate. Clegg cites the rather atypical example of Nazi extermination camps to argue that inmates would not organize resistance for fear of failure and certain death. Yet the personal experience of Primo Levi (1987a, 1987b) suggests that forms of resistance did occur even in these brutalizing conditions. In such cases, resistance could even take the form of suicide. Death becomes one means of escaping from the horror. Burrell (1984) has also revealed how homosexual relationships still emerged despite attempts by the Nazis to ensure their eradication. Perhaps a better example of how knowing can limit workplace resistance is in the case of managers who provide trade union officials with confidential, 'off the record' information that cannot be used or communicated to members. This often has the effect of reducing the possibility of resistance. However, Clegg's analysis at best provides only a partial account. The relationship between subjectivity and resistance can be the exact opposite of that which he suggests. In some cases 'not knowing' may facilitate resistance and the determination to see a challenge through. There are significant material and symbolic costs and pressures associated with resistance, many of which may be unfamiliar to those who decide to resist. In such cases initial ignorance could facilitate resistance rather than impair it [...]. Yet in Clegg's analysis, there is no space for these non-rational aspects of subjectivity and motivation. Indeed, there is no analytical space for the examination of motives whatsoever (see also n. 13 below).

4   While workers may not be fully cognisant of bureaucratic procedures, they often control technical, performance-related knowledge. It was precisely this control that Taylor sought to eliminate through scientific management principles (see also Manwaring and Wood 1985; Davies and Rosser 1986). Moreover, in his earlier work, Clegg (1979) himself highlighted workers' 'discretionary knowledge power' as a facilitator of workplace resistance. Ten years later, however, he talks of subordinates being 'ignorant', rather than about various types of knowledge producing different effects. Multiple knowledges have an important role within oppositional practices, as the case studies will outline later.

5   Since a great deal of resistance draws on a thorough knowledge of the technical and social organization of production, securing data on resistance can be difficult for researchers of organizations who may not possess such detailed information and understanding about routine practices. Equally, in some cases employees' statements are more oppositional than their practices. In other cases, it is not so much what respondents say, but more how they act that reveals grievances and workplace tensions. Hence, resistance

often occurs at a highly informal, concealed and subterranean level that is deeply embedded in organizational practices. A great deal of time, effort and perseverance is necessary for researchers to develop the relationships of trust and familiarity that would make employees willing to reveal their covert practices of resistance. Like managers, employees may have strong reasons for restricting information to outside researchers. Hence, we often find considerable resistance to the study of resistance in organizations.

6   This was the headline on the first edition of the new house magazine designed to herald the culture change in the organization. It refers to the American managing director who is encouraging people to recognize management's open door policy.

7   He elaborated, 'What they do is, they keep us in the dark and then shit on us occasionally. That's how you grow mushrooms!'

8   Paradoxically, resistance through distance could also include managerial practices undertaken by shop stewards and workers. Indeed, workers' knowledge in various ways resulted in them managing the production process despite their oppositional discourses. Moreover, some workers managed their own businesses outside work. For example, one worker ran an off-licence selling alcohol and confectionary and another owned a fish and chip shop. The ways in which shopfloor workers managed production are elaborated in Collinson (1992a).

9   In an insurance office, as on the shopfloor of an engineering factory, resistance through distance can take many forms. For example, Jane could have: avoided dealing with telephone enquiries; spent longer periods in the toilet, picked up files off her desk under the pretext of researching a difficult problem and then left the department to talk with friends in other areas (see [. . .] Collinson 1993). Generally, Jane could have worked much more slowly than she had done previously and for which she had received strong praise in her annual appraisals.

10 Accordingly, what is an exercise of power/control and what is an exercise of resistance becomes difficult to disentangle. This is particularly so since resistance is not merely the prerogative of those most subordinated in organizations for even managers can engage in oppositional practices (see [. . .] Collinson et al. 1990). However, particular practices are invariably located in specific conditions of power asymmetries and inequalities which in turn largely determine whether they are best seen as an exercise of power or resistance.

11 It could be argued that this contradictory and mutually embedded character of consent and resistance is simply a condition and consequence of the contradictory nature of the capitalist labour process in which conflict and interdependence coexist (Cressey and Macinnes 1980; Hyman 1987). However, as Knights (1990) has argued in his criticisms of Cressey and Macinnes, an explanation of the reproduction of these contradictory features of employee behaviour requires a critical analysis of subjectivity as well as power.

12 The foregoing case-study material was presented in order to explore the relationship between resistance and knowledge in particular. There was not the space to develop a more detailed analysis of subjectivity (see Collinson 1992a). Suffice it to say here, that viewing subjectivity as contradictory, ambiguous and shifting has important methodological and analytical implications. Case studies cannot claim to constitute an objective representation of 'organizational reality' Such notions of objectivity deny the phenomenological processes and power relations at work in the conduct of research (see Collinson 1992b). Hence the foregoing empirical analysis was merely one version among several that could have been presented. When presenting case-study material it is therefore important to be explicit in outlining one's assumptions and analytical framework. It is then for the reader to decide on the plausibility of the argument by

critically examining the coherence and integration of the theoretical and empirical analysis. The value of case-study material lies in its potential to question the validity of more abstract constructs while also illustrating and 'breathing life' into these analytical themes.

13   This neglect, however, is justified by Clegg (1989), where he highlights the methodological problems of trying to access 'the internal mental and intentional well-springs of another's causal actions' (p. 3). He argues that intention should not be associated with 'the private mental states of persons' (p. 210) but rather with 'currently "fixed" representations for making sense of what people do' (p. 210). For Clegg, since these 'vocabularies of motive' (Mills 1940) are determined by current social rules (Clegg 1989: 10), it is to an examination of rules and structures which we should turn. He contends that any resource to the actor's own account as an explanation will be fundamentally flawed (p. 3). While acknowledging that there is no perfect access to the subjective accounts of respondents (or of oneself, for that matter), I would reject this view. To argue that actors' accounts have no explanatory value is to reproduce the deterministic analytical perspective for which Braverman has been so heavily criticized and to derogate the subject in Giddens's (1979) terms. Even if accounts are to some extent rationalizations of practices, they may still shape future conduct (Mills 1940: 907) and are nonetheless instructive and useful in innumerable ways. A reliance on these accounts would be problematic, but as a resource they can enhance our understanding of organizational processes. Indeed, some of the most valuable studies of organizations in the past twenty years have been ethnographies that have taken accounts into consideration and examined them critically, locating them within broader conditions and consequences. It seems strange that Clegg acknowledges the 'embodied agency of subordinates' (p. 194), but then rejects any value in actors' accounts and rationalizations as at least a partial explanation of their discursive practices. Paradoxically, Clegg's position does not seem to restrict him from imputing (overly rationalist) motives and intentions on to those about whom he writes.

14   Like Clegg, Burawoy's analysis of employee consent fails to examine workers' accounts of their practices (see Collinson 1992a). *Manufacturing Consent* is a study of observed workplace practices by a researcher tied for long periods to a particular machine. It therefore does not explore the subtleties and complexities of worker subjectivity, meaning and discourses that are the condition and consequence of these practices. Far from privileging subjectivity as some have claimed, Burawoy neglects it both empirically and analytically. Although Burawoy (1979: 229) is critical of Marxism and Althusserian structuralism for their reduction of 'wage labourers to objects of manipulation; to commodities bought and sold in the market' (p. 77), Burawoy's own account tends towards a deterministic analysis that derogates workers who are seen to be embroiled in and hoodwinked by the game of 'making out' in the wider capitalist society. In various places, and particularly in the footnotes, Burawoy does acknowledge his neglect of any discussion of subjectivity or what he terms 'explicit psychology' and 'theory of human nature' (pp. 125, 157, 237). However, he seeks to justify this omission on the grounds that, 'presenting individuals as carriers or agents of social relations . . . captures the essential quality of existence under capitalism. Within such a context psychology can be reduced to a theory of needs: how capitalism generates needs, what these needs are in the different phases of its development, and whether capitalism can satisfy the needs it produces' (p. 236). In Burawoy's analysis, then, agency is reduced to an essentialist needs theory determined by the functionalist requirements of surplus value appropriation in an all-pervasive capitalist system.

Social forces are given complete analytical primacy while human agency and subject-ivity are neglected.

15 In the engineering factory, those workers who articulated a more explicit discourse of consent also criticized certain managers for their failure to live up to the 'hard but fair' image that they held of the ideal-typical authority figure. In their eyes, 'real' managers should be tough but reasonable. This negation of individual managers has been termed 'idealized substitution' by Sennett (1980). In this process, particular managers or leaders were criticized, but in ways that implicitly confirmed the legitimacy of hierarchy and control. As a result, many of these workers decided to stop informing supervisors and managers on ideas to improve working materials and product design. In addition, consent was often interpreted by these workers as a form of opposition to the majority of colleagues who they argued were intent on 'causing trouble' or 'skiving' from work.

16 Feminist ethnographies have demonstrated how the resistance of organized male labour can simultaneously constitute forms of oppression against women (e.g. Cock-burn, 1983, 1991; Walby 1986). Seeking to exclude or segregate women in order to protect the male 'breadwinner wage', men workers' resistance is clearly revealed to be a simultaneous exercise of power and control over women.

17 For example, Stanley Adams and his wife suffered severe consequences for his whistle-blowing. In 1973, before resigning as world-product manager of the Swiss-based drug company Hoffman-La Roche, Adams revealed the multinational's involvement in illicit price fixing, market sharing with competitors and oppressive control of the worldwide vitamin market. Roche was subsequently fined $430,000 by the European Economic Community. However, the company accused Adams of industrial espionage and treason. He was arrested in Switzerland, charged and given a three-year suspended sentence. During Adams's detention, his wife committed suicide (Adams 1984; Made-ley 1986). [A] spate of 'whistleblowing' in UK public-sector organizations in the 1980s [...] resulted in the government considering the introduction of 'gagging clauses' into employment contracts, for example in the National Health Service.

18 Michael Muetzelfeldt and Jill Graham have both suggested certain similarities between the two strategies of resistance explored [here] and Hirschman's (1970) categories of 'exit' and 'voice'. Hirschman argues that in responding to organizational decline, individuals will either resign/escape from (exit) or try to change (voice) products, conditions or processes which they find objectionable. Focusing heavily upon con-sumer behaviour, however, this perspective fails to acknowledge the distinctive nature of power relations *within* employment. Its economistic orientation is based on a rationalistic and voluntaristic notion of the subject that ignores the social and cultural dynamics of workplace power relations. This in turn reflects and reinforces Hirsch-man's underestimation of the costs *and* overestimation of the possibilities of *both* exit and voice (see also Ahrne 1990; Flam 1993). His rather static and one-dimensional categories do not allow for the possibility of more subtle, multiple, ambiguous and contradictory employee discursive practices such as resistance through distance which combines elements of both exit and voice. Hence I would argue that similarities with Hirschman's approach are actually more superficial than they might at first appear.

REFERENCES

Ackers, P. and J. Black (1992), 'Watching the detectives: shop stewards' expectations of their managers in the age of human resource management', in A. Sturdy, D. Knights, and H. Willmott, eds, *Skill and Consent* (London: Routledge), pp. 185–212.

Adams, S. (1984), *Roche versus Adams* (London: Jonathan Cape).

Ahrne, G. (1990), *Agency and Organization* (London: Sage).

Beynon, H. (1980), *Working for Ford* (Harmondsworth: Penguin).

Braverman, H. (1974), *Labour and Monopoly Capitalism* (New York: Monthly Review Press).

Brown, G. (1977), *Sabotage: A Study in Industrial Conflict* (Nottingham: Spokesman Books).

Brown, R. (1965), *Social Psychology* (New York: Free Press).

Brown, R. K. (1992), *Understanding Industrial Organisations* (London: Routledge).

Burawoy, M. (1979), *Manufacturing Consent* (Chicago: Chicago University Press).

Burawoy, M. (1985), *The Politics of Production* (London: Verso).

Burrell, G. (1984), 'Sex and organisational analysis', *Organization Studies*, vol. 5, no. 2, pp. 97–118.

Clawson, D. and R. Fantasia (1983), 'Review essay: beyond Burawoy: the dialectics of conflict and consent on the shopfloor', *Theory and Society*, vol. 12, no. 3, pp. 671–80.

Clegg, S. R. (1979), *The Theory of Power and Organisation* (London: Routledge & Kegan Paul).

Clegg, S. R. (1987), 'The power of language and the language of power', *Organization Studies*, vol. 8, no. 1, pp. 60–70.

Clegg, S. R. (1989), *Frameworks of Power* (London: Sage).

Clegg, S. R. (1990), *Modern Organisations* (London: Sage).

Clegg, S. R. and D. Dunkerley (1980), *Organisation, Class and Control* (London: Routledge & Kegan Paul).

Cockburn, C. (1983), *Brothers* (London: Pluto Press).

Cockburn, C. (1991), *In the Way of Women* (London: Macmillan).

Cohen, S. and L. Taylor (1992), *Escape Attempts* (London: Routledge).

Collinson, D. L. (1988), 'Engineering humour: masculinity, joking and conflict in shopfloor relations', *Organization Studies*, vol. 9, no. 2, pp. 181–99.

Collinson, D. L. (1992a), *Managing the Shopfloor: Subjectivity, Masculinity and Workplace Culture* (Berlin: Walter de Gruyter).

Collinson, D. L. (1992b), 'Researching recruitment: qualitative methods and sex discrimination', in R. Burgess, ed., *Studies in Qualitative Methodology*, vol. 3 (Greenwich, CT: JAI Publications), pp. 89–122.

Collinson, D. L. (1993), 'Introducing on-line processing: conflicting human resource policies in insurance', in J. Clark, ed. *Human Resource Management and Technical Change* (London: Sage), pp. 155–74.

Collinson, D. L., D. Knights and M. Collinson (1990), *Managing to Discriminate* (London: Routledge).

Cressey, P. and J. Macinnes (1980), 'Voting for Ford: industrial democracy and the control of labour', *Capital and Class*, vol. 11, pp. 5–33.

Davies, C. and J. Rosser (1986), 'Gendered jobs in the health service: a problem for labour process analysis', in D. Knights and H. Willmott, eds, *Gender and the Labour Process* (Aldershot: Gower), pp. 94–116.

Davies, S. (1990), 'Inserting gender into Burawoy's theory of the labour process', *Work, Employment and Society*, vol. 4, no. 3, pp. 391–426.

Ditton, J. (1976), 'Moral horror versus folk terror: output restriction, class and the social organisation of exploitation', *Sociological Review*, vol. 24, pp. 519–44.

Dubois, P. (1979), *Sabotage in Industry* (Harmondsworth: Penguin).

Dunphy, D. C. and D. A. Stace (1988), 'Transformational and coercive strategies for planned organisational change', *Organizational Studies*, vol. 9, no. 3, pp. 317–34.

Edwards, P. K. (1986), *Conflict at Work: A Materialist Analysis of Workplace Relations* (Oxford: Basil Blackwell).

Edwards, P. K. (1990), 'Understanding conflict in the labour process: the logic and autonomy of struggle', in D. Knights and H. Willmott, eds, *Labour Process Theory* (London: Macmillan), pp. 125–52.

Edwards, P. and H. Scullion (1982), *The Social Organisation of Industrial Conflict* (Oxford: Basil Blackwell).

Edwards, R. (1979), *Contested Terrain: The Transformation of the Workplace in the Twentieth Century* (London: Heinemann).

Emmett, I. and D. H. J. Morgan (1982), 'Max Gluckman and the Manchester shop-floor ethnographies', in R. Frankenberg, ed., *Custom and Conflict in British Society* (Manchester: Manchester University Press), pp. 140–65.

Flam, H. (1993), 'Fear, loyalty and greedy organizations', in S. Fineman, ed., *Emotions in Organizations* (London: Sage), pp. 58–75.

Foucault, M. (1977), *Discipline and Punish* (London: Allen & Unwin).

Friedman, A. L. (1977), *Industry and Labour* (London: Macmillan).

Giddens, A. (1979), *Central Problems in Social Theory* (London: Macmillan).

Goffman, E. (1959), *The Presentation of Self in Everyday Life* (Harmondsworth: Penguin).

Goffman, E. (1968), *Asylums* (Harmondsworth: Penguin).

Goffman, E. (1961), *Encounters* (Harmondsworth: Penguin).

Gouldner, A. W. (1954), *Patterns of Industrial Bureaucracy* (New York: Free Press).

Grey, C. (1993), 'A helping hand: self-discipline and management control', delivered at the 11th Annual Labour Process Conference, Blackpool, March.

Henriques, J., W. Hollway, C. Unwin, C. Vein and V. Walkderdine, (1984), *Changing the Subject* (London: Methuen).

Hirschman, A. O. (1970), *Exit, Voice and Loyalty* (Cambridge, MA: Harvard University Press).

Hyman, R. (1987), 'Strategy or structure? Capital, labour and control', *Work, Employment and Society*, vol. 1, no. 1, pp. 25–55.

Hyman, R. (1989), *Strikes* (London: Macmillan).

Jermier, J. (1988), 'Sabotage at work: the rational view', in N. DiTomaso and S. Bacharach, eds, *Research in the Sociology of Organisations*, vol. 6 (Greenwich, CT: JAI Publications), pp. 101–34.

Klein, J. (1964), *The Study of Groups* (London: Routledge & Kegan Paul).

Knights, D. (1990), 'Subjectivity, power and the labour process', in D. Knights and H. Willmott, eds, *Labour Process Theory* (London: Macmillan), pp. 297–335.

Knights, D. and D. L. Collinson, (1985), 'Redesigning work on the shopfloor: a question of control or consent?', in D. Knights, H. Willmott and D. Collinson, eds, *Job Redesign* (Aldershot: Gower), pp. 197–226.

Knights, D. and D. Collinson (1987), 'Disciplining the shopfloor: a comparison of the disciplinary effects of managerial and financial accounting', *Accounting, Organisations and Society*, vol. 12, no. 5, pp. 457–77.

Knights, D. and A. J. Sturdy (1990), 'New technology and the self-disciplined worker in insurance', in I. Varcoe, M. McNeil and S. Yearly, eds, *Deciphering Science and Technology* (London: Macmillan), pp. 126–54.

Kondo, D. (1990), *Crafting Selves: Power, Discourse and Identity in a Japanese Factory* (Chicago: Chicago University Press).

Kotter, J. P. and L. A. Schlesinger (1979), 'Choosing strategies for change', *Harvard Business Review*, March/April.

Kreitner, R. (1986), *Management* (Boston: Houghton Mifflin).

Kusterer, K. (1978), *Know How on the Job* (Boulder: Westview Press).

Lazega, E. (1992), *Micropolitics of Knowledge: Communication and Indirect Control in Workgroups* (New York: Walter de Gruyter).

Levi, P. (1987a), *If This is a Man* (London: Abacus).

Levi, P. (1987b), *If Not Now, When?* (London: Abacus).

Lewin, K. (1951), *Field Theory: Social Science* (New York: Harper & Row).

Linstead, S. (1985), 'Breaking the purity rule: industrial sabotage and the symbolic process', *Personnel Review*, vol. 14, no. 3, pp. 12–19.

Littler, C. R. (1982), *The Development of the Labour Process in Capitalist Societies* (London: Heinemann).

Littler, C. R. (1990), 'The labour process debate: a theoretical review 1974–1988', in D. Knights and H. Willmott, eds, *Labour Process Theory* (London: Macmillan), pp. 46–94.

Lupton, T. (1963), *On the Shopfloor* (Oxford: Pergamon).

McBarnet, D., S. Weston, and C. Whelan (1993), 'Adversary accounting: strategic uses of financial information by capital and labour', *Accounting, Organizations and Society*, vol. 18, no. 1, pp. 81–100.

Madeley, J. (1986), 'Whistle-blower paid high price', in P. J. Frost, V. F. Mitchell and W. R. Nord, eds, *Organisational Reality: Reports from the Firing Line* (Glenview, IL: Scott, Foresman & Company), pp. 228–30.

Mann, M. (1986), *The Sources of Social Power*, vol. 1: *A History of Power from the Beginning to A.D. 1760*, (Cambridge: Cambridge University Press).

Manwaring, T. and S. Wood (1985), 'The ghost in the labour process', in D. Knights, H. Willmott and D. Collinson, eds, *Job Redesign* (Aldershot: Gower), pp. 171–98.

Mars, G. (1982), *Cheats at Work* (London: Allen & Unwin).

Martin, J. (1990), 'Deconstructing organizational taboos: the suppression of gender conflict in organizations', *Organization Science*, vol. 1, no. 4, pp. 339–59.

Mayo, E. (1933), *The Human Problems of an Industrial Civilization* (New York: Macmillan).

Mills, A. J. and J. J. Murgatroyd (1991), *Organisational Rules: A Framework for Understanding Organisational Action* (Milton Keynes: Open University Press).

Mills, C. W. (1940), 'Situated actions and vocabularies of motive', *American Sociological Review*, vol. 5, pp. 904–13.

Mitchell, T. (1990), 'Everyday metaphors of power', *Theory and Society*, vol. 19, no. 5, pp. 545–78.

Nichols, T. and H. Beynon (1977), *Living with Capitalism* (London: Routledge & Kegan Paul).

Phillips, A. and B. Taylor (1980), 'Sex and skill: notes towards a feminist economics', *Feminist Review*, vol. 6, pp. 79–83.

Plant, R. (1987), *Managing Change and Making it Stick* (London: Fontana).

Polanyi, M. and H. Prosch (1975), *Meaning* (Chicago: Chicago University Press).

Ramsay, H. and N. Howarth (1989), 'Managing the multinationals: the emerging theory of the multinational enterprise and its implications for labour resistance', in S. R. Clegg, ed., *Organisation Theory and Class Analysis* (Berlin: Walter de Gruyter), pp. 275–97.

Rose, N. (1989), *Governing the Soul* (London: Routledge).

Roy, D. (1952), 'Quota restriction and goldbricking in a machine shop', *American Journal of Sociology*, vol. 57, no. 5, pp. 427–42.

Scott, J. C. (1985), *Weapons of the Weak: Everyday Forms of Peasant Resistance* (New Haven: Yale University Press).

Scott, J. C. (1990), *Domination and the Arts of Resistance: Hidden Transcripts* (New Haven: Yale University Press).

Sennett, R. (1980), *Authority* (London: Secker & Warburg).

Sennett, R. and J. Cobb (1977), *The Hidden Injuries of Class* (Cambridge: Cambridge University Press).

Sewell, G. and B. Wilkinson (1992), ' "Someone to watch over me": surveillance, discipline and the just-in-time labour process', *Sociology*, vol. 26, no. 2, pp. 271–89.

Sprouse, M., ed. (1992), *Sabotage in the American Workplace* (San Francisco: Pressure Drop Press).

Stallybrass, P. and A. White (1986), *The Politics and Poetics of Transgression* (London: Methuen).

Storey, J. (1985), 'The means of management control', *Sociology*, vol. 19, no. 2, pp. 193–211.

Sturdy, A., D. Knights, and H. Willmott, eds (1992), *Skill and Consent* (London: Routledge).

Taylor, F. (1947), *Scientific Management* (New York: Harper & Row).

Taylor, L. and P. Walton (1971), 'Industrial sabotage: motives and meanings', in S. Cohen, ed., *Images of Deviance* (Harmondsworth: Penguin), pp. 219–45.

Thompson, P. (1990), 'Crawling from the wreckage: the labour process and the politics of production', in D. Knights and H. Willmott, eds, *Labour Process Theory* (London: Macmillan), pp. 95–124.

Thompson, P. and E. Bannon (1985), *Working the System: The Shop Floor and New Technology* (London: Pluto Press).

Walby, S. (1986), *Patriarchy at Work* (Cambridge: Polity Press).

Walby, S. (1990), 'Theorising patriarchy', *Sociology*, vol. 23, no. 2, pp. 213–34.

Walker, C. R. and R. H. Guest (1952), *The Man on the Assembly Line* (Cambridge, MA: Harvard University Press).

Willis, P. E. (1977), *Learning to Labour* (London: Saxon House).

Willis, P. E. (1980), 'Shopfloor culture, masculinity and the wage form', in J. Clarke, C. Critcher and R. Johnson, eds, *Working Class Culture* (London: Hutchinson), pp. 185–98.

Willmott, H. (1990), 'Subjectivity and the dialectics of praxis: opening up the core of labour process analysis', in D. Knights and H. Willmott, eds, *Labour Process Theory* (London: Macmillan), pp. 336–78.

Willmott, H. (1993), 'Strength is ignorance; slavery is freedom: managing culture in modern organizations', *Journal of Management Studies*, vol. 30, no. 4, pp. 215–552.

Zuboff, S. (1988), *In the Age of the Smart Machine* (New York: Basic Books).

Part IV

After Class

Introduction

Part IV of the book moves from scepticism about the prevalence of consensus to scepticism about the predominance of class. Until the 1970s most studies of work were wholly focused on particular forms of identity – in effect working-class men, especially those working in factories. Since that time a much greater degree of interest and research has switched to the two major alternative constructions of identity: ethnicity and gender, but also to the very notion of identity itself. This should not be taken as the exit sign for social class, for without doubt social class remains an important element of identity. For instance, the disposable income for the median household in the UK is around £250 per week. Yet at the same time Sam Chishol, formerly of BskyB, earned around £150,000 per week as the UK's highest paid director. Nor is he alone, for forty-nine directors of the country's 350 largest companies received more than a million pounds in pay and bonuses in 1998, with the best paid director in each of the FTSE 100 companies receiving an average of £800,000 a year (Buckingham 1998: 21). Such inequalities prompted the General Secretary of the Communication Workers' Union, Derek Hodgson, to call such 'over-paid' bosses 'greedy bastards' (quoted in the *Guardian*, 19 September 1998). However, it is worth pondering here on the disparity between the 'greed' of the bosses and the 'value for money' earned by pop stars and football players – the disparity between the rich and the poor may be identical, but the perception of the justice of that disparity can often be markedly divergent.

Against this background the inequalities of social class also persist in health – for example the 'unskilled' are almost five times more likely to die of lung cancer and almost three times more likely to suffer coronary heart disease than the 'professional' class (Boseley 1998: 3).

But there is a strong sense of *déjà vu* in all this for sociologists in particular have been unveiling such gross disparities of wealth, health and influence for generations. Thus it is not because social class is irrelevant that I have chosen not to concentrate upon it, but rather that we should take social class as a given, an aspect of identity and life already well recorded and discussed. What remains is to consider what else is important and why.

If the construction of employee identity is an increasing concern for employers is there any evidence that ethnic identity is decreasingly relevant for work purposes? Well, not in Britain, at least not for most non-whites. The reading by Tariq Modood reviews the data and suggests that while some progress has been made, especially by Chinese and African Asians, there is little evidence that the life-chances of Pakistanis and Bangladeshis have improved over the last few decades relative to the white population, while marginal progress has been achieved by Indians and Caribbeans.* However, the precise link between ethnic identity – or 'race' – and work experiences is also complicated by the links to gender, culture and religion. Moreover, most young people (eighteen- to twenty-four-year-olds) in Britain appear to think that race relations will worsen over the next five years, and this is noticeably so for young black people (Ward 1998: 4).

Modood considers the extent to which ethnic minorities are under-represented in the highest occupational categories and over-represented among manual work, but also how different groups fare quite differently in the labour market, with Chinese men and women exceeding the job levels of white men while Caribbean, Pakistani and Bangladeshi men come off worst. The historical entry point of many minorities into the labour force still prevails in particular areas, with many Caribbean men undertaking shift-work in the public sector, and few of any minority in a supervisory position over whites. And while Bangladeshi, and to a lesser extent Chinese, men are disproportionately at work in the catering industry, the largest single occupational grouping of minority women is of Caribbeans in the health services.

Earnings are similarly skewed, with Chinese male earnings identical with white males and Bangladeshi earnings the lowest of any male group. This pattern is also reflected among female earnings, to the extent that Pakistani and Bangladeshi women earn the lowest of all, but not with regard to any other group since the rest earn more than white women – though at a lower rate than their male equivalents. And the most significant way that employed minorities have been able to increase their earnings has been education. In effect, and to quote Tony Blair out of context, the three most important things are: education, education, education.

One manifestation of the general position of minorities in Britain is their high degree of self-employment, with the exceptions of Caribbeans and Bangladeshis, and also the distribution of this work, with a large proportion in retail or catering compared with the white self-employment strongholds in construction, agriculture and manufacturing. But exactly what self-employment entails depends, among other things, on the particular group. For example, Caribbeans have a low rate of self-employment but relatively high rewards, while the opposite is true for Pakistanis, though again we should beware of assuming that ethnic group determines work – it simply does not. Nevertheless, Modood concludes that the least disadvantaged male minorities are the Chinese and African Asians, while the most disadvantaged are the Pakistanis and Bangladeshis; somewhere between these two extremes lie the Indians and Caribbeans. For minority women the positions are

---

* This is a radically cut version of Modood's original work: material covering unemployment and trade unions has been excluded.

similar, though Caribbean women are relatively less disadvantaged compared with Caribbean men. Precisely why these divisions and positions exist is still subject to much debate, though it seems clear that the history of British colonialism, and the production and reproduction of discrete stereotypes by the white population rooted in racial, cultural and religious factors, bears a significant responsibility – as does the economic restructuring that continuously alters the demand for labour.

Since much of that restructuring has eliminated many of the manual and manufacturing jobs that certain groups have historically depended on, we should not be surprised to see some changes in their relative fortunes, and in theory such developments should have boosted the position of women at all levels of work. To some extent this is the case, for women now comprise almost half the workforce in Britain and, to some extent, women have entered the ranks of management in much greater numbers. From some points of view, the assumption that women are essentially different from men – and that difference facilitates certain gendered tendencies in managerial style – proceeds to claim not just that women managers are different but they are more suitable than men for running contemporary organizations that have moved away from command and control management systems common in the nineteenth and twentieth centuries. If that is the case then we have difficulty in explaining the relative dearth of women at the most senior levels of management. For example, in 1999 there were only two female CEOs leading Fortune 500 companies and only eighty-three of the top 2267 top corporate officers in the USA were women. And while women comprised 11 per cent of board seats in the Fortune 500 companies, only 1 per cent of the total were women of colour. In the UK just under 4 per cent of directors are women and while women have made progress at the lower and middle management levels there is precious little evidence of them making further inroads at the very top. It is not for want of trying or education that progress is so limited: in 1998 almost 60 per cent of law students in the UK were women but the vast majority of senior legal professionals remain men. It is not that women fail to secure promotion because of discrimination: as Booth et al. (1998) suggest, women are receiving more promotions than men in general, but they still receive lower salaries even after promotion, primarily because they are unable to exploit the external labour market to secure subsequent salary increases in the way that men do. In effect, it is women's inability to get beyond the 'sticky floor' of initial promotion that constrains them, rather than the 'glass ceiling' that prevents them securing promotion in the first place. Indeed, between 1988 and 1998 the gap between the full-time wages of men and women actually widened.

Judy Wajcman's reading confronts the assumption that it is the gendered differences that explain the gap head on, and she contends that there is no 'female' management style because the similarities between male and female managers far outweigh the differences between them. Wajcman suggests that there is no significant difference between successful male and female managers, despite the contrary assertion by the likes of Rosener (1990) among others. This is not to say that the respondents to her questionnaire are identical; on the contrary, the women managers were more likely to be single, divorced or separated and less likely to have children than their male counterparts. However, in terms of responsibilities for childcare, the opposite was the case, with almost all the women who had children being primarily responsible for their care, while only 15 per cent of men were similarly responsible. Yet there were only marginal differences in terms of the hours spent at work, while women were slightly more concerned with power and slightly less motivated by money than men. The attitude of male and female managers to each other was also only marginally gendered: while women were far more committed to the view that women had 'positive skills' to bring to the workplace, few of either gender preferred to work for a female manager. It might seem paradoxical, then, to note that most of the managers – of both genders – described their own management styles in terms of the consultative and people-oriented styles deemed appropriate to the 1990s and the twenty-first century – but also allegedly closer to female than male styles. Yet, as Wacjman makes clear, what people say about themselves and their organizations may not be how they are perceived by others, and when analysed a little more closely it seems that the preferred styles of men and their organizations are rather different from those espoused in the corporate rhetoric. In sum, although Wacjman suggests that her sample of successful female managers was very close in style to that of male managers, this does not mean that management is gender-neutral. On the contrary, since management is a male-dominated work arena, success for all is still over-dependent upon displaying a male-oriented management style. Furthermore, even if a 'female management' style was valued, there is nothing to prevent men from monopolizing it and adding such an approach to their existing 'male' model, thus further inhibiting the quest for gender equality.

9   Race and Ethnicity

Employment

TARIQ MODOOD

Introduction

The [...] migration to Britain from the Caribbean and the Asian subcontinent [after the Second World War], while based upon imperial ties, was very much driven by economic imperatives. The rebuilding of the war-shattered economy created a demand for labour that could not be satisfied by the British population alone. The demand was particularly acute in the National Health Service, in public transport and in many sectors of manufacturing; qualified and unqualified labour, especially young single men, were invited from the Caribbean and the subcontinent to fill the vacancies. Early studies of these migrants in the British economy show that, regardless of their social origins and qualification levels, Caribbean and Asian people were confined very largely to low-paid manual work. Racial discrimination in recruitment was widespread, even after being outlawed (Daniel 1968; Smith 1977).

The predecessor to [this] survey, undertaken in 1982, found that, while some progress in relative job levels and earnings among these non-white groups had occurred, they were suffering disproportionately from high levels of unemployment, despite some groups participating in the burgeoning self-employment (Brown 1984). Moreover, racial discrimination in the labour market seemed as prevalent if not as overt as before (Brown and Gay 1985). The Labour Force Surveys of the late 1980s (Jones 1993) and the 1991 Census (Ballard and Kalra 1994) confirmed the trends of the early 1980s: the minorities were upwardly mobile and expanding into self-employment, but had much higher levels of unemployment than whites. It was abundantly clear, however, that each of these conditions applied to some rather than all Caribbean and Asian ethnic groups. Economic differences between migrants have become more pronounced and better substantiated by statistical data than was the case [in 1982].

Yet the central thrust within the sociology of race has been to argue against claiming that too much has changed:

> Very few writers on race would dispute the facts of racial disadvantage, particularly in relation to economic disadvantage. The data on employment show migrants, particularly Black migrants, as well as the Black British population, to be at the bottom of the occupational and income scale. Despite a number of differences between various groups, such as Asians and African-Caribbeans and between men and women, there exists none the less a class distribution effect. (Anthias and Yuval-Davis 1992: 62)

There has been increasing emphasis on indirect forms of discrimination, and it has been argued that the processes of racial discrimination in employment have become so routine and subtle as to be 'invisible' even to those engaged in discriminating practices (Wrench and Solomos, eds, 1993: 159). Others, however, have denied that non-white people could any longer be analysed as a unitary class (Miles 1987). This opens the way for new plural analyses of race, and linkages between race and other bases of discrimination, such as gender (Anthias and Yuval-Davis 1992; Bhavnani 1994), and culture and religion (Modood 1992) have been offered to explain facets of the new ethnic diversity.

In a related way it has been argued that racial exclusion in British society works in a different way regarding Caribbeans and South Asians (Cross 1989, 1994). Alternatively, and in a more radical vein, it has been argued that the British [...] economy is more open and meritocratic than analysts sometimes assume, and that 'race' is of declining salience in explaining opportunities and outcomes in employment (Iganski and Payne 1996). In contrast, work has been done to show that despite a long-term trend in the reduction of differences in job-levels achieved, there is a more or less constant 'ethnic penalty' paid by non-white people measured in terms of the jobs that similarly qualified people achieve (Heath and McMahon 1995). That is to say, ethnic minorities may be getting better jobs, but they are still doing so to a lesser extent than white people with the same qualifications. This sort of analysis, however, also reveals considerable diversity between minority groups, with some having a rate of success closer to whites than to other non-whites.

This [reading] present[s] the findings on employment. The length and complexity of the presentation are based on the belief that employment is at the centre of the issues of life-chances and equality, and also that the nature of the findings is not susceptible to simple black–white analysis, for the differences between the various minority groups are as important for analysis as the points of commonality. The long presentation is followed by a discussion of the implications for ideas such as racial disadvantage, ethnic penalty and differential racisms. In the 1970s and 1980s theorists sought to explain racial inequality; this survey makes clear that what needs to be explained are racial inequality and ethnic diversity. For insofar as there is a fundamental divide in employment by ethnicity, it is not a black–white divide, but a divide between whites, Chinese and African Asians on the one hand, and Bangladeshis and Pakistanis on the other, with Indians and Caribbeans in perhaps an intermediate position.

[...]

Employment

This section examines the distribution of the different ethnic groups between different types of employment. However, we need to bear in mind that the combination of low activity rates and high unemployment rates means that only about four in ten adult, non-retired Pakistani and Bangladeshi men have any form of paid employment. The figure for Caribbean men is about half. Nearly two-thirds of white men are in employment: a higher figure than that for Indians but slightly lower than the one for African Asians and the Chinese.

Generally women were less likely than men to be in paid employment, although the proportion for Caribbean women was the same as for Caribbean men. However, only 15 per cent of Pakistani and 8 per cent of Bangladeshi non-retired women were in paid employment. Although some of the sample sizes are rather small, we nevertheless need to remember that women from these groups who have jobs are unusual.

Type of work

Previous studies have found strong ethnic disparities in type and level of employment, with most of the minorities under-represented in the highest occupational categories. Except for African Asians and Caribbean women, minorities are over-represented in manual work. There has, however, also been evidence over time of a movement up the hierarchy, and from manual to non-manual work, in the workforce as a whole, but this has been more marked for ethnic minorities and for some groups in particular (Brown 1984: 175; Jones 1993: 82–4).

The definitions of what constitutes manual and non-manual work were drawn up in an era when there were clear differences between the two groups. Broadly, manual workers worked with their hands, mainly in manufacturing industry, mining and utilities, with some jobs in services, particularly local government. Few formal educational qualifications were required, and the work was often dirty. Non-manual workers typically worked in shops or offices, and needed formal educational qualifications, at least to school-leaving level. They worked in clean environments and wore either their own clothes or staff uniform. However, in a service economy with a high technology manufacturing sector, these simple categories become less helpful. For example, shelf stackers in supermarkets are non-manual workers, while technicians educated to HND level may be classified as manual workers. A young man with career aspirations in the 1990s would generally do better qualifying as an electrician than entering clerical work. This background should be borne in mind in the discussion that follows, since sample numbers do not allow detailed analysis by complex job categories. It also needs to be recalled that for women manual work is very much the exception in the economy as a whole. Most types of work traditionally done by women are non-manual. The main exceptions are cleaning, hairdressing and mechanized sewing.

Table 9.1 Job levels of men (base: male employees and self-employed)

column percentages

Socio-economic group	White	Caribbean	Indian	African Asian	Pakistani	Bangladeshi	Chinese
Prof./managers/ employers	30	14	25	30	19	18	46
Employers and managers (large establishments)	11	5	5	3	3	0	6
Employers and managers (small establishments)	11	4	11	14	12	16	23
Professional workers	8	6	9	14	4	2	17
Intermediate and junior non-manual	18	19	20	24	13	19	17
Skilled manual and foreman	36	39	31	30	46	7	14
Semi-skilled manual	11	22	16	12	18	53	12
Unskilled manual	3	6	5	2	3	3	5
Armed forces or not available	2	0	3	2	2	0	5
Non-manual	48	33	45	54	32	37	63
Manual	50	67	52	44	67	63	31
Weighted count	*789*	*365*	*349*	*296*	*182*	*61*	*127*
Unweighted count	*713*	*258*	*356*	*264*	*258*	*112*	*71*

Men

Our survey found that white men in work were quite evenly divided between non-manual and manual work and that the position of Indians and African Asians was similar (table 9.1), while two-thirds of Chinese men were in non-manual work. In contrast about two-thirds of Caribbeans, Pakistanis and Bangladeshis were in manual work.

The Caribbeans at 14 per cent had the lowest representation in the top category of professionals, managers and employers, while nearly half the Chinese men were in this category. Both whites and African Asians had around a third in this group, with Indians a little lower at a quarter. The proportion of most groups in the skilled manual or foreman category was between 30 and 40 per cent. For Pakistanis it was higher at nearly half the total, and for Bangladeshis and Chinese it was markedly lower, although the sample sizes were small, particularly for the former. All ethnic groups had very small proportions who were unskilled manual workers. The most striking differences were in the incidence of semi-skilled manual

Table 9.2 Proportions of male self-employed and employees, by two job levels

column percentages

	White	*South Asian/Chinese*
Employers and managers – small establishments		
Employees	55	30
Self-employed	45	70
Weighted count	*87*	*138*
Unweighted count	*76*	*136*
Skilled manual and foreman		
Employees	66	49
Self-employed	34	51
Weighted count	*283*	*304*
Unweighted count	*247*	*322*

work. Over half the Bangladeshi men in work were in semi-skilled manual work compared with one in five Caribbeans, one in six Indians and Pakistanis and one in ten whites, Chinese and African Asians.[1]

All the minorities were distinctly less likely than white men to be employers and managers of large establishments. Indeed, insofar as South Asians and Chinese were well represented in the broad professional, managerial and employers category it was significantly because of the contribution of self-employment. For table 9.2 shows that, while white employers and managers in small establishments were more likely to be employees than self-employed, these minorities were more than twice as likely to be self-employed. The fairly strong presence of ethnic minority men (except Bangladeshis and Chinese) in the top manual work category is also partly explained by a higher incidence of self-employment compared with whites.

Job levels were strongly related to the possession of academic qualifications, but not strictly so. Table 9.3 offers an analysis of job levels of male employees by highest British qualification. As self-employment is often far less determined by formal entry criteria or the possession of qualifications, the self-employed are excluded from the analysis.[2] Even using rather broad qualification levels, we might expect a similar pattern between whites and ethnic minorities and between minorities. However, this expectation is only partially fulfilled. For example, 40 per cent of whites and African Asians with A-levels or a higher qualification were in the top non-manual category, as were over half the Chinese. However, only a third of the Indians and Pakistanis, and only a fifth of the Caribbeans with A-levels or above were in the top occupational category. A much higher proportion of South Asian men than white men with these qualifications were in the lower non-manual category. Nearly half of the highest qualified Caribbean men were in manual work compared with a third of the whites and a fifth of the others. However, in interpreting these findings we need to bear in mind the caveat that the

TARIQ MODOOD

Table 9.3 Job levels of male employees, by highest British qualification (base: male employees excluding self-employed)

column percentages

	White	Caribbean	Indian	African Asian	Pakistani/ Bangladeshi	Chinese
% in professional, managerial and employers category						
A-level or higher	40 (12)[1]	15 (18)	30 (16)	40 (26)	34 (22)	61 (36)
O-level/CSE/other	21	15	21	17	11	–
No qualification	11	2	10	13	3	9
% in other non-manual category						
A-level or higher	24	29	43	34	36	20
O-level/CSE/other	26	25	37	37	26	62
No qualification	12	2	13	24	11	22
% in skilled manual category						
A-level or higher	27	36	12	20	15	9
O-level/CSE/other	28	37	18	11	9	–
No qualification	43	37	33	31	34	–
% in semi-skilled and unskilled manual category						
A-level or higher	9	20	15	6	16	10
O-level/CSE/other	25	23	24	35	54	38
No qualification	33	60	44	32	51	68
Weighted count	*612*	*314*	*241*	*205*	*167*	*83*
Unweighted count	*561*	*219*	*262*	*189*	*266*	*48*

1 The figures in parentheses apply to professional workers.

skilled manual category in particular includes an increasing proportion of jobs requiring relatively high-level qualifications. Nonetheless, one in five Caribbean men with higher qualifications were in unskilled or semi-skilled manual jobs, as were one in six Indians, Pakistanis and Bangladeshis.

The distribution of men with O-level or equivalent qualifications across types of jobs also shows some variation, albeit less than at the higher qualifications level. Since a reasonable proportion of both the other non-manual and the skilled manual categories will require qualifications at this level, the evidence for under-use of qualifications is likely to be found at semi-skilled and unskilled manual levels. Around a quarter of whites, Indians and Caribbeans with these qualifications had semi-skilled or unskilled jobs, as did around a third of Chinese and African Asians. The most marked difference occurred with the Pakistanis/ Bangladeshis, where more than half had semi-skilled jobs.

There were differences between the groups in the division of those educated to O-level standard between skilled manual work and intermediate and junior non-manual work. The whites were evenly divided. The Caribbeans had over a third in the skilled manual and only a quarter in the other non-manual category. The Chinese (on a small sample) had none in the skilled manual category and nearly two-thirds in the other non-manual. All the South Asian groups had twice the proportion in other non-manual work compared with skilled manual, although the Pakistani/Bangladeshi proportion was lower than for the other groups because of their concentration in semi-skilled manual work.

Ethnic minority men with higher qualifications were more likely than their white peers to be professionals. This could reflect differential career preferences, or that it is easier for ethnic minorities to get a return on their qualifications where higher qualifications are more likely to be a necessary part of a job description. It also seems to be the case that there is a greater propensity among qualified South Asian and Chinese men for non-manual over manual work compared with Caribbeans and whites. For example, more than a third of white men with higher qualifications were in manual work but a quarter or less of Chinese, African Asians and Indians. The latter groups, where they do not achieve employment in the top non-manual category, are more likely to have lower level non-manual work.

Women

Turning to women, it is immediately apparent from table 9.4 that far fewer women than men were in the top professional, managerial and employer category. Overall the proportion was around half that of men. The variation across groups was, however, similar to that of the men. Chinese women, at 30 per cent, were almost twice as likely as whites to be in this category. Just over one in ten of all the South Asian women in employment, but only one in twenty Caribbeans were in the top occupational group.[3] Unlike men, however, a large majority of women in all groups were in non-manual work, ranging from the Chinese (76 per cent) to the Indians (58 per cent). This means that more than half of working women in each ethnic group were in intermediate or junior non-manual work, rising to nearly two out of three for Caribbean and African Asian women. This reflects the economy-wide concentration of women in clerical/secretarial and sales occupations.

For women, as with men, the Pakistani and Indian women's presence in the top non-manual work category was strongly influenced by self-employment, as the figures in parentheses in table 9.4 reveal. Excluding the self-employed, only around 6 per cent of Pakistani and Indian women were in the top non-manual category, less than the African Asians (10 per cent) and much less than white (15 per cent) and Chinese (25 per cent) women. On the other hand, the overwhelming majority of women of all groups who were in skilled manual work were self-employed. Apart from the top non-manual category and its mix between employees and self-employed, the differences in job levels between women of different ethnic origins were considerably less than the differences among men, and there was not the division between minorities. This suggests that gender divisions in the labour market may be stronger and more deeply rooted than differences due to race and ethnicity.

Table 9.4 Job levels of women in work (base: female employees and self-employed)

column percentages

	White	*Caribbean*	*Indian*	*African Asian*	*Pakistani*	*Chinese*
Professional, managerial and employers	16 (15)[1]	5 (5)	11 (7)	12 (10)	12 (6)	30 (25)
Intermediate non-manual	21	28	14	14	29	23
Junior non-manual	33	36	33	49	23	23
Skilled manual and foreman	7 (2)	4 (2)	11 (3)	7 (3)	9 (3)	13 (–)
Semi-skilled manual	18	20	27	16	22	9
Unskilled manual	4	6	4	1	4	2
Armed forces/ inadequately described/not stated	0	1	1	1	0	0
Non-manual	70	69	58	75	64	76
Manual	29	30	42	24	35	24
Weighted count	*734*	*452*	*275*	*196*	*60*	*120*
Unweighted count	*696*	*336*	*260*	*164*	*64*	*63*

1 The figures in parentheses are exclusive of self-employed.

Nevertheless, both men and women in nearly all the minority groups shared one fundamental difference from white men and women. They were much less likely to be in the top occupational category, and when they were, they were much less likely to work in large establishments. The explanations for this are likely to be complex. There may be some direct discrimination, but part of the explanation could lie in the continued importance of social-educational networks associated with public schools and Oxbridge in the filling of higher-level jobs.

[O]ne significant difference between the sexes is the much larger number of women in part-time work, though here too the difference was not just one of gender but one of ethnicity too. These differences persist when job levels are allowed for. Table 9.5 shows the percentage of women in part-time work. It shows that over a third of white women in non-manual jobs and over half in manual jobs were working less than thirty hours a week. The proportion of Caribbean women working part-time was around half that of white women in each type of job. Around a quarter of South Asian women in all occupational groups were part-time.

Table 9.5 Female employees who work part-time, by job levels (base: women employees, excluding self-employed)

cell percentages

	White	Caribbean	South Asian
Non-manual	36	17	26
Senior and intermediate	28	14	27
Junior	45	19	25
Manual	55	35	26
Weighted count	*1100*	*388*	*336*
Unweighted count	*1049*	*277*	*312*

Table 9.6 Job levels of female employees, by highest British qualification (excluding self-employed)

column percentages

	White	Caribbean	Indian	African Asian	Pakistani	Chinese
% in professional, managerial and employers category						
A-level or higher	24 (4)[1]	11 (1)	12 (6)	19 (12)	11 (6)	32 (26)
O-level/CSE/other	8	10	6	9	–	14
No qualification	10	–	4	1	–	17
% in other non-manual category						
A-level or higher	60	75	77	77	81	63
O-level/CSE/other	66	74	74	79	58	67
No qualification	44	36	27	39	19	45
% in skilled manual category						
A-level or higher	–	1	4	5	3	–
O-level/CSE/other	2	2	2	5	8	–
No qualification	6	6	3	5	3	–
% in semi-skilled and unskilled manual category						
A-level or higher	17	12	7	–	5	5
O-level/CSE/other	25	23	18	6	34	19
No qualification	39	59	65	54	78	38
Weighted count	*669*	*432*	*233*	*178*	*57*	*88*
Unweighted count	*633*	*322*	*226*	*149*	*66*	*48*

1 The figures in parentheses apply to professional workers.

The impact of qualifications is shown in table 9.6. White and Chinese women had a broadly similar occupational pattern with about a quarter of those qualified to A-level or above in the professional, managerial and employer category;

African Asians were not far behind, at one in five. For all the other groups the proportion was closer to one in ten. As with the men, a much larger proportion of the highest qualified ethnic minorities (excluding Caribbeans) in the top jobs category, when compared with whites, were professionals rather than managers. At the other extreme, around one in six whites with A-levels or higher qualifications was in semi-skilled or unskilled manual work. This was much higher than for any other group. The Caribbeans, with one in nine, were the closest. For all other groups the proportion was closer to one in twenty. This may reflect different participation decisions. Qualified South Asian women with poor job prospects may choose to remain inactive rather than take unskilled work.[4]

With the exception of Pakistanis, more than three-quarters of employed women from minority groups with O-levels were in intermediate or junior non-manual work. Pakistani women had the smallest proportion of women without qualifications in non-manual work, and the highest proportion with O-levels in semi-skilled manual work. In this instance their pattern resembles that of their male counterparts rather than other women (see table 9.3).

Hours worked, shifts worked and supervision

Among those who worked more than thirty hours a week, there was not much difference in the hours worked by different job levels, except that the highest weekly hours were declared by men and women in the top non-manual category. This is consistent with the general pattern in the Labour Force Survey. Nor were there significant differences between the South Asian groups. Men work about five hours more than women on average, and whites work slightly more than the minorities (figure 9.1). Interestingly, the hours worked by white men and women are the same as they were in 1982. Among Caribbean men there has been an increase of nearly an hour, and among Caribbean women and South Asian men and women there has been a decrease of almost two hours (Brown 1984: 211). The gap between white and ethnic minority men was greater in the public sector.

There has been a relative decline in the proportion of South Asians doing shift-work. Earlier surveys found that Caribbeans and South Asians were much more likely to be doing shifts than white workers. The position in 1994 was that, while Caribbean men were still much more likely to be doing shift-work than whites, this was no longer true of South Asian men, and South Asian women were least likely to be working shifts (figure 9.1). This may be because many jobs, such as those in the textile industry, which involved shift-work, and in which Pakistani men were concentrated, disappeared during the 1980s, or it may be because of the increased non-manual profile of South Asians, especially Indians and African Asians – or both.

In our survey shift-work was more common among all men, and among Caribbean women, in the public sector. Shift-working is, of course, common in a number of public sector industries, most notably the health service, the emergency services and public transport. The PSI analysis of the Labour Force Survey data for 1988–90 found that the likelihood of ethnic minorities being engaged in

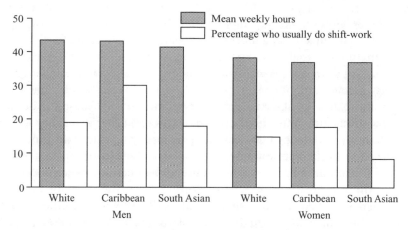

Figure 9.1 Hours and shift-work of full-time employees

Table 9.7 Supervisors as a proportion of employees, by job type (excluding self-employed)

cell percentages

	White	Caribbean	Indian	African Asia	Pakistani/ Bangladeshi	Chinese	All ethnic minorities
Non-manual							
Men	68	47	47	53	43	61	50
Women	37	37	28	30	(27)	(40)	34
Manual							
Men	28	28	15	17	12	*	20
Women	11	21	4	(6)	*	*	12
All							
Men	49	34	30	37	22	46	33
Women	30	33	18	24	18	34	27
Weighted count							
Men	*623*	*315*	*242*	*207*	*168*	*90*	*1022*
Women	*672*	*439*	*237*	*180*	*58*	*88*	*1001*
Unweighted count							
Men	*569*	*220*	*263*	*192*	*268*	*51*	*994*
Women	*636*	*326*	*228*	*151*	*67*	*48*	*820*

*indicates that the cell size is too small; if the cell size approaches 40, the figure is given in parentheses.

shift-work declines sharply the younger the workers (Jones 1993: 74). We found in this survey that sixteen- to thirty-four-year-old Caribbean men, unlike South Asians, were just as likely to be doing shift-work as their elders; younger Caribbean women, however, were much less likely to do shift-work than their elders.

Another measure of job level is the extent to which people have supervisory responsibilities and whom they supervise. Table 9.7 shows that those in non-manual jobs were much more likely to supervise others than those in manual jobs, and that within each of these categories men were much more likely to be supervisors than women. This was true for all groups. There were, however, group differences. Ethnic minority male non-manual employees (except the Chinese) were only two-thirds as likely to supervise as white men. Among male manual workers there was little difference between whites and Caribbeans, but in varying degrees all the Asian groups were less likely to supervise, with Pakistanis/Bangladeshis the least likely. Interestingly, taking only those working in the private sector, the Caribbean manual workers were more likely to be supervisors than any other ethnic group.

Among female employees the Chinese and Caribbeans were a little more likely to be supervisors than whites, and the South Asians were much less likely to be and had very little likelihood of supervising in manual work. Caribbean women in manual work, on the other hand, were twice as likely as white female manual workers to be in supervisory posts. The Caribbeans were the only group in which, taking all employees, women were as likely to supervise as men. This was explained by their strong presence in the public sector, where all women were more likely to have supervisory responsibilities.

Industry

About a third of white men work in manufacturing industries. This is about the same as Caribbeans, Indians and African Asians, though this figure is exceeded by Pakistanis. The Bangladeshi and Chinese, on the other hand, have a much lower representation in manufacturing (table 9.8). Caribbean and Indian men are disproportionately concentrated in engineering, including the motor industry. One in three of all Pakistani male employees is in other manufacturing (including one in ten in textiles). More than half of Bangladeshi men work in hotels and catering, as do a quarter of the Chinese. Most of the minority groups have a much larger presence in transport and communication than whites, but only the African Asians do so in retailing. More than one in eight of white men is in the financial sector, and this is matched or exceeded by African Asians and Indians.

Our findings are broadly consistent with the PSI analysis of the Labour Force Survey of the late 1980s, although there has been a further decline in manufacturing and an increase in financial services (Jones 1993: table 4.8; cf. OPCS 1994: table 14).[5] The situation, then, at this broad-brush level of analysis, is that different minority groups have quite distinct industrial distributions. None is quite like any other or akin to white males. Moreover, not only does each minority have some economic sectors in which it is particularly concentrated, but each has a more restricted distribution than do white men, although the distribution of Caribbean men is fairly close to that of white men.

214

Table 9.8 Male employees, by industry (excluding self- employed)

column percentages

	White	Caribbean	Indian	African Asian	Pakistani	Bangladeshi	Chinese
Agriculture, forestry, fishing, energy and water supply	5	0	0	1	1	0	0
Extraction of minerals, metal manufacture	5	9	4	3	3	0	0
Metal goods, engineering and vehicles	11	13	12	6	12	2	2
Other manufacturing	16	14	19	20	30	11	10
Construction	6	7	7	3	1	2	3
Retail distribution	9	6	8	23	11	6	15
Hotels and catering	2	3	2	2	6	60	23
Transport and communication	9	17	18	13	15	0	5
Banking and finance	14	5	13	17	5	1	8
Public administration	9	10	5	4	2	4	5
Education	4	4	3	2	5	1	10
Hospitals	4	5	3	4	2	2	10
Other services	6	7	8	4	8	11	7
Weighted count	*601*	*310*	*239*	*206*	*117*	*50*	*90*
Unweighted count	*552*	*216*	*260*	*190*	*172*	*93*	*51*

Bangladeshis show the most extreme pattern, being concentrated in just one sector, catering. This, combined with their manual work profile, means that more than half of all employed Bangladeshi men have just one occupation: waiting and kitchen work in restaurants. As there is a limit to the availability of these jobs, especially in a given area, this occupational segregation helps to explain the very high levels of Bangladeshi unemployment.

There is, however, only one industrial sector in which all minority groups are consistently under-represented. That is the composite category of agriculture, forestry, fishing, energy and water supply. It is a relatively small sector of the economy, accounting for only 5 per cent of all male employees, but it is one in which ethnic minority men are virtually absent.

Compared with white men, white women are particularly concentrated in retail, medical care and education. Women generally have a much smaller

Table 9.9   Female employees, by industry (excluding self-employed)

column percentages

	White	Caribbean	Indian	African Asian	Pakistani	Chinese
Agriculture, forestry, fishing, energy and water supply	1	0	0	3	0	0
Extraction of minerals, metal manufacture	0	1	1	1	0	0
Metal goods, engineering and vehicles	2	2	5	3	0	5
Other manufacturing	6	4	21	14	20	11
Construction	1	0	0	2	0	0
Retail distribution	17	6	13	22	11	4
Hotels and catering	5	4	4	2	9	19
Transport and communication	3	4	5	9	2	3
Banking and finance	15	9	11	15	4	13
Public administration	7	15	12	7	14	6
Education	13	9	9	4	18	0
Hospitals	21	39	12	13	8	30
Other services	8	7	6	4	14	9
Weighted count	*663*	*434*	*235*	*180*	*51*	*88*
Unweighted count	*627*	*322*	*226*	*151*	*55*	*47*

presence in manufacturing, though South Asian women, especially Indians, work in manufacture much more so than whites and Caribbeans (table 9.9). A fifth of Indian and Pakistani women employees are in other manufacturing (half of them in clothing and footwear). Women from most groups are found in large numbers in retail and in finance, though ethnic minorities, except the African Asians, less so than whties.

Four out of ten Caribbean women work in hospitals and medical care, double the proportion of white women. This helps to explain the high level of shift-working noted earlier. They are also, with Pakistanis and Indians, twice as numerous as whites in public administration. While women from all groups except the Chinese had a higher proportion than men working in education, Pakistani women had the highest proportion there. This, however, was not the finding of the PSI analysis of the Labour Force Survey (Jones 1993: table 4.9). That showed few Pakistani women working in education and strongly suggests that our small sample may be biased, and probably under-represents Pakistani women in 'other manufacturing' (primarily clothing and footwear) and in retail. Additionally, compared with that analysis and the 1991 Census, our survey has a much larger proportion of women from all ethnic groups working in hospitals and fewer in engineering.

Table 9.10 Proportion of full-time employees in the public
sector

cell percentages

	White	Caribbean	South Asian
Men	26	33	27
Women	38	61	39
Weighted			
Men	*606*	*157*	*313*
Women	*364*	*171*	*145*
Unweighted			
Men	*554*	*103*	*359*
Women	*355*	*120*	*138*

The public sector, comprising central and local government, health authorities, nationalized industries and so on, has contracted as an employer in recent years, with the transfer of ownership and functions to the private sector. It nevertheless still accounts for about a third of those in employment. It is a particularly important source of employment for Caribbeans, as shown in table 9.10. This emphasizes the unusual employment pattern of Caribbean women, 61 per cent of whom work full time in the public sector, especially in health and local government. They are concentrated in intermediate non-manual jobs, including, particularly, nursing.

There were, however, a number of further interesting contrasts in relation to the public sector and ethnicity. For example, ethnic minority men in the public sector were more likely to be in non-manual work compared both with white men and with ethnic minority men in the private sector. Yet those in the private sector have a much better chance of being in the top non- manual category (table 9.11).

The disparities identified in table 9.11 apply with greater force to those who are employers and managers in large establishments, although the public sector is likely to have a bigger proportion of large employers. This is an interesting finding given the perception that it is the public sector, especially local government, that has taken the lead in implementing equal opportunity policies. This is not necessarily to say that equal opportunity measures have not been set up; rather, their effectiveness depends upon there being vacancies, and the contraction of the public sector may mean there have been insufficient vacancies, especially in high-level positions, to have a noticeable effect (Ward and Cross 1991). The situation of women was somewhat different: ethnic minority women's chances of being in the top category were equal between the two sectors, but white women's chances were better in the public sector.

Table 9.11 Proportion of men in higher non-manual jobs, private and public sectors (excluding self-employed)

cell percentages

	White		Caribbean		South Asian	
	Private	*Public*	*Private*	*Public*	*Private*	*Public*
	29	27	17	(5)[1]	20	13
Weighted	449	157	95	52	215	75
Unweighted	408	146	64	39	239	81

1 Figure in parentheses denotes small cell size.

Earnings

Survey respondents were asked about their earnings by being shown a card with sixteen bands of earnings, each of which was labelled with a random letter of the alphabet. Respondents were asked to state the letter which labelled the band in which their gross weekly earnings fell. While there was a good response from some groups, there was, as shown in tables 9.12 and 9.13, a high refusal rate among South Asians, about a quarter of whom, excluding Bangladeshis, declined to indicate their earnings. The comparative earnings analyses offered here need to be read with this limitation in mind. The non-respondents in each ethnic group were spread across the job levels, though the relatively few white and Chinese non-respondents were more likely to be non-manual employees, and South Asians' rate of refusal was higher when they chose to be interviewed in English only. It is possible, therefore, that the aggregate average earnings presented here are a little reduced because of the composition of the non-respondents.[6]

This section looks mainly at the earnings of full-time employees. [...] While the comparison of employees' earnings provides a basis for comparison with previous surveys, and an indication of equality of opportunity, the complete picture on the financial returns of employment has to include the contribution of self-employment to the relative position of various groups.

Table 9.12 compares the weekly earnings of male employees in two different ways. The upper part of the table shows the distribution of the respondents between the different condensed earnings bands. The lower part gives the mean weekly earnings, calculated from the midpoints of each of the original sixteen earnings bands. The mean figures show that the average for all ethnic minority men was below that for white men. However, there was parity between whites, African Asians and Chinese. Caribbean men were a little behind, with Indians even more so, and the Pakistanis and Bangladeshis a third or more below whites.

For some groups the mean is likely to be depressed because of a higher refusal rate among the higher earners; the figure for Indian men in particular is more depressed than one might have expected given their job-level distribution, as

Table 9.12 Male employees' earnings (base: male full-time employees)

	White	Caribbean	Indian	African Asian	Pakistani	Bangladeshi	Chinese	Hindu	Sikh	Muslim	All ethnic minorities
Weekly earnings											
Less than £116	4	1	9	6	13	41	2	6	9	23	7
£116–£192	14	16	22	18	39	29	23	20	24	31	22
£193–£289	33	36	30	34	28	10	24	31	38	24	31
£290–£385	19	28	16	13	9	8	15	15	14	10	18
£386–£500	14	11	13	4	4	4	25	6	10	6	10
More than £500	15	8	10	25	6	8	10	23	5	6	12
Mean weekly earnings[1]	£336	£306	£287	£335	£227	£191	£336	£338	£249	£223	£296
Weighted count	541	255	154	152	76	42	72	162	84	140	751
Unweighted count	493	179	169	144	113	78	42	154	84	233	726
Refusal/can't say	6	6	29	16	26	8	3	21	31	18	16

1 Means calculated from midpoints of sixteen earnings bands.

shown earlier in table 9.1. The distribution between bands is particularly interesting in the case of the Caribbeans, for they are fewest in the worst-off as well as the best-off band, and therefore have a more equal distribution of earnings than other groups. African Asian men, by contrast, are much more widely distributed among the earnings bands. Hence even though they are easily the best represented in the highest band of gross earnings of more than £500 a week, being two-thirds more likely to be in that band than whites, their average is the same as that for whites.

The inclusion of religious groups in table 9.12 allows one to see that the addition of Indian and African Asian Muslims to Pakistanis and Bangladeshis raises the Muslim mean weekly earnings from what it might otherwise be; and the difference between the mean earnings of Hindus and Sikhs is quite substantial, mainly because Sikhs had only 5 per cent in the top earnings band as opposed to 23 per cent of Hindus (though both groups, and especially the Sikhs, had a high refusal rate).

This comparative position of African Asians and Hindus compared with other South Asians is a striking new development which has not been properly recorded before. At the time of the PSI Second Survey of Racial Minorities in 1974, it was clear that the African Asians, many of whom were recent refugees from East Africa, were much better qualified, had a better facility in English and were more likely to be in non-manual work than Indians; correspondingly, Indians were in a much better position than the Pakistanis (Smith 1977). On the other hand, perhaps partly because of their recent arrival in Britain, and perhaps because of their larger numbers in white-collar work in which overtime and shift-work premiums were not available, the median gross weekly earnings of African Asian men were 15 per cent below those of whites, 10 per cent below that of Indians, and the lowest for all groups (Smith 1977: 83).

The PSI Third Survey in 1982 found that, while average earnings for Asian men were nearly 15 per cent below those of white men, there was little difference between Indians and African Asians, or between Hindus and Sikhs – both these pairs of Asian groups being much better off than Pakistanis and, especially, Bangladeshis (Brown 1984: tables 109 and 114). The position now is that, while the pattern of earnings differentials between whites, Indians and Pakistanis appears still in place as it has been for two decades, African Asian men have moved from the bottom to the top of the distribution. Two decades ago they were averaging less than the Pakistanis, a decade ago they were equalling Indians, and now they seem to have caught up with the whites.

Similarly, a decade ago Hindu and Sikh men averaged the same earnings, but now Hindus have more than a quarter more than Sikhs. It has to be re-emphasized, however, that these findings are based on high non-response rates, and moreover that the main difference between African Asians and Indians and Hindus and Sikhs respectively is that the former in each pair (which, of course overlap with each other) have a very high proportion of top earners. Nevertheless, the earnings position of African Asians found here is consistent with earlier findings about their job levels. As a group they were always highly qualified and were largely in the professions, administration and business in East Africa. After the period of being political refugees and rebuilding their livelihoods and establishing themselves in Britain, they seem to have made considerable progress in re-creating their prosperity.

Table 9.13 Female employees' earnings (base: female full-time employees, excluding self-employed)

column percentages

	White	Caribbean	Indian	African Asian	Pakistani/ Bangladeshi	Chinese	Hindu	Sikh	Muslim	All ethnic minorities
Weekly earnings										
Less than £116	10	6	19	13	21	16	19	16	19	11
£116–£192	31	20	25	31	46	23	27	36	34	24
£193–£289	30	39	33	29	23	20	27	34	28	33
£290–£385	15	24	9	12	4	19	8	7	11	18
£386–£500	10	7	4	5	7	8	6	3	5	6
More than £500	4	5	11	9	0	14	14	5	4	7
Mean weekly earnings[1]	£244	£267	£252	£254	(£181)	(£287)	£258	£223	(£221)	£259
Weighted count	345	278	103	90	34	48	93	65	46	552
Unweighted count	337	206	94	72	36	28	81	50	47	436
Refusal/can't say	6	12	29	23	18	–	27	30	10	16

1 Means calculated from mid-points of 16 earnings bands. Figures in parentheses denote small sample.

The position of full-time women employees was very different to that of men. Female weekly earnings were considerably lower than men's in all ethnic groups, but the biggest gender gap was among whites (table 9.13). The average earnings of ethnic minority women were higher than those of white women, although this is likely to be inflated by high levels of non-participation by those Pakistani and Bangladeshi women whose potential earnings were very low (Heckman and Sedlacek 1985), and the greater likelihood of higher qualified white women working part-time rather than full-time. This is, nevertheless, an important finding which shows the limits of the idea of 'double discrimination', the view that, besides the general disadvantage of women, non-white women suffer an additional inequality in comparison to white women (Bhavani 1994). The highest average earnings were of Caribbean women (the Chinese women's were higher but the sample size is small).

The differences between groups of women, however, were less than in the case of men. The averages for Indians and African Asians were similar, yet the earnings for Sikh women were significantly less than those for Hindus. This was because Hindus had a very much higher proportion of top earners than Sikhs, or indeed whites. As with men, however, there were high non-response rates among South Asians.

The Labour Force Survey started asking an earnings question shortly before our survey, and findings for the same period of time as our fieldwork (December 1993 to November 1994) have now been published (Sly 1995). The two sets of findings cannot, however, be compared in any detail, given the use of different bands. While the LFS analysis is based on much smaller ethnic minority sample sizes than ours, it is perhaps worth noting that the two data sources present a consistent pattern of male differentials. This is complicated, however, by the fact that the LFS adds Black Africans to Caribbeans to create a 'black' category and includes African Asians as Indians. The LFS found that black and Indian men earned about 10 per cent less than white men, similar to our finding in relation to Caribbean men and Indians/African Asians. The LFS finding that Pakistani/ Bangladeshi men earn about a third less than white men is comparable to our finding if Pakistanis are considered alone, but is too optimistic for Pakistani and Bangladeshi men taken together. The one ethnic minority category of men with higher average earnings than white men in the LFS was 'Mixed/Other origins', which includes the Chinese, suggesting, as we found, that male Chinese and white earnings are broadly similar. The overall average for ethnic minority men in the LFS was 89 per cent of male white earnings; in our survey it was 88 per cent.

Our survey, on the other hand, leaving aside the Pakistani/Bangladeshi women on account of the small sample sizes, consistently found that ethnic minority women earned more than white women, whereas the LFS found that while black women earned 6 per cent more than white women, Indian/African women earned 10 per cent less (Sly 1995).

The differentials are of course partly the result of the different job-level profiles of groups. Our sample was not large enough for an analysis of earnings by job levels by each group, but we are able to compare whites and ethnic minorities taken together by the main socio-economic levels in order to investigate a little

Table 9.14 Gross weekly earnings, by job levels (base: full-time employees excluding self-employed)

	Whites		Ethnic minorities		Differential	Differential 25–54 years old only	Differential in 1982[1]
	Weighted count		Weighted count				
Prof./managers/employers							
Men	£467	(165)	£430	(146)	−8%	−8%	−18%
Women	£327	(68)	£412	(61)	+26%	+21%	(+14%)[2]
Other non-manual							
Men	£325	(112)	£302	(172)	−7%	−8%	−4%
Women	£243	(209)	£260	(355)	+7%	+3%	+5%
Skilled manual and foremen							
Men	£278	(170)	£290	(198)	+4%	−3%	−8%
Women	(£183)	(13)	(£245)	(12)	(+34%)	(+22%)	+11%
Semi- or unskilled manual							
Men	£208	(85)	£211	(229)	+1%	−6%	−9%[3]
Women	£162	(55)	£177	(117)	+9%	+7%	+10%

1 Brown 1984.
2 Non-count figures in parentheses denote small cell sizes.
3 Semi-skilled only.

further as to where the differences lie. This is done in table 9.14. Earnings are very clearly stratified by job levels (and so any group, such as the Caribbeans, which is under-represented in the highest job levels will have a lower average), but what is also interesting is that the male ethnic minority disadvantage is only in the non-manual group. In the manual group (in which ethnic minority men are dispro-portionately represented, table 9.1), ethnic minorities have the advantage over white men in semi- or unskilled manual work. More strikingly, however, among women, ethnic minorities earn more than whites at each job level. As before, we need to exercise caution with this finding, given the propensity of women with very low potential earnings to remain outside the labour force altogether.

Table 9.14 also presents the differentials as they were in our 1982 survey. In the whites–minorities comparison the basic pattern across job levels for each sex has held over this time. More generally, there has been an upward movement among ethnic minorities, with men reducing the size of their disadvantage (except for the other non-manual group) and women increasing their advantage.

The finding of 1982 that ethnic minority women full-time employees had higher average earnings than their white counterparts has been criticized for overlooking the fact that many ethnic minority women, especially in the clothing and hosiery industries, are 'homeworkers' (Bruegel 1989; Bhavnani 1994). That is to say, they manufacture items at home, usually on machines bought by themselves, from materials delivered by an employer or contractor, and are paid a piece rate. The rates of pay are extremely poor, so that any sample which under-represents such workers will overestimate the average pay of groups among whom the incidence of homeworking is high. The suspicion that the 1982 survey may have done this is strengthened by some local studies in places such as London, Leicester and Coventry that found the pay of ethnic minority women to be lower than that of white women (Bruegel 1989; Duffy and Lincoln 1990; Gray et al. 1993). We do, however, believe that in our national surveys we are comparing like with like, especially as the new survey supports the earlier one.

All the evidence we have suggests that our survey is representative of the populations from which it was drawn. It is therefore most unlikely that we have seriously under-represented homeworkers in our sample. The question, then, is where are they in our analysis? The women in question could have described themselves as self-employed, but far fewer South Asian than white and Caribbean self-employed women work at home. They could have described themselves as part-time employees, but, as we have seen, far fewer ethnic minority than white women work part-time; and as part-time work is not as well paid as full-time work (absolutely, as well as per hour), to include it in the same analysis would depress white women's averages more than that of the ethnic minorities. It is possible that the answers given by some homeworkers have resulted in their being classified either as full-time employees or (as Bruegel 1989: 50–1 suspects in the case of the 1982 survey) as unemployed or economically inactive. If in the former, they are included in the earnings analysis. If in either of the other categories, provided they did not work full-time, their inclusion does not invalidate the comparison of earnings of full-time employees. In any case, the most striking earnings comparison does not affect South Asian women at all, but only Caribbeans and whites.[7]

Influences on earnings

There are, then, differing patterns of earnings between groups and between men and women, and these clearly relate to job levels, age and a number of other factors. However, in order to understand the patterns we need to look at these effects simultaneously. This enables us to establish, for example, whether the observed disparities between different ethnic and age groups can perhaps be explained by different qualification rates between younger and older people in different ethnic groups.

We undertook some simple regression analysis to examine the simultaneous effects on average weekly earnings of age, local unemployment rates, qualifications, social class, fluency in English, presence of dependent children and ethnic origin. These regressions assume that the effect of any one variable, for example age, is the same for all ethnic groups. Small sample sizes preclude separate analysis for the different groups. We recognize that this may be a problem, since the PSI survey of 1974 found that white and ethnic minority male earnings were differently related to age. In 1974 older manual workers were disproportionately represented among the low earners, but, because the ethnic minority population was much

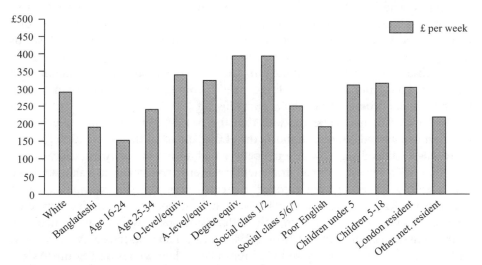

Figure 9.2 Influences on male earnings, 1997

younger than whites, minority average earnings appeared to be higher if age was not taken into account. On the other hand, for young manual workers, another low-paid group, minority average earnings were higher than for whites. However, since the simultaneous effect of qualifications, family structure and occupational distribution were not considered, the observed differences may not have been related to age as such. In any case, we believe that the advantages of considering several factors together outweigh the disadvantages, and should give a reasonable indication of the factors that are the most important in explaining earnings differences.

Bangladeshis were the only group of men to have lower weekly earnings than other men of the same age with similar qualifications, social class, family circumstances and local labour market conditions (figure 9.2). The differences between the earnings of all other ethnic minority men and white men could be accounted for by their different occupational pattern, qualifications, family circumstances and age as well as local labour market conditions.

Taking all groups together, the youngest men had the lowest earnings and the over thirty-fives the highest. Living in area of high unemployment led to lower earnings, as did a poor standard of English (irrespective of the possession of any formal qualifications). All types of qualifications had a positive effect on earnings, but particularly degrees. Those in the highest professional and managerial category earned the most, followed by those in other non-manual and skilled manual employment. Semi-skilled and unskilled manual workers earned the least. Men with children earned slightly more per week than those without.

In 1974, when twenty-five- to fifty-four-year-old male workers were compared, the earnings of semi- and unskilled minority workers were no different from those of whites. However, for other occupational groups, but especially at professional and managerial level, the white advantage was apparent (Smith 1977: 84–5). When the analysis was replicated a decade later, the white advantage at the highest level considerably narrowed, suggesting that the minorities were making inroads into the highest paid jobs, but slightly widened or remained the same at all other levels (Brown 1984: table 111). Our findings suggest that the earnings of ethnic minority men, except Bangladeshis, reflect their qualifications and occupational status (although, as we saw earlier, their occupational status is not always commensurate with their qualifications, so that the job level itself may represent the outcome of a discriminatory process). Nonetheless, this is encouraging and suggests that there has been some progress since the early 1980s.

Moreover, it is no longer the case that the pay of ethnic minority men looks comparatively good because of shift-work. In 1982 part of the explanation for why there was a relatively narrow pay gap between white and minority manual workers was that shift-workers earned considerably more than other manual workers. White shift-workers actually enjoyed a greater premium, but because a larger proportion of minority employees worked shifts it raised the latter's average by a larger amount and suggested that the difference in basic wages was greater than in the actual amounts earned (Brown 1984: 168). The situation now, as we saw earlier, is that substantially more Caribbean men than whites and South Asians regularly work shifts. The proportions of shift-workers among manual workers are in fact very similar, about a third in each group. South Asian male manual workers who never work shifts are the poorest, and those who regularly work shifts earn nearly a quarter more. This is a higher differential for shift-work than among other groups, but it does not alter the overall pattern, which is that South Asians were the poorest paid shift- as well as non-shift-workers, and Caribbean men were the highest paid in both categories. The earnings advantage of minority male manual workers over white male manual workers is therefore quite independent of shift-work; it is a reflection of the high earnings of Caribbean men in manual work.

As far as the data on women are concerned, it is more difficult to perform multiple regression to disentangle the effects of different factors such as age, qualifications, job levels, family circumstances and local labour market conditions. For women the difference between weekly and hourly earnings is more important, since it is predominantly a result of the differences in hours worked. Unfortunately, this information was missing in so many cases that we were unable to include it as an explanatory variable. On the other hand, the choice of whether to work full- or part-time depends in part on the potential rewards from doing so. It is usual in more complex analyses of women's earnings to model the decision to participate in the labour market (and to work full- or part-time where appropriate) as part of the same process. That is because those with the lowest potential earnings will tend to remain outside the labour market altogether, and the exclusion of their (zero) earnings from the analysis produces an upward bias in the results.

We have not followed this procedure here, mainly because its technical complexity is a deterrent to the general reader, and have confined the analysis to full-time employees. However, it means that the results for women will be biased towards those who have the highest potential earnings, because they are the ones who gain the greatest net advantage from working. In principle, as we are looking at women separately from men, provided those with similar characteristics from

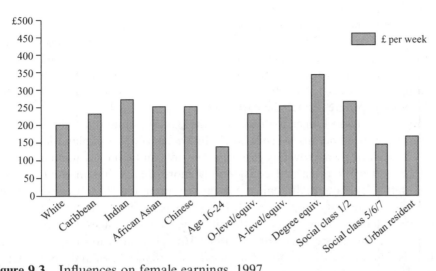

Figure 9.3 Influences on female earnings, 1997

all ethnic groups remain economically inactive, then there will be no effect on the intergroup comparisons. However, if higher inactivity rates for some groups are associated with differential labour market disadvantage, then our findings will tend to understate that disadvantage. As the analysis of women's economic activity rates strongly suggested that the decision to participate in the labour market varied between ethnic groups, the following analysis has to be read with this qualification in mind.

As with men, earnings increased with qualifications and with occupational level (figure 9.3). Caribbean, Indian, African Asian and Chinese women had higher earnings than those from other ethnic groups of a similar age, and with similar qualifications, job levels, family circumstances and labour market background. The position of Pakistani and Bangladeshi women was not significantly different from that of white women, and this was also true of women with dependent children. However, in view of their low participation rates, those from the former two groups who do have jobs may be unrepresentative. The pattern overall, therefore, is one where there is no apparent earnings discrimination: different groups with similar qualifications doing the same types of jobs in the same areas are paid the same amounts. In fact white women earn substantially less on average than most other groups.[8] The key issue then becomes whether possession of qualifications allows access to better jobs on the same terms as for whites. The analysis of job levels above suggests that it does not always. However, if the differences were large they would be expected to show up in the analysis by increasing the effect (positive or negative) of ethnic group to a point where it becomes statistically significant, and they have not done so [. . .].

These findings, therefore, are encouraging, since they suggest that the apparent labour market advantages of Caribbean women, and the progress made by Indian and African Asian women, are genuine.

Table 9.15 Comparison of earnings of full-time employees and self-employed

	White	Caribbean	Indian	African Asian	Pakistani	Bangladeshi	Chinese	All ethnic minorities
Men								
Employees	£336	£306	£287	£335	£227	£191	£336	£296
Self-employed	£308	(£347)[1]	£361	£321	£232	(£238)	(£466)	£327
Employees and self-employed	£331	£311	£302	£331	£229	£198	£368	£303
Weighted count								
Employees	*541*	*255*	*154*	*152*	*76*	*42*	*72*	*751*
Self-employed	*110*	*33*	*41*	*53*	*44*	*7*	*23*	*202*
Combined	*651*	*288*	*195*	*205*	*120*	*49*	*96*	*953*
Women								
Employees	£244	£267	£252	£254		(£181)	£287	£259
Self-employed	£242	(£349)	(£370)	(£219)		(£251)	(£249)	£290
Employees and self-employed	£244	£270	£268	£251		£189	£274	£262
Weighted count								
Employees	*345*	*278*	*103*	*90*		*34*	*48*	*552*
Self-employed	*46*	*10*	*15*	*9*		*4*	*25*	*64*
Combined	*391*	*288*	*118*	*99*		*38*	*73*	*616*

1 Figures in parentheses denote small cell sizes.

In the 1970s it was argued that qualifications did little to improve the earnings prospects of minority groups (Smith 1977: 87). This no longer appears to be true in the 1990s. The possession of qualifications has positive effects for all groups, and the higher the qualification, the greater the impact. This suggests that the strategy pursued by some ethnic minority groups, especially some South Asian groups, of encouraging young people to maximize their qualifications has been the right one, and has been an important factor in the changing pattern of earnings among minority groups. Put at its simplest, higher qualifications double the earnings of Pakistanis and Bangladeshis and enable Indians to catch up with, and African Asians to overtake, white men. They seem to have a similar value for the Chinese. For women the possession of a degree, as compared with A-levels, adds around two-thirds to earnings.

A comparison between the earnings of employees and self-employed is interesting. [...] [S]ome minority groups have a larger (and some smaller) than average rate of self-employment. It has been argued that, on account of a lack of opportunities in paid employment, partly because of racial discrimination, some groups have invested disproportionately in self-employment (Aldrich et al. 1981). A consequence may be that the employees' average earnings for those groups are depressed because a higher proportion of qualified and resourceful persons from that group are self-employed. It may also be the case that earnings from self-employment are lower than those from paid employment for those with equivalent qualifications, and so self-employment is confirmed as a second-best option, at least from the point of view of earnings.

Table 9.15 compares the earnings of employees and the self-employed. While white male employees earned more than their self-employed counterparts, the reverse was true of ethnic minorities apart from African Asian men. Taken as a whole, self-employed ethnic minority men earned more than whites, and so self-employment, like qualifications, contributes to narrowing the earnings gap,[9] especially for Indians and Caribbeans (and places Chinese men as the highest earners, though the sample is too small for confidence). As with paid employment, ethnic minority women in self-employment on average earned more than their white peers (though the sample sizes are relatively small) and so female self-employment consolidates the earnings advantage of ethnic minority women (except Pakistanis and Bangladeshis). As regards average earnings, self-employment is not a second-best option for the minorities – in fact it is relatively attractive for above-average earners.

[...]

Equal opportunities and discrimination

For several decades now concern about the extent and nature of racial discrimination in the economy has been central in discussions about ethnic minorities. This topic has been directly explored in the previous surveys in [the National Survey of

Table 9.16 Belief about what proportion of employers would refuse someone a job for racial/religious reasons (base: currently economically active)

column percentages

	White	Caribbean	Indian	African Asian	Pakistani	Bangladeshi	Chinese	All ethnic minorities
Most	5	24	16	13	19	8	7	18
About half	22	31	21	25	20	9	14	24
Fewer than half	44	30	22	29	27	20	22	27
Hardly any	13	4	2	5	2	6	7	4
Some but can't say how many	6	5	4	2	3	8	10	5
None	5	2	16	15	12	21	23	12
Can't say	5	3	19	10	16	29	17	12
Weighted count	*1717*	*555*	*375*	*288*	*237*	*67*	*125*	*1627*
Unweighted count	*1590*	*400*	*370*	*266*	*293*	*131*	*70*	*1524*

Ethnic Minorities in Britain] series and was reinvestigated in the Fourth Survey. At the time of the last survey in 1982, anti-discrimination legislation and the Commission for Racial Equality were in place, but it has been only in the [1990s] that positive equal opportunity policies have acquired some prominence. We sought the views of white and minority people on the extent and character, and from minority people details of personal experience of discrimination.

Ninety per cent of economically active white people thought that employers refuse people jobs for racial/religious reasons (table 9.16). This was more than any ethnic minority group except the Caribbeans, 95 per cent of whom believed that such discrimination existed. About 60 to 75 per cent of most of the other minority groups thought that discrimination in the jobs market existed. The exception was the Bangladeshis, about half of whom thought it existed and nearly a third could not answer the question, perhaps reflecting the group's low participation rate in the labour market. While the analysis is only of the economically active, there is some correlation between a group's belief in discrimination and its economic participation rate, though the Indians and Chinese have a lesser belief than their participation rate might suggest and the Chinese were most likely to give the response that employers do not discriminate.

While ethnic minority respondents were less likely than white people to believe in the existence of discrimination, it is interesting that, where they did perceive it, the ethnic minorities believed that it was more widespread. Table 9.16 also gives the proportion of employers people believed discriminate. While the Caribbeans were most likely to believe that most employers discriminate, one in five of all ethnic minorities believed this, but only one in twenty whites. Even so, more than a

Table 9.17 Persons refused a job for perceived racial/religious reasons (base: those who have ever been economically active)

cell percentages

	Caribbean	Indian	African Asian	Pakistani/ Bangladeshi	Chinese	All ethnic minorities
Perceived discriminatory refusal	28	15	19	5	7	19
Of whom:						
refused more than once	71	67	78	87	49	72
refused in last 5 years	43	39	40	67	32	44
Weighted count	*675*	*469*	*327*	*315*	*151*	*1937*
Unweighted count	*507*	*461*	*296*	*469*	*85*	*1818*

quarter of whites believed that half or more of employers discriminate and more than 40 per cent of the ethnic minorities thought this happened. In general the views of the South Asians were very similar, except for the Bangladeshis, who estimated the lowest levels of discrimination. The Chinese thought more discrimination took place than the Bangladeshis, and were closest in their views to the whites. A further breakdown is not tabulated, but not only did the economically active think that more employers discriminated than the inactive, but the unemployed in all groups, including the Caribbeans, thought that discrimination was less prevalent than the employed.

The answers given mark a significant increase since the previous survey in the belief that employers discriminate, by about a fifth among whites and Caribbeans, and by about a half among South Asians, with an even larger increase in the number of people who believe that half or more employers discriminate (Brown 1984: 219–20). With this increase in perception of discrimination, it is not surprising that over four-fifths of ethnic minority people thought that the present laws on racial discrimination should be enforced more strictly. The same proportion thought that there should be new, stricter laws. These figures were the same for Caribbeans and South Asians and represent a very high level of consensus on the need for political action on racial discrimination. It is perhaps of some interest that the South Asians and Chinese were more likely to concur on the need for stricter laws against discrimination than to state that employers discriminate.

The views of some of the minority respondents were based on personal experience. Table 9.17 shows the number of people who said they had been refused a job for a reason to do with their race or religion. A fifth of those who had ever been economically active thought this had happened. Few Bangladeshis and Chinese reported this experience, while over a quarter of the Caribbeans thought this had happened to them. Again (though not presented in the table) the unemployed were less likely to report discrimination than those in employment. About three-quarters of those who reported suffering racial discrimination in seeking work thought this had happened to them more than once, the South Asians, except the Indians, being more likely than the others to think so. Nearly half said that the most recent time they believed this had happened to them was in the previous five years. This was less so for the Chinese, but two-thirds of Pakistanis and nearly all of the Bangladeshis said that their (last) experience of discrimination was in this recent period. Also consistent with the increase in perceptions of discrimination, it is interesting that all the minorities taken together reported discrimination varied little by age, even though the different age groups had spent a varied number of years in the labour market. In fact, younger Caribbeans were more likely to have perceived discrimination than their elders; among Indians it was the oldest work-ers and among the other South Asians it was the middle age group, those thirty-five to forty-nine years old. There was a very slight increase in the reports of these perceived acts of discrimination among the Caribbeans in comparison to 1982, but about a 50 per cent increase among South Asians (Brown 1984: 218).

On the whole, then, the belief that employers discriminate is much more wide-spread than the experience of discrimination; increases are shown in both cate-gories, but the increase in belief is larger. This is not surprising. Testing for discrimination has shown that most acts of discrimination take place without individuals knowing they have been discriminated against (Brown and Gay 1985). As awareness of discrimination grows, it will be the case that the knowledge that it exists will outstrip the actual experience of it. Individuals may also be more likely to attribute discriminatory motives than before. So increases in reports of discrimination are compatible with stable, or even, declining levels of discrimina-tion. Objective tests suggest that the proportion of white people who are likely to carry out the most basic acts of discrimination has been stable at about a third for several decades (Daniel 1968; Smith 1977; Brown and Gay 1985; Simpson and Stevenson 1994). Nor is there any simple correlation between the reports of discrimination and socio-economic disadvantage. Despite their socio-economic difference, South Asians reported comparable levels of discrimination, except that the Bangladeshis, despite (or because of) being the most disadvantaged, reported very little discrimination. Yet the Caribbeans, whose economic position is in the middle range, were seven times as likely to report discrimination as the Bangladeshis.

The fact that these reports have increased in a period when the position of minorities has generally improved, and that the groups in which they have increased the most are those which have made the most progress, suggests that reports of discrimination may be linked to an awareness of the issue and whether the climate of opinion is receptive to such reports. A climate in which equal opportunities issues are being addressed may, at least initially, increase complaints of discrimination and perceptions about the prevalence of discrimination. More-over, the experience of discrimination may be more linked to competition for prized jobs than relative disadvantage *per se*. For a precondition of the encounters

Table 9.18 Perceived reasons for the refusal of a job

column percentages

	All ethnic minorities	Caribbean	Indian	African Asian	Pakistani/ Bangladeshi	Hindu	Sikh	Muslim
Race	65	75	55	51	48	51	51	51
Religion	6	8	2	1	11	–	5	7
Both of these	26	15	37	40	39	38	44	39
Can't say	3	2	6	6	2	9	2	2
Weighted count	*400*	*203*	*70*	*67*	*50*	*69*	*45*	*55*
Unweighted count	*339*	*148*	*67*	*56*	*62*	*56*	*100*	*99*

in which discrimination may occur is competition for the same jobs, and that assumes some commonality in qualifications, skill levels and employment experience. As ethnic minorities become more effective competitors for more prized jobs and professions, the salience of the issue of discrimination may, ironically, increase.

Respondents who reported discrimination were asked whether they thought the refusal of the job(s) was on account of their race or their religion, or due to both of these. Three-quarters of the Caribbeans and half of the South Asians thought it was because of their perceived race (table 9.18). Very few thought it was a result of their religion alone, though one in ten of the Pakistanis/Bangladeshis, and, interestingly, nearly the same number of Caribbeans did, while fewer Sikhs and no Hindus believed this was the case.

The most interesting finding, however, is that a quarter of all the ethnic minority persons who believed that they had been discriminated against in a job application believed that it was for a mixture of reasons to do with their race and religion. In fact over 40 per cent of South Asians, evenly spread across ethnic and religious groups, believed this combination of reasons to be operative. Moreover, younger South Asians were more of this view than the older age groups. This suggests that, for South Asians, the idea of racial discrimination is of a more complex character than it is in many equal opportunities policies, in which it is assumed that racial discrimination is unfair treatment simply of 'people of colour'. Moreover, the perception of South Asians that their religion is relevant to their experience of racial discrimination is not to do with an older generation with limited encounters with British society, but seems to be on the increase. These matters relate to the place which South Asians give to colour and religion in their definition of themselves, and in how they think white people perceive them [. . .].

Pursuing further the topic of what people think is the basis of hostility against minority groups, we asked all groups which racial, ethnic or religious group faces most prejudice today. They could give any answer they chose, but they had to name just one group. The answers are presented in table 9.19. What is really

Table 9.19 Views on which racial, ethnic or religious group faces most prejudice

column percentages

	White	Caribbean	Indian/African Asian	Pakistani	Bangladeshi	All South Asians	Chinese	All ethnic minorities
Asians	32	37	11	11	10	11	10	19
Muslims	10	8	19	30	5	21	12	16
Pakistanis	12	2	1	4	1	2	5	2
Indians	3	3	1	–	–	1	1	2
Bangladeshis	–	1	1	1	6	1	–	1
Caribbeans/Blacks/Africans	14	19	10	3	4	8	30	13
Some other answer	10	8	17	13	17	14	13	13
Don't know	21	23	40	38	57	41	29	34
Weighted count	2867	783	1037	420	138	1595	195	2574
Unweighted count	2867	614	988	584	289	1861	104	2579

interesting is the contrast between how whites and Caribbeans, on the one hand, identify the victim group, and how the victim group is identified by the others. For whites and Caribbeans the victim group is identified as 'Asians'. Yet, except for the Bangladeshis (the majority of whom were not able to answer the question), the South Asians do not primarily think that the prejudice directed against them is aimed mostly at their Asianness. Almost twice as many Indians/African Asians and three times as many Pakistanis think that it is Muslims, rather than Asians, who face the most prejudice. The Chinese too were of the view that Muslims as a group face more prejudice than Asians as a group, but they were exceptional in identifying 'black' people, people of African descent, as the group which faces the most prejudice (considerably more so than the Caribbeans did).

The point here is that there is now a consensus across all groups that prejudice against Asians is much the highest of any ethnic, racial or religious group; and it is believed by Asian people themselves that the prejudice against Asians is primarily a prejudice against Muslims. To date, however, there has been virtually no research on religious discrimination in Britain, nor on how perceptions of religion and race interact to create distinctive forms of prejudice (e.g. stereotypes about 'fundamentalist Muslims') and discrimination. It had been assumed that religious discrimination is quite separate from racial discrimination and is confined to Protestant–Catholic relations in Northern Ireland.[10] Indeed, the UK legislation against religious discrimination is strictly confined to Northern Ireland and does not extend to mainland Britain. In recent years, however, it has been argued that anti-Muslim prejudice is a central and growing strand of racism (Modood 1992), and the Commission for Racial Equality and others have asked the Home Secretary to revise anti-discrimination laws so that they can more effectively protect ethno-religious minorities (CRE 1991; UKACIA 1993; Runnymede Trust 1996: 11–12). Perhaps it is equally important to note that as many Sikhs and Hindus as Muslims who reported having been discriminated against in recruitment thought their religion was a factor held against them.

Employees had a more positive view of their own employer than they did of some other employers. Nearly half of the ethnic minority employees felt that 'there are real equal opportunities for everyone regardless of race, colour, or religious or cultural background' where they worked. Those under thirty-five years old were more likely to believe they had personally experienced discrimination but that there were equal opportunities where they worked.

There were also some interesting contrasts in the answers between those who worked in the private and the public sectors. There was in fact no real difference between whites and ethnic minorities combined, or between men and women. Yet there were considerable differences between the views of the minorities. For example, much larger proportions of African Asian, Pakistani and Bangladeshi men in the private sector thought there were equal opportunities where they worked than did Caribbean and Indian men. Within the public sector, South Asian and Caribbean women took radically different views: only a third of Caribbean but two-thirds of South Asian women thought there were real equal opportunities where they worked. However, one area within the public sector where the ethnic minorities took one view, but white people quite another, was in health: three-quarters of white employees but only a third of the minority employees thought there were equal opportunities in their health authority or hospital. Indeed, of the thirty-two Caribbean women employees in this sector, twenty-five denied there were equal opportunities where they worked. This is particularly worrying as the health services are a major employer of ethnic minorities, but is entirely consistent with the results of a large-scale PSI study of the experiences of nurses (Beishon, Virdee and Hagell 1995).

[...]

Upward mobility and racial disadvantage

The findings of this [reading] depict a pattern of inequality, but also of a divergence in the circumstances of the main minorities. Many aspects of this diversity are not new. The radically differing economic–educational profiles of African Asians and Indians, on the one hand, and Pakistanis and Bangladeshis, on the other, were apparent in the 1970s (Smith 1977). They were somewhat obscured in the 1980s, when attention came to be focused on the disproportionate impact of unemployment upon the ethnic minorities and there was a tendency to overgeneralize from the condition of the worst-off groups to the minorities as such; the 'black–white' divide therefore seemed to dwarf other distinctions. Now that the differences between minorities seem as evident as the similarities, it is worth examining whether the differences are consistent over time, and, if not, whether they are narrowing or widening. Are some groups experiencing more mobility across job levels than others?

Table 9.20 presents male job levels as found in the 1982 PSI survey of ethnic minorities and as found in this survey. For the sake of comparison with 1982, the self-employed are not included. The table shows that the period 1982 to 1994 was one of structural change and that all groups, though in differing degrees, participated in the change. The main change is an upward occupational shift. In 1982 a fifth of white and African Asian male employees who were in work were in the top employment category. In 1994 it was over a quarter, though with whites overtaking the African Asians. The Caribbeans and Indians, starting from a much lower base, have roughly doubled their representation in the top category of employees, but the mobility of Pakistani employees has been more modest and for Bangladeshis it may even have been proportionately downwards. There are no 1982 data for the Chinese, but our survey confirms the Census records that, of the groups under discussion, the Chinese are most represented in professional and managerial employment.

For all groups other than Pakistanis there has been a contraction in work for skilled manual employees and foremen. For all the minorities junior and intermediate non-manual work has grown rapidly, and for Indians, African Asians and Pakistanis the proportion engaged in semi- and unskilled manual work has

Table 9.20 Job levels of male employees, 1982 and 1994[1]

column percentages

	White		Caribbean		Indian		African Asian		Pakistani		Bangladeshi		Chinese
	1982	1994	1982	1994	1982	1994	1982	1994	1982	1994	1982	1994	1994
Professional/ managerial/ employers	19	30	5	11	11	19	22	26	10	14	10	7	41
Other non-manual	23	21	10	20	13	28	21	31	8	18	7	22	26
Skilled manual and foremen	42	31	48	37	34	23	31	22	39	36	13	2	5
Semi-skilled manual	13	14	26	26	36	22	22	17	35	28	57	65	20
Unskilled manual	3	4	9	6	5	7	3	3	8	4	12	4	8
Non-manual	42	51	15	31	24	47	43	57	18	32	17	29	67
Manual	58	49	83	69	75	52	56	42	82	68	82	71	33

1 For the sake of comparison with 1982, the self-employed are not included.

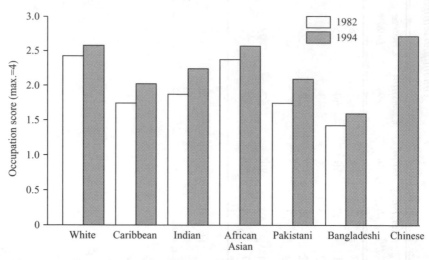

Based on average job-level score derived from the following scale: 4: Professional, managerial, employers; 3: Other non-manual; 2: Skilled manual and foreman; 1: Semi-skilled manual; 0: Unskilled manual

Figure 9.4   Relative improvement in job levels of male employees between 1982 and 1994

declined. With the exception of the African Asians, in 1982 about four-fifths of employed South Asians and Caribbean men were in manual work; now it is about two-thirds. The group whose employment profile has shifted most substantially in this period are Indian men. At the start of the 1980s they were preponderantly in manual work, like the Caribbeans, Pakistanis and Bangladeshis. However, while these three groups are still largely in manual work, the Indian profile is now much closer to that of the whites, African Asians and Chinese.

A good way of capturing this lessening of disadvantage among male employees is by scoring the job levels on a common scale. An average can then be derived for each ethnic group for 1982 and 1994 and the degree of movement measured. This has been done, and is presented in figure 9.4, from which can be seen that all the minority groups made more relative improvement in this period than whites, though only African Asians have achieved parity with whites (the Chinese are best off in 1994 but, again, there are no 1982 data for them).

It is worth reminding the reader that, in this period, there has also been a growth in self-employment. Moreover, this too has benefited ethnic minority men, both within the non-manual and the manual job levels self-employment marks an upward movement for this group. Most of this self-employment, as we have seen, is not of a nominal kind – for example, masking underemployment or employment arrangements whereby employers contract out work to (former) employees.

The women's pattern of movement across job levels has some parallels with that of the men, especially in the growth of non-manual work, which has been greater for women than men, and for some minorities more than white women (table 9.21). Taking full-time employees only, while all women continue to have

Table 9.21 Job levels of full-time female employees, 1982 and 1994

column percentages

	White 1982	White 1994	Caribbean 1982	Caribbean 1994	Indian 1982	Indian 1994	African Asian 1982	African Asian 1994	Pakistani 1994	Chinese 1994
Prof./managerial/employers	7	21	1	4	5	3	7	14	7	38
Intermediate and junior non-manual	55	58	52	76	35	61	52	66	60	55
Skilled manual and foremen	5	3	4	2	8	2	3	3	3	–
Semi-skilled manual	21	17	36	18	50	32	36	17	29	7
Unskilled manual	11	1	7	1	1	3	3	–	–	–
Non-manual	62	79	53	80	40	64	59	80	67	93
Manual	37	21	47	21	59	37	42	20	32	7

a smaller proportion than men in the professional, managerial and employers category, there has been a significant increase among white women. The position of African Asian women seems to be slightly better than in 1982, but the other minority women are much more poorly represented in this category, and Indians possibly less so than a decade ago. The exception are the Chinese, who were not included in the 1982 survey, but who were very much concentrated at the top end of the job levels in 1994.[11] Intermediate and junior non-manual work has grown substantially since 1982 for all minority groups for whom data allows a comparative analysis, and Caribbeans, Indians and African Asians are now disproportionately in this category. Pakistani and Indian full-time women employees are still, however, disproportionately manual workers, especially at the semi-skilled level (they, together with Chinese women, are more likely to be skilled manual as self-employed rather then employees). Our findings, then, about job levels are consistent with the general trends of upward mobility, and from manual into non-manual work, identified in successive Labour Force Surveys (Jones 1993) as well as in the 1991 Census, although they are not as sanguine about the presence of Pakistani and Bangladeshi men, and ethnic minority women in general, in the top jobs category. The general pattern, however, is one of declining differentials between whites and the main ethnic minority groups, as has recently been argued in an analysis which compares LFS data for 1966 with 1991 (Iganski and Payne 1996). This has happened, as Iganski and Payne point out, during a period of substantial growth in the numbers from these groups in the labour market, and so the gains have had to be sustained for many more people (Iganski and Payne 1996: 118). Moreover, given [. . .] that all the ethnic minorities have higher, sometimes much higher, levels of participation in post-compulsory education and increasing levels of admission into higher education, it is most likely that the minorities will continue to improve their relative position in the economy. The differentials between minorities may also become more pronounced as some groups consolidate the advantaged profile they have begun to develop.

If today the ethnic minorities cannot be described collectively as being disproportionately confined to low-skill, low-paid work, it is largely because they are returning to their pre-migration occupational levels. It is sometimes asserted that migrants 'have tended to be from the poorest and most underprivileged groups of their countries of origin' (Anthias and Yuval-Davis 1992: 77). This is almost certainly not the case. An analysis of 1972 data from the Nuffield Social Mobility Survey found that nearly a quarter of the non-white migrants had professional-class origins, predominantly higher professional, which was twice the proportion of the native English; and more than half had social origins in either the petty bourgeoisie or the farming classes (the figure for the English was 16 per cent, Heath and Ridge 1983). The analysis shows that there was, however, a serious downward social mobility as people of professional origins failed to secure professional posts, and the petty bourgeoise was 'proletarianized': children of self-employed traders, artisans and farmers met the demand for labour in British factories (Heath and Ridge 1983).

Earlier PSI studies, too, found that the initial effect of migration was downward social mobility, as the overwhelming majority of migrants could get only manual

Table 9.22 Employment disadvantage of ethnic minority men[1]

	Chinese	African Asian	Indian	Caribbean	Pakistani	Bangladeshi
Employers and managers in large establishments	0.5	0.3	0.5	0.5	0.3	0.01
Professionals, managers and employers	1.5	1.0	0.8	0.5	0.6	0.6
Supervisors	0.9	0.8	0.6	0.7	0.4	0.4
Earnings	1.0	1.0	0.9	0.9	0.7	0.6
Unemployment rates	0.6	0.9	1.3	2.1	2.5	2.8
Long-term unemployed[2]	–	(1.6)	3.1	5.9	7.7	7.7

1 Disadvantage is expressed as a relation to white men, who are taken to represent 1. A figure below 1 gives, therefore, the degree of under-representation in that category compared with whites. The figures include the self-employed.
2 Those unemployed for more than two years as a proportion of economically active in the ethnic group, relative to white men.

work; this included persons with academic qualifications, even degrees, and who may have been in white-collar work before migration (Daniel 1968: 60–1; Smith 1977). Studies in other countries, such as the USA, with large immigrant populations have found similar patterns. We have seen in this survey that, among the first generation, Indian men were among the most qualified, and one might conjecture, therefore, suffered particularly from the racial bias operating in entry into non-manual work. The initial downward mobility was accepted because it still offered much higher earnings than were available in the countries of origin, but it is not surprising that those individuals who have been able to surmount the proletarian character ascribed to migrant labour and their families should have endeavoured to do so. It is, therefore, not inappropriate to see the above-average upward social mobility among some minorities as a process of reversal of the initial downward trend produced by migration and racial discrimination in the early years of settlement in Britain.

There is, then, an overall trend of progress in the job levels of ethnic minorities and a narrowing of the differentials between the ethnic majority and the minorities. We saw the same trend in the earlier analysis of earnings. Yet this certainly has not developed to a point where there is an ethnic parity or where the concept of racial disadvantage is redundant. Table 9.22 sets out the extent of the employment disadvantages of ethnic minority men compared with white men. Six key indicators of advantage/disadvantage have been chosen out of the previous analyses from this [reading]. The figures in table 9.22 are derived from treating the position of whites as a baseline against which the minorities are given a score. Where the positions are the same, this is represented by a 1; where a minority group is under- or over-represented relative to whites, a figure is given showing the

Table 9.23   Employment disadvantage of ethnic minority women[1]

	Chinese	African Asian	Indian	Caribbean	Pakistani	Bangladeshi
In paid work[2]	1.1	1.0	1.0	0.9	0.3	0.1
Professionals, managers and employers	1.9	0.3	0.8	0.7	0.8	–
Higher and intermediate non-manual	1.4	0.9	0.7	0.8	1.1	–
Supervisors	1.1	1.1	0.8	0.6	0.6	–
Earnings	–	1.1	1.0	1.0	–	–
Unemployed	0.7	2	1.3	1.3	4.3	4.4

1 Disadvantage is expressed as a relation to white women, who are taken to represent 1. A figure below 1 gives, therefore, the degree of under-representation in that category compared with whites. The figures include the self-employed.
2 Proportion in paid work based on all women aged 16–60 not in retirement, full-time education or long-term illness.

scale of the representation in relation to whites. Table 9.22 shows that most, but not all, the groups are still disadvantaged, but not evenly so. There is in fact only one circumstance in which all the minorities are disadvantaged: they are all substantially under-represented in the most elite jobs, namely as employers and managers in large establishments. This could be said to be a 'glass ceiling' that affects all non-white men equally.

Beyond that, the differences between the minorities are as important as their position in relation to whites. For, by the rest of the measures, the Chinese are more advantaged than whites, and the African Asians are broadly similar to whites. The Indians are somewhat disadvantaged, but are closer to whites than to the remaining three minority groups, who, despite any progress they may have made, continue to be significantly disadvantaged. Caribbean men at some points are in a similar position to, or more advantaged than Indians but are significantly more disadvantaged in relation to job levels and unemployment. The Pakistanis are in all respects more disadvantaged than the Caribbeans except that owing to their much higher level of self-employment, which as we have seen yields on average low incomes, they score slightly higher for presence in the professional, managerial and employer category. Finally, the Bangladeshis are as a group the most disadvantaged. Ethnic minority men fall, therefore, into two broad groups, those who are close to parity with whites (the Chinese, African Asians and Indians) and the others who are significantly disadvantaged. It is also possible to represent these six groups of men in three bands, with the Indians and Caribbeans occupying the middle band.

Table 9.23 offers a similar analysis of employment disadvantage for women. The key measures used in this table are not the same as those used for men but reflect the fact that the low participation rate of some groups of women is an indicator and source of disadvantage. Moreover, too few women are managers and employers in large establishments to generate large enough sample sizes for analysis. Table 9.23 shows that the scale of differentials between women of different ethnic groups is much smaller than is the case for men, but otherwise the ethnic groups are stacked up in a similar order as for the men. There are, however, two distinctive features in the comparative circumstances of women. Firstly, the low economic activity rates for Pakistani and Bangladeshi women create a division between these groups of women and all others which does not exist for men. It could though be said to have some parallel with the high levels of Pakistani and Bangladeshi male unemployment, which also exist among women from these groups. What both Pakistani and Bangladeshi men and women have in common is very low levels of paid work, especially as employees (though, as has been noted, there is a strong anecdotal impression that many self-declared economically inactive women from these groups are engaged in homeworking for the clothing industry). The second difference in employment disadvantage between men and women is that the position of Caribbean women relative to white and other women is much better than that of Caribbean men. While Caribbean women are grossly under-represented in the top jobs category and have a high rate of unemployment, they are strongly represented in intermediate non-manual work, and as a result have an above average share of supervisory posts and above-average earnings.

If we combine the position of the sexes, the position of the minorities in employment relative to whites seems to fall into three bands:

1 disadvantage confined to top jobs in large establishments: the Chinese and African Asians;
2 relative disadvantage: the Indians and Caribbeans;
3 severe disadvantage: the Pakistanis and Bangladeshis.

Ethnic penalties

Racial disadvantage, then, continues to be a fact, even if it does not apply to all ethnic minority groups. Moreover, this disadvantage is attributable partly to discrimination in employment. Controlled tests, whereby white and ethnic minority persons respond to advertised vacancies for which they are equally suitable, have been conducted since the 1960s and tend to reproduce the result that at least one third of private employers discriminated against Caribbean applicants, Asian applicants or both (Daniel 1968; Smith 1977; Brown and Gay 1985; Simpson and Stevenson 1994). Discrimination is found not just in face-to-face encounters, or in telephone calls, but also in tests using written applications where it is clear from the applicant's name or biographical details that they are or are not white (Noon 1993; Esmail and Everington 1993). The Commission for Racial Equality continues every year to publish findings of direct or indirect discrimination in the practices of specific employers, and sometimes whole professions or industries, such as accountancy (CRE 1987) or hotels (CRE 1991). The number of complaints of racial discrimination made by individuals to the CRE and to industrial tribunals has risen over the years (CRE annual reports), and [. . .] the belief that some employers discriminate is held by 90 per cent of white people and three-quarters of minority ethnic persons. One in five of the minority ethnic respondents said they had been refused a job on racial grounds, nearly half of whom had had this experience at least once in the previous five years.

One of the alternative ways of relating the socio-economic diversity of ethnic minorities with the idea of racial discrimination and disadvantage is to argue that all non-white groups, regardless of qualification and the position of groups in the jobs hierarchy, suffer 'an ethnic penalty' (Heath and McMahon 1995). 'Ethnic penalty' refers to 'all the sources of disadvantage that might lead an ethnic group to fare less well in the labour market than do similarly qualified whites . . . [because] discrimination is likely to be a major component' (Heath and McMahon 1995, 1). Heath and McMahon submitted data from the 1991 Census to a logistic modelling, in which age and qualifications were strictly controlled, and found that male migrants with higher-level qualifications in groups that appeared to be successful in the jobs market such as the Chinese and African Asians/Indians were significantly less likely to be employees in higher or intermediate non-manual work than either British-born white people or Irish-born migrants. While the African Asians/Indians and Chinese were more successful than the other groups of non-white men, nevertheless 'their high qualifications effectively masked their difficulty in gaining access to the salariat' (Heath and McMahon 1995: 18). Migrant women from non-white groups were even more likely to pay an 'ethnic penalty', except for the Caribbean women, who were more successful than Irish-born women.

Heath and McMahon went on to carry out the same logistic regression for the British-born members of the various ethnic groups. Again, while there were differences between groups, there was a clear tendency for second-generation non-white men and women to pay significant ethnic penalties in the competition for the better non-manual jobs. Moreover, the advantage that the first-generation Caribbean women had is not repeated for the second generation, leading Heath and McMahon to suggest that the first-generation pattern was owing to rather special recruitment efforts by the National Health Service to secure nurses from the Caribbean (Heath and McMahon 1995: 26). They conclude, therefore, that, for non-white groups, being born in this country is not associated with any improvement in competitive chances, for 'the second generation experienced the same pattern and magnitude of ethnic penalties in the British labour market as the first generation did' (Heath and McMahon 1995: 29).

There may, then, be a declining racial difference in outcomes, as demonstrated by Iganski and Payne (1996), which as they suggest may be owing to an increase in the supply of the better non-manual jobs and to more 'open', 'meritocratic' competition, but it may still be the case that even the 'over-achieving' groups are being 'under-rewarded' – that is to say, that typically, for the more competitive posts, ethnic minority individuals have to be not just as good but better than their white competitors in order to get the job.

Explaining diversity

The fact of an ethnic penalty, which Heath and McMahon emphasize includes probably the effects of discrimination but also other forms of disadvantage, suggests that there might be a greater degree of commonality among the non-white groups than the data might at first suggest. Yet, even after controlling for birth in Britain, age and qualifications, Heath and McMahon found that the chances of entry into the salaried posts varied between non-white groups. Black Africans, a group not included in our survey, have only about one-third the chance of success of their white peers, while 'Black-Other' (mainly people of at least part Caribbean ancestry who prefer a self-description such as 'Black British' which does not refer to the Caribbean) have almost the same chance as whites, with African Asians/Indians and Pakistanis in between these two groups (Heath and McMahon 1995: 30; the Chinese and Bangladeshi samples were not large enough to be included in this analysis). A similar analysis using LFS data from the 1983–9 surveys also showed diversity in its results: for example, the Chinese suffered no ethnic penalty, the African Asians a small one, but the Indians a much larger one, with Caribbeans and Pakistanis placed in the middle (Cheng and Heath 1993). Comparable analyses of similarly qualified candidates for similar courses in higher education found that Caribbeans and Pakistanis had lower chances of entry to the 'old' universities than other candidates (Modood and Shiner 1994), while, for medical schools, not having a European surname was a stronger predictor of lower chances of entry than not being white (McManus et al. 1995).

How is this diversity in the structure of inequality to be explained? The question has been posed as one of how to 'explain the disparity between groups which share similar skin colour' (Robinson 1990: 284). Robinson suggests the existence of three possible lines of enquiry. One approach 'stresses the differential incorporation or marginalisation of the groups and the impact that this might have upon the desire for social mobility in a society which is perceived as alien' (Robinson 1990: 284). Malcolm Cross, for example, has distinguished between class exclusion and class segmentation as two different socially structured forms of racial inequality (Cross 1994). While high levels of representation among the unemployed and low paid are a symptom of class exclusion, class segmentation takes place when a group is allowed to enter the higher occupational classes, but is confined to an inferior subset of the higher occupations (Cross 1994: 232). Cross believes that the Caribbeans are subject to class exclusion, while the racism against Asians within British employment practices has the effect of incorporation through segmentation of the existing class structure.

The distinction between class segmentation and class exclusion may be an important one, but Cross's application of it through an Asian–Caribbean dichotomy is unfeasible. The 'catching up' by African Asians and the prospect of overtaking whites, with already a stronger representation at the higher earnings levels, does not suggest that they are being confined to an inferior subset of the better-classes. On the other hand, Pakistanis and Bangladeshis fit much better Cross's definition of the excluded as given above, especially as the high levels of Pakistani unemployment predate those of the Caribbeans and consisted of actual job losses as the textile and related industries collapsed during the 1970s and early 1980s. For the Caribbeans unemployment rose more gradually as successive cohorts of school leavers found that the supply of jobs, especially for those without qualifications, had dried up. Hence Robinson found that, while 5 per cent of all workers who had a job in 1971 did not have one in 1981, 8 per cent of Caribbeans did not, but the figure for Pakistanis was 19 per cent (Robinson 1990: 280).

The reason why Cross thinks that the longer-term prospects of the Pakistanis and Bangladeshis are of class segmentation rather than exclusion is because, in contrast to the Caribbeans, economic marginalization has not led to a socio-political alienation. The Pakistanis and Bangladeshis are still committed to economic advancement; the young will acquire, he believes, qualifications that will enable them to compete for the kind of jobs that will be available. The impact of racism and economic disadvantage seems, however, to have blunted the motivation of a sizeable proportion of younger Caribbeans (Cross 1994: chapters 8 and 10). While there is some truth in this contrast, the prediction that Pakistanis and Bangladeshis will develop a similar class profile to other South Asians grossly understates the current scale of the disadvantage of Pakistanis and Bangladeshis, and takes no account either of the cultural differences between South Asians (Modood, Beishon and Virdee 1994; see also Nazroo 1997), or of a political alienation, sometimes expressed in terms of a political Muslim identity, which is itself a product of and further stimulates anti-Muslim prejudice (Modood 1990), or of anxiety about a possible trend of criminalization among young Pakistanis and Bangladeshis, which in some ways parallels the experience of Caribbean male youth (Nahdi 1994).

In any case, the position of young Caribbean men (and to some extent women) is itself paradoxical: they are among those with the highest rates of unqualified and unemployed and yet also among the highest average earners. It is possible that the high earnings averages are a product of the high unemployment, for, by taking out of the earnings sample more potentially lower earners, the sample is biased compared with other groups in favour of higher earners, especially among manual workers. Yet it does not have this effect upon Pakistanis and Bangladeshis who also have high rates of unemployment among sixteen- to thirty-four-year-olds. It is more likely that the paradoxical findings are pointing to an economic polarization among young Caribbean men, who are to be disproportionately found both among the long-term unemployed and the middle band of earners. Indeed, in this respect the Caribbeans may be becoming more like the Pakistanis and Bangladeshis, rather than vice versa. For the aspect of these latter groups that probably suggests to Cross that they will progress like the other South Asians is the presence within them of a highly qualified professional and business class.[12] Yet this class is not new among Pakistanis and Bangladeshis: it was picked up in the PSI surveys of the 1970s and 1980s (Smith 1977; Brown 1984), and what is remarkable is that it has hardly grown between 1982 and 1994 (see table 9.20). Indeed, if the unemployed are added back into the figures on which the analysis is based, there is no growth at all among Pakistanis and Bangladeshis, in contrast to other groups, in the proportion of men in the top jobs category (the 1991 Census, though, does suggest growth). At a time of general upward mobility for men, this would in fact be a relative decline.

In examining the educational qualifications of migrants, the internal polarity among those from the subcontinent, with a disproportionate number having degrees and a disproportionate number having no qualifications and many speaking little English, was a strong contrast to the relative homogeneity of the Caribbeans. This tendency among Caribbeans of disproportionate grouping around the middle is also found in Robinson's longitudinal study of social mobility between 1971 and 1981 (Robinson 1990), as also in the findings about earnings in this [reading]. The paradoxical statistics about young Caribbean men may be pointing to a post-migration, indeed, a relatively recent, internal polarization among Caribbeans, while the class divisions among Pakistanis and Bangladeshis, and the divisions between these two and the other South Asian groups, have deepened by the collapse of those industries that provided jobs to the Pakistanis in the 1970s, but in fact stretch back to pre-migration origins.

So while Cross is right not to want to conflate the disadvantaged profiles of Caribbeans with the disadvantaged profiles of Pakistanis and Bangladeshis, the differences in question cannot be captured by his differential use of exclusion and segmentation, and give no grounds for his Caribbean–Asian dichotomy or for projecting an optimistic view of upward social mobility for Pakistanis and Bangladeshis. If we wanted to explore these questions further, we could perhaps proceed by asking how differently post-industrial long-term unemployment would impact on excluded groups if one was composed of tightly knit, hierarchically organized families and communities and ongoing connections with the country of origin, and the other was not. Such a reformulation would not be a basis for reliable predictions (for there are too many other variables to take into account, especially in relation to changes in the economy), but it would bring us closer to raising some of the issues that lie behind Cross's discussion. It also leads us to a form of explanation identified by Robinson.

A second possible explanation for the disparity between minorities 'stresses the groups' histories prior to migration, and the traditions and resources they can therefore mobilise to gain mobility' (Robinson 1990: 284). This is an approach that has been developed most to explain the phenomenon of immigrant self-employment, as found in many countries, especially in North America, and which is often critical in facilitating upward social mobility (Waldinger, Aldrich and Ward 1990). It connects with a sociological tradition that arose through studies of European migration to the large American cities in the early part of this century (Lal 1990). While the resources in question are of a complex sort and relate to culture, religion and gender, one simple measure is qualifications. There does seem to be a strong correlation between the qualifications of the first generation [. . .], and the extent of current disadvantage depicted in tables 9.22 and 9.23. This lends particular support to the general view that the post-migration social mobility of groups consists of the re-creation of a comparable class profile to the one the group had in the country of origin before migration. We have, of course, seen that similar qualifications do not yield similar occupational advantages for all groups, and that it is likely that some of the differences are explained by forms of direct and indirect discrimination.

This relates to the third possible explanation of disparities mentioned by Robinson: that different groups are stereotyped differently, perhaps influenced by the roles allotted to groups during British colonial rule (Robinson 1990: 285). An important piece of research on middle managers' perceptions of minority workers and their ethnicity in the early 1980s found that stereotypes (not always negative) related to two groupings, Caribbeans and South Asians, and that radically different stereotypes were held of the two groups. The most common view expressed of Caribbean workers was that they were lazy, happy-go-lucky or slow, while the most common view of Asians was that they were hard workers (Jenkins 1986). It has been argued that similar antithetical images of the main non-white groups are in fact pervasive in commonsense and media representations (Bonnett 1993). In the last decade or so, it has increasingly been argued that contemporary racism cannot be understood in terms of an undifferential colour racism, but that additionally groups are racialized, and praised or condemned, on the basis of alleged cultural traits rather than any kind of biology (Barker 1981; Gilroy 1987; Cohen 1988), and that groups such as South Asian Muslims suffer a distinctive and complex kind of racism (Modood 1992 and 1997). In this [reading] we have seen how nearly half of South Asians who complain of racial discrimination in recruitment believe that their religion was a factor in the discrimination; and so do a quarter of Caribbeans, further suggesting the complex nature of discrimination as perceived by those who believe they have direct experience of it. We have also seen that all groups now believe that the most prejudice is directed at Asians and/or Muslims. [. . .]

It has to be said that it would be wrong to expect racial disadvantage, both its decline and its persistence, to be only, or even primarily, explained in terms of 'race', discrimination or ethnic differences. There is a general agreement that the most important fact is economic restructuring. The changes in job levels for the minorities, no less than for the majority population, are above all a consequence of the continuing loss of jobs in manufacturing, especially those that require low levels of skills, in favour of the service sector, which has seen a continuous growth in higher-level jobs and lower-level part-time work. It is this fundamental and continuing shift, together with the demographic shortages that have increased job opportunities for women and some minorities, that is the cause of the differential advantage and disadvantage experienced by the different minority groups, and it is the context in which the more specific factors that have been discussed are played out.

NOTES

From T. Modood (1997), 'Employment', in T. Modood, R. Berthoud, J. Lakey, J. Nazroo, P. Smith, S. Virdee and S. Beishon, *Ethnic Minorities, in Britain* (London: Policy Studies Institute), pp. 83–149, which acknowledges Pam Meadows, Director of the Policy studies Institute, for her assistance.

1   There may, however, be some uncertainty about the profile of Pakistanis and Bangladeshis, for the 1991 Census figures, based on 10 per cent of the Census, show the
Pakistanis and Bangladeshis to have a distinctly higher presence in the top non-manual
category, and for the Pakistanis to have a smaller presence in the top manual category
than we found. This may just reveal the changed circumstances of 1991 and 1994, or it
may reflect on our smaller but more targeted sample structure, which was designed to
include to a greater degree some of the 'hard-to-find' population that it is estimated that
the Census missed (Simpson, 1996). Because the Census under-represents these groups it
is not clear whether our sample is more representative of the underlying population, or
whether it is skewed in the other direction. The Labour Force Survey over many years
has strongly suggested that the Pakistani and Bangladeshi male jobs level profile continues to have a manual skew and a distinctly smaller representation in the top employment category than the African Asian and Indians (e.g. Jones 1993: 99), and that is what
our survey too reports. However, our male skilled manual and foreman figures, particularly for Pakistanis, seem higher than they should be, given that there is a very distinct
downward trend in the numbers of manual workers.

2   As a matter of fact, in some groups the self-employed were better qualified than
employees.

3   The 1991 Census reports that women of all ethnic minorities except the Chinese have a
greater presence in the top jobs category, with the result that there is little difference
between South Asian and white women. The Census found also that while there was a
smaller proportion of Caribbean than other women in the top category, they were as
well represented as white women, and much better than all other groups, among
employers and managers in large establishments (3 per cent) (OPCS 1993b, table 16;
Abbot and Tyler 1995, table x). South Asian and Chinese women, in contrast, were
more likely to be professional workers. The difference between our findings and those of
the Census may be that our survey includes more women from the 'hard-to-find'
categories, such as those with poor facility in English, and as they are more likely
to be in manual work (though they are even more likely to be economically inactive)
their inclusion will depress the proportion of women of certain minorities in the top
category.

4   The high Pakistani and Bangladeshi female inactivity also suggests that the poorly
qualified are more likely to be keeping house than be in paid manual work outside the
home.

5   There is one important aspect in which our Chinese sample is not consistent with the
LFS 1988–90 and the 1991 Census. They found that over half of Chinese men and nearly
half of the women were in distribution and catering, which is substantially more than in
our sample.

6   It is not unusual for higher earners to be under-represented in surveys of income. It is a
long-established feature of the Family Expenditure Survey, for example, which is known
to exclude the top 5 per cent (Kemsley, Redpath and Homes 1980).

7   It has further been argued that the female full-time employees' earnings differentials in
the analysis of the 1982 data were misleading, for minority women worked longer hours
and were not earning more than white women on an hourly pay comparison (Bruegel
1989, 52; Bhavnani 1994, 84). Maybe this was so in 1982, but, as we have seen, the
finding of this survey is that ethnic minority women in full-time work do fewer hours
than whites (figure 9.1); an hourly pay analysis would widen the gap.

8   For more detailed investigation of comparative earnings, see the follow-up study by
Berthoud and Casey (1997).

TARIQ MODOOD

9   This is achieved at a cost. A further study of a subset of the sample of self-employed
    South Asians suggests that they work much longer hours than Asian employees
    (Metcalf, Modood and Virdee 1996, 88).
10 Interestingly, in Britain, prejudice against a religious minority does not seem to be
    connected to a strong religious affiliation. The survey found that people who said
    religion was important to them were much less likely to say that they were prejudiced
    against ethnic minorities or Muslims.
11 The reader will recall that the presence of Indian, and to a lesser extent Pakistani,
    women in the top non-manual category was very much because of their self-
    employment, as was seen in table 9.4. A further difference between the two tables is
    that the analysis under consideration (table 9.21) is only of full-time employees. This
    makes a significant difference to the profile of white women, for not only are they more
    likely to be in part-time work, but as most white women in manual work are part-
    timers (as we saw in table 9.5), analysis of only full-time workers increases white
    women's comparative representation in non-manual work, especially in the top cate-
    gory. The opposite proved to be the case for Indian women in our survey: an unusually
    high proportion of Indian women employees in the top jobs category were part-timers.
12 Anecdotal evidence suggests that this class is from urban Pakistan and, to a lesser
    extent, rural Punjab: in contrast, the majority of Pakistanis in Britain are from rural
    Kashmir, especially Mirpur – one of the poorest and least economically developed
    areas in the region.

REFERENCES

Abbott, P. and M. Tyler (1995), 'Ethnic variation in the female labour force: a research
    note', *British Journal of Sociology*, vol. 46, no. 2, pp. 339–51.
Aldrich, H. E., J. C. Cater, T. P. Jones and D. McEvoy (1981), 'Business development and
    self-segregation: Asian enterprise in three British cities', in C. Peach, V. Robinson and S.
    Smith, eds, *Ethnic Segregation in Cities* (London: Croom Helm).
Allen, S. and C. Wolkowitz (1987), *Homeworking: Myths and Realities* (London: Macmillan).
Anthias, F. and N. Yuval-Davis (1992), *Socialised Boundaries: Race, Nation, Gender,
    Colour, Class and the Anti-Racist Struggle* (London: Routledge).
Ballard, R. (1996), 'The Pakistanis: stability and introspection', in C. Peach, ed., *Ethnicity
    in the 1991 Census*, vol. 2: *The Ethnic Minority Populations of Britain* (London: HMSO).
Ballard, R. and V. S. Kalra (1994), *The Ethnic Dimensions of the 1991 Census: A Prelimin-
    ary Report* (University of Manchester, Census Dissemination Unit).
Barker, M. (1981), *The New Racism* (London: Junction Books).
Basu, A. (1995), *Asian Small Businesses in Britain: An Exploration of Entrepreneurial
    Activity*, University of Reading, Discussion Paper no. 303, Series A, vol. 7.
Beishon, S., S. Virdee and A. Hagell (1995), *Nursing in a Multi-Ethnic NHS* (London:
    Policy Studies Institute).
Benson, S. (1996), 'Asians have culture, West Indians have problems: discourses of race and
    ethnicity in and out of anthropology', in T. Ranger, Y. Samad and O. Stuart, eds (1996),
    Culture, Identity and Politics (London: Avebury).
Bhavnani, R. (1994), *Black Women in the Labour Market: A Research Review* (London:
    Equal Opportunities Commission).
Bhopal, R. (1995), 'Ethnicity, race, health and research: racist black box, junk or enligh-
    tened epidemiology', paper presented at Society for Social Medicine Scientific Meeting,
    London.

Bonnett, A. (1993), *Radicalism, Anti-Racism and Representation* (London: Routledge).

Bruegel, I. (1989), 'Sex and race in the labour market', *Feminist Review*, vol. 32, pp. 49–68.

Brown, C. (1984), *Black and White Britain* (London: Heinemann).

Brown, C. and P. Gay (1985), *Racial Discrimination: 17 Years after the Act* (London: Policy Studies Institute).

Cheng, Y. and A. Heath (1993), 'Ethnic origins and class destinations', *Oxford Review of Education*, vol. 19, no. 2, pp. 151–65.

Cohen, P. (1988), 'The perversions of inheritance: studies in the making of multi-racist Britain', in P. Cohen and H. S. Bains, eds, *Multi-Racist Britain*, (London: Macmillan).

Coleman, D. J. Salt, eds (1996), *Ethnicity in the 1991 Census*, vol. 1: *Demographic Characteristics of Ethnic Minority Populations* (London: HMSO).

Commission for Racial Equality (1987), *Chartered Accountancy Training Contracts: Report of a Formal Investigation into Ethnic Minority Recruitment.* (London: CRE).

Commission for Racial Equality (1991), 'Second review of the Race Relations Act 1976: consultative paper' (London: CRE).

Cross, M. (1989), 'Afro-Caribbeans and Asians are affected differently by British racism', *New Statesman and Society*, 7 April, p. 35.

Cross, M. (1994), *Ethnic Pluralism and Racial Inequality*, (Unpublished dissertation, University of Utrecht).

Daniel, W. W. (1968), *Racial Discrimination in England* (Harmondsworth: Penguin).

Donald, J. and A. Rattansi, eds (1992), *'Race', Culture and Difference* (London: Sage).

Drew, D. (1995), *'Race', Education and Work: The Statistics of Inequality* (Aldershot: Avebury).

Drew, D., J. Gray and N. Sime (1992), *Against the Odds: The Education and Labour Market Experiences of Black Young People,* England and Wales Youth Cohort Study, Report R&D no. 68, Youth Cohort Series no. 19, Employment Department.

Duffy, K. B. and I. C. Lincoln (1990), *Earnings and Ethnicity* (Leicester: City Council).

Esmail, A. and S. Everington (1993), 'Racial discrimination against doctors from ethnic minorities', *British Medical Journal*, vol. 306, pp. 691–2.

Gilroy, P. (1987), *There Ain't No Black in the Union Jack* (London: Hutchinson).

Gray, P. et al. (1993), *Access to Training and Employment for Asian Women in Coventry* (Coventry: City Council).

Hagell, A. and C. Shaw (1996), *Opportunity and Disadvantage at Age 16* (London: Policy Studies Institute).

Hakim, C. (1993), 'The myth of rising female employment', *Work, Employment and Society*, vol. 7, no. 1, pp. 97–120.

Heath, A. and D. McMahon (1995), *Education and Occupational Attainments: The Impact of Ethnic Origins*, paper 34, (London: Centre for Research into Elections and Social Trends).

Heath, A. and J. Ridge (1983), 'Social mobility of ethnic minorities', *Journal of Biosocial Science Supplement*, vol. 8, pp. 169–84.

Heckman, J. J. and G. Sedbcek (1985), 'Heterogeneity', aggregation and market wage functions: an empirical model of self selection in the labour market', *Journal of Political Economy*, vol. 93, no. 6.

Iganski, P. and G. Payne (1996), 'Declining racial disadvantage in the British labour market', *Ethnic and Racial Studies*, vol. 19, no. 1.

Jenkins, R. (1986), *Racism in Recruitment* (Cambridge: Cambridge University Press).

Jones, T. (1993), *Britain's Ethnic Minorities*, (London: Policy Studies Institute).

Kemsley, W. F. F., R. V. Redpath and M. Homes (1980), *Family Expenditure Survey Handbook*, (London: HMSO).

Lal, B. B. (1990), *The Romance of Culture in an Urban Civilisation* (London: Routledge).

McEvoy, D., T. P. Jones, J. Cater and H. Aldrich (1982), 'Asian Immigrant Businesses in British Cities', paper presented to the British Association for the Advancement of Science, London: annual meeting, September.

McManus, I. C., P. Richards, B.C. Winder, K. A. Sproston and V. Styles (1995), 'Medical school applicants from ethnic minority groups: identifying if and when they are disadvantaged', *British Medical Journal*, vol. 310, pp. 496–500.

Metcalf, H., T. Modood and S. Virdee (1996), *Asian Self-Employment: The Interaction of Culture and Economics in England* (London: Policy Studies Institute).

Miles, R. (1987), 'Class relations and racism in Britain in the 1980's', *Revue européenne des migrations internationales*, vol. 3, nos 1–2.

Modood, T. (1990), 'British Asian Muslims and the Rushdie affair', *Political Quarterly*, vol. 61, no. 2, pp. 143–60; reprinted in J. Donald and A. Rattansi, eds (1992), *'Race', Culture and Difference* (London: Sage), pp. 260–7.

Modood, T. (1992), *Not Easy Being British: Colour, Culture and Citizenship* (Stoke on Trent: Runnymede Trust and Trentham Books).

Modood, T. (1997), 'Difference, cultural racism and anti-racism', in P. Werbner and T. Modood, eds, *Debating Cultural Hybridity: Multi-cultural Identities and the Politics of Anti-racism* (London: Zed Books).

Modood, T., S. Beishon and S. Virdee (1994), *Changing Ethinic Identities* (London: Policy Studies Institute).

Modood, T. et al., eds, *Ethnic Minorities in Britain: Diversity and Disadvantage* (London: Policy Studies Institute).

Modood, T. and M. Shiner (1994), *Ethnic Minorities and Higher Education: Why are there Differential Rates of Entry?* (London: Policy Studies Institute).

Nahdi, F. (1994), 'Focus on crime and youth', *Q-News*, vol. 3, no. 3 pp. 15–22.

Nazroo, J. Y. (1997), 'Health and Health Services', in Modood, T. et al., eds, *Ethnic Minorities in Britain Diversity and Disadvantage* (London: Policy Studies Insitute).

Noon, M. (1993), 'Racial discrimination in speculative applications: evidence from the UK's top one hundred firms', *Human Resource Management Journal*, vol. 3, no. 4, pp. 35–47.

OPCS (1993), *1991 Census: Ethnic Group and Country of Birth (Great Britain)* (London: HMSO).

Payne, J. (1996), *Education and Training for 16–18-Year-Olds: Individual Paths and National Trends*, (London: Policy Studies Institute).

Peach, C. ed. (1996), *Ethnicity in the 1991 Census*, vol. 2: *The Ethnic Minority Populations of Britain* (London: HMSO).

Phizacklea, A. and C. Wolkowitz (1995), *Homeworking Women: Gender, Racism and Class* (London: Sage).

Rafiq, M. (1992), 'Ethnicity and enterprise: a comparison of Muslim and non-Muslim owned Asian businesses in Britain', *New Community*, vol. 19, no. 1, pp. 43–60.

Ram, M. (1992), 'Coping with racism: Asian employers in the inner-city', *Work, Employment and Society*, vol. 6, no. 4, pp. 601–18.

Robinson, V. (1990), 'Roots to Mobility', *Ethnic and Racial Studies*, vol. 13, no. 2, pp. 274–86.

Robinson, V. (1993), 'Ethnic minorities and the enduring geography of settlement', *Town and Country Planning*, March, pp. 53–6.

Runnymede Trust (1996), *The Multi-Ethnic Good Society: Vision and Reality* (London: Runnymede Trust).

Schmitt, J. and J. Wadsworth (1995), *Why are 2 Million Men Inactive? The Decline in Male Labour Force Participation in Britain*, Centre for Economic Performance Working Paper no. 338, London School of Economics and Political Science.

Simpson, A. and J. Stevenson (1994), *Half a Chance, Still? Jobs, Discrimination and Young People in Nottingham*, (Nottingham and District Racial Equality Council).

Simpson, S. (1996), 'Non-response to the 1991 Census: the effects on ethnic group enumeration', in D. Coleman and J. Salt, eds, *Ethnicity in the 1991 Census*, vol. 1, (London, HMSO).

Sly, F. (1995), 'Ethnic groups and the labour market: analyses from the spring 1994 labour force survey', *Employment Gazette*, vol. 102, pp. 251–61.

Smith, D. J. (1977), *Racial Disadvantage in Britain* (Harmondsworth: Penguin).

UKACIA (1993), *Muslims and the Law in Multi-Faith Britain: Need for Reform.* A Memorandum to the Home Secretary.

Virdee, S. and K. Grint (1994), 'Black self-organization in trade unions', *Sociological Review*, vol. 42, no. 2, pp. 202–25.

Waldinger, R. H. Aldrich and R. Ward (1990), *Ethnic Entrepreneurs* (London: Sage).

Ward, R. and M. Cross (1991), 'Race, employment and economic change', in P. Brown and R. Scase, eds, *Poor Work: Disadvantage and the Division of Labour* (Buckingham: Open University Press), pp. 116–31.

Werbner, P. (1990a), *The Migration Process* (Oxford: Berg).

Werbner, P. (1990b), 'Renewing an industrial past: British Pakistani entrepreneurship in Manchester', *Migration*, vol. 8, pp. 7–39.

Wrench, J. and J. Solomos, eds (1993), *Racism and Migration in Western Europe* (Oxford: Berg).

Wrench, J. and S. Virdee (1995), 'Organising the unorganised: "race", poor work and trade unions', in P. Acker, C. Smith and P. Smith, eds, *The New Work Place and Trade Unions* (London: Routledge).

10   Gender

It's Hard to be Soft: Is Management Style Gendered?

JUDY WAJCMAN

Traditionally, men have been seen as better suited than women to executive positions. The qualities usually associated with being a successful manager are 'masculine' traits such as drive, objectivity and an authoritative manner. Women have been seen as different from men, as lacking the necessary personal character- istics and skills to make good managers. The entry of women into senior levels within organizations over the last decade or so has brought such stereotypes into question. One of the issues generating debate is whether women bring a distinct style of management to organizations as we enter the twenty-first century.

If a participative, co-operative management style is in the ascendancy, this style is more closely associated with women than men. So there is much at stake. Recent developments in organization theory, such as human resource management and Japanese management, have moved away from the hardness of quantitative methods and deterministic conceptions of corporate strategy. According to the new orthodoxy, effective management needs a softer edge, a more qualitative, people-oriented approach. If women really have a 'natural' proclivity for this style, concerns about their career prospects may be misguided. Because they more closely fit the new criteria for success in management, women will flourish as never before.

This examines the thesis that management style is itself gendered. It asks whether there are sex differences in how women and men manage, and what this means in terms of defining the skills necessary for managerial success. My data show that the women who have made it into senior positions are in most respects indistinguishable from the men in equivalent positions. In fact, the similarities between women and men far outweigh the differences between women and men as groups. This finding leads me to argue that there is no such thing as a 'female' management style. However, my data also suggest that gender stereotypes are still deeply entrenched. Despite the current enthusiasm for a 'feminine' style of man- agement, women have to adopt the style associated with male management in order to succeed. Style is after all an intrinsic part of the managerial job which, as I have argued, is itself gendered male.

The 'feminine' in management

Recently there has been a positive re-evaluation of gender stereotypes of women managers. This development is due largely to the fact that standard renditions of women's leadership qualities are in tune with current fashions in management theory.

During the 1980s management theory underwent a paradigm shift, reflecting a growing recognition that managerial processes had damaged the competitive position of US business. A central theme has been how to adapt Japanese management techniques to Western economies. Leadership, just-in-time management, teamworking and total quality control all entered managerial discourse alongside more general concerns about flexibility, new technology and niche marketing (see reviews by Wood 1989; and Sisson 1994). This 'new wave' of management theory criticizes American management practice as placing too much weight on a centrally imposed rationality, expressed through undue emphasis on the measurable, involving the manipulation of complex structures of compliance. In Japanese business, the emphasis is on the creation of a strong cohesive culture of collective commitment to achieve organizational goals. The Americans had neglected this 'transformational' leadership in favour of a shorter-term, 'harder' transactional style. 'The lesson was clear: cultural management that secured the commitment of employees as valued assets – hallmarks of the "soft" human resource management model – should be the order of the day' (Legge 1994: 403). Successful firms are described as people oriented and decentralized, uncluttered by rigidly hierarchical and bureaucratic layers of management. Leadership is now concerned with fostering shared visions, shared values, shared directions and shared responsibility.

In the more popular versions of these new wave theories, gender images are commonly deployed. They are used to suggest that women have a more consensual style of management, and that this will be an advantage in post-industrial corporations. According to management gurus Peters and Waterman (1982), managers need 'irrational, intuitive' qualities for success, qualities that are explicitly described as feminine. They challenge the masculine image of the rational manager by demonstrating that seemingly feminine characteristics are actually potent managerial tools. Similarly, in its report *Management Development to the Millennium*, the British Institute of Management (1994) argues that 'female ways of managing will be more appropriate in the millennium' In the future, they say, organizations will be less hierarchical, will rely more on teamwork and consensus management, and 'feminine' skills of communication and collaborative working will come to the fore. *Enterprising Nation: Report on Leadership and Management Skills*, published by the Australian government (1995), concurs that managers need to embrace women's 'soft' skills: 'In this new way of managing, increasing recognition is given to factors such as relational rather than competitive values, the need for firms to seek interdependence rather than dominance in the market-place and for business opportunities to be nurtured in an "emergent" manner through affiliation and cooperation rather than rationality, separation and mani-pulation' (p. 8). So the advantage men formerly enjoyed in 'command-and-con-trol' style organizations will pass to women in these new organizations.

This controversy about gendered management style also resonates with key preoccupations of feminist theory [. . .]. During the 1970s feminist authors often minimized or even denied differences between men and women, in order to argue that women had the same potentialities as men and should have equality of opportunity at work. Since the 1980s, however, many feminist scholars have begun to emphasize women's difference and to celebrate what they see as specific-ally female values and ways of behaving, feeling and thinking (Gilligan 1982). The new and fundamentally feminist twist in the argument is that difference is no longer equated with inferiority or hierarchical ordering. For example, Ferguson's (1984) radical feminist case against male bureaucracy rests on the assumption that women-centred modes of organization are more democratic and participatory. Questioning whether the aspiration for equality is too limited a goal, such writers claim superiority for women's ways of doing things and are positive about the possibility of social change through the revaluing of gender differences.

The literature on women in management reflects this shifting emphasis. Much of the early research was aimed at discrediting the idea that women themselves lacked the necessary attributes to succeed in management (Hennig and Jardim 1979; Marshall 1984). These critics targeted psychologically based theories which viewed women's personality traits as ill-suited to the managerial role. Studies of women in management using this perspective argued that there were no essential differences between men and women, refuting notions that women are less effect-ive as managers than men.

The feminine stereotype is now being challenged. The debate was sparked off by an article in the *Harvard Business Review* (Rosener 1990), questioning whether women have a different style of management from men, and what its significance might be for management practice in general. Rosener argues that women execut-ives are now making it to the top, 'not by adopting the style and habits that have proved successful for men but by drawing on the skills and attitudes they devel-oped from their shared experience as women. . . . They are succeeding because of – not in spite of – certain characteristics generally considered to be "feminine" and inappropriate in leaders' (pp. 119–20). In contrast to the command-and-control leadership style associated with men, she describes women's style as 'transforma-tional and interactive' because they actively encourage participation, share power and information, enhance the self-worth of others and stimulate enthusiasm about work. Loden (1985) and Martin (1993) similarly argue that female managers, because of biology and socialization, are ideally suited to today's decentralized organizations where teamwork and delegation, rather than hierarchy and direc-tion, are the key.

The conclusion drawn in this literature is that, rather than women managers modelling themselves on men, the norm of effective management should be based on the way women do things. Accordingly, men will need to acquire the skills and qualities of 'feminine leadership' if they are to maintain their position. In the words of Tom Peters: 'Gone are the days of women succeeding by learning to play men's games. Instead the time has come for men on the move to learn to play women's games' (Fierman 1990: 71).

Although much of this literature is from the US, it finds a resonance among British feminists, who have embraced this notion of women's different style in response to the limited achievements of equal opportunity policies. They argue that the 'sameness' approach, embodied in equality policies, leads to women succeeding only on men's terms. For example, Ashburner says that 'the consequence of highlighting the differences between men and women, far from further marginalising them, is to challenge the view that women do not conform to the "norm", and to put the emphasis onto the issue of changing management style and structures. Minimising differences avoids any challenge to the predominant male value system' (1994: 193–4). This discussion of women's different style mirrors a shift in the language of equal opportunities from a concern with equality to 'valuing diversity', in this case a valuing of diversity in management styles (Liff and Wajcman 1996).

Managers of reason

When I reflect on the copious literature on leadership style, I am struck by the way in which it is permeated by gender stereotypical oppositions, such as that between hard and soft, reason and emotion. Instead of challenging the gendered nature of the dichotomies, they simply invert them. Leadership traits that correspond with male traits like dominance, aggressiveness and rationality are now presented negatively, while formerly devalued feminine qualities like the soft and emotional are presented positively. This simple inversion hardly signals a great step forward for women's prospects in management. Have feminist scholars in business schools adopted the correct strategy by embracing these new business fashions and using them to promote the cause of women managers? I have my doubts.

My book *Feminism Confronts Technology* (1991) presents a critical analysis of the way scientific and technological practices are depicted as detached, objective activities appropriate to men. Similarly, the discourse on management rationality has operated to legitimate and normalize masculine authority and to exclude women. In both cases, the central problem is that the patriarchal construction of gendered subjects, of what it is to be a man or woman, continues to be mapped on to a set of symbolic polarities like culture versus nature, mind versus body, reason versus emotion, objectivity versus subjectivity, the public realm versus the private realm, and read in a gendered hierarchy.

For well over a decade, feminist philosophers have exposed the way this symbolic dualism feeds into essentialism, or the assertion of fixed, unitary and opposed female and male natures (Lloyd 1984; Harding 1986). These writers point to the historical specificity of such gender metaphors, in that there is no behaviour or meaning which is universally and cross-culturally associated with, for example, either rationality or intuition. Both 'masculinity' and 'femininity' are socially constructed and are in fact constantly under reconstruction. Furthermore, it must be stressed that the values being ascribed to women originate in the historical subordination of women. The association of women with nurturance, warmth and intuition lies at the heart of traditional and oppressive conceptions of womanhood. They are meanings and values ascribed to women in a world where men are more powerful than women. Definitions of the feminine are profoundly distorted by the male-dominated structure of society.

Feminist organization theorists are seeking to apply this epistemological analysis in their deconstruction of the rational model of management and organizations. Taking issue with the concept of 'bounded rationality', which is often used in organization theory to critique the notion of 'pure rationality', Mumby and Putnam (1992) argue that it too is grounded in male-centred assumptions that exclude alternative modes of organizing. Bounded rationality acknowledges that rationality, typically defined as intentional, reasoned, goal-directed behaviour, is limited by organizational actors and their institutional practices. As these authors point out, however, even this concept of rationality positions other forms of reasoning such as intuition and judgement as non-rational, and decisions based on emotions as irrational. Emotional experience defined as feelings, sensations and affective responses to organizational situations is devalued and marginalized, or treated as inappropriate in the work context.

The merits of Mumby's and Putnam's project are summed up thus: 'Deconstructing the dichotomy between rationality and emotionality debunks organizational efforts to reify certain experiences and behaviours as either masculine or feminine' (1992: 480). They contrast bounded rationality with their concept of 'bounded emotionality', which refers to an alternative mode of organizing in which nurturance, caring, community, supportiveness and interrelatedness shape organizational experience. Emotions, then, should be integral to organizations.

These authors recognize that rationality is a social phenomenon in which emotion plays a central role, and draw on the feminist discussion of the knowledge-producing dimension of emotion (Jaggar 1989; Smith 1987). Nevertheless, their work ultimately rests on a gendered conception of emotion. What counts as 'emotion' is still defined within a discourse of gender difference. For them, emotionality constitutes positive feelings of mutual affection, cohesion, interrelatedness, tolerance of ambiguity. They do not see that organizations are already founded on emotion: the emotions of aggression, fear and anxiety, and that 'emotions' may be key in terms of the constitution of gendered management (Jackall 1988; Van Maanen and Kunda 1989). Neither the management literature nor this feminist analysis successfully challenges the dialectic of emotionality and rationality, or considers how such distinctions interrelate with the construction of masculinity and femininity in an organizational context.

A more innovative approach is possible if we turn from asking 'What are the emotions?' to the question 'In what situations and in what ways can the emotions be considered acquired responses, determined by socio-cultural prescriptions and behaviour?' (Gherardi 1995: 153). A sociological perspective shifts attention from emotion as a physiological experience to the learning of the language of emotions, and to the cultural variability of emotions and their expression. That is, emotions can be understood only in their social and institutional context. The same emotions in the public world of work and in the private sphere acquire very different meanings. Being aggressive at home may be defined as being emotional, but being aggressive in the public sphere may be seen as effective leadership. Fundamentally, the terms 'rational' and 'emotional' derive their meaning from their specific connection with the domains of the public and private. The point here is not whether men are necessarily less or more emotional than women, but how these feelings are *expressed, perceived* and *interpreted* within organizations.

To return to the question of leadership style, the central issue is that different interpretations are placed upon apparently identical modes of behaviour. The point at which a decisive move becomes precipitative, or a tactful decision becomes a cave-in, depends on the interpretative framework, not on the behaviour itself. Any action may be interpreted in a radically different way depending on whether the actor is a man or a woman. For example, a particular action or experience might be defined as 'firm', 'decisive' and 'rational' when constructed in relation to a man, and as 'bossy', 'hysterical' and 'irrational' where a woman is involved. A woman exercising a democratic leadership style may be seen as soft or indecisive. The common description of men as more aggressive and competitive managers than women can be recast as a description of men being more emotional than women. Yet uncontrolled competition and aggression are seen as rational when in pursuit of organizational goals. The same leadership behaviour will be interpreted differently depending on the gender of the leader.

This points to a major problem with the leadership literature generally. The central fallacy of leadership studies is that they reduce the study of power and leadership to the individual. Like power, leadership is not simply a trait which people possess. It is a structural asset that is exercised through a social network and is dependent upon the accounts and responses of those who are assessing the actions of a manager in particular situations. My study shows that organizational constraints rather than individual personality traits determine management style.

Many of the ideas canvassed above, particularly in relation to questions of management style and gender difference, have been elaborated in the absence of a firm empirical foundation. A major weakness of the empirical research that does exist is its tendency to treat women managers in isolation from men. The failure to examine the experience of men within the same organization inevitably limits our understanding of how managers are made. This study aims to correct the imbalance by presenting comparative material on the attitudes and experiences of women and men managers. Firstly, I investigate the extent to which female and male managers subscribe to conventional views about women managers. I then go on to consider whether women and men have distinct styles of management, and how managerial stereotypes match with gender stereotypes. I argue that a danger with the recent theoretical turn towards accentuating gender difference is that it may serve to reproduce gender stereotypes and, in doing so, divert attention from continuing sex discrimination in organizations.

Attitudes towards women managers

Given the marked increase in women managers in recent years, one might expect representations of the managerial position in terms of gender to have been radically transformed. Studies of the relationship between sex, managerial stereo-types and gender stereotypes were first conducted in the early 1970s in the US. In 1973 Schein reported findings that strongly influenced the thinking of industrial and organizational psychologists working in the area of sex bias and discrimination. Using a ninety-two-item attribute inventory to characterize gender stereo-types, she asked male managers at nine insurance companies across America to characterize 'women in general', 'men in general' and 'successful middle managers'. She found that 'successful middle managers' possessed an abundance of characteristics generally associated with men rather than with women. Moreover, successful managers were viewed as more like men than women in terms of attributes considered critical to effective work performance, such as leadership ability, self-confidence, objectivity, forcefulness and ambition. These results indicated that women were perceived as lacking the qualities essential for success in management positions.

Several studies replicating Schein's research fifteen years later by Heilman et al. (1989) demonstrate that managerial stereotypes held by male managers have remained essentially the same. They persist in viewing women in general as far more deficient in the attributes necessary for success as a manager than men in general. Moreover, even with the manager label firmly affixed, women are thought to differ in important ways from men and successful managers, most notably in their leadership ability and business skills, attributes central to managerial performance. The authors conclude that 'assumptions of progress as a result of social, legal, and organizational changes are unwarranted ... women still appear to be burdened by perceptions depicting them as unfit for effectively enacting the managerial role' (Heilman et al. 1989: 942).

Evidence about women managers' attitudes is less conclusive. Some studies indicate that, unlike women in the 1970s, contemporary female managers do not sex-type the managerial position but view women and men as equally likely to possess characteristics necessary for managerial success (Brenner et al. 1989). Other studies do not find a significant difference between men and women. For example, Powell (1993: 154) reports that in a study of undergraduate business students about 70 per cent of both women and men still described a good manager in predominantly masculine terms. Virtually no one preferred a 'feminine' good manager. In sum, it would seem that men, and to a lesser extent women, continue to describe good managers as being endowed with typical masculine traits rather than feminine traits. Negative images of women managers have deep roots, are widely shared and are remarkably resistant to change.

Given the resilience of sexual stereotypes, it is important to establish what currency they have for the managers in my study. I found no major differences between the views of women and men in response to more general questions about

Table 10.1 Percentage distribution of respondents' attitudes towards women managers

		Strongly agree	Agree	Disagree	Strongly disagree
Women managers	Men	41	56	3	–
have positive skills	Women	80	19	1	–
Male managers are	Men	1	13	65	21
more committed	Women	2	7	39	52
There should be	Men	1	10	45	44
positive discrimination	Women	2	10	56	32
Women should not	Men	1	10	51	37
combine career and	Women	–	3	35	62
motherhood					
All managers should be	Men	38	47	12	2
treated the same	Women	42	39	17	2
Difficult to work for a	Men	1	9	49	41
woman manager	Women	1	3	42	54

the role of women in management. Asking people to respond to stock statements along a scale is somewhat crude as it may promote conventional answers. However, I included this exercise for comparison with an earlier British survey. The following set of statements mirrors the set asked by Coe (1992) in a report on members of the British Institute of Management: 'women managers have positive skills to bring to the workplace'; 'male managers are more committed to the organization than women managers'; 'there should be positive discrimination for women managers'; 'women should not combine a management career and motherhood'; 'all managers should be treated the same, regardless of family responsibilities'; 'I do find it/would find it difficult to work for a woman manager'. The results are set out in table 10.1.

Overall there is not much difference between the views of women and men in relation to these statements, both being overwhelmingly positive about women managers' skills, commitment, and right to combine a career with motherhood. However, as in Coe's survey, some differences emerge at the extremes. Twice as many women as men 'strongly agree' that women managers have positive skills to bring to the workplace; well over twice as many women as men 'strongly disagree' that male managers are more committed to the organization than women; a higher proportion of women 'strongly disagree' with the statement that women should not combine a management career and motherhood; and men are more likely than women to 'strongly disagree' with the statement that there should be positive discrimination for women managers. In fact, there is very little support for positive discrimination among men or women.

In answer to a separate set of questions about preferences for male or female managers they work *with* or *for*, most men and women express no preference. In addition, most respondents (86 per cent) say that neither men nor women make better managers. In this context it is worth noting that 45 per cent of the managers report that they have actualy worked for a woman manager, with a slight tendency for women to report it more.

However, in sharp contrast to these views, when respondents were asked whether they would prefer to work for a manager of their own sex, a sizeable proportion (21 per cent) of men say that they would prefer to work for a male manager. In the words of one male respondent, who had himself never worked for a female manager, his preference is still for a male boss: 'it's just a comfort zone thing'. Interestingly, 10 per cent of women also say that they prefer to work for male managers. Neither men nor women express a preference for a woman manager. This would indicate that women are still far from being fully accepted in senior management positions.

Managing to differ?

Claims about women and men having distinct styles of management are difficult to investigate empirically, let alone substantiate. A comprehensive review of this research, most of which is North American and is set largely within a social psychological perspective, is provided by Eagly and Johnson (1990). They demonstrate that most of the evidence for sex differences in leadership style is derived from two types of study, namely laboratory experiments and assessment studies. The data usually come from responses to fixed-choice questions, such as whether leaders have a task-oriented versus an interpersonal style, or a directive versus a participative style. The subjects are either college students or people not in management positions. They are typically placed in artificial environments; and they interact as strangers on a short-term basis, without the constraints of established organizational roles. Consequently, they evince great ambiguity about how to behave. Gender expectations may provide stronger cues than they otherwise would, producing gender-stereotypical outcomes.

The strength of my research is that it examines practising managers anchored in their own institutional context. It compares the perceptions and attitudes of senior men and women who are at the same managerial level. Furthermore, rather than the more usual feminist approach which asks only women about management style, it sets the views of women alongside those of men. No previous British research has asked men their views about gendered management styles. Moreover, a defining feature of my research is that, rather than relying exclusively on standardized questionnaire data, I elicit respondents' own understandings of management style by means of open-ended questions and face-to-face interviewing. The survey data are complemented by substantial qualitative material based on interviews undertaken in the case study company known as 'Chip', a multi-national computer firm [...]

Let me begin by presenting my survey findings from typical questions about gender and leadership. Initially, I found that a high proportion of both women and men express the view that sex differences in management style *do* exist. On the whole they describe women's difference in positive terms. Asked generally about whether there are identifiable 'male' and 'female' styles of management, 69 per cent of women and 41 per cent of men think that there is a difference in style. It is interesting to note that a much higher proportion of women than men endorsed the view that there are sex differences in management style. Perhaps because women managers are in such a minority, they are more conscious of their difference from the men who predominate in management.

Typical descriptions by both men and women of the male style include: 'directive', 'self-centred/self-interested', 'decisive', 'aggressive', 'task oriented'. Adjectives used to describe the female style are: 'participative', 'collaborative', 'co-operative', 'coaching style', 'people oriented', 'caring'. Several women elaborated on this theme.

> The qualities that women bring to management tend not to be heavily control and power oriented, they tend to be more towards empowering people and getting the workers on board as opposed to telling them what to do . . . I don't think many women feel comfortable with an authoritarian style.
>
> Women are generally more concerned to get a job done quickly and efficiently and are less concerned with pushing themselves forward and making a mark in the organization. Men are more likely to look outside their department to play politics and ensure that they are noticed by the people that matter. Women prefer everybody to be as contented as possible whereas men are better able to put up with a hostile, aggressive atmosphere which is often a feature of business.
>
> I think there are what I would call feminine and masculine characteristics that people have and I've experienced male managers who predominantly only portray what I call male characteristics – domineering, very task oriented, directive, impatient, those sort of things, and the more female characteristics I would describe as more encouraging, inclusive, mentoring type of way of managing somebody. Now in the past I would have said males tend to portray the male characteristics and women the female, though it's not exclusive. I see much more of the female characteristics being used by everybody nowadays and there are a few women I see who are using the male characteristics as well.

A number of men similarly describe differences in management style, identifying what they regarded as strengths in women's approach and decrying men's preoccupation with status and hierarchy.

> Women have well-tuned antennae to the needs of other people, they have been brought up to deal with the needs of other people, almost above their own. So they are better managers of people . . . the female style is more sell – selling an idea they want you to do, whereas the male style is more tell – go and do it.
>
> Males are status aware. Women are there to do a good job and be recognized and rewarded for that job, and they're actually not so bothered where they sit in the hierarchy. Men are very bothered about where they sit in the hierarchy and they're not necessarily so interested in the work, they're just more interested in the progress, because their status outside the company is so much reflected in what they do. People

ask you what job you do, how big's your budget, how big's your factory, is your factory bigger than my factory?

Women deal well with detail and I think a lot of low-quality work in business is done because people don't deal with things at the right level of the detail because of being overconfident, which is something I would criticize myself for doing.

The other set of oppositions respondents draw upon to describe sex differences in managerial style are those to do with reason versus emotion. Some men were particularly perceptive about the limitations of prevailing stereotypes and are concerned to emphasize that they do not fit the management style of women and men in their firm. These men see difference, but are inclined to reverse the standard terms by which women's difference is defined. For example,

Inevitably women do tend to handle things from a slightly different tack...sort of rational...they tend to come at things from a much quieter perspective and particularly men can tend to go at things aggressively whereas women will argue their point more logically and retain their temper more consistently.

The views of the former head of human resources are interesting in this context because, although he appears to subscribe to the popular version of women's management style, he goes on to paint a more complex picture. He begins by saying that 'women's management style is coaching, enabling and nurturing rather than controlling and directing', and that this is the style of the future. He then proceeds to describe women first as rational and then as emotional, all the while deconstructing the standard dichotomy.

Men and women are different in terms of the way they think and the way they act. Men are conditioned to be action oriented, what we call in Chip 'the ready-fire-aim syndrome'. So you get lots of smoke and clouds and dust and not a lot happens at the end of it. Whereas women have got a much more objective, rational approach; they are not so caught up in the emotion of 'let's make something happen'. They are actually able to be more rational and objective and logical towards the problem. Men are more often driven by power and status and ego needs.

Reflecting further on the question of sex differences, he acknowledges that men too are emotional but covertly so:

I do find women more emotional than men *externally*, in the sense that they are more able to show their emotions than men. Does that mean they're more emotional than men? Don't know. I know lots of men who churn over internally all the bloody time and never let it show. So what is the definition of emotional?

By contrast, some women respondents thought that women managers take a more holistic approach, 'stepping back from the nitty gritty detail and seeing the whole thing and making linkages between apparently separate things, they have a more systematic view of the world. I experience this when I sit in a meeting'. The same interviewee attributes this female characteristic to 'the way women are brought up, they see their mothers doing a lot of things in parallel, and it's to do with men having single-track minds and focusing on getting one thing done before they move on to the next'.

Other women took up this theme of women's ability to cope with multiple tasks.

> Women are better managers because they juggle with their life anyway. I mean women are naturally better at coping with multiple tasks than men because they have to. More and more women work now, therefore if they have arranged their home life such that they have to play the role of the wife/mother and worker then they have to juggle and women just seem to be more adept at it. I mean I think if you put a man, most men in a woman's situation, the situation I'm in, they would fail dismally after about a week. They just don't have this ability to juggle. And I think that makes us women better at managing because we have this ability to have three or four or five plates spinning at any one time and that's the norm.

In fact, although these respondents regard these qualities as feminine ones, they are more specifically connected with responsibility for childrearing. The last two quotes are from women who are themselves mothers, which is atypical of the sample in which less than a third of women managers are mothers. These women attach value to skills learnt in the home, reflecting what has been and continues to be an important thread in feminist strategies to improve women's position in the labour market. Equal value or 'comparable worth' legislation developed to deal with the fact that many women's skills are drawn on by employers but are not remunerated at the rate of men's equivalent skills.

Feminist theorizing about skill argues that a major reason that women have failed to achieve recognition of the skills required for their work is that skills are not technically but socially determined (see, for example, Cockburn 1985; Phillips and Taylor 1980; Wajcman 1991). That is, the categories for evaluating skill definitions are themselves gender biased. The very recognition of a job as skilled reflects competencies possessed by men, not women. Skilled status has been traditionally identified with masculinity and with work that women do *not* do, whereas women's skills have been defined as non-technical and hence undervalued.

A key reason for the undervaluing of women's skills is that some skills are regarded by employers as 'natural' female attributes rather than skills developed through training and experience. The household, the place in which these skills are often acquired, either transmitted by other women or developed in the course of childrearing, is not recognized as a valid training ground. In an innovative piece of Australian research on job evaluation schemes, Cox and Leonard take the notion of a skills audit and broaden it to include all those skills that women learn and practise in their unpaid work but that remain unacknowledged. Their project shows that in their household and community-based work many women develop 'technical, management, finance, interpersonal and organizational expertise which is transferable into paid work situations' (1991: 5). From my own survey it is evident that many of the qualities that both men and women attribute to a feminine style are associated with mothering. Indeed, better managers are frequently now cast in the mould of mothers. Yet most women who *are* mothers are still absent from the ranks of senior management.

Saying It soft, doing It hard: management in practice

When we examine how respondents to the survey describe *their own* management style, either as 'participative style, people-handling skills, developing subordinates' or as 'leading from the front, drive, decisively directing subordinates', we find no significant difference between the men's and women's responses. As many as 81 per cent of all respondents describe their management style as 'participative style, people-handling skills, developing subordinates'. Only 19 per cent describe themselves as 'leading from the front, drive, decisively directing subordinates'. Similarly, both men and women equally cite 'people management' as the most important skill required to do their jobs successfully.

These findings reveal the extent to which people characterize themselves in terms of dominant cultural values. Research shows that men and women tend to sterotype their own behaviour according to learned ideas of gender-appropriate behaviour, just as they stereotype the behaviour of other groups (Epstein 1988). An integral part of the identity of men and women is the perception that they possess, respectively, masculine and feminine qualities. So it is not surprising that women and men respondents subscribe to gender stereotypes of management styles. At the same time, respondents describe themselves in terms that accord with the prevailing orthodoxy of good management practice, now strongly associated with a consultative style and a high level of interpersonal skills. Subscribing to a people-centred approach happens to correspond with the current vogue for 'soft' human resources management (see, for example, Blyton and Turnbull 1992; Storey 1992).

What is ironic is that the participatory and co-operative leadership style with which the majority of both men and women identify also corresponds to current notions about a 'female management style'. If true, it would suggest that, rather than women having to become like men to be effective managers, men are already becoming more like women. Clearly the problem with these data is that they are based on self-identification. Other studies have highlighted the limitations of leaders' self-reports (see reviews by Ferrario 1994; Powell 1993). We might expect managers' self-perceptions in this study to be similarly biased. Unfortunately, little research has been conducted on subordinates' responses to their own managers, especially in business settings. It may well be that managers of both sexes who perceive themselves as having a participatory style may, in practice, use the command-and-control style.

Certainly the picture that emerges at the more detailed case-study level is more complicated than the survey evidence suggests. Perhaps in a survey people answer in terms of what they would like their organizations to be like rather than what they are really like. The rise of 'management speak' makes it much more difficult to conduct research in this area, because managers of large multinationals now tend to use the language of the human resource management model. Indeed, this language may even be used by senior management to mask the high degree of uncertainty and ambiguity that characterizes the current situation of many organizations.

When managers are asked to discuss more specifically their own work practices, a gap between beliefs and behaviour emerges. The evidence from my qualitative case-study material confirms that a major discrepancy exists between the rhetoric of 'soft' management and the 'hard' reality of practice. As Sisson argues, while the management 'rhetoric may be the people-centred approach of the "soft" version: the reality is the cost reduction approach of the "hard" version' (1994: 15). Many of my interviewees commented that with the almost continuous 'downsizing' of companies, management is returning to a more traditional hierarchical structure. Macho management is again in the ascendancy. As the most senior woman manager in one company explained:

> The culture of the organization is becoming much more directive, much more con-trolled from head office . . . flexibility, empowerment, those sort of values, are not high on people's priorities just at the moment because of the crisis the company is going through . . . when things are tough people like to be in control and pull back con-trol . . . there's much more structure, much more rigidity. The word that is being used is discipline . . . and these changes in management style favour a male style . . . manage-ment say the right things on diversity issues but their actions are less clear. The actual tangible results are getting worse.

It is symptomatic of the business environment that she and several of the other senior women are leaving the company where they had initially prospered.

Male managers also expressed concern about the changes that were taking place. According to one respondent, 'we have returned to the 1960s military style of management by brutality, shouting louder, hit them harder and threaten them to death until they're frightened and they do what they're told.' He went on to contrast this with his preferred 'SAS or Israeli crack troops' style of leadership, which he described as 'working in very tight teams without massive hierarchies and lots of bullying. Simple pragmatism that says we are the best, this is our vision, and these are the goals we have to attain'.

The most pressing issue for managers at the time of my interviews was the problem of downsizing. Making people redundant was a frequent activity. Coping with uncertainty within the organization was also a constant theme. All my respondents found this process difficult and no obvious gender differences in managerial style emerged in how they accomplished the task. Likewise, when I asked people to talk about how they handled difficult and conflictual issues, no gender differences emerged. Rather both men and women related similar stories about dealing with such issues as pay, performance and retrenchment. As one female manager said:

> I hate having to make people redundant but I've been doing it for five years. I still don't find it any easier. But that's not true, I find I *can* detach myself more emotionally from it than I used to be able to. Nobody likes doing that. I'm used to giving feedback both good and negative and I do think it's important people know. I've had to sack people, so I've been through all that side too. I've had to deal with an alcoholic, I've had to deal with somebody moonlighting. I can't say it's very pleasant but I felt I had to deal with it. Why should they get away with it when all the other people are working hard?

A male told me that his worst experience as a manager had been reducing the income of a group he managed.

> I was a manager at the Aberdeen office at the time and the prices of houses were more expensive than London. So the guys got an Aberdeen allowance, which amounted to an extra 15 per cent of their salary. And then the company decided to remove that allowance, quite a huge percentage to lose. And I felt it was the hardest time for me because I was a manager in the company and therefore I had to carry out the company's wishes. The house prices had fallen, these guys had high mortages and the company had taken away the support to help. So that was a difficult time – a bit emotional for me. I certainly fell out with my bosses at that time.

Managing had become extremely difficult in this fast-contracting company. Many managers had not received a substantial pay rise for years. Indeed, at the time of my interviews, the company had implemented a corporate-wide pay freeze throughout the UK. As a result good performance could not be rewarded adequately. The context made it hard to deal with subordinates who were not performing well. Several managers recounted stories around this theme. The first is from a woman attempting to discipline someone when retrenchment packages are ripe for the taking. She describes it as her 'worst management decision'.

> I inherited a guy and I felt that we should have fired him rather than making him redundant, but I could never quite tie him down. He never ever performed, but I couldn't prove it a hundred per cent. Somehow I could never quite get the goals to actually reflect whether it was his doing, or somebody else's, no matter how much I tried. Basically the guy walked out with a large sum of money when he didn't really deserve it. He should have been on disciplinary. I didn't manage that too well and what really upset me was he wrote to me thanking me for the large cheque I'd just given him.

The next two stories typically illustrate the harsh environment in which managers are now operating. The first account is from a woman manager and the second from a man.

> I do have a situation where a particular person is supposed to do quite a lot of marketing communications work for me. Two or three times there's been bad delivery of the work and I had to sort it. But I don't have time to do that now, and to go on and on suggesting training courses, books to read – some people just do not want to learn. It's got very hard now. If all the work gets outsourced then he will be made redundant.
>   There's less people management time available now. Motivation levels have changed over the last few years. People aren't getting rewarded the same as they used to in terms of salary, and there's less time available to spend with them on things that bother them. They work longer hours which affects their home life, there's less flexibility to do the things they might have done. You're having to screw down on what their core role is and cut down on what's good to do, nice to do, in order to concentrate on what they're really here for.

Finally, I recount at length how a male manager describes following the routine set of mediating procedures that the company has in place for dealing with questions of performance. Fair and proper procedures are time-consuming, and he too ends his account by acknowledging that his managerial style has hardened because of the current situation.

> I had an individual here who was working hard but not actually doing the job that I wanted him to do. We had a meeting and went through the plan and direction, and what he felt he should be doing. There was a clear mismatch. The outcome of that meeting was that we both decided to think about it for another day or so and then get back to the round table and come up with reasons why we felt so strongly. When we met again I was able to present more evidence of what I thought he should be doing, and why. He wasn't and it was the same after the next meeting, which ended with me just saying, 'Well, I'm sorry, that's the way it is and you're just going to have to accept it or find yourself another job'. Now he was annoyed at the time but since then he's come around to my way of thinking and he's actually doing the job that I wanted him to do and that worked very well. But it took quite a lot of time and quite a lot of effort and I'm not sure if that situation happened again that I would actually do the same thing. I think it was the right thing to do. I think I'd be more inclined *these days* to turn around and say, 'That's the way it is'. It's bad news, but that's the reality.

The business context of continuous restructuring and job losses has greatly intensified pressures for senior managers. Insecurity about the future is pervasive. The traditional career-for-life model, based on employment security and promotion prospects, has been replaced by a climate of fear and anxiety about the very real prospect of redundancy in many organizations. These conditions are not conducive to sustaining work relationships based on high levels of trust and co-operation. Rather, the logic of survival results in heightened individualistic competition for a dwindling number of career opportunities. In this economic climate, both men and women feel the need to conform to the male stereotype of management because it is still, in practice, the only one regarded as effective.

This situation was summed up neatly in the words of a male respondent who clearly felt so constrained:

> In any organization there is a norm for success and everyone has to conform to that. In some organizations that norm is very male, white macho in style; women are expected to adhere to that norm. I am not saying that it is the only norm in Chip, but the white, Western, male macho culture is ingrained. ... Macho means not being willing to look at yourself, being closed to certain things, being certain about everything in life. Attitudes such as: I cannot possibly allow my defences to come down; it's impossible to talk to anyone honestly about how I feel. And never allowing people to see me cry.

You can't take the 'man' out of management

There are thus powerful organizational imperatives that dictate management style and goals and permit few substantial modifications in management approach. This point is particularly important in relation to Rosener's argument discussed at the outset of this [reading]. Her survey is based on managers in medium-size, non-traditional organizations in which, significantly, women have come to management via unconventional career paths. My research is based on five male-dominated multinational corporations whose organizational structure and institutional politics are very different. Furthermore, the vast majority of managers have had conventional internal career paths in these companies. Respondents have moved around within the company. Over 80 per cent of both men and women were recruited to their present post through internal promotion. So both groups have had equal exposure to the promotion system in their company.

In sharp contrast to Rosener's sample, selection processes and organizational socialization have fundamentally shaped the management approach of both women and men managers in my study. Senior managers of either sex, who hold positions with equivalent status and power in their companies, behave in broadly similar ways. Whether a diversity of management styles is accepted and successful in less conventional organizations, or at lower levels of management, remains an open question.

Given these constraints, it should come as no surprise that many women managers adapt and survive by being more male than the men. The statement of one man in my survey is typical:

> In general female managers prefer a participative, consensual style of management but at *senior* level in my experience there is a 'Thatcher factor' – a tendency to be more stereotypically male than typical male managers. That is, decisive, even aggressive, and avoiding any interacting except in formal professional contexts often associated with 'I never needed equal opportunities to get where I did so why do they?' approach.

This comment partly reflects the 'iron maiden' stereotype of strong women working in male-dominated organizations who do not conform to the more usual feminine roles, so well described by Kanter. However, as Kanter argues, it also reflects a strategy adopted by some women in order to succeed: 'some women try to stay away from the role traps by bending over backwards not to exhibit any characteristics that would reinforce female stereotypes. This strategy, too, is an uneasy one, for it takes continual watchful effort, and it may involve unnatural self-distortion' (1977: 237).

Although I have been emphasizing the ways in which the symbolic representation of management is sharply gendered as male, it is precisely because there is substance to these stereotypes that they continue to have such enduring force. In general, women and men tend to conform in practice to their gender roles. Women who deviate by adopting the male role pay a heavy price. Even if there are no consistent gender differences in management style, there are certainly profound gender differences in experience [. . .].

The crucial point to be borne in mind is that the strength of the ideology of sex difference is precisely its capacity to be flexible. To say that management is identified as male does not imply that there is a single uniform idea of what good management is. Indeed, participatory involvement was seen as the key characteristic of management during the Human Relations movement of the 1930s and 1940s. Even so, this precursor of the current fashion for 'transformational management' was entirely identified as a male leadership style. Ideas of what constitutes effective management will necessarily change over time. The point is that the qualities associated with effective management are not gender neutral. While current debates reflect a blurring of the familiar set of oppositions in which hard management is male and soft management is female, it is still men who are best placed to lay claim to whatever characteristics are seen to be the desirable ones.

It is important not to confuse the issue of valuing 'feminine' qualities in management with the issue of including more women in senior positions. The revaluing of the female style and a stress on diversity rather than equality will not necessarily improve women's prospects of success. Instead of producing an influx of women into senior management, it is just as likely that men will appropriate this rediscovered 'feminine' style and add it to their traditionally male repertoire. Indeed it could be said that performing a 'feminine' style has a completely different meaning for men than for women. For men this style is not naturalized as part of the self, and is therefore rewarded and can be mobilized as an occupational resource. Whereas men will be advantaged by adding new qualities to those they are already deemed to have, women will continue to be seen as offering feminine qualities only.

The danger is that by focusing on women's individual characteristics rather than the structural barriers they face, the recent managerial discourse about gendered management styles may mask the extent to which women are losing out in the current business climate. It is naive to believe that the revaluing of women's 'difference' will succeed where 'equal' opportunities have failed. A stress on women's difference leaves untouched the mythical male figure of the rational, instrumental manager. It therefore slides easily into a reinforcement of traditional sex stereotypes of managers and may even contribute to new regimes of gender hierarchy within organizations. Whichever way women play it, we will never make the grade as men.

NOTE

From J. Wajcman (1998), 'It's Hard to be Soft' in her *Managing Like a Man* (Cambridge: Polity).

REFERENCES

Ashburner, L. (1994), 'Women in management careers: opportunities and outcomes', in J. Evetts, ed., *Women and Career* (London: Longman).

Australian Government (1995), *Enterprising Nation: Report on Leadership and Management Skills* (Canberra: Australian Government Publishing Service).

Blyton, P. and P. Turnbull, eds (1992), *Reassessing Human Resource Management* (London: Sage).

British Institute of Management (1994), *Management Development to the Millennium* (London: BIM).

Cockburn, C. (1985), *Machinery of Dominance* (London: Pluto Press).

Cockburn, C. (1991), *In the Way of Women: Men's Resistance to Sex Equality in Organizations* (London: Macmillan).

Coe, T. (1992), 'The key to the men's club', British Institute of Management Report, London.

Cox, E. and H. Leonard (1991), 'From Ummm...to Aha!: recognising women's skills', Women's Research and Employment Initiatives Program (Canberra: Australian Government Publishing Service).

Eagly, A. and B. Johnson (1990), 'Gender and leadership style: a meta-analysis', *Psychological Bulletin*, vol. 108, no. 2, pp. 233–56.

Epstein, C. Fuchs (1988), *Deceptive Distinctions: Sex, Gender, and the Social Order* (New Haven: Yale University Press).

Ferguson, K. (1984), *The Feminist Case against Bureaucracy* (Philadelphia: Temple University Press).

Ferrario, M. (1994) 'Women as managerial leaders', in M. Davidson and R. Burke, eds, *Women in Management* (London: Paul Chapman).

Fierman, J. (1990), 'Do women manage differently?', *Fortune*, 17 December, pp. 71–4.

Gherardi, S. (1995), *Gender, Symbolism and Organizational Cultures* (London: Sage).

Giddens, A. (1992), *The Transformation of Intimacy* (Cambridge: Polity Press).

Gilligan, C. (1982), *In a Different Voice: Psychological Theory and Women's Development* (Cambridge, MA: Harvard University Press).

Harding, S. (1986), *The Science Question in Feminism* (Ithaca, NY: Cornell University Press).

Heilman, M., C. Block, R. Mantell and M. Simon (1989), 'Has anything changed?: current characterizations of men, women, and managers', *Journal of Applied Psychology*, vol. 74, no. 6, pp. 935–42.

Hennig, M. and Jardim, A. (1979), *The Managerial Woman* (London: Pan Books).

Jackall, R. (1988), *Moral Mazes: The World of Corporate Managers* (New York: Oxford University Press).

Jaggar, A. (1989), 'Love and knowledge: emotion in feminist epistemology', in A. Jaggar and S. Bordo, eds, *Gender/Body/Knowledge: Feminist Reconstructions of Being and Knowing* (New Brunswick: Rutgers University Press).

Kanter, R. M. (1977), *Men and Women of the Corporation* (New York: Basic Books).

Kanter, R. M. (1992), *The Challenge of Organizational Change* (New York: Free Press).

Legge, K. (1994), 'Managing cultures: fact or fiction?', in K. Sisson, ed., *Personnel Management* (Oxford: Blackwell).

Liff, S. and J. Wajcman (1996), '"Sameness" and "difference" revisited: which way forward for equal opportunity initiatives?', *Journal of Management Studies*, vol. 33, no. 1, pp. 79–94.

Lloyd, G. (1984), *The Man of Reason* (London: Methuen).

Loden, M. (1985), *Feminine Leadership, or How to Succeed in Business without being One of the Boys* (New York: Times Books).

Marshall, J. (1984), *Women Managers: Travellers in a Male World* (Chichester: John Wiley).

Marshall, J. (1995), *Women Managers Moving On* (London: Routledge).

Martin, P. (1993), 'Feminist practice in organizations', in E. Fagenson, ed., *Women in Management* (Newbury Park: Sage).

Mead, G. (1934), *Mind, Self and Society* (Chicago: University of Chicago Press).

Mumby, D. and L. Putnam (1992), 'The politics of emotion: a feminist reading of bounded rationality', *Academy of Management Review*, vol. 17, no. 3, pp. 465–86.

Pateman, C. (1988), *The Sexual Contract* (Cambridge: Polity Press).

Pateman, C. (1989), *The Disorder of Women* (Cambridge: Polity Press).

Peters, T. and R. Waterman (1982), *In Search of Excellence* (New York: Harper and Row).

Phillips, A. and B. Taylor (1980), 'Sex and skill: notes towards a feminist economics', *Feminist Review*, vol. 6, pp. 79–88.

Powell, G. (1993), *Women and Men in Management* (Newbury Park: Sage).

Rosener, J. (1990), 'Ways women lead', *Harvard Business Review*, December, pp. 199–225.

Schein, V. (1973), 'The relationship between sex role stereotypes and requisite management characteristics', *Journal of Applied Psychology*, vol. 57, pp. 95–100.

Schein, V. (1994), 'Managerial sex typing: a persistent and pervasive barrier to women's opportunities', in M. Davidson and R. Burke, eds, *Women in Management: Current Research Issues* (London: Paul Chapman).

Sisson, K. (1994), 'Personnel management: paradigms, practice and prospects', in K. Sisson, ed., *Personnel Management* (Oxford: Blackwell).

Smith, D. (1987), *The Everyday World as Problematic* (Milton Keynes: Open University Press).

Storey, J. (1992), *Developments in the Management of Human Resources* (Oxford: Blackwell).

Van Maanen, J. and G. Kunda (1989), 'Real feelings: emotional expression and organizational culture', *Research in Organizational Behaviour*, vol. 11, pp. 43–103.

Wajcman, J. (1981), 'Work and the family: who gets the best of both worlds?', in Cambridge Women's Studies Group, ed., *Women in Society: Interdisciplinary Essays* (London: Virago).

Wajcman, J. (1991), *Feminism Confronts Technology* (Cambridge: Polity Press; University Park: Penn State Press).

Wajcman, J. (1996), 'Women and men managers: careers and equal opportunities', in R. Crompton, D. Gallie and K. Purcell, eds, *Changing Forms of Employment* (London: Routledge).

Wood, S. (1989), 'New wave management?', *Work, Employment and Society*, vol. 3, no. 3, pp. 379–402.

Part V

The Future of Work

Introduction

In the final part of the book I switch direction once more to look beyond the contemporary world of work and peer into the future – albeit 'through a glass darkly'. Much of the debate around the future of work is often constructed through a relatively simple lens that perceives the changes across time as shifting from one dominant trend to another, often led by different countries or trading blocks. Thus while during the 1960s and 1970s there were some arguments that a global management style was emerging – but it was wholly American in origin – an equivalent argument in the 1980s replaced the US domination by Japanese domination. And if the 'American era' was one of Fordism then the 'Japanese era' has been one of post-Fordism. In effect, it is argued, there has been a shift from the giant corporations dominating through the advantages of scale to an array of more versatile or even virtual companies dominating through the advantages of 'flexible specialization'.

The reading by Fiorenza Belussi and Francesco Garibaldo dissects this controversy by first considering the political support for the contending patterns on offer and noting how the supporters of flexible specialization – small-scale, highly skilled niche production – were also faced with the apparent growth of 'lean production', that is large-scale, highly automated Japanese production methods. Their contention is that any single global trend towards the organization is simply inadequate to the complexities of the situation. However, they do suggest three trends that underlie contemporary developments

- the priority given to saving time;
- the change in labour's status from a cost to a resource;
- and the increasing significance of collective learning and knowledge.

This combination of developments leads them to assert that there are four, not one, possible futures for work: a slightly modified Fordism that has provided the basis for Anglo-American work systems; a European approach configured around highly skilled labour and the co-determination of work that typifies the German approach; a core-periphery model framed around the Japanese experience; and a non-Fordist skill-based hierarchy of firms that has its origins in networks of small firms in parts of northern Italy. Moreover, even these four, relatively discrete, models are themselves subject to widespread hybridization as organizations adopt processes and systems from across the globe in an effort to survive and prosper in what is an increasingly global market place. Finally Belussi and Garibaldo suggest that, notwithstanding the power of the global market, the conditions set by local and regional political authorities are critical to maximizing growth and minimizing the tendency to assume that the market determines the future of work.

We end, as we began, by considering the nature of change itself in Stephen Barley's and Gideon Kunda's reading on rational and normative ideologies of control. Change, like history, sometimes does seem to be 'one damn thing after another' and indeed it may well be that we cope with such a confusing maelstrom of events by imposing a pattern upon the material to make better sense of it. Of course, that pattern may simply be wishful thinking and it is quite possible that there is no 'key' to change, that the past and the future of work are inherently unpredictable.[*]

Barley and Kunda set out to overturn the traditional assumption that the development of (American) managerial control can be described as a three-part transition from coercive, through rational to normative control. In its place they suggest the changes are better understood as pendulum swings between normative and rational rhetorics of control that are linked to the limits of language and symbols – specifically the way these are premised upon binary opposites (good–bad, light–dark, scientific–normative) and economic long waves of development. In their account, normative ideologies appear more effective during economic depressions when labour is weak, and rational ideologies dominate when economic growth occurs and labour is strong. In other words, and to return us to the first reading in this book, there has been no linear development but rather a cyclical movement – though the authors are keen to point out that rational ideologies are usually dominant among the managerial population. Dividing US managerial ideologies into five phases they begin by describing the first (1870–1900) as 'Industrial Betterment', a normative form with roots into the Protestant notion of (employer) responsibility for remaking the employee into a sober and co-operative servant. However, by the turn of the century the engineering and scientific predilections of the next generation overthrew the first phase and replaced it with 'Scientific Management' that lasted from 1900 to 1923. This was a rational form of control where science displaced norms to generate a more efficient, effective and systematic form of work organization. Under the tutelage of F. W. Taylor, and the American Society for Mechanical Engineers, the 'efficiency craze' shook industry out of its normative complacency and oversaw the beginning of the time and motion revolution. Yet, by the end of the First World War the limits of this fashion became exposed as labour resistance increased and the third phase began: Human Relations (1925–55). This marked a return to the

---

[*] See Grint (1994) and Grint (1997: 31–58) on the issue of historical patterning to work change.

normative patterns of control in the guise of group-oriented developments, particularly those developed in the Hawthorne Experiments under Elton Mayo and later through the ideas of Maslow (Grint 1998: chapter 4). By the mid-1950s a raft of developments in technology, and the perceived weakness of the US, had generated a reaction to this normative approach and ushered in the 'Systems Rationalism' that lasted until 1980. Once again scientific and rational ideologies prevailed as computers and statistical methods took over and courses in systems behaviour, financial and accounting practices filled MBA courses. By 1980 the systems revolution appeared to be producing marginal rewards as the Japanese economy moved into top gear, apparently grounded in employee motivation and dedication, not systems behaviour. As such the fifth pattern emerged, 'Organizational Culture and Quality' which, one could argue, is now under direct threat from an attempted shift to a sixth wave linked to the re-engineering shake-out of the early 1990s, the global financial headaches of the late 1990s, and the dot.com craze of the early twenty-first century. If Barley and Kunda are right, we should expect a return to science and rationality as legitimations of managerial strategies, and these may manifest themselves through greater reliance on automated and computerized systems and through a closer appreciation of financial imperatives at the expense of human resource management philosophies as the global economy expands.

Precisely what form of managerial ideology will dominate in the early part of the twenty-first century may be of little interest to the majority of the global population. According to the United Nations 1998 report, the gross inequalities between the rich and poor nations are increasing – with 20 per cent of the world's population accounting for 86 per cent of the world's consumption. Indeed, the richest 225 people have a combined wealth equal to the annual income of 47 per cent of the entire global population.[*] As ever, there remains a huge amount of work for us all to do.

---

[*] According to the UN report Bill Gates alone has more wealth than the 106 million poorest Americans. Though we should all be wary of throwing stones here: it is further suggested that if the money the West spends per year on pet food and perfumes was redirected it could provide education, food, water and sanitation for all those who are currently without in the world.

11   Globalization

Variety of Pattern of the Post-Fordist Economy:
Why are the 'Old Times' still with us and the 'New Times' yet to come?

FIORENZA BELUSSI AND FRANCESCO GARIBALDO

[...]

Despite the complex changes which the economies of the most industrialized countries have undergone, current interpretations of the evolution of the economic system remain extraordinarily simplistic. The popular view, sustained by an impressive number of academic publications during the 1980s, has been that 'Fordism', at the heart of the continued development of the capitalist world since the Second World War, is no longer the driving force of the economy (Aglietta 1987; Doray 1988; Lipietz 1987, 1992a, 1992b; Boyer 1985, 1988, 1989; Dunford 1990; Sayer 1988, 1991).

Yet, according to this view, a historically different solution was ready to be established: an alternative 'flexible specialization' path based on craft principles of production and on the repopulation of mature industries by numerous, small, competitive and technologically advanced firms. This 'new industrial divide' was publicized by the influential work[1] of Piore and Sabel (1984). Their theories were rooted in the industrial districts of modern Europe, and especially of northern Italy. In examining these areas, Piore and Sabel observed a distinctive pattern of development in some traditional sectors, and in the machine tool industry a trend towards a small-firm-based industrial structure dominated by the so-called flexibly specialized enterprise with a highly qualified workforce, spontaneously co-ordinated by the invisible hand of the market (Sabel et al. 1989; Brusco 1982, 1989; Leborgne and Lipietz 1988).

This reconceptualization of the historical pattern of transformation of modern capitalism could be used to provide support both for the advocates of the true 'market economy' as an alternative to the dominant power of political bureau-cracies and economic oligopolies, and for the aspirations of progressivists (Williams et al. 1987; Harrison 1989a). In the latter case, the model could be seen as the route to the 'promised land' of a democratically controlled economic environment characterized by evenly matched power relations within the productive sphere and by new models of work organization which could break the old methods inherited from Fordist practice.

In short, this perspective struck a chord not only with the supporters of aggressive micro-capitalism, but also with sophisticated left-wing commentators who felt that political institutions had a part to play in promoting the development of democratic 'small-business-based' industrial structures. The message of Piore and Sabel was thus a blend of empirical observations and prophecies.

As regards the analysis of Piore and Sabel, there are two main questions. First, was the pattern of development of small businesses (or, as we have called them in figure 11.1, 'non-Fordist skill-based' organizations) a long-term feature of contemporary (post-Fordist) capitalism or simply a short-term trend of economic decentralization? Was it a political message and an ethical hope, or a reality?

Second, was the aura of *magic and miracle* that surrounded the growth of small business in peripheral areas of Europe purely an economic phenomenon driven by *local policy makers*, or rather was it the consequence of a historical co-evolution of a socio-economic institutional system? If the latter was the case, as argued by the proponents of the 'Third Italy' model, then the development of a small-enterprise structure depended first on the presence of certain prerequisites (such as a network of small towns endowed with tertiary functions, a structure of agricultural families with entrepreneurial capabilities, artisan traditions, technical skills formed around some pilot industrial initiatives, etc.), and later on a set of local/regional and national macro regulative promotional activities (legislation, consortia, public infrastructures, etc.) and some positive social and relational structures, all of which might enable the development of a favourable social climate (diffused trust among economic operators, economic and social co-operation among local collective agents such as trade unions and employers' associations, growth-oriented local economic institutions, etc.), rather than merely a (nationally based) large rate of growth in aggregate demand (Weiss 1988; Belussi 1993c).

We are dealing not with a universal model but with idiosyncratic, territorial systems of production, partially untransferable and rapidly evolving (Belussi 1993c; Bull forthcoming; Benko and Lipietz 1992; Harrison 1994; Franchi 1994).

A second very influential meta discourse emerged later in the international discussion, after the mid-1980s, and focused on new principles of 'lean production'. The 'departure' from the Fordist methods was here depicted in the context of the transformation of the giant firms of the automobile industry. Thus, in 1990, Womack, Jones and Roos announced the emergence of an international pattern in organizing production – the Japanese model of production (Wood 1991; Freeman 1987; Coriat 1991; Dore 1987).

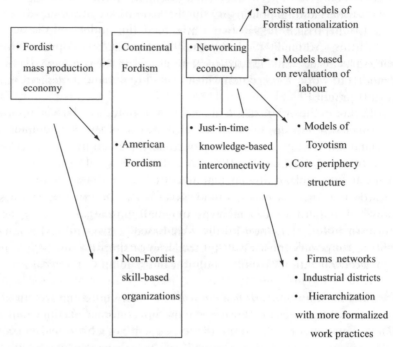

Figure 11.1   Models of post-Fordist societies

These two views of the process of industrial restructuring provide conflict-ing messages to the observer. On the one hand, small firms localized within industrial districts represent a new industrial paradigm of more cohesive economic environments. On the other, in contrast, a deterministic, dominant organizational paradigm influences the changing landscape of corporate power.

But can the pattern prevailing in the international automobile industry provide a more general model for the restructuring of the economic system? Even the most elementary analysis of technology has contrasted small batch, large batch and mass production (see the pioneering analysis of Woodward 1958). And is the Japanese model so revolutionary, then, in terms of demonstrat-ing to the world a new and progressive example of anti-Taylorist practices, worthy of being applied in a *ready-to-use* form? (Dhose et al. 1985; Garibaldo 1988, 1994a).

This [reading] presents a framework of analysis which will principally discuss three main issues.

1   The restructuring of the industrial system needs to be interpreted in terms of the 'governance' of different production systems (Harrison and Storper 1991). We strongly believe that any metaphor which reduces the complexity of organizational structure to a potentially dominant industrial stereotype must be rejected. Small firms and large firms seldom appear to be the sole,

alternative modes of production (Belussi 1992a). Large, vertically integrated organizations and small firms are simply the two extremes of a wide range of production possibilities (Brusco 1993), including industrial districts,[2] network firms (Antonelli 1987; Butera 1991; Sako 1989; Cooke et al. 1992), semi-verticalized firms (Enrietti 1987), global firms (*Business Week* 1986; Belussi and Festa 1990; Barba Navaretti and Perosino 1993), network districts (Gordon 1992; Longhi and Quere 1991), etc. The move towards a post-Fordist era in the organization of production should not be held to mean the *end of mass production* (Williams et al. 1987). Worldwide manufacturing is still characterized by large production volumes, albeit in an orgy of product differentiation (Henderson 1989; Bergsten and Grahm 1993). In recent years, for instance, Sony has manufactured more than 300 versions of its basic Walkman, and Seiko is renowned for its ability to introduce a new model of watch every day (Hayes and Pisano 1994). However, the post-Fordist revolution has opened the door to a still more diverse set of possibilities, ranging from the custom-made single product through a *flexible mass production* model to the continuous upgrading of products.[3]

2   The tendency in implementing new methods of work organization is towards the massive debureaucratization of work. This has been happening in a non-Taylorist context – in the case of the typical producer of machine tools of the Emilia Romagna region (Fiorani et al., eds, 1993) or the Baden Württemberg district, for instance. However, it has also occurred in intensified Taylorist schemes, as described by Kobayashi (1990) and Dhose et al. (1985). In particular, there is a growth in cognitive and relational work (Garibaldo 1994a, 1994b; Koike 1989; Simon 1982, 1991). This is the feature which most characterizes 'post-industrial' manufacturing, rather than any ideological end of the *capitalistic division of labour*.

3   The globalization of national economic systems will not render the concept of *localism* redundant. However, any local/regional system using locally ingrained specific resources must be viewed in a context of global relations. More and more firms will face global markets, global finance, global technologies (Amin 1994). What is left partially undetermined is the possibility of reinterpreting and restructuring local factors of competitiveness. Local systems can decide to compete in various ways. Such competition could be on the basis of lowering input costs, or focused on the means of increasing creativity, on the search for synergies between firms, and on global networks. They can seek to create additional nodes of intelligence within their structure and move in the direction of more value-added productions.

In short, a confrontation with some general worldwide trends has occurred, but a process of metabolization will generate diversity, cumulative growth, bifurcations, path dependency, etc. In this context, social and institutional actors will play a vital role in differentiating the performances of various local systems in terms of stimulating innovation, industrial cooperation, etc. (Bianchi 1994).

Eclectic configuration of production systems in post-Fordist times

In modern times, the coexistence of large, incumbent firms alongside small and dynamic organizations is the dominant characteristic of economic development.

In the economic literature we can clearly trace (for an extensive discussion, see Belussi 1992a) three separate phases which have accompanied the study (and the discovery) of the permanent existence of the small-firm model within the industrial structure of developed nations: (a) studies on the economic 'subordination' of small firms to large firms (Brusco 1975); (b) the discovery of autonomy, which dates back to early studies on peripheral development (Piore and Sabel 1984; Bagnasco 1977); and (c) the analyses of the 1980s on economic complementarities between small and large firms (Harrison 1994; Dore 1986, 1987; Pavitt 1984; Freeman 1982).

While in the neo-classical tradition firms are considered as atomistic agents immersed in a world of pure and perfect competition, contemporary economics has rather emphasized those factors, explaining the increase in firm-like organizations (Williamson 1975), endowed with specific resources (Richardson 1972), market power technological capabilities (Pavitt 1984; Nelson 1990; Rummelt 1974) and specific competences (Foray and Freeman 1993; Pilotti 1993; Rosenberg 1976). The growth of firms is thus related to the development of their competitiveness, and to the valorization of scale and scope economies (Chandler 1990). The concept of the evolving firm (Nelson and Winter 1982; Winter 1991) helps to explain the eclectic configuration of local production systems. Firms are differentiated organizations with varying levels of niche market power, living in a world of technological pluralism.

As emphasized by Coase (1937), firms are hierarchical organizations of governance. The existence of small firms and large firms is the inevitable result of several factors. These include the process of task decentralization; the use of specific specialized suppliers; and the nature of the market, where firms produce for particular niches. Firms can be thought of as productive networks (Harrison and Storper 1991) whose borders are mobile or more or less expanded (Belussi 1987). They are differentiated agents using differentiated resources. On a local level, the factors which influence the process of growth are the interfirm division of labour, the development of technology and the level of task hierarchization (with the use of subcontracting) (Belussi 1993b, 1993c).

All local production systems are a blend of firms of different sizes. The industrial dynamics (Geroski 1991) stem from the continuous creation of new firms which experiment with new business ideas, introducing new products and new methods into the market. Many small firms lack market autonomy. They have instead developed a particular efficient capability in dealing with productive tasks decentralized to them by larger firms.

Local production systems evolve very quickly. In many areas considered to be ideal sites for small-firm development, large networks have grown up (Belussi, 1992b, 1993c). The rapid evolution of firms and the ever-changing landscape of local production systems seem to be a constant characteristic of post-Fordist times. The typical industrial district as defined in the literature of the Third Italy model, based only on a dense network of independent small firms, will tend to be a rarity. More complex dynamics are on the way.

Debureaucratization of work

The international debate on changes in the organization of work brought about by new technologies and by new developments in capitalism has involved an ongoing dispute, resulting in an intellectual situation characterized by – to use the words of Leborgne and Lipietz (1991, 1992) – *conceptual fallacies* and *open questions*.

On one hand, the 'new times' thesis was celebrated and welcomed. Any move away from Fordist practices was seen as the promised land following the crisis of socialism. The de-skilling (*à la* Braverman) versus re-skilling (*à la* Piore and Sabel) debate took up much of the available space, for instance, in regional studies or in development economics.

On the other hand, the diffuse perception of a technologically deterministic causal sequence from technology to skills and from skills to work organization, made it difficult to define the new tendencies in terms of a dominant pattern (on this issue see Belussi 1993a). In fact, it made it hard even to agree on the nature of some common properties. Were these changes post-Fordist or neo-Fordist?[4] Were these models the inevitable consequence of the shifting of the technological paradigm (*à la* Dosi) or, more deeply, of the regime of capitalistic accumulation (*à la* Aglietta)?

Our contribution to the analysis starts with a simple statement of the growing relevance of cognitive and relational work (Koike 1989; Schon 1979; Aoki et al. 1989). In it we have sketched those features that refer to a new 'cognitive construction' of work on problems setting and framing (Garibaldo 1988: 53), where we note a clear shift towards: an intense debureaucratization of work; more 'human-centred' work design (Ehn 1988); the management of events; the interactive performances; the creative use of work; strong collective learning; and more participatory industrial relations.

How is work organization changing?

The past	*The future*
Bureaucratic work	Debureaucratization of work
Technologically determined tasks	Human-centred systems
Division of work into fixed elementary tasks	Management of events
Additive performance	Interactive performance
Division of tasks between execution and conception	Use of the workers' proposals
Speed of the task's execution	Speed of collective learnings
Confrontational models where the system is designed to minimize the influence of human variability	More participative industrial relations

285

The broad perspective adopted here is based on three principles which in our view are transforming contemporary organizations: (a) the conception of time (and of its saving) which is producing a new idea of productivity and of post-manufacturing industrial structure (see also figure 11.1); (b) the definition of labour, which becomes a qualitative input of production, a strategic resource rather than a cost; and (c) the collective dimension of individual learning, which emphasizes the role of co-operation (Aoki 1984, 1988; Axelrod 1985; Bonazzi 1991; Capecchi 1990; Iwata 1992; Kumon and Rosovsky 1992; Rohlen 1992; Butera 1993), the importance of evolution in changing routines (Dore 1986) and the part external factors (environment, externalities, institutions, etc.) play in determining the economic performance of any organization.

In this vision organizations are oriented more towards the holistic control of the *process* (Butera 1993), and towards the management of turbulence and innovation through programmes of action learning (directed to the improvement of quality, training, new procedures for cost reduction, etc.).

The mid-1980s and the beginning of the 1990s signify a profound breakthrough in the design of new organizations. The availability of a range of informational and co-ordinating tools has resulted in a reassessment of the importance of human capital within economic organizations, and of the relevance of intellectual skills in establishing satisfactory performances.

This perspective should certainly not be interpreted as implying a *future stand-ardization of all work practices*, either in terms of a shift towards more qualified and skilled work in a post-Taylorist world of production (as is commonly perceived by the post-Fordist literature), or as a shift towards a clear-cut, neo-Fordist, flexible and de-skilling, way of organizing production – as appears in works which emphasize the elements of 'Toyotism' emerging from the new methods of organizing assembly lines in Japanese (Belussi 1993a) and in some leading European firms. As regards the clothing industry, see the clear example represented by the Benetton case – discussed by Belussi (1992b, 1993d) – or the Norwegian case (Skorsatad 1992).

In figure 11.1 we have defined the major features of what we have called the future *networking economy*. This economy is based on interconnectivity, knowledge-based organizations and the application of just-in-time techniques. We did not conclude with just one *best practice*. On the contrary, in trying to analyse the post-Fordist experience, we have arrived at a definition of *four* basic models applicable worldwide. These are: (a) the continuation of the Fordist model as we have known it, with just some minor or incremental modifications; (b) the expansion of models based on the revaluation of labour, in line with the European tradition; (c) the introduction of Toyotism or of *core–periphery models*; and (d) the evolution of non-Fordist skill-based economies towards more formalized working practices and towards a hierarchization of firms.

The evolutionary pattern of this fourth type is perhaps still unclear. However, as regards the patterns of work organization seen in small firms, for instance in the Emilia Romagna region, recent research shows a major formalization of functions (Franchi forthcoming). This is not to say that the industrial structure in such cases will no longer be based on craft production, but simply that the observable trend is not towards any intensification of the 'flexible specialization' model. In contrast, the division of tasks between executive and conceptual activities appears to become ever more sharply defined.

Let us introduce a (somewhat artificial) distinction between short-term and long-term transformations. We can then analyse the data set out in the three columns below, where we have identified those short-term changes which have occurred in some large Italian organizations (that is to say that a large part of the organizational structures investigated during the course of our research were still functioning on the basis of only slightly modified Taylorist schemata).

The modifications identified here have occurred in three areas:

- the introduction of a significant process of interfirm division of labour;
- the elimination of the most extreme forms of demarcation on the shopfloor through a process of partial recomposition (job enrichment, rotation, enlargement); and
- the introduction of innovative practices for the development of entrepreneurial skills among managers, and at the highest strata of the firm's hierarchy (Camuffo and Costa 1992).

The question which must be raised is whether or not a unique model of work organization, either post-Fordist or neo-Fordist, will emerge in the near future (Leborgne and Lipietz 1988). As one of us has previously emphasized (Garibaldo 1994b), we are not in the presence of an already realized new model applicable to every sector, a superior rationality represented by the firm and its managers, which we need to study and understand. We are rather confronting a common core of new ideas: ideas on what an industrial activity is nowadays; on what constitutes an adequate service sector; and on the standards set by international demand. However, what all this means in terms of the organization of production, economy and

Modifications observed in the short term within Fordist or post-Fordist work organization models

Features that remain	Features abolished	Features modified
Task analysis		
Division of labour within the firm	Task fragmentation	Division of labour among firms
Differentiation of status between blue-collar workers and white-collar workers	Piece-work payment	Introduction of new styles of management for executives and professionals
Managers' power over personnel		
Hierarchical system		
Technocentrical structure		
Passive use of labour force		

287

society is still not certain. This appears to be not only a classic political problem – and for that reason a matter for conflict between visions, classes and nations – but also an open process of learning for all social actors, based on concrete experience. In a similar way, as we show in figure 11.1, the methods of Fordism were applied in at least three very different institutional contexts: Anglo-American Fordism; continental Fordism (based on better qualified workforces and on co-determination practices); and the new developments of non-Fordist organizations (see, for instance, the Italian model of 'industrial districts'), which coexisted with 'pure' forms of Fordism (Coriat 1991). It is thus difficult to say just where an ideal-type, labelled 'Fordism', has ever existed. Indeed, in a very provocative essay, Clark (1992) argues that Fordism did not live beyond the 1920s. Perhaps it is better simply to acknowledge that pure models are generally overwhelmed by local 'hybrids' and that this process in fact represents an important mechanism of evolution and selection in new social forms of production.

In this sense, Jürgens's (1993a, 1993b) description of the restructuring of the German car industry provides a clear example of how the realization of the lean production concept is currently taking place within the framework of that country's system of co-determination. The influence of collective agreements and the way in which labour is regulated produce a hybrid of the various models of production organization.

Consider, for example, subassembly modules, where in a typical German firm we can observe work cycles ranging generally from fifteen to forty-five minutes. In Japanese lean manufacturing, they are no longer than one/two minutes. In contrast, the Swedish experience is remarkable for its introduction of an autonomous work group at the assembly phase (Ellegard 1993). These three models are set out below.

Three models of work and production organization

Swedish model	*German model*	*Japanese model*
Semi-skilled workers with high initial training	Skilled worker deployed on direct production jobs	Semi-skilled workers with generally high starting qualification
Work totally uncoupled from production cycle	Work partially uncoupled from the production cycle	Work tied to the production cycle
Holistic tasks with long work cycles (one hour)	Job enlargement with work cycles below one hour	Highly repetitive work: cycle times around 1 minute on the assembly lines; around 5 minutes in the machining areas where multi-machine work is the norm
Homogeneous groups	Mixed teams of specialists	Homogeneous groups

High partial autonomy for teams through process layout	Little partial autonomy for teams through automation and module production	No partial autonomy for the teams through just-in-time design
De-hierarchization with elected speaker and self-regulation of group affairs	Controversial role of group speaker/leader and of degree of self-regulation	Strong hierarchical structures, group leader appointed by management, no group self-regulation

In 1992 the German Employers' Association formulated [a body of] principles for the application of 'lean production', which show a surprising degree of continuity with the postwar co-determination approach:

- increase work motivation;
- use the benefits of teamwork;
- integrate tasks with *simultaneous engineering*;
- deploy human-centred technologies;
- increase workers' qualifications;
- make work time more flexible; design a system of remuneration that supports performance as well as co-operation;
- design health technologies;
- emphasize information and participation of workers;
- co-operation with the factory works' council;
- practise firm leadership.

The German case shows a specific trend in the labour regulation model (Locke 1993; Locke and Camuffo 1993). The de-Taylorization of work has been realized through the role of institutions such as trade unions and government agencies, and thanks to the use of skilled workers facilitated by a national system of training based on the apprentice. These elements of the national model overlapped the specific firm's pattern but were clearly distinguishable.

Kelly's and Brooks's (1988) analysis of the state of computerized automation in US manufacturing also provides support for an eclectic approach to matters of work organization. As expected, the most widespread form found among firms is that of neo-Taylorist organization (nearly half the sample studied). This is followed by firms sharing control with their employees. There is also a marginal presence of post-Fordist (worker-centred) organizations.

For some time to come, organizational changes will continue to be confronted with a complex pattern of firm divergence, given the differing levels of inertia embedded in organizations as regards the debureaucratization of work, and their different capacities for designing new, rapidly evolving organizational forms (Dosi and Tonielli 1992).

Often, the old and the new will be blurred together. Anti-Taylorist practices may sometimes emerge, but, we suspect, more as a result of conscious social planning – as in the case of the car industry in Germany or in Sweden (AA VV

1993), or again in the US Saturn Project – rather than as a spontaneous effect of market forces.

Some elements will obviously be commonly applied: waste elimination, techno-logical improvements of products and processes, work intensification, continuous organizational improvements, new quality goals, better use of suppliers and more involvement in customers needs in accordance with the principles of the just-in-time system and total quality management (Sayer 1988; Marchisio 1994; Gar-ibaldo forthcoming).

Nevertheless, as we have tried to demonstrate, the question appears to be neither one of the emergence of an ideological *new work order* (Appelbaum and Batt 1994), nor of whether these changes will be introduced or not, but rather one of how such changes will influence work organization (Delbridge and Turnbull 1992; Garibaldo 1994c).

Globalization of 'local systems'

Since the mid-1970s, developments among small-sized organizations in certain semi-developed areas of Europe have fuelled a growing interest in 'local models of small firms'. This process has been perceived either as an increasing delocalization of the manufacturing system from the congested metropolitan areas to peripheral parts of the economy, or as a more general process of economic deconcentration. The positive economic performance of peripheral regions of Europe during the 1980s reinforced the belief that future economic developments would take place exclusively on a small scale, due to the flourishing of local communities sustained by a growing swarm of small and independent organizations (Sabel 1989).

The development of industrial districts (Brusco 1993) and the expansion of peripheral areas – local productive systems, specialized areas or system areas in Garofoli's topology – indicated the nature of the forthcoming paradigm: the territorial disintegration of production.

In the vast literature built around the 'Third Italy' model – the origins of which were clearly anti-neo-classical – the 'industrial district' and the Marshalian *industrial atmosphere* became a general model for economic thinking (Rullani and Beccatini 1993). But what can be said, then, about the phenomenon of globalization of the international economy? (Bergsten and Grahm 1993; Simon 1982; Amin and Thrift 1994; Chase Dunn 1989; Dicken 1993; Dunning 1988, 1993; Chalmin et al. 1988).

Despite strong interest in these forms of endogenous growth (whose extension is still limited, as has been documented by Sforzi (1990) in Italy, in a 'tentative' study of the localization of specialized districts) there has been an underlying process of economic centralization. Large firms are 'coming out of the corner' – becoming more flexible and efficient (Harrison 1994). So, while some economic activities are systematically decentralized, big firms continue to be in control in many strategic and advanced sectors (Pavitt and Patel 1988, 1994). Powerful multinational cor-porations are refocusing on their core business, and in doing so can retain their market power through the development of leading technologies, marketing and advertising etc. Scale economies are now shifting from production to marketing (Pavitt and Patel 1988).

As regards the power of multinationals, Costello et al. (1989) calculated that the turnover of the 200 largest multinationals today covers 30 per cent of the value of all international production. The intensification of economic exchanges and the broad growth of communications has helped to set international standards and regulations in most high-tech industries – telecommunications, aerospace, financial services, pharmaceuticals, the automobile industry, etc. (Camagni 1989; Henderson 1989; Teece 1991). In the foreseeable future, at least half of all products sold will be sold in a global market place – from cars, clothes, electronic gadgets, washing machines and televisions to international services.

Naturally, the globalization of the economy has had many implications (Archibugi and Michie forthcoming). These include the global exploitation of technology (firms have access to technology through diffusion), the internationalization of markets, and the development of scientific and technological co-operation. Local economic systems are part of this new post-Fordist model of 'flexible accumulation', where the power of oligopolies is destined to last, but where new forms of hierarchization are changing the relative competitive position of many specialized districts. The dynamic growth of hierarchical economic networks seems to be substituting for the confused fragmentation of powerless horizontal networks (Martinelli and Schoenberger 1992). During the 1980s, many local networks underwent this transformation with the emergence of leading firms (Harrison 1994).

This has happened in many Italian districts. Examples include the silk area in Como (see the role of Ratti), the ceramic district (with the dominance of the Marazzi group), the glass frame district of Belluno (with the Lux ottica), the footwear areas of Brenta (with the Rossi moda firm; Camagni and Rabbellotti 1994; Belussi 1994), and of Marche (with Diego della Valle), the many mechanical districts of Emilia Romagna (Franchi 1994; Belussi forthcoming) and, of course, the clothing industry, where the network firm model (Benetton, Stefanel, Carrera; Belussi 1992b) has challenged the slow, continuous development of the sector during the 1970s.

Today we can find an extensive range of different economic aggregations in every local context. There are various small-firm systems (Sartore 1992), traditional industrial districts (Schmitz 1992), system areas (Garofoli 1983; Scott and Storper 1986), hierarchical organizations, metropolitan economies (Scott and Storper 1986) and district networks (Veltz 1990). The growth of local economies and the emergence of the peripheral areas [...] has not taken place in isolation from wider developments. On the contrary, local development is now becoming global (Perulli 1993).

A suggested approach to policy

In the post-Fordist model, how do macro-economic policies influence the evolution of the socio-economic system? (Streeck 1992) It is well known that public policies (in terms of innovation policies – see Freeman 1982; Nelson 1982; 1993;

291

Johnson 1982; Malerba 1993; Archibugi et al. 1992 – and public provision of utilities and services – see Nomisma 1991, 1992; Brusco and Righi 1989; Bauer 1992; Bartolozzi 1993; Fraschi 1992) contribute a great deal to the overall efficiency of economic systems. The same holds true when we analyse the collective strategies of social actors (Capecchi 1990; Carrieri 1993). The development of knowledge in the society (Nelson et al. 1967) and the ability to impose adequate standards of services and industry regulation (OTA 1994) contribute to the creation of welfare in the same way as does possession of a competitive industrial structure (Porter 1990). The perspective which we have outlined raises many questions, the most important being the following: is it really plausible to suggest that one clearly dominant model of industrial organization, combining particular styles of production with a particular political and economic context, will emerge? If such a model should emerge, how far will it conform to a well-defined post-Fordist model? (Boyer and Freyssenet 1994). Or, to turn to a more complex methodological issue, is it possible to identify any crucial variables which may determine the final result?

Our perspective on possible future social changes can be summed up in this way.

1 We believe that we must avoid a discussion mainly focused on a theoretical comparison of different paradigmatic models – such as Fordist versus post-Fordist. On the contrary, it is necessary to accept, as a starting-point, the possibility of hybridization with the recent Japanese experience of managing firms and organizations. Our main thesis is that the diffusion of this Japanese experience will not lead to the dominance of one 'best way'. The key point is rather to shift from a 'catch-up' approach – which until now seems to have been not successful at all – to a strategy firmly oriented towards the creation of innovative and self-sustaining processes of development.

2 In order to create such innovative and self-sustaining processes, firms, regions and nations must reassess their culturally embedded, idiosyncratic factors of production and their particular regulatory practices. Differences between organizational models should not be eradicated. On the contrary, the most competitive countries and/or regions will be those which are able to create a virtuous circle based on their own cultural identity and on the more generally applicable knowledge resulting from the Japanese experience.

3 The full development of the potential of these virtuous circles can be mapped out, starting with the removal of weak points inherited from the past, such as:

- the systematic underutilization of human resource management (which has penalized the use of the most important factor of production, the labour force);
- the low level of importance assigned to customer-driven production processes;
- the inadequate regulatory relationships existing between firms and government authorities, and between employers and unions (on a local, national and European level).

In this context it may be relevant to summarize the conclusion of the LOM evaluation report of 1992:

> In contrast to the American model based on individual firms and private consultancy services, but without accompanying research and support structures at the macropolitical level, two generative mechanisms are especially striking, which may well constitute necessary preconditions for furthering and diffusing innovation:
>
> - public research providing a critical evaluation of processes of change within organizations and their positions *vis- à-vis* the competitive environment;
> - social discourse as an essential determinant of rational and consensual action in terms of broad-based mobilization of resource potential. (pp. 122–3)

It should be noted that the Clinton administration programme concerning the workplace of the future seems to aim to change the traditional American way of thinking (Reich 1991).

In order to achieve such a goal, public authorities must accept responsibility for supporting the social process by which a minimum set of criteria for the organizational renewal of the production system is selected, and for creating a setting for the process of change (Ires Materiali 1993). We have in mind a strategy whose aim is not to implement a predefined model of organization but rather to provide a way of keeping the process under control and therefore not inhibiting the participatory dimension (Garibaldo 1994c; Fondazione europea 1992).

Epilogue

This reading was intended to present an examination, based on the Italian experience, of present and future changes in international socio-economic systems. Our hypothesis challenges the all too simplistic view of the 'old' and 'new' times thesis (Womack et al. 1990; Hall and Jacques 1989). We have argued that transformations occurring in the post-Fordist societies incorporate elements of the old system. In some cases old and new are blurred together. However, the main topic discussed is the relationship between the core of technical and organizational changes based on a new form of networking economy and the evolution of different 'modes of production', whether neo-Fordist, post-Fordist, or non-Fordist.

NOTES

From F. Belussi and F. Garibaldo (1996), 'Variety of Pattern of the Post-Fordist Economy: why are the "Old Times" still with us and the "New Times" still to come?', *Futures*, vol. 28, no. 2, pp. 153–71; © 1996 Elsevier Science Ltd.

1   The flex-spec thesis, deriving from the work of Piore and Sabel, has been extensively discussed. See, for instance, Sabel and Zeitlin 1985; Sabel 1989; Wood, ed., 1989; Amin

1988, 1989; Belussi 1992a, 1992b; Hirst and Zeitlin 1992; Williams et al. 1987; Winterton 1992; Jessop 1991; Bagguley 1988; Gilbert, Burrows and Pollert, eds, 1992; Piore and Sabel 1984.

2   The literature on this issue is now vast. See, for instance, Bagnasco and Trigilia, eds, 1984; Becattini 1979, 1989; Brusco 1993; Pyke, Becattini and Sengenberger, eds, 1990; Pyke and Sengenberger, eds, 1992; Amin and Robins 1990; Harrison 1989b, 1990; Amin 1991, 1993; Anastasia, Corò and Occari 1993; Moussanet and Paolazzi eds, 1992; Bortolotti, ed., 1994.

3   This appears to be the main result of the studies that Belussi conducted during his years of empirical analysis on the evolution of firms in the 'Third Italy' model with regard to the Veneto region (1988) the evolution of the Modena districts (1990), the changing pattern of firms in the Alessandria provincia (Belussi and Guidi 1992) and in Reggio Emilia (Belussi forthcoming).

4   As discussed by Lipietz (1992a, 1987) in neo-Fordist theories, there is an attempt to transform work and organizations within the Taylorist or Fordist paradigm, whereas post-Fordism implies a move towards the manufacture of specialized goods, employing flexible technologies and innovative forms of work organization. On the same topic, see also Winterton 1992 and Di Bernardo and Rullani 1992.

REFERENCES

AA VV (1993), *Auto e lavoro* (Rome: Ediesse).
Aglietta, M. (1987), *A Theory of Capitalistic Regulation: The US Experience* (London: New Left Books).
Amin, M. (1988), 'Specialisation without growth: small firms in an inner-city area of Naples', mimeo, Centre for Regional and Urban Development Studies.
Amin, M. (1989), 'Flexible specialisation and small firms in Italy: myths and realities', *Antipode*, vol. 27, no. 1.
Amin, A. (1991), 'These are not Marshallian times', in R. Camagni, ed., *Innovation Networks: Spatial Perspectives* (London: Belhaven Press).
Amin, A. (1993), 'The difficult transition from informal to Marshallian district', mimeo, University of Newcastle upon Tyne.
Amin, A. (1994), 'Globalisation and the local economy', paper presented at the conference 'Industrial Districts and Local Development in Italy', Bologna, 2–3 May.
Amin, A. and K. Robins (1990), 'Industrial districts and regional development: limits and possibilities', in Pyke et al., eds, op. cit.
Amin, A. and N. Thrift (1994), 'Living in the global', mimeo, Centre for Regional and Urban Development Studies.
Anastasia, B., G. Corò and F. Occari (1993), 'Valutazioni e simulazioni sui "criteri ufficiali" per la delimitazione geografica dei distretti', *Oltre il ponte*, p. 42.
Antonelli, C. (1987), 'Dall'economia industriale all'organizzazione industriale', *Economia politica*, vol. 2.
Aoki, M. (1984), *The Co-operative Game of the Firm* (Amsterdam: Elsevier Science).
Aoki, M. (1988), *Information, Incentives and Bargaining in the Japanese Economy* (Cambridge: Cambridge University Press).
Aoki, M., B. Gustafsson and O. E. Williamson, eds (1989), *The Firm as a Nexus of Treaties* (London: Sage).
Appelbaum, E. and R. Batt (1994), *The New American Workplace* (New York: IRL Press).

Archibugi, D., R. Evangelista and M. Pianta (1992), 'Il sistema innovativo italiano: punti di forza e di debolezza', paper presented at the conference 'Ritardo tecnologico ed integrazione europea', 16 December.

Archibugi, D. and J. Michie, 'The globalisation of technology: myths and realities', *Cambridge Journal of Economics*, forthcoming.

Axelrod, R. (1985), *The Evolution of Cooperation* (New York: Basic Books).

Bagguley, P. (1988), 'The post-Fordism enigma: theories of labour flexibility', working paper, University of Lancaster, 1988, p. 29.

Bagnasco, A. (1977), *Le tre itali: la problematica territoriale dello sviluppo* (Bologna: IL Mulino).

Bagnasco, A. and C. Trigilia, eds (1984), *Società e politica nelle aree di piccola impresa* (Venice: Arsenale Editrice).

Barba Navaretti, G. and G. Perosino (1993), 'Global firm strategy, foreign investment, and trade policy in the Italian textile and clothing industry', paper presented at the conference 'Innovation in the Traditional Sectors and the Survival of Old Technologies', Venice, 28–9 May.

Bartolozzi, P. (993), 'Le politiche industriali e di sostegno all'impresa PM—Artigianato delle autorita regionali in Emilia Romagna, Marche, Toscana, Veneto, Fruili', mimeo, Ires Emila Romagna, Bologna.

Bauer, W. (1992), 'Vincoli ed opportunita per lo sviluppo: considerazioni conclusive', in C. Tolomelli, ed., *Le politiche industriali regionali: esperienze, soggetti, modelli* (Bologna: Clueb).

Becattini, G. (1979), 'Dal settore industriale al distretto industriale: alcune considerazioni sull'unità di indagine in economia industriale', *Economia e politica industriale*, vol. 1.

Becattini, G. (1989), *Modelli locali di sviluppo* (Bologna: IL Mulino).

Belussi, F. (1987), *Benetton: Information Technology in Production and Distribution*, SPRU occasional paper, 25, Sussex University.

Belussi, F. (1988), 'La diffusione delle innovazione: modelli ed analisi dell'impatto del cambiamento tecnologico nei settori *supplier-dominated*', in F. Belussi, ed., *Innovazione tecnologica ed economic locali* (Milan: Angeli).

Belussi, F. (1990), 'Alcune riflessioni sullo sviluppo industriale della provincia di Modena', mimeo, Provincia di Modena.

Belussi, F. (1992a), 'Piccole imprese e capacità innovativa: le radici di un dibattito teorico ed alcune evidenze empiriche', *Small Business*, vol. 3.

Belussi, F., ed. (1992b), *Nuovi modelli di impresa, gerarchie organizzative ed imprese rete* (Milan: Angeli).

Belussi, F. (1993a), 'Industrial innovation and firm development in Italy: the Veneto case', SPRU, PhD thesis, University of Sussex.

Belussi, F. (1993b), 'The evolutionary theory of the firm: models of technological learning and development of firm capabilities', working paper, 8, Sire (Economica dei sistemi reticolari), University of Udine.

Belussi, F. (1993c), 'Imprese e gerarchie, distretti industriali e reti globali verso un nuovo paradigma dell'economia industriale?', *Ires Materiali*, vol. 9.

Belussi, F. (1993d), 'The transformation of the 1980s: the growth of network companies or the return of flexibility in large business?', *International Journal of Technology Management*, November.

Belussi, F. (1994), 'Il distretto industriale della Rivera del Brenta: tipologia delle imprese e tendenze evolutive', *Oltre il ponte*, p. 43–4.

Belussi, F. 'L'evoluzione dei comparti produttivi nella provincia di Reggio Emilia' (Rome: Ires Materiali, forthcoming).

Belussi, F. and M. Festa (1990), 'L'impresa rete del modello veneto: dal post-fordismo al toyotismo? Alcune note illustrative sulle strutture organizzative dell'indotto Benetton', *Oltre il ponte*, p. 31.

Belussi, F. and M Guidi, (1992), 'Imprenditoria alessandrina: matrici e cultura', in V. Castronovo, ed., *L'economia alessandrina dal Secondo Dopoguerra ad oggi*, (Alessandria: Cassa di Risparmio).

Benko, G. and A. Lipietz, eds (1992), *Les régions qui gagnent* (Paris: Presses Universitaires de France).

Bergsten, C. F. and E. M. Grahm (1993), *The Globalisation of Industry and National Economic Policies* (London: Longman).

Bianchi, P. (1992), 'Sentieri di industrializzazione e sviluppo regionale negli anni '90: strategie politiche di intervento pubblico nella nuova fase competititiva post-fordista', in F. Belussi, ed., *Nuovi modelli di impresa* (Milan: Angeli).

Bianchi, P. (1994), 'New approaches to industrial policy at the territorial level', paper presented at the Conference on Industrial Districts and Local Economic Development in Italy: Challenges and Policy Implications, Bologna, 2–3 May.

Bonazzi, G. (1991), *Storia del pensiero organizzativo* (Milan: Angeli).

Bortolotti, F., ed. (1994), *Il mosaico e il progetto* (Milan: Angeli).

Boyer, R. (1985), *Capitalism fin de siècle* (Paris: Presses Universitaires de France).

Boyer, R. (1988), 'Technical change and the theory of "regulation"', in G. Dosi et al., eds, *Technical Change and Economic Theory* (London: Pinter).

Boyer, R. (1989), *The Regulation School: A Critical Introduction* (New York: Columbia University Press).

Boyer, R. and M. Freyssenet (1994), 'Processus d'emergence de nouveaux modèles industriels', mimeo, CNRS, Paris.

Brusco, S. (1975), 'Sindacato e piccola impresa, strategia del capitale ed azione sindacale del decentramento produttivo, a cura dell'FLM' (Bari: De Donate).

Brusco, S. (1982), 'The Emilian model: productive disintegration and social integration', *Cambridge Journal of Economics*, vol. 6, no. 2, pp. 167–84.

Brusco, S. (1989), *Piccole imprese e distretti industriali* (Turin: Rosenberg and Sellier).

Brusco, S. (1993), 'Il modello emiliano rivisita il distretto', *Politica ed economia*, July.

Brusco, S. and E. Righi (1989), 'Enti locali, politica per l'industria e consenso sociale: l'esperienza di Modena', in S. Brusco, ed., *Piccole imprese e distretti industriali* (Turin: Rosenberg and Sellier).

Bull, A. C. 'Synchronic and dyachronic approaches to the industrial districts theory: a comparison between Como and Rome', mimeo, New York University, *Industrial and Corporate Change*, forthcoming.

Business Week, 'The hollow corporation', 3 March 1986.

Butera, F. (1991), 'Gestire la crescita di un'impresa inconoscibile: la piccola e media impresa come pacchetto di organizzazioni co-esistenti e come nodo di "reti organizzative"?, *L'industria*, vol. 7.

Butera, F. (1993), 'Nuove strutture flessibili per governare i processi', *L'impresa*, vol. 7.

Camagni, R. (1989), 'Accordi di cooperazione, e alleanze strategiche: motovizioni, fattori di successo ed elementi di rischio', *Rassegna economica LBM*, vol. 4, suppl., December.

Camagni, R. and R. Rabellotti (1994), 'Footwear production systems in Italy: a dynamic comparative analysis', paper presented at IVth Gremi Meeting, Grenoble, 11 June.

Camuffo, A. and G. Costa (1992), 'Strategic human resource management: The Italian way', mimeo, Cà Foscari.

Capecchi, V. (1990), 'A history of flexible specialisation of industrial districts in Emilia Romagna', in F. Pyke and W. Sengenberger, eds, *Industrial District and Inter-firm Cooperation in Italy* (Geneva: ILO).

Carrieri, M. (1993), 'The impact of participation on the system of industrial relations', paper presented at the conference 'The social shaping of new technology', at Ravello, 13–15 October.

Chalmin, P., J. Gambeard and C. Prager (1988), *The Global Markets* (New York: Prentice Hall).

Chandler, A. D. (1990), *Scale and Scope: The Dynamics of Capitalism* (Cambridge, MA: Belknap Press).

Chase Dunn, C. (1989), *Global Formation: Structures of the World Economy* (Cambridge, MA: Basil Blackwell).

Clark, S. (1992), 'Strange bedfellows: Ford and Keynes', in N. Gilbert, R. Burrows and A. Pollert, eds, *Fordism and Flexibility: Division of Labour and Change* (Basingstoke: Macmillan).

Coase, R. (1937), 'The nature of the firm', *Economics*, vol. 4.

Cooke, P. et al. (1994) *Towards Global Localisation: The Computing Industries and Telecommunications in Britain and France* (London: UCL).

Coriat, B. (1991), *Penser à l'envers* (Paris: Christian Bourgois).

Costello, N., J. Michie and S. Milne (1989), *Beyond the Casino Economy* (London: Verso).

Delbridge, R. and P. Turnbull, eds (1992), *Reassessing Human Resource Management* (London: Sage).

Dhose, K., U. Jürgens and T. Malsh (1985), 'From "Fordism" to "Toyotism"? The social organisation of the labour process in the Japanese automobile industry', *International Review of Economic, Political and Social Development*; also in *Politics and Society*, vol. 14, no. 4.

Di Bernardo, B. and E. Rullani (1992), 'Cicli lunghi e morfogenesi del capitalismo industriale: teoria dell'innovazione o teoria dell'evoluzione', in F. Belussi, ed., *Nuovi modelli di impresa* (Milan: Angeli).

Dicken, P. (1993), *Global Shift in the Internationalization of Economic Activity* (London: Paul Chapman).

Doray, D. (1988), *From Taylorism to Fordism: A Rational Madness* (London: Free Association Books).

Dore, R. (1986), *Flexible Rigidities: Industrial Policy and Structural Adjustment in Japan* (London: Athlone).

Dore, R. (1987), *Taking Japan Seriously: A Confucian Perspective on Leading Economic Issues* (London: Althone).

Dosi, G. and P. A. Tonielli, eds (1992), *Technology and Enterprise in an Historical Perspective* (Oxford: Press).

Dunford, M. (1990), 'Theories of regulation', *Society and Space*, vol. 8, no. 3.

Dunning, J. H. (1988), 'International business, the recession and economic restructuring', in N. Hood and J. E. Vahlne, eds, *Strategies in Global Competitions* (London: Croom Helm).

Dunning, J. H. (1993), *The Globalisation of Business* (London: Routledge).

Ehn, P. (1988), *Work-oriented Design of Computer Artifacts* (Stockholm: Arbeitslivscentrum).

Ellegard, K. (1993), 'The creation of a new production system at the Volvo automobile assembly plant in Udevalla', mimeo, Göteborg University.

297

Enrietti, E. (1987), 'La dinamica dell'integrazione verticale alia Fiat', *Economia e politica industriale*, vol. 55.

Fiorani, G., M. Franchi and V. Rieser, eds, *Le piccole imprese crescono: una ricerca sulle piccole imprese metalmeccaniche nella provincia di Modena* (Modena: Snamm-Cna).

Fondazione europea per il miglioramento della condizioni di vita e di lavoro (1992), *Partecipazione al cambiamento, nuove tecnologie e coinvolgimento dei lavoratori*, ed. P. Cressey and R. Williams, The Information Booklet Series, 11, Dublin.

Foray, D. and C. Freeman, eds (1993), *Techology and the Wealth of the Nations* (London: Pinter).

Forzi, F. (1990), 'The Italian districts in the Italian economy', in F. Pyke, G. Becattini and W. Sengenberger, eds, *Industrial Districts and Inter-firm Cooperation in Italy* (Geneva: ILO).

Franchi, M. (1994), 'Developments in the districts of Emilia Romagna', paper presented at the Conference on Industrial Districts and Local Economic Development in Italy: Challenges and Policy Implications, Bologna, 2–3 May.

Franchi, M. (forthcoming), 'La convergenza dei modelli organizzativi d'impresa', *Sociologia del lavoro*.

Fraschi, A. C. (1992), *Centri di servizi alle imprese in Toscana*, mimeo, Dipartimento Attivita produttive, Turismo, Formazione Professionale, Servizi alle imprese', mimeo, regione Toscana, Florence, October.

Freeman, C. (1982), *Industrial Innovation* (London: Pinter).

Freeman, C. (1987), *Technology Policy and Economic Performance: Lessons from Japan* (London: Pinter).

Garibaldo, F. (1988), *Lavoro, innovazione, sindacato* (Genova: Costa and Nolan).

Garibaldo, F. (1994a), 'Organizzazione del lavoro e riduzione d'orario', *Nuovo rassegna sindacale*, p. 22–3.

Garibaldo, F. (1994b), 'Globalizzazione e contesti nazionali', *Spazio impresa*, vol. 30.

Garibaldo, F., ed. (1994c), *Il lavoro tra memoria e futuro* (Rome: Ediesse).

Garibaldo, F. (forthcoming) 'Total quality management', *Spazio impresa*.

Garifoli, G. (1983), 'Le aree-sistema in Italia', *Politica ed economica*, vol. 11, pp. 57–70.

Garofoli, G. (1992), 'Les systèmes de petites enterprises: un cas paradigmatique de developpement endogene', in G. Benko and A. Lipietz, eds, *Les régions qui gagnent* (Paris: Presses Universitaires de France).

Geroski, P. A. (1991), *Market Dynamics and Entry* (Oxford: Blackwell).

Gilbert, N. R. (1991) Burrows and A. Pollert, eds (1992) *Fordism and Flexibility: Division of Labour and Change* (Basingstoke: Macmillan).

Gordon, R. (1992), 'State, mileu, network: systems of innovation in Silicon Valley', paper presented at the workshop 'Systems of Innovations', Bologna, 5–6 October.

Hall, S. and M. Jacques (1989), *New Times: The Changing Face of Politics in the 1990s* (London: Lawrence and Wishart).

Harrison, B. (1989a), 'The big firms are coming out of the corner', working paper 39, Carnegie Mellon University Pittsburgh, PA.

Harrison, B. (1989b), 'Concentration without centralisation', paper presented at a conference on employment and local development, Tokyo, 12–14 September.

Harrison, B. (1990), 'Industrial districts: old wine in new bottles?', working paper 90, Carnegie Mellon University, Pittsburgh, PA

Harrison, B. (1994), *Lean and Mean* (New York, Basic Books).

Harrison, B. and M. Storper (1991), 'Flexibility, hierarchy, and regional development: the changing structure of the industrial production system', *Research Policy*, vol. no. 5.

Hayes, R. and G. Pisano (1994), 'Evolving capabilities', *Harvard Business Review*, January–February.

Henderson, J. (1989), *The Globalisation of High-tech Production: Society, Space, and Semiconductors in Restructuring the Modern World* (London: Routledge).

Hirst, P. and J. Zeitlin (1992), 'Specializzazione flessibile e post-fordismo: realtà e implicazioni politiche', in F. Belussi, ed., *Nuovi modelli di impresa* (Milan: Angeli).

Ires Materiali (1993), *Organisation and Framework for Managing the Social Dimensions of Change* (Rome: Ires Nazionale).

Iwata, R. (1992), 'The Japanese enterprise as a unified body of employees', in S. Kumon and H. Rosovsky, eds, *The Political Economy of Japan: Cultural and Social Dynamics* (Stanford, CA: Stanford University Press).

Jessop, B. (1991) 'Fordism and post-Fordism: a critical reformulation', mimeo, University of Lancaster.

Johnson, C. (1982), *Miti* (Stanford, CA: Stanford University Press).

Jürgens, U. (1993a), 'Differenze specifiche nazionale e aziendali nell'organizzazione del lavoro di produzione nell'industria automobilistica', in *Auto e lavoro* (Rome: Ediesse).

Jürgens, U. (1993b), 'Lean production and co-determination: the German experience', paper presented at Wayne State University, 20–2 May.

Kelly, M. and H. Brooks, (1988), *The State of Computerised Automation in US Manufacturing* (Cambridge, MA: John Kennedy School University Press).

Kobayashi, H. (1990), 'L'operaio giapponese alia catena', *Politica ed economia*, vol. 3.

Koike, K. (1989), 'Intellectual skill and the role of employees as constitutent of large firms in contemporary Japan', in M. Aoki, B. Gustafsson and O. Williamson, eds, *The Firm as a Nexus of Treaties* (London: Sage).

Kumon, S. and H. Rosovsky, eds (1992) *The Political Economy of Japan: Cultural and Social Dynamics* (Stanford, CA: Stanford University, Press).

Leborgne, D. and A. Lipietz (1988), 'New technolgoies, new modes of regulation: some spatial implications', *Society and Space*, vol. 6.

Leborgne, D. and A. Lipietz (1991), 'Two social strategies in the production of new industrial spaces', in G. Benko and M. Dunford, eds, *Industrial Change and Regional Development: The Transformation of New Industrial Space* (London: Pinter).

Leborgne, D. and A Lipietz (1992), 'Conceptual fallacies and open questions on post-Fordism', in M. Storper and A. Scott, eds, *Pathways to Industrialization and Regional Development* (London: Routledge).

Lipietz, A. (1987), *Mirages and Miracles: The Crisis of Global Fordism* (London: Verso).

Lipietz, A. (1992a) *Towards a New Economic Order: Post-Fordism, Ecology and Democracy* (Cambridge: Polity Press trans. of *Choisir l'audace*, Paris: Editions La Découverte, 1989).

Lipietz, A. (1992b), *Berlin, Bagdad, Rio: Le 21 siècle est commencé* (Paris: Quai Voltaire).

Locke, R. (1993), 'Modifiche strutturali delle imprese ed organizzazioni del lavoro per moduli autoregolati, le lezioni del passato', paper presented at Bologna, 5–7 May.

Locke, R. and A. Camuffo (1993), 'Italian industrial relations: searching for a new "national model" in a world where they no longer exist', mimeo, Sloane School of Management, MIT.

LOM (1992), 'Evaluation report', Science Center, Berlin (WZB).

Longhi, C. and M. Quere (1991), 'Local systems of production and innovation: the case of Sophia-antinopolis', mimeo, Latapes.

Malerba, F. (1993), 'Italy: the national system of innovation', in R. Nelson, ed. *National Innovation Systems* (Oxford: Oxford University Press).

Marchisio, O. (1994), *La mobilità come prodotto* (Milan: Franco Angeli).

Martinelli, F. and E. Schoenberger (1992), 'Les oligopoles se portent bien, merci! Elements de reflexion sur l'accumulation flexible', in G. Benko and A. Lipietz, eds, *Les régions qui gagnent* (Paris: Presses Universitaires de France).

Moussanet, M. and L. Paolazzi, eds (1992), *Gioielli, bambole, coltellii: viaggio nei distretti produttivi italiani* (Milan: II Sole 24-Ore).

Nelson, R. et al. eds (1967), *Technology, Economic Growth, and Public Policies* (Washington, DC: Brookings Institution).

Nelson, R. (1982), *Government and Technical Progress: A Cross-industry Analysis* (New York: Pergamon).

Nelson, R. (1990), 'Capitalism as an engine of progress', *Research Policy*, vol. 19, no. 3.

Nelson, R., ed. (1993), *National Innovation Systems* (Oxford: Oxford University Press).

Nelson, R. and S. Winter (1982), *An Evolutionary Theory of Economic Change* (Cambridge, MA: Belknap).

Nomisma (1991), *Strategic e valutazione nella politica industriale* (Milan: Angeli).

Nomisma (1992), *centri di servizio reale alle imprese: stato dell'arte e repertorio delle esperienze italiane*, mimeo, Bologna: Nomisma.

OTA (1994), *1994 Report: The Electronic Enterprise* (Washington, DC: Government Printing Office).

Pavitt, K. (1984), 'Sectoral pattern of technological change: towards a taxonomy and a theory', *Research Policy*, vol. 13, no. 6.

Pavitt, K. and P. Patel (1988), 'The international distribution and determinants of technological activities', *Oxford Review of Economic Policy*, vol. 4.

Pavitt, K. and P. Patel (1994), 'Technological competences in the world's largest firms: characteristics, constraints and scope for managerial choice', Steep discussion paper, vol. 13.

Perulli, P., ed. (1993), *Globale e locale* (Milan: Angeli).

Pilotti, L. (1993), 'Origini e natura dell'apprendimento nei sistemi di impresa: scatola nera, strategia o evoluzione?' working paper, 7, Sire (Economica dei sistemi reticolari), University of Udine.

Piore, M. J. and C. F. Sabel (1984), *The Second Industrial Divide: Possibilities for Prosperity* (New York: Basic Books).

Porter, M. (1990), *The Competitive Advantage of Nations* (Cambridge, MA: MIT Press).

Pyke, F., G. Becattini and W. Sengenberger, eds (1990), *Industrial Districts and Inter-firm Co-operation in Italy* (Geneva: ILO).

Pyke, F. and W. Sengenberger, eds (1992), *Industrial Districts and Local Economic Regeneration* (Geneva: ILO).

Reich, R. (1991), *The Work of Nations* (London: Simon & Schuster).

Richardson, G. B. (1972) 'The organisation of industry', *Economic Journal*, vol. 82.

Rohlen, T. (1992), 'Learning: the mobilisation of knowledge in the Japanese political economy', in S. Kumon and H. Rosovsky, eds, *The Political Economy of Japan: Cultural and Social Dynamics* (Stanford, CA: Stanford University Press).

Rosenberg, N. (1976), *Perspectives on Technology* (Cambridge: Cambridge University Press).

Rullani, E. and G. Becattini (1993), 'Sistema locale e mercato globale', paper presented at conference in Milan, 12–13 November.

Rummelt, R. P. (1974), *Strategy, Structure, and Economic Performance* (Boston: Harvard University Press).

Sabel, C. (1989), 'Flexible specialization and the reemergence of regional economies', in J. Zeitlin, ed., 'Local Industrial Strategies', *Economy and Society*, vol. 18, no. 4.

Sabel, C., G. Herrigel, G. Deeg and R. Kazis (1989), 'Regional prosperities compared: Massachussetts and Baden-Württemberg in the 1980s', in J. Zeitlin, ed. 'Local Industrial Strategies', *Economy and Society* vol. 18, no. 4.

Sabel, C. and J. Zeitlin (1985), 'Historical alternatives to mass production: politics, markets and technology in nineteenth century industrialization', *Past and Present*, vol. 108.

Sako, M. (1989) 'Neither markets nor hierarchies: a comparative study of the printed circuit board industry in Britain and Japan', paper presented at the conference 'Comparing Capitalist Economies', Bellagio, 29 April–2 May.

Sartore, M. (1992) 'La flessibilita non governata: i sub-contractors dipendenti dell'area del Basso Polesine', in F. Belussi, ed., *Nuovi modelli di impresa* (Milan: Angeli).

Sayer, A. (1988), 'Post-Fordism in question', *International Journal of Urban and Regional Research*, vol. 3, no. 4.

Sayer, A. (1991), 'New developments in manufacturing: the just in time system', in A. Sayer and R. Walker, *Divided and Unruly: Reworking the Division of Labour* (London: Basil Blackwell).

Schmitz, H. (1992), 'Industrial districts: models and reality in Baden-Württemberg, Germany', in F. Pyke and W. Sengenberger, eds, *Industrial Districts and Local Economic Regeneration* (Geneva: ILO).

Schon, D. (1979), 'Generative metaphor: a perspective on problem setting in social policy', in A. Ortony, ed., *Metaphor and Thought* (New York: Cambridge University Press).

Scott, A. and M. Storper, (1986) *Production, Work, Territory: The Geographical Anatomy of Industrial Capitalism* (Boston: *Allen and Unwin*).

Sforzi, F. (1990), 'The Italian districts in the Italian economy', in F. Pyke, G. Beccatini and W. Sengenberger, eds, *Industrial Districts and Inter-firm Cooperation in Italy* (Geneva: ILO).

Simon, H. (1982), *Models of Bounded Rationality* (Cambridge, MA: MIT Press).

Simon, H. (1991), 'Organizations and markets', *Journal of Economic Perspectives*, vol. 2, pp. 25–42.

Skorsatad, E. (1992), 'From Taylorism to Toyotism in the Norwegian textile industry', in A. Kasvio, ed., *Industry without Blue-collar Workers: Perspectives of European Clothing Industry in the 1990s* (Tampere: University of Tampere Press).

Streeck, W. (1992), *Social Institutions and Economic Performance* (London: Sage).

Teece, D. (1991), 'Politiques d'appui aux industries strategiques: impact sur les economies nationales', in OECD, *Les industries strategiques dans une economic globale: questions pour les années 90* (Paris: OECD).

Veltz, P. (1990), 'Nouveaux modèles d'organisation de la production et tendances de l'economie territoriale', in G. Benko, ed., *La dynamique spatiale de l'economie contemporaine* (La Garenne-Colombes: Editions de l'Espace européen).

Weiss, L. (1988), *Creating Capitalism: The State and Small Business since 1945* (Oxford: Basil Blackwell).

Williams, K., C. Haslam and J. William (1987), 'The end of mass production?', *Economy and Society*, vol. 6, no. 3, pp. 404–38.

Williamson, O. E. (1975), *Markets and Hierarchies* (New York: Free Press).

Winter, S. (1991), 'On Coase, competence, and corporation', in O. Williamson and S. Winter, eds, *The Nature of the Firm* (New York: Oxford University Press).

Winterton, J. (1992), 'The transformation of work? Work organization in the UK clothing industry', in A. Kasvio, ed., *Industry without Blue-collar Workers: Perspectives of European Clothing Industry in the 1990s* (Tampere: University of Tampere Press).

Womack, J. P., D. T. Jones and D. Roos (1990), *The Machine that Changed the World* (New York: Rawson Associates).

Wood, S. ed. (1989), *The Transformation of Work?* (London: Unwin Hyman).

Wood, S. (1991), *Japanization and/or Taylorism* (London: LSE).

Woodward, J. (1958), *Management and Technology* (London: HMSO).

12 Change

Design and Devotion: Surges of Rational and Normative Ideologies of Control in Managerial Discourse

STEPHEN R. BARLEY AND GIDEON KUNDA

[...]

Modern American industrial history is marked not only by the rise of large corporations and the professionalization of management (Chandler 1977) but by the formulation of theories that minister to one of management's central problems: the control of complex organizations. Although managerial theories can be assessed as sets of propositions, they may also be treated as rhetorics or ideologies. By an ideology we mean a stream of discourse that promulgates, however unwittingly, a set of assumptions about the nature of the objects with which it deals. In this sense, all theories have an ideological component, since all theorists must adopt some ontological stance in order to proceed with their work. The objects of rhetorical construction in managerial theories have typically been corporations, employees, managers and the means by which the latter can direct the other two.

Although some scholars have suggested that managerial theorizing has produced little more than a plethora of perspectives (Koontz 1961), most have detected more orderly development. In what may still be the most influential study of managerial ideology, Bendix (1956) wrote of an increasing preoccupation with the social-psychological aspects of work. Bendix argued that rhetorics of social Darwinism typical of the nineteenth century had gradually but steadily given way to the belief that managers could better secure compliance by shaping workers' attitudes and sentiments. A number of managerial theorists have offered similar readings of managerial history (Scott 1959; Wren 1972), as have some of management's most vociferous critics (Mills 1951; Whyte 1956; Edwards 1979). In fact, despite serious theoretical and political differences, scholars have converged on a common vision of how American managerial thought has evolved.

The dominant view posits a succession of phases (Jacoby 1991) that parallels Etzioni's (1961) taxonomy of compliance and control. During the first phase,

Table 12.1 The succession of managerial ideologies since 1870

Ideology	Era of ascent	Tenor
Industrial betterment	1870–1900	Normative
Scientific management	1900–1923	Rational
Welfare capitalism/human relations	1923–1955	Normative
Systems rationalism	1955–1980	Rational
Organizational culture	1980–1992	Normative

which ended in the late 1800s, managerial discourse sought to legitimate coercive shopfloor practices (Bendix 1956; Nelson 1975; Edwards 1979). The rhetoric of this early regime justified harsh discipline and even threats of violence by appealing to an individualistic ethic of success. By the turn of the century, early forms of mass production and a wave of corporate consolidations had set the stage for a second phase, during which utilitarian rhetorics became increasingly popular (Haber 1964; Wren 1972; Edwards 1979). Culminating in the work of Frederick Taylor, rational theories of management dominated managerial discourse by the First World War. The workforce was now said to be more effectively controlled by streamlining production processes and by appealing to the worker's self-interest. The Depression is widely held to mark the beginning of the third phase (Bendix 1956; Wren 1972). As the white-collar labour force grew, managerial discourse began to emphasize normative control: the idea that managers could more effectively regulate workers by attending not only to their behaviour but to their thoughts and emotions. By winning the hearts and minds of the workforce, managers could achieve the most subtle of all forms of control: moral authority. Although developments in managerial thought since the 1950s have yet to be rigorously analysed, the recent explosion of interest in schemes for increasing employee loyalty and commitment are often read as evidence for the continuing vitality of the normative orientation that began with the Human Relations movement.

Although the thesis of a progressive shift toward normative control has considerable elegance, it rests on a reading of history that underplays events in the late nineteenth century and that ignores streams of thought that gained prominence after the Second World War. Rectifying these oversights warrants a different interpretation of the historical record. Rather than having evolved linearly, managerial discourse appears to have alternated repeatedly between ideologies of normative and rational control. Table 12.1 summarizes our thesis.

Since 1870 five distinct rhetorics have left their mark on American managerial thought and practice. The second column of the table provides a rough estimate of the period during which each rhetoric surged into managerial discourse. Although it is difficult to date the beginning and end of such surges with precision, the notion of a surge corresponds roughly to the era when a rhetoric was articulated and diffused to a wider audience. However, unlike a passing fad, the five rhetorics with which we are concerned have never disappeared. Instead, images and practices central to each rhetoric were gradually institutionalized. It therefore seems that American managerial discourse has been elaborated in consecutive waves.[1] Moreover, as the final column of table 12.1 suggests, these rhetorical waves seem to have been of two broad types. The three that we label 'industrial betterment', 'human relations' and 'organizational culture' were grounded in an ideology of normative control. In contrast, 'scientific management' and 'systems rationalism' reflected an ideology of rational control. Even more critically, the two ideological orientations seem to have alternated through time, at least insofar as instances of one or the other were considered to be at the cutting edge of managerial thought. Each of the rational rhetorics surged to prominence in the wake of a normative rhetoric's heyday, and vice versa. Consequently, at least in broad contour, the history of American managerial thought appears less a progression than a continued wrestling with counterpunctual themes.

This [reading] explains and justifies the categorizations of managerial thought summarized in table 12.1. Our aim is to substantiate the timing of each rhetoric's surge, to identify its ideological underpinnings as either normative or rational, and to explain why the alternations occurred and what might have triggered them.

Eras of managerial ideology since 1870

Industrial betterment, 1870–1900

Surge Historians concur that, with few exceptions, American employers paid little attention to working conditions or to the welfare of employees prior to the Civil War (Baritz 1960; Cameron 1960; Wren 1972; Nelson 1975; Jacoby 1991). During the first half of the nineteenth century a handful of visionaries such as Robert Owen and James Montgomery wrote tracts espousing the ethos that would become known as 'industrial betterment' and, later, 'welfare capitalism' (Owen 1813; Montgomery 1832). However, industrialists largely ignored Owen's and Montgomery's message until the 1870s, when a generation of reformers popularized their work as part of a movement to alter industrial conditions. The movement consisted of a loose coalition of clergy, journalists, novelists, academics and capitalists. Prominent among the early spokespersons was Washington Gladden a Congregationalist minister who linked religious visions of morality to a 'new stage of industrial evolution' premised on the 'principle of co-operation' and characterized by 'industrial partnerships' that would improve 'the mental and moral qualities of the working-people' (Gladden 1876: 44–50). Similar ideas appeared in widely read novels of the time, such as Charles Reade's *Put Yourself In his Place*, which is reputed to have influenced a number of prominent businessmen (Buder 1967: 36). However, industrial betterment's most important advocates were without doubt the prominent industrialists who sought to apply Gladden's philosophy in their own businesses.

Experiments with industrial betterment began in the railroad industry. During the 1870s Cornelius Vanderbilt and other railroad magnates began founding

Young Men's Christian Associations (YMCAs) along trunk lines to minister to the railroaders' physical and spiritual needs. The railroads hoped that the YMCAs would stem drunkenness and foster a more reliable workforce (Latta 1906; Hopkins 1951). By 1879 thirty-nine YMCAs employing twenty full-time welfare secretaries had been founded (Brandes 1970: 15).[2] During the 1880s and 1890s industrial betterment spread beyond the railroads to a variety of industries. Popular activities included building libraries and recreational facilities, offering classes for employees and their families, establishing social clubs, instituting profit-sharing and benefit plans, and improving the aesthetics and sanitation of factories (Gilman 1899; Olmstead 1900). Some industrialists, such as George Pullman, founder of the Pullman Palace Car Company, and N. O. Nelson, owner of the N. O. Nelson Manufacturing Company, went so far as to build entire communities for their employees (Buder 1967).

News of such experiments spread by word of mouth and by the popular press. Not only did newspapers and magazines such as *Scribners* and *Harpers* routinely extol the virtues of industrial betterment but, by the turn of the century, several books and governmental reports on betterment programmes had been published in hope of promoting similar experiments elsewhere (Gilman 1889, 1899; Olmstead 1900; Tolman 1900; Stevens and Hatch 1904). Associations formed to promote reform further disseminated the betterment movement's philosophy. Alfred T. White, a noted architect who wrote an influential tract on building homes for the 'labouring classes' (White 1879), began the Model Tenement movement in the 1880s (Buder 1967). In 1898 Josiah Strong and William Tolman founded the League for Social Service, later named the American Institute for Social Service (Brandes 1970). The National Civic Federation, which served in part as a clearing-house for information on industrial betterment and which administered an employment service for welfare secretaries, was chartered in 1904 (Nelson 1975). By the turn of the century, industrial betterment had become so widely touted as the wave of the future that the Paris Exposition of 1900 showcased an exhibit on the betterment practices of American corporations (Tolman 1900).

Although records of industrial practices were collected far less systematically during the late 1800s than today, a sense of industrial betterment's acceptance can be gleaned from several publications from the turn of the century that include rosters of firms that had established some type of betterment programme. Gilman (1899) mentioned seventy-six companies, while Olmstead (1900) named forty-one additional firms. Several years later, Stevens and Hatch (1904) surveyed 110 firms that had instituted some type of welfare programme in New York State alone. Many of these firms were among the largest and best known of the day: for instance, National Cash Register, US Steel, McCormick and Pullman.

Rhetoric The rhetoric of industrial betterment reflected the context in which it evolved. The late 1800s were a time of considerable social change. The period witnessed a revolution in technology that enabled mass manufacturing and, ultimately, corporate growth and consolidation (Hounsell 1984). As firms grew, owners found face-to-face management more difficult. To meet the spiralling demand for labour, owners turned to recent immigrants, who often brought with them foreign customs and behaviours, including alien notions of work and employment relations (Korman 1967). Labour relations became increasingly confrontational: not only were strikes and lock-outs relatively common, but radical labour unions, influenced by the immigrants' European notions of socialism, emerged. As a result, many prominent Americans began to fear social upheaval.

Because the ferment seemed to revolve around employment relations, reformers maintained that modifying industrial conditions would alleviate the threat to society. However, because most reformers accepted the sanctity of private property and an ethic of individualism (Laslett and Lipset 1974; Davis 1986), they sought to assuage the situation without challenging the prerogatives of free enterprise. For instance, Gilman (1899: 2–3) began his influential book on welfare capitalism by assuring his readers that he was no 'advocate of the workingman' and that he considered factory owners to be a 'natural aristocracy' based on 'the leadership of the competent'. When linked to religious and moral values, the objective of preserving the prerogatives of ownership forged the rhetoric of industrial betterment.

Industrial betterment's rhetoric pivoted on several themes that were loosely knit into a vision for what George Pullman heralded as 'a new era... in the history of labor' (Buder 1967: 45). At its core was a decidedly Protestant notion of duty. Because industrialists had achieved wealth and position through the work of others, they were morally bound to shoulder responsibility not only for the economy but for the individual and collective well-being of their employees. Gladden (1876: 175–81) preached:

> So long as the wage system prevails... employers of labor will be, to some degree, responsible for the well-being of the mechanics and operatives. The power that wealth gives them... is a power that carries with it heavy obligations. ... First among them is the obligation to care for the physical health and comfort of his work-people.... The Christian law is, that we are to do good to all men as we have the opportunity; and certainly the employer's opportunity is among his employees.

This Protestant vocabulary of motive was entwined with a second theme that signalled the movement's goal: to change the employee. Early advocates of industrial betterment spoke of improving the 'conditions of the workingmen' (Olmstead 1900: 1117) rather than of improving working conditions. Reformers argued that a lack of frugality, industriousness and temperateness lay at the root of industrial unrest (Gladden 1876: 44–50). Hence, it was the employer's duty to educate the workforce and, if necessary, 'Americanize' the worker's habits and character (Korman 1967). As the following excerpt from an 1883 article published in the *New York Sun* illustrates, advocates of industrial betterment routinely drew their readers' attention to the middle-class demeanour of employees who had been bettered:

> The scenes which the streets and public resorts of the village present after nightfall are entertaining in the extreme and prove perhaps more conclusively than anything else the fact that Mr. Pullman's estimate of human nature is far from wrong. After the evening

meal the people made their appearance on the streets. They are presentable almost without exception and most of them are surprisingly neat in their dress and circumspect in their manners. The women and children in clothing and deportment present such a striking contrast to the people of their class in the noisy and dirty city that having seen the two modes of life, an observer may be pardoned for doubting that Pullman is made up almost exclusively of mechanics and laborers and their families. (cited in Buder 1967: 93)

The goal of remaking workers was cast as the path to a new order whose tenor was captured by a third motif: systems based on co-operation are more advanced than systems based on conflict. Reformers argued that if the firm could become the hub around which the employee's life revolved, communal order and industrial peace could be achieved. Accordingly, the most celebrated experiments sought to create total institutions by furnishing the infrastructure of community: houses, schools, churches, libraries, stores and recreational facilities.

Industrial betterment's final motif was profitability. As the treasurer of the Waltham Watch factory proclaimed in the late 1890s, 'Anything that tends to lighten the strain of labor upon the mind, or serves to promote cheerfulness and contentment, is an economic advantage' (Gilman 1899: 211). Similar sentiments were echoed by almost every advocate of industrial betterment who put pen to paper. In short, the path to profit, control and industrial peace lay in bringing the workers' interests, values and beliefs in line with those of the owner.

Challenge to the rhetoric   The spread of industrial betterment brought with it growing criticism. The violent strike at the Pullman Palace Car Company in 1894 strengthened the hand of those who questioned the utility of betterment programmes. Doubters observed that Pullman had done more for his employees than almost anyone else, yet it appeared that even his efforts were insufficient to avert the rising tide of labour militancy (Buder 1967). The depression of 1896 cast further doubt on the promise of an economic utopia, since reform-oriented firms appeared to weather the depression no better than less enlightened firms.

By the 1890s journalists, academics and trade unionists had begun to attack industrial betterment on moral grounds. For instance, in 1885 Richard T. Ely, professor of economics at Johns Hopkins and founder of the American Economic Society, published an early critique of Pullman in *Harpers New Monthly Magazine*. Ely warned that Pullman was a 'gilded cage' for the working man, 'a benevolent, well wishing feudalism which desires the happiness of the people but in such a way as shall please the authorities' (Ely 1885: 466). However, no challenge to industrial betterment was more significant than that mounted by the growing cadre of industrial and mechanical engineers.

Scientific management, 1900–1923

Surge   While industrialists such as Pullman were busy promulgating industrial betterment, a radically different response to contemporary trends was brewing on the shopfloor. Known as the 'systematic management' movement, the response consisted of attempts by managers with engineering backgrounds to apply the principles of their discipline to the organization of production. The experimenters claimed that industry's growing complexity had undermined management's ability to plan and regulate. Firms were losing control, not because social conditions were deteriorating but because administration had become 'increasingly chaotic, confused, and wasteful' (Litterer 1963: 15). Accordingly, industry's problems could be solved by developing more rational methods for managing the shopfloor.

In the late 1880s and early 1890s a number of books and papers appeared outlining schemes for improving management's co-ordination and control (Metcalfe 1885; Towne 1886, 1889; Halsey 1891). These schemes were of three types: cost accounting systems, production control systems and wage payment plans (Litterer 1963). As Shenhav (1994) suggested, their common denominator was an attempt to enhance productivity by specifying cause and effect in the production process. Significantly, the drive for systematics occurred in conjunction with mechanical engineering's emergence as a distinct occupation. Founded in 1880, the American Society for Mechanical Engineers (ASME) rapidly became the primary forum for disseminating information on systematic management. In 1886 Henry Towne argued before the ASME that because no management associations existed, the ASME should fill such a role (Towne 1886). By 1900 Towne's vision was largely fact. Most papers on systematic management appeared in such engineering journals as the *American Machinist* and the *Transactions* of the ASME. Nelson (1975: 45) has documented the increasing frequency of such papers during the late 1800s: 'Only 15 articles appeared before 1880. After that ... the number increased rapidly. From 1880 to 1885, 60 articles appeared, between 1885 and 1890, 93, in the next five years, 68, and in the last five years of the century, 185.' Yet, despite the movement's growing influence, its impact before 1900 was largely confined to managerially oriented members of the ASME. The situation changed with the advent of 'scientific management'.

Fathered by Frederick Taylor and nurtured by a loose band of disciples during the first decades of the twentieth century, scientific management supplied the systematic management movement with a coherent ideological foundation. By 1885 Taylor had worked his way to the position of chief engineer at the Midvale Steel Company. Like many of his contemporaries, he had devised various schemes for improving shopfloor production. Taylor claimed that his ideas for broader industrial reform crystallized around 1882. However, he did not begin to disseminate his views until 1895, when he published an article on the piecc rate, the text of a talk delivered to the ASME (Taylor 1895).

Scientific management subsequently become influential in three stages. From 1895 to 1901 Taylor and his associates worked with few firms and published exclusively in engineering journals. After 1901, Taylor began to promulgate his ideas more widely (Nelson 1980). During the first decade of the century, Taylor delivered numerous public lectures and attempted to sell scientific management to interested industrialists. He published his first book, *Shop Management*, in 1903. It was also during this period that Henry Gantt, Carl Barth, Harrington Emerson and other of Taylor's protégés and admirers began to market their own variants of scientific management (Nelson 1980: 120–36). Between 1901 and 1911 at least eighteen firms adopted some variant of Taylor's system (Nelson 1975: 71). In 1908 the Harvard Business School declared Taylor's approach the standard for modern management and adopted it as the core around which all courses were to be organized. Taylor himself began to lecture at Harvard in 1909 (Nelson 1980). In 1910 the Carnegie Commission drew on Taylor's work to prescribe reform in higher education, thereby proclaiming the philosophy's utility beyond the factory (Cooke 1910). Thus, by the end of the first decade of the twentieth century scientific management had gained considerable support among the industrial elite. However, it did not obtain widespread notoriety until after 1910.

A series of events between 1910 and 1912 transformed scientific management almost overnight into what may have been the first American business fad. In 1910 the Eastern Railroad requested a rate increase from the Interstate Commerce Commission. The request caused widespread anger among the middle class and among industrialists who felt that rates were already too high. Louis Brandeis agreed to represent a group of industrialists who challenged the increase before the ICC. Brandeis argued that had the railroad been managed more efficiently it could have met its costs without raising prices (Nelson 1980). To support his claim, Brandeis solicited testimony from key Taylorites. Their testimonies not only became the centrepiece of the hearings and created a national audience for Taylor's ideas but the term 'scientific management' was apparently coined during the hearings (Haber 1964).

Taylor and his protégés used the Eastern rate case to further popularize their views. Immediately afterwards, Taylor (1911) published *The Principles of Scientific Management*, which became a best seller. Emerson, by now a self-proclaimed spokesman for the movement, published two even more popular books lauding the benefits of efficiency (Emerson 1912, 1914). The Society to Promote the Science of Management (later called the Taylor Society) and Emerson's Efficiency Society were both founded in 1911.

These and other developments occasioned a public mania known among historians as the 'efficiency craze'. Rhetorics of efficiency became so popular in America that in 1914 an 'efficiency exposition' was held in New York City with Taylor as the keynote speaker. The exposition drew a crowd estimated at 69,000 (Haber 1964: 61). The Progressives, in particular, saw in Taylor's ideas a platform for promoting their political agenda (Haber 1964). Taylor's emphasis on the superiority of scientific reasoning and his insistence on the authority of expertise lent credence to the Progressives' claim that society would be better governed by a college-trained elite. By embracing scientific management, the Progressives ushered Taylor's ideas into the mainstream of American political thought during the second decade of the century.

Rhetoric   Taylor explicitly forged scientific management as a two-edged sword to solidify the engineering movement while challenging the ideological underpinnings of industrial betterment. Taylor thought his perspective more reasonable than welfare capitalism: he not only cast his system as a 'partial solution of the labor problem' (Taylor 1895) but actively criticized betterment programmes and their notion of charity. Taylor professed an intense dislike for welfare secretaries and considered welfare programmes a 'joke' (Nelson 1975: 59). 'No self-respecting workman', Taylor wrote, 'wants to be given things, every man wants to earn things' (Taylor 1903: 1454).

The philosophy of scientific management has been so well documented that little explication is required. Although at times more nuanced than critics admit, scientific management's rhetoric revolved around three tenets: (1) an unshakeable belief in the utility and morality of scientific reasoning; (2) the axiom that all people are primarily rational; and (3) the supposition that all people view work as an economic endeavour. Drawing on these premises, Taylor argued that when placed in jobs appropriate to their abilities and when fairly paid, even the least-skilled worker could immediately recognize the superiority of rationally optimized work procedures. Rationalization would not only make work less arduous and more productive, it would result in greater earnings for workers and industrialists alike. The question of how to organize work properly was viewed as a technical problem whose solution could be obtained by following the canons of science, by applying the criterion of efficiency, and by offering a fair day's pay for a fair day's work. Because scientific solutions were, by definition, incontrovertible, effective management reduced to nothing more, or nothing less, than the exercise of demonstrably valid expertise. However, achieving such goals, Taylor insisted, would require a 'mental revolution' especially among employers who had grown accustomed to managing by caprice (Taylor 1911). Thus, for Taylor, scientific management was more a way of thinking than a set of techniques, however crucial these might be.

Challenge to the rhetoric Enthusiasm for efficiency cooled after the First World War. A number of developments indexed the cooling. The successful diffusion of practices popularly associated with scientific management gradually dulled the rhetoric's novelty. By the 1920s elements of Taylor's system, such as the piece rate and time–motion studies, had become widely accepted (Baritz 1960). As the practices were institutionalized, they no longer required justification. Of equal importance, by the 1920s several widely publicized and respected government studies had cast doubt on Taylor's claims (Hoxie 1915; Federated American Engineering Societies 1921). The efficiency movement's inability to substantially reduce waste and lower costs, as well as its more obvious failure to bring about an industrial utopia, led many advocates to modify their stance.

Even before the war a number of Taylor's devotees had begun to admit that scientific management was no panacea for industry's ills. Lillian Gilbreth and Henry Gantt, in particular, advocated paying more attention to 'human factors'. After the war, other Taylorites, notably Morris L. Cooke, broke dramatically with scientific management's orthodoxy by supporting collective bargaining and union participation in corporate governance (Cooke 1920). By the early 1920s even the Taylor Society had begun to advocate a more conciliatory stance toward organized labour (Haber 1964). The shift mirrored the changing concerns of the business community. Stimulated in part by fear of the Bolshevik revolution, industrialists evinced a new willingness to co-operate with labour. The Progressives also began to meld notions of expertise drawn from scientific management

311

with the rhetoric of industrial betterment. As a result of the shift in climate, betterment practices enjoyed a resurgence. Data on the founding of betterment programmes indicate that they enjoyed two periods of popularity: one that peaked in the early 1890s and a revival that peaked in the 1920s (Brandes 1970). In fact, even though the rhetoric of industrial betterment was first articulated and disseminated during the late nineteenth century, its associated practices were more widely implemented in the 1920s.

Human relations, 1923–55

Surge   The resurgence of welfare capitalism after the First World War marked the rekindling of interest in normative control. However, the revival of welfare practices was not accompanied by a revival of the rhetoric that had legitimated the industrial betterment movement. Instead of the old themes of communalism and improved working men, the new rhetoric focused on entitlements and improved working conditions. For instance, the US Bureau of Labor Statistics' survey of welfare practices in 1919 concerned itself almost exclusively with vacations, sick leaves, healthcare, sanitation and pension funds – topics we would now term employee benefits – rather than the social programmes that attracted so much attention during the 1880s. More importantly, the report eschewed appeals to morality or duty in favour of appeals to efficiency, the watchword of scientific management. Thus the resurgence of welfare capitalism in the 1920s is best viewed as an attempt to modify and extend rationalism's promise to the realm of employment relations. The upshot was the birth of personnel administration (Jacoby 1985).

By 1920 not only had the National Personnel Association been formed but the National Civic Federation had begun to speak of 'personnel directors' instead of 'welfare secretaries' (Baritz 1960). In 1917 the first general text on applied psychology was published (Hollingworth and Poffenberger 1917), as was the first issue of the *Journal of Applied Psychology*. The journal's lead article was tellingly entitled 'Human engineering' (Fish 1917). As the title implies, the two most influential variants of the new industrial and personnel psychology – testing and ergonomics – remained firmly grounded in a Taylorist ethos. The testing movement, which grew out of the War Department's support for ability assessment, sought procedures for selecting and placing employees, an objective consistent with Taylor's notion of a 'first class man' (Taylor 1903). Ergonomists, who were heavily influenced by Gilbreth's work, attributed differences in performance to environmental and physiological factors, thereby sustaining scientific management's emphasis on individualism, rationalism and scientific intervention. Thus, although managerial discourse took a normative turn during the 1920s, it did so hesitantly, through a rhetoric crafted out of a modified Taylorism. Yet, by legitimating a concern with human factors in the workplace, the industrial psychologists and personnel workers of the 1920s paved the way for the emergence of a new ideology of normative control: the group-oriented rhetoric of the Human Relations movement.

312

Between 1929 and the end of the Second World War, managerial theorists fashioned a rhetoric of control that turned on the imagery of depth psychology and group behaviour. Although Oliver Sheldon (1923) and Mary Parker Follett (1918, 1924) had written of the social-psychological aspects of work during the 1920s, their work was overshadowed by interest in testing and human factors. Follett's work, in particular, remained obscure until long after Elton Mayo was ensconced as the Human Relations movement's founder. Unlike most managerial theorists of the day, Mayo brought to the problems of industry a multi-disciplinary perspective. He began his career with an interest in fatigue, but by the late 1920s his interest had gravitated to clinical psychology, in particular the work of Freud and Janet. Mayo was convinced that psychodynamics drove work behaviour and that labour conflict was a form of group psychopathology. Mayo's clinical vision caught the fancy of a number of prominent businessmen and academics, who offered Mayo financial and institutional support. With the help of his patrons, Mayo was appointed to the faculty of the Harvard Business School in 1926, where he soon became involved in the ongoing studies of human factors at Western Electric's Hawthorne plant (Trahair 1984).

Mayo quickly realized that environmental and physiological factors could not account for the anomalies that the researchers had uncovered. At Mayo's urging, the team abandoned its ergonomic perspective and enlisted the aid of William Lloyd Warner, who had been influenced by Malinowski and Radcliffe-Brown. Warner advocated the observational studies of work groups for which the Hawthorne studies are famous. In making sense of these studies, Mayo subsequently blended ideas from clinical psychology, sociology and anthropology into a novel explanation for shopfloor dynamics. Crucial to these dynamics, Mayo argued, was the amplification of individual psychopathologies by group processes and the role of the first-line supervisor, whose behaviour presumably determined whether a group would advance or hinder a firm's objectives.

As with scientific management, interest in human relations grew slowly over several decades. The principles of human relations were initially formulated during the 1930s. Mayo revealed his interpretation of the Hawthorne studies in 1928 (Trahair 1984: 237). However, the first published report on Hawthorne did not appear until 1930 (Pennock 1930) and was followed, over the next decade, by a stream of articles and books written by Mayo and his colleagues (Mayo 1930, 1931, 1933; Roethlisberger and Dickson 1934, 1939; Whitehead 1936, 1938). A number of these publications garnered considerable attention. Mayo's *The Human Problems of Industry* became a best seller and was reviewed favourably in both the popular and academic press (e.g., Park 1934). Roethlisberger and Dickson's *Management and the Worker* was considered important enough to be abstracted by *Reader's Digest* (Trahair 1984: 263)

Yet, it was not until the 1940s that the Human Relations movement garnered substantial institutional support. As with scientific management, educators played a prominent role in spreading the gospel. During the 1940s a number of applied human relations research programmes were founded. The University of Chicago established the Committee on Human Relations in Industry in 1943 to promote a multi-disciplinary approach to industrial research (Wren 1972). In 1945 Kurt

313

Lewin formed the Research Center for Group Dynamics at the Massachusetts Institute of Technology, and Rensis Likert founded the Institute for Social Research at the University of Michigan. In 1947 Leland P. Bradford established the National Training Laboratory in Bethel, Maine, an institute dedicated to training managers in human relations techniques. Each of these programmes elaborated and disseminated human relations' theory and practice.

After the Second World War corporate experimentation with strategies for enhancing loyalty, motivation and satisfaction blossomed almost overnight. Shop-floor interventions rapidly expanded beyond counselling and supervisory training, modelled on programmes Mayo had begun at Western Electric, to include innovative compensation systems (Lesieur 1958), schemes for participatory decision-making and job enrichment (Lewin 1951; Whyte 1955; Hertzberg 1966), attitude surveys and even such esoteric techniques as psychodrama and sociometry (Moreno 1946; Van Zelst 1952). The philosophy of the Human Relations movement also shaped American labour relations. During the late 1940s a number of industrial relations centres were established, including the New York State School of Industrial and Labor Relations at Cornell, the Yale Labor-Management Center, and the Institute of Labor and Industrial Relations at the University of Illinois. As supposedly neutral bodies, the centres were charged with institutionalizing a system of collective bargaining. A number of prominent spokespersons for the Human Relations movement joined these centres and subsequently moulded visions of collective bargaining in directions compatible with the human relations ideology. As a result, the collective bargaining system's emphasis shifted from solely structuring conflict through due process to include the potential for collaboration (Walton and McKersie 1965).

By the late 1950s the rhetoric of human relations was well established. Consultants and consulting firms whose business entailed selling organizations expertise in such areas as organizational development, work redesign and personnel management proliferated (Amon 1958; Kubr 1986). Organizational behaviour, industrial relations and personnel administration were emerging in business schools as distinct disciplines specializing in the human side of enterprise. Mid-level managers and corporate executives had even begun to partake of leadership training and management development experiences designed to enhance self-awareness and interpersonal skills.

Rhetoric   Human relations ultimately became a catchphrase for an assortment of philosophies ranging from Mayo's and Lewin's interest in work groups to Maslow's (1954) and Rogers's (1961) theories of self-actualization. Yet, despite such variation, most of the discourse promoted a similar view of workers, managers and organizations. In direct opposition to scientific management's rationalism and individualism, human relations theorists argued that workers were primarily social beings driven by a need for belonging and acceptance. Social interaction and group affiliation were deemed necessary for human fulfilment and, by implication, harmony in the workplace. Following Mayo (1935), human relations' advocates claimed the locus of commitment in the workplace was the work group, whose norms emerged from ongoing interaction. However, precisely because group norms were emergent, there was no guarantee of their consistency with managerial objectives. Accordingly, human relations theorists claimed that effective management was synonymous with leadership: only by influencing social dynamics and gaining the consent of the workforce could managers ensure a healthy and productive organization. Leadership entailed leashing the power of normative systems to enhance a firm's integration. Since primary work groups were the ultimate point of integration, managers all the way down to first-line supervisors were said to require communication skills, sensitivity in interpersonal relations, methods for instilling if not inspiring motivation and knowledge of how to mould the dynamics of a group.

The rhetoric of human relations resembled that of industrial betterment in several key respects. Like proponents of industrial betterment, human relations theorists equated effective organizations with cohesive collectives. Both construed conflict as pathological. And, like the advocates of industrial betterment, spokespersons for the human relations perspective attributed the lack of cohesion in modern organizations to a runaway division of labour and the anomie it spawned. But whereas industrial betterment sought to address industry's problems by socializing employees through the communities in which they lived, the Human Relations movement sought to transform the firm itself and, more importantly, management into a cohesive collective.

Challenge to the rhetoric As the rhetoric and practices of human relations became increasingly institutionalized, criticism grew. Observers of corporate life warned that the cost of cohesive organizations was the loss of individualism and a homogenizing mediocrity, especially among white-collar employees (Mills 1951; Whyte 1956). Such claims were popularized by a number of widely read novels, including Wilson's (1955) *The Man in the Grey Flannel Suit* and Marquand's (1961) *The Point of No Return*. Critics pointed to practical problems as well. The unintended consequences of cohesion and loyalty were said to limit the firm's capacity to respond when conditions required creative thought and novel behaviour (Janis 1972). At the same time, organizations were accused of undermining the values of a democratic society and of contributing to the disintegration of families and communities (Whyte 1956). However, the most important challenge to the Human Relations movement came from managers themselves. Managerial spokespersons began to claim that human relations practices were costly and delivered few results (Baritz 1960: 172). As technically trained MBAs swelled the ranks of general management, it became increasingly popular to denigrate the 'happiness boys' and 'touchy-feely techniques' (see Pettigrew 1985).

The rising tide of criticism coincided with three developments that catalysed a new surge of managerial theorizing. First, even though computers were developed in the 1940s, it was not until the late 1950s that corporations bought them in appreciable numbers. The spread of the mainframe computer not only launched a new technical infrastructure, it popularized the language of cybernetics, which would provide a new lexicon for managerial discourse (Beniger 1986). Second, the launching of Sputnik in 1957 raised fears that the Soviets might best the US in the technical competition that underwrote the Cold War. As a result, the federal government intensified its space and weapons programmes, which, in turn, subsidized the high-technology industries that were to become the growth sectors of the American economy over the next twenty years. Science and engineering once again became economically and culturally central. Finally, in 1959 the Ford Foundation and the Carnegie Corporation issued influential reports critical of business schools (Gordon and Howell 1959; Pierson 1959). Both reports argued that managerial education lacked a coherent core and that managerial training should be as rigorous as other professional training. Both recommended that the MBA degree be made a prerequisite for a managerial career and that business schools stiffen their curricula with courses in statistics and quantitative methods. Together, these developments created a context hospitable to a wave of managerial theorizing in a more rational key. The swell occurred simultaneously on three fronts: the rise of operations research and management science; the search for general managerial principles; and the birth of organizational theory.

Systems rationalism, 1955–80

Surge During the Second World War, the British and American military employed teams of mathematicians, physicists and statisticians to devise methods for solving logistical problems (Crowther and Whiddington 1948; Trefethen 1954). Working with early computers, these 'operations research teams' were so successful that after the war each of the services established its own operations research unit (Wren 1972). Operations research (OR) quickly spread from the military to industry. The Arthur D. Little consulting company began applying OR techniques to managerial problems in the early 1950s. The Operations Research Society of America was established in 1952 and, a year later its sister organization, the Institute for Management Science, was formed. Both organizations dedicated themselves to developing and applying quantitative techniques to problems of planning and control (Burack and Batlivala 1972). Hertz estimated that by 1954 at least twenty-five firms had established formal OR groups and that as many as 300 analysts worked in industry (cited in Burack and Batlivala 1972). By the mid-1960s queuing theory, network analysis, simulation techniques and theories of linear and dynamic programming were sufficiently well developed to be used by large corporations, and a number of universities had already established programmes leading to doctoral degrees in operations research (ORSA 1971). In fact, by the end of the decade the Ford and Carnegie commissions' educational vision was largely realized: operations research, management science, finance, accounting and statistics were now the core of the curriculum at elite business schools.

As OR and management science grew more prominent, the general tenor of managerial discourse began to change. Theorists again began to search for an 'orderly body of knowledge' to guide the manager (Luthans 1973: 67). During the 1950s Newman (1951), Drucker (1954), Koontz and O'Donnell (1955) and others published volumes detailing the 'principles' and 'functions' of management. Like Taylor, these theorists sought universal dictums that managers could employ in the course of their work. However, unlike their predecessors, the new system-atizers wrote of general processes rather than specific practices (Wren 1972). Process theorists equated management with setting objectives and designing systems for meeting those objectives. Planning, forecasting and controlling were to be the manager's watchwords. Process theories thereby provided management with a definition of itself consistent with the tools of OR and management science. In fact, the process theorist's recommendations were decidedly calculative even when they were not quantitative. For instance, management by objectives (MBO), originally proposed by Drucker in 1954, did not become popular until Odiorne (1965) published a step-by-step manual for constructing and implementing an MBO system.

Organizational behaviour also began to shed the rhetoric and practices of the Human Relations movement during the late 1960s. The change was heralded by the advent of contingency theory (Luthans 1973) and furthered by the subsequent separation of organizational theory from organizational behaviour. Thompson (1967), Lawrence and Lorsch (1967) and other contingency theorists proclaimed that the adequacy of an organization's structure depended on the specifics of its environment and technology. Furthermore, with an appropriately analytic orientation and knowledge of contingent relations, managers were led to believe that they could consciously design more effective firms by manipulating structures and decision processes (Galbraith 1977). Although most organizational theorists followed March and Simon (1958) in arguing that humans were boundedly rational and, hence, less omniscient than earlier rationalists presumed, the difference was one of degree. There might be no 'one best way', as Taylor had proposed, but some ways were clearly better than others. Implicit in such theories was the notion that employees are instrumentally motivated and that efficiency is a matter of means/ends calculations or inducement/contribution ratios (Simon 1960). Organizational theory's revitalizing of rational action, in turn, influenced micro-organizational behaviour, as psychological studies of organizations were now called. During the 1970s previously popular affective theories of motivation (Maslow 1954; McGregor 1960) were replaced by motivational schemes grounded in rational calculation and 'cognitive decision-making'.

Because systems rationalism became popular in an age when the indexing of publications became systematized, it is possible to chart the ideology's trajectory using bibliometric techniques. One such measure, constructed from the *Business Periodicals Index* (*BPI*), is displayed in figure 12.1. The solid line plots the annual frequency of articles pertaining to general and specific techniques advocated by systems rationalists. The measure was constructed by counting the number of articles listed in the *BPI* from 1960 to 1989 under the following subject headings: cost benefit analysis, financial analysis, job analysis, management by objectives, management information systems, operations research, work design, job descriptions and job evaluation. The index shows slow growth in the 1960s, explosive growth [after 1975] a peak in 1979–80 and subsequent decline.

Rhetoric Management science, operations research, process theory and contingency theory were each instances of a broader trend that we dub 'systems

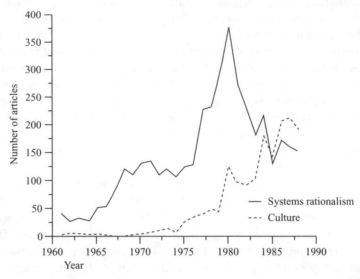

Figure 12.1   Annual frequency of articles associated with systems rationalism and culture indexed in the *BPI*

rationalism'. Unlike earlier managerial rhetorics, systems rationalism had no titular spokesperson and lacked the character of an integrated movement. Instead, rhetorics of systems rationalism were articulated simultaneously by several camps that sometimes drew sharp distinctions between themselves. Nevertheless, the camps explicitly or implicitly subscribed to a set of precepts that transcended their differences.

As a group, systems rationalists expressed antipathy toward human relations. Odiorne (1965: 8), for example, referred to the 'human relations era' as the 'age of the good-off' and promised to move beyond fuzzy visions of a 'sunny atmosphere' to practical action. In a similar vein, Vroom (1973: 66–7) wrote:

> We began with the normative question. What would be a rational way of deciding on the form and amount of participation in decision making that should be used in different situations? We were tired of debates over the relative merits of Theory X and Theory Y and of the truism that leadership depends on the situation. We felt that it was time for the behavioral sciences to move beyond such generalities. . . . Our aim was to develop a set of ground rules for matching a manager's leadership behavior to the demands of the situation. It was critical that these ground rules be operational, so that any manager could determine how he should act in any decision-making situation.

Analogous passages that prescribe rational and calculative activities as antidotes for human relations' excesses litter the management literature of the late 1960s and early 1970s.

All systems rationalists regardless of discipline peddled programmatic techniques or universal principles that would enable managers to plan, forecast and act more effectively. Accordingly, each camp drew moral, if not technical inspiration from scientific management. Throughout the period, noted systems rationalists

318

attempted to exonerate Taylor's reputation (Fry 1976; Locke 1982). Drucker (1954: 280), for example, proclaimed scientific management 'the most powerful contribution America has made to Western thought since the Federalist Papers'. Other theorists simply appropriated the Taylorites' achievements. For example, the Critical Path Method (CPM) and the Programme Evaluation and Review Technique (PERT), popularized by operations researchers in the 1960s, were direct extensions of the Gantt Chart developed by Henry Gantt in the early 1900s (Archibald and Villoria 1967).

Like the Taylorites, the systems rationalists turned to science and engineering for ideas. But whereas scientific management drew on mechanical engineering, systems rationalism appropriated concepts from electrical engineering and computer science. Computer metaphors and 'systems thinking' became the lingua franca of endeavours as disparate as linear programming and organizational design. During the 1960s general systems theory became increasingly prominent in managerial discourse. Proponents argued that, like computer programs, organizations could be controlled by managing boundaries between 'sub-units' and by regulating the 'input/output interfaces' between the organization and its environment (Boulding 1956; Miller and Rice 1967; Buckley 1967). By the 1970s 'box and line' diagrams depicting organizations as programmes had become common in texts and journals. The rhetoric intimated that management was simply a form of systems analysis, albeit one with a broader perview.

Accordingly, to be successful, managers once again needed to be experts. However, because systems analysis was so abstract, the new vision of expertise differed from the 'functional' expertise that Taylor had advocated. Systems analysis was depicted as a general skill. Managers who understood an organizational system could presumably control a firm's performance without knowing details. Moreover, because details were irrelevant, trained managers could presumably apply their skills to almost any organization or problem they encountered.

Finally, systems rationalism lacked an explicit model of the workforce. Aside from top management and the occasional staff expert, employees were largely absent in texts written by systems rationalists. In some areas of organizational theory, it even became popular to write as if the actions of employees and the decisions of managers were irrelevant to an organization's fate (e.g., Aldrich 1979). As in economics, when the workforce was considered, employees were portrayed either as automatons who responded mechanically to structural changes or as rational actors whose involvement in work was instrumental.

Challenge to the rhetoric   By 1980 systems rationalism was not only well institutionalized but its promise had tarnished. For the first time since the Second World War, American industry faced significant foreign competition, especially from Japan and West Germany, whose products had gained an international reputation for quality. Asymmetric trade policies and the advantage of lower labour costs in South-East Asia allowed the Japanese, in particular, to market their goods at prices lower than those produced in the US. At the same time, the US had encountered a period of relatively high inflation coupled with periods of recession linked, in part, to worldwide shocks in the oil market. With the decline of traditional industries and the rise of the service economy (Bluestone and Harrison 1985) came an increasing number of professional and semi-professional workers whose identities were tied to occupations that extended beyond the organization. The expertise of such occupations was said to be more specialized, more obscure, and less amenable to control than that of the traditional labour force (Von Glinow 1988). Moreover, having matured during the 1960s, many professional workers and their blue-collar contemporaries seemed less willing to accept authority or view work as a central life interest (Bellah et al. 1985). It appeared as if loyalty to the firm could no longer be taken for granted, even among the professional labour force. Thus, in the guise of social and economic change, managers found themselves confronting problems for which systems rationalism seemed ill suited. A variety of commentators began to argue that curing industry's ills would demand a rededicated workforce as well as greater flexibility and creativity (Peters and Waterman 1982; Piore and Sabel 1984). It was in this context that discourse on organizational culture and employee commitment began to attract attention.

Organizational culture and quality, 1980–[92]

Surge   Theorists associated with the Human Relations movement spoke of organizational climates and occcassionally noted that organizations had cultures (Jacques 1951; Schein 1969). However, the idea that organizations might profitably be viewed as cultures did not attract sustained attention until the late 1970s, when the notion entered managerial discourse via two paths. The first was through the work of theorists who argued that organizations should be viewed as socially constructed systems of meaning (Wilkins 1979; Pettigrew 1979; Van Maanen 1979; Dandridge et al. 1980; Louis 1981; Martin 1982; Pondy et al. 1983). Influenced by anthropology and symbolic interactionism, these scholars sought to counterbalance systems rationalism by promoting an alternate paradigm for organizational analysis. The second and more influential path was through the work of consultants and applied researchers who wrote primarily for practitioners (Silverzweig and Allen 1976; Peters 1978; Ouchi and Price 1978; O'Toole 1979; Baker 1980; Schwartz and Davis 1981). Although the second group used images similar to the first, their claim was more pragmatic: by heeding the symbolics of leadership and by attending to employees' values, managers could enhance their firm's competitiveness. The practitioner literature explicitly linked organizational culture to Japanese competition. Japan's industrial ascent was popularly attributed to the Japanese corporation's ability to inspire commitment without sacrificing flexibility and performance. Commentators suggested that American firms would do well to emulate the Japanese by developing 'strong' cultures that fostered concern for quality, flexibility and service (Pascale and Athos 1981; Ouchi 1981).

Both camps gathered momentum slowly until 1982, when interest in organizational culture suddenly exploded. The groundswell of interest was sparked by cover stories in *Business Week* (1980), *Fortune* (Uttal 1983) and other popular magazines, as well as by the back-to-back commercial success of three books that spoke of culture under various guises: Ouchi's *Theory Z* (1981), Peters's and

Waterman's *In Search of Excellence* (1982) and Deal's and Kennedy's *Corporate Cultures* (1982). By the mid-1980s the practitioner-oriented view had become dominant, even in academic circles (Barley, Meyer and Gash 1988). By the end of the decade, notions of culture and commitment had become entwined with a variety of efforts to revitalize American industry, such as the 'Total Quality movement' and the movement for 'World Class Manufacturing'. Quality was seen as the product of a state of mind that required a revolution in the way both managers and workers viewed their jobs. Commitment was to quality as calculation was to efficiency.

Evidence that cultural rhetorics have begun to compete with systems rationalism can be garnered from observations of managerial practice. Not only have numerous managers [...] written about cultural change in their own organizations (e.g., Cunningham 1981; Brown 1982; Boyle 1983; Shapiro 1983; Bice 1984; Kanarick and Dotlich 1984; Koerner 1984; Malinconico 1984) but studies indicate that self-conscious attempts to formulate corporate cultures have become part of organizational life (Schein 1985; Van Maanen and Kunda 1989). In his ethnography of a firm widely celebrated as the possessor of a strong culture, Kunda (1992) noted that employees not only talked about culture but the firm also sent its employees to culture seminars. The organization even employed a corporate ethnographer charged with documenting and disseminating a managerially sanctioned interpretation of life in the firm.

More systematic evidence can be gleaned from an analysis of articles published in the business press. Figure 12.1 also plots the frequency of articles indexed annually by the *Business Periodicals Index* under subject headings associated with the rhetoric of corporate culture: commitment, employee motivation, organizational loyalty, teamwork, culture and morale. As the graph indicates, the frequency of such articles began to grow in the late 1970s and had not plateaued by 1989. In fact, the graph suggests that by the late 1980s discourse on corporate culture may have become as common as discussions of systems rationalist techniques.

Rhetoric Culture's popularizers openly attacked systems rationalism. In the rush to adopt rational systems of control, firms were said to have sacrificed moral authority, social integration, quality and flexibility. Although rationalization may have streamlined production, it was criticized for rewarding specialization, parochialism and calculative involvement at the expense of loyalty and commitment. Culture's proponents claimed that rampant systematization posed few problems in a period of surplus and stability but that the costs of relying on systemic controls materialized when environments became turbulent. Critics argued that under such conditions exclusive reliance on rational controls might even exacerbate anomie to the point where further rationalization would actually occasion declines in productivity (Masuch 1985). The point was succinctly articulated by Baker (1980: 53) in his thumbnail diagnosis of a typical firm's ills:

> Despite continuing profitability costs were higher... Management tried to take corrective action, but the new marketing programs were not properly implemented. They

reorganized only to find that the new structure had little impact.... They increased their spending on research and development, but nothing substantial developed. The culture thwarted most of their actions.... Frustrated by their inability to get employees to take needed actions, top managers tightened their employees further, increasing management's frustration and provoking still tighter controls. In one organization, the vicious cycle ended only with bankruptcy.

The postulate of rationality's declining returns underwrote culture theory's first tenet: economic performance in turbulent environments requires the commitment of employees who make no distinction between their own welfare and the welfare of the firm. Texts on culture argued that 'unity' and 'loyalty', the primary attributes of 'strong' cultures, could counteract the unintended consequences of rational design. Although shared beliefs and values might blur the boundaries between self and organization, such commitment was said to imply no loss of individualism or autonomy. In fact, strong cultures were said to actually enhance autonomy, since well-socialized employees could be trusted to act in the organization's best interest. The image of autonomy within the confines of value conformity was central to Peters's and Waterman's (1982: 15–16) image of an 'excellent company':

Excellent companies are both centralized and decentralized. For the most part ... they have pushed autonomy down to the shopfloor.... On the other hand, they are fanatic centralists around the few core values they hold dear. 3M is marked by barely organized chaos.... Yet one analyst argues: 'The brainwashed members of an extremist political sect are no more conformist in their central beliefs.'

Ultimately, advocates promised, strong cultures would transform organizations into full-fledged collectives. As Kanter (1983: 119) proclaimed of employees in strong-culture companies:

They gain an experience of ... communitas ... which lifts them out of the humdrum ... of their place ... [it] may be the closest to an experience of community [that many workers may have].... What imbues this with meaning ... is not just the sense of being part of a group, but ... the feeling of pride and accomplishment at building ... something relevant to the larger organization.

The rhetoric's second tenet was that strong cultures can be consciously designed and manipulated. Enlightened managers were said to be capable not only of formulating value systems but of instilling those values in their employees. Management was advised to exorcise unwanted thoughts and feelings from the workforce and to replace them with beliefs and emotions that benefited the organization. To make the point, proponents employed an imagery of cults, clans and religious conversions (see Ouchi and Price 1978; Deal and Kennedy 1982; Donnelly 1984; Pascale 1984). Authors exhorted managers to become the 'high priests' of their organization's values to appoint 'mythical heroes' and to fabricate 'sagas' (Deal and Kennedy 1982). The following passage is typical:

The manager who attempts to change the organizational culture must assume... the role of a missionary. If the manager is successful in converting key personnel to the new set of values, then appropriate symbolic change should follow.... As with any new proselyte, organizations which are converting their cultures can be helped in this process by institutionalizing new rituals, symbols, languages, and heroes.... This will take the form of memos and directives from top management... and reward systems which praise those who serve the new values. (Ulrich 1984: 126)

Of course, culture's champions did not advocate controlling values simply for its own sake. The third tenet was that value conformity and emotional commitment would foster financial gain. Most spokespersons vaguely promised that strong cultures would result in some form of economic advantage. However, those more familiar with their audience's hard-nosed pragmatism attempted to quantify the gain. Deal and Kennedy (1982: 15), wrote in no uncertain terms: 'The impact of a strong culture on productivity is amazing... we estimate that a company can gain as much as one or two hours of productive work per employee per day.'

Explaining alternations in the tenor of managerial thought

Cultural antinomies

The historical record thus seems to suggest that since 1870 five reasonably distinct rhetorical waves successively embellished American managerial discourse. Moreover, these five waves appear to cluster coherently into two thematically contrasting sets. The rhetorics of industrial betterment, human relations and organizational culture emphasized normative control. Proponents of each claimed that organizations are, or should be, collectives. Whether the dominant image was of community, group or culture, each depicted the organization as a locus of shared values and moral involvement. Accordingly, all three blurred the boundaries between work and non-work and between managers and workers. Because advocates of each envisioned cohesion and loyalty as the ultimate source of productivity, they exhorted managers to be leaders: to set an example, to inspire, to motivate and to provide for the employees' welfare. As sentient, social beings, employees were said to perform more diligently when they were committed to a collective whose ideals they valued. Control therefore rested on shaping workers' identities, emotions, attitudes and beliefs.

In contrast, the second set of rhetorics emphasized rational control. Proponents of scientific management and systems rationalism argued that productivity stemmed from carefully articulated methods and systems. Each portrayed the firm as a machine, either mechanical or computational, that could be analysed into its component parts, modified and reassembled into a more effective whole. Both rhetorics exhorted managers to be experts: to bring rational analysis and a body of empirical knowledge to bear on the firm's problems. Furthermore, both assumed that employees were calculative actors with instrumental orientations to work. Employees were said either to understand the economic advantages of an

323

efficient system or to be powerless to resist a well-designed structure. Since compliance was therefore unproblematic, control could be readily exercised by manipulating systems.

The five rhetorics' sequence suggests an alternation between normative and rational ideologies of control. Although it is impossible to date ideological surges precisely, it seems safe to say that the normative rhetoric of industrial betterment captured the attention of prominent industrialists after 1870, when spokespersons first began to articulate the philosophy, and before 1900, when betterment practices had become sufficiently institutionalized to be showcased at an international exposition. Similarly, the rational rhetoric epitomized by scientific management moved beyond engineering circles to the larger managerial community between 1900 and the early 1920s. The resurgence of welfare capitalism and the rise of industrial psychology during the 1920s marked a return to normative theorizing that gathered full force in the Human Relations movement, whose ideas were well institutionalized by the late 1950s. The rhetoric of systems rationalism, inspired by the rise of general systems theory in the mid- to late 1950s, came to dominate managerial discourse, if not practice, by the late 1970s. Finally, during the early 1980s the rhetorics of organizational culture, commitment and quality gathered force as American managers once again evoked a normative ideology in the face of foreign competition and global dependency. The alternating pattern of elaboration (normative, rational, normative, rational, normative) strongly suggests that American managerial ideology has evolved within the confines of a bipolar ideational structure.

Structural anthropologists (Lévi-Strauss 1963, 1967; Needham 1973; Maybury-Lewis and Almagor 1989) have long maintained that cultures revolve around core ideas that are oppositional or dualistic in structure. These dualisms are said to define the ontological dilemmas that undergird everyday life. They suffuse the culture's dominant symbols, validate cleavages in social structure and fuel the semantics of everyday speech (Eisenstadt 1989). In pre-industrial societies, pivotal dualisms often encode naturalistic and religious enigmas: life versus death, good versus evil, and so on. Most anthropologists agree that although industrial cultures are less dualistic than pre-industrial cultures, oppositions still continue to play a crucial role (Maybury-Lewis 1989). For instance, with respect to images of the social order, no antinomy has been more salient in Western culture than the contrast between communalism and individualism or mechanistic and organic solidarity.

Writing in the period 1876 to 1922, which spanned the eras of industrial betterment and scientific management, Marx (1906), Tönnies (1957), Durkheim (1933) and Weber (1968) each sensed that industrialization was problematic because it juxtaposed two contrasting paradigms for social order. These two forms of social organization were given different names by different scholars. Weber wrote of the 'communal' and the 'associative', Durkheim contrasted 'mechanistic' with 'organic' solidarity, and Tönnies used 'Gemeinschaft' and 'Gesellschaft'. However, the essence of their vision was the same. In a Gemeinschaft, people share a common identity, are bound by common values and traditions, and partake of a way of life that contrasts sharply with the competition, individualism and calculative self-interest associated with Gesellschaft. The central dilemma identified by the early social theorists concerned the integrity of the social fabric. How could relations based on utilitarianism and rational calculation remain integrated and socially fulfilling? It seemed that increasing differentiation would beget crises of integration and that increasing integration would beget crises of differentiation.

The question of how to balance these opposing processes not only continues to motivate much sociological research, it appears to have become a central motif in Western culture. Several anthropologists and sociologists have recently argued that all Western societies treat traditionalism/rationalism and communalism/individualism dualistically (Eisenstadt 1989; Abbott 1990). Associated with the antinomies' poles are opposing solutions to the problem of control: normative control and regimes of trust versus rational control and regimes of self-interest. For those who run corporations, this dualism often evinces itself in the practical issue of how to prevent anomie, construed as lack of commitment, while reaping the benefits of the very rationalization that exacerbates anomie. It should therefore come as no surprise that managerial ideologies traffic in notions of both normative and rational control. However, as structural anthropologists note, because cultural dualisms are ontologically incompatible, they can never be resolved even by the most cunning theory. All one can expect is to cope with the incommensurates.

After examining the anthropological literature on cultural dualism, Maybury-Lewis (1989) concluded that 'alternation' or 'temporal segregation' is one of a small set of strategies by which societies have sought to manage incommensurates.[3] Temporal segregation entails emphasizing alternate poles of an antinomy during successive time periods. Maybury-Lewis observed that alternation has been particularly prominent in Anglo-American cultures where, among other things, it underwrites the institution of two-party politics.

The trajectory of American managerial thought seems consistent with the Anglo-American pattern. One might therefore explain the alternation between rhetorics of normative and rational control as follows. Like most other people, managerial theorists are constrained by their culture's repertoire of images and ideas. As in most Western cultures, Anglo-American visions of social order rest on an opposition between organic and mechanistic solidarity, associated, respectively, with normative and rational ideologies of control. Thus, when constructing theories of how best to manage firms, theorists are more or less obliged to work within a broadly bipolar framework. Perhaps also for cultural reasons, American theorists have broached the duality of mechanical and organic solidarity by emphasizing either one or the other. But because the two visions form a duality, any ideology that emphasizes normative action is vulnerable to charges of ignoring rational action and vice versa. Hence, temporal segregation offers an inherently unstable resolution. The instability may remain latent so long as the current ideology provides a plausible interpretation for events and so long as the managerial community appears to be coping reasonably well with socio-economic conditions. However, when conditions change and the practices associated with the prevailing ideology seem to become inadequate, the cultural repertoire constrains theorists to search for alternatives nearer the pole of the antinomy least recently emphasized. Accordingly, managerial discourse evolves in alternating waves.

Although a theory of cultural constraint may be able to explain why the innovative edge of managerial discourse alternates between ideologies of normative and rational control, it cannot account for the timing of each new wave. Theories of cultural dualism imply that pressures for change flow from within the system of ideas. Tensions internal to the system may well offer proponents of change a blueprint for criticism, but because conceptual tensions are theoretically omnipresent, the mere fact of their existence cannot trigger a surge. To account for the timing of alternations one must therefore invoke forces exogenous to the culture's conceptual repertoire.

Timing

Because most scholars of managerial discourse have focused on one or two particular rhetorics, they have tended to offer historically contextualized accounts of each ideology's ascent. Without doubt, each wave of discourse reflected and perhaps even shaped the events and practices of an era. For instance, industrial betterment's emergence cannot be fully understood apart from the socio-economic conditions of the late nineteenth century. Similarly, one can hardly imagine how the imagery and techniques of systems rationalism could have developed without the computer. Yet, however bound a particular rhetoric's content might be to the specifics of an era, to account for surges solely in terms of contextual factors would be to imply that normative and rational theorizing have alternated more or less by coincidence. Although serendipity and historical confluence have surely played a role in the evolution of managerial discourse, the strong pattern of alternation begs for the consideration of more systematic explanations.

Levels of labour activity   Derber (1970), Edwards (1979) and other scholars have linked changes in managerial ideology to the shifting quality of labour relations in the United States. Although some commentators claim that all managerial ideologies are a means of repressing labour, a few have offered interpretations cued to the substantive differences between rhetorics (Salvati 1984). Sanford Jacoby reasoned that because normative rhetorics have emphasized employment relations, they should have become attractive when labour relations seemed especially troublesome.[4] Conversely, because rational rhetorics have ignored employee relations, they should have gained popularity during periods of relative calm. By this logic, the three normative rhetorics should have surged during periods of relatively high labour activity, while the two rational rhetorics should have grown prominent during lulls.

Labour activity can be measured in a variety of ways (Stern 1978). Figures 12.2 and 12.3 display time series for two such indices: the number of unions founded annually between 1870 and 1975 (figure 12.2) and the frequency of strikes between 1880 and 1988 (figure 12.3). Data on union births were drawn from Hannan and Freeman's (1987: 925) study of the foundings of US labour unions.

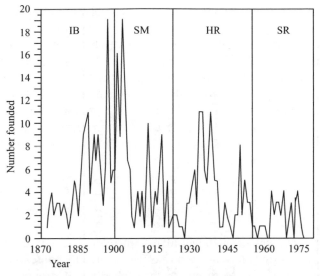

Note: IB = Industrial betterment; SM = Scientific management;
HR = Human relations; SR = Systems rationalism.

Figure 12.2   Unions founded annually, 1870–1975

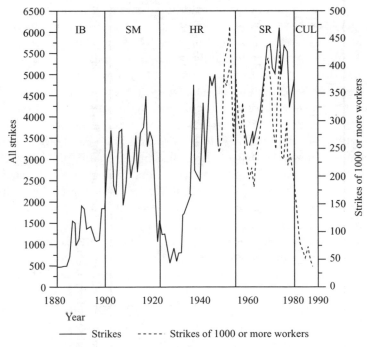

——— Strikes   - - - - - Strikes of 1000 or more workers

Note: IB = Industrial betterment; SM = Scientific management;

HR = Human relations; SR = Systems rationalism;

CUL = Organizational culture.

Figure 12.3   Annual frequency of strikes, 1880–1988

Table 12.2 The timing of longwaves, according to six analysts

	Schumpeter (1934)	Kondratieff (1935)	Rostow (1978)	Mandel (1980)	Van Duijn (1983)	Sterman (1990)	Average
First wave							
Expansion	1787–1814	1790–1817	1790–1815	–	–	–	1789–1818
Contraction	1814–1843	1817–1851	1815–1848	1826–1847	–	–	1818–1847
Second wave							
Expansion	1843–1870	1851–1875	1848–1873	1847–1873	1845–1872	–	1847–1872
Contraction	1870–1898	1875–1896	1873–1896	1873–1893	1872–1892	1870–1894	1872–1894
Third wave							
Expansion	1898–1925	1896–1920	1896–1920	1893–1913	1892–1929	1894–1923	1894–1921
Contraction	–	–	1920–1935	1913–1948	1929–1948	1923–1938	1921–1944
Fourth wave							
Expansion	–	–	*	–	1948–1973	1938–1973	1944–1971
Contraction	–	–	*	–	1973–[1992]	1973–[1992]	1971–[1992]

* As explained in n. 6, because Rostow's estimates for later periods are based on a method that departs radically from that used by other theorists, we exclude his estimates from the table.

Data on the frequency of strikes were compiled from the *Handbook of Labor Statistics* (US Department of Labor, 1942, 1980, 1989).[5] The figures also indicate the periods (given in table 12.1) during which each managerial rhetoric is thought to have surged (data on the percentage of the workforce that struck between 1880 and 1988 replicate the patterns discussed below).

Figures 2 and 3 challenge the thesis that normative rhetorics prospered during periods of labour turmoil and that rational rhetorics flourished in eras of labour peace. Of the three normative rhetorics, only industrial betterment clearly co-incided with a period of increasing unionization and strike activity. Heightened labour activity may also have fanned interest in human relations during the 1940s. However, rhetorics of organizational culture and commitment unambiguously arose in an era of declining labour militancy. Moreover, of the two rational rhetorics, only systems rationalism surged during a period of labour calm. Scient-ific management moved beyond engineering circles as union foundings were reach-ing an all-time high and flowered when strikes were more common than at any previous time. Nevertheless, the labour-activity hypothesis remains elegant pre-cisely because it relates the pattern of alternation to trends relevant to the sub-stantive themes that distinguish between normative and rational ideologies of control. In fact, no contrast could be more prominent: normative rhetorics stress the employee's relation to the firm, while rational rhetorics do not. The labour-activity hypothesis may therefore fail not because it emphasizes the wrong dis-tinction but because it neglects to specify the distinction fully.

The hypothesis frames the issue solely in terms of the tenor of the normative rhetorics. This one-sidedness directs attention to trends that may warrant an interest in normative control but not to trends that may warrant an interest in rational control. In effect, the labour-activity hypothesis assigns rational rhetorics to a residual category by claiming that they should surge whenever conditions do not merit normative appeals. The timing of normative and rational surges may be better explained by a process that would explicitly elicit normative rhetorics during certain times and rational rhetorics during others. Expansions and con-tractions of the economy may be such a process.

Economic expansions and contractions Rational and normative rhetorics both promise managers greater productivity and profitability but advocate radically different means for obtaining these ends. Rational rhetorics stress the efficient use of structures and technologies, while normative rhetorics stress employee rela-tions. Therefore one might argue that rational rhetorics should surge when profit-ability seems most tightly linked to the management of capital. Conversely, normative rhetorics should surge when profitability seems to depend more on the management of labour. The literature on 'Kondratieff cycles' or 'economic longwaves' provides support for this line of reasoning.

Students of longwaves contend that over the last 200 years Western economies have experienced four broad cycles of expansion and contraction, each with a period of approximately fifty years (Schumpeter 1934; Kondratieff 1935; Rostow 1978; Mandel 1980; Van Duijn 1983; Sterman 1990). Table 12.2 displays estimates of the timing of each wave as well as an average calculated from the estimates.[6] Of particular interest are the second, third and fourth waves, which span the eras under discussion. The second expansion is said to have begun in the late 1840s and continued until the early 1870s, when the economy entered a slow decline that ended with the depression of 1896. During the late 1890s Western economies once again began a boom that lasted until the early 1920s. The subsequent contraction ceased with the end of the Great Depression, which some scholars locate before and others after the Second World War. In either case, by the end of the war the West had entered a fourth expansion, which lasted until the 1960s. By the early 1970s Western economies had again embarked on a downturn, which has yet to end. Although evidence of longwaves can be found in economic data from most Western nations, the evidence is particularly strong for the United States (Van Duijn 1983).

Longwave theorists concur that escalating levels of capital investment (Forrester 1973, 1977; Rostow 1978; Mandel 1980) spurred by fundamental shifts in the technical infrastructure (Schumpeter 1934; Kuznets 1953; Mensch 1979; Kleinknecht 1987) have driven each expansion. Contractions occurred when the supply of capital outstripped its demand, which typically coincided with the saturation of markets stimulated by the technologies that underwrote the expansion. Scholars have shown that the second wave swelled with the rise of the railroads, steampowered machinery and replaceable parts; that the third wave coincided with the spread of electricity and the internal combustion engine; and that the fourth wave paralleled the diffusion of electronics, air transportation and synthetic materials (Mensch 1979; Rostow 1980; Van Duijn 1983). These technologies became infrastructural, in part, because they allowed industries to automate different aspects of the production process (Coombs 1984a, 1984b). Steam-powered machinery and replaceable parts enabled automated fabrication, which became common during the course of the second wave. Transfer processes remained largely manual until the spread of electric motors, internal combustion engines and conveyor belts during the third wave. Finally, during the fourth wave, electro-mechanical technologies were widely used to automate control systems.

Each wave and its associated technology thus engendered a 'paradigm of automation' (Coombs 1984a) that triggered a quantum leap in the rationalization of production. The techniques and technologies associated with each paradigm spread rapidly during upswings and were partially responsible for the expansions' escalation (Mensch 1979; Coombs 1984a; Kleinknecht 1987). However, as the downturns set in, further automation began to yield declining returns and the paradigms stagnated. It stands to reason that managers should be attracted to rhetorics that emphasize rational procedures and structures when profits hinge easily on capital investment and automation. But when returns on capital begin to decline, managers should show greater interest in rhetorics that focus on the utilization of labour, industry's second factor of production. One might therefore expect rational rhetorics to have surged during the upswings of longwaves and normative rhetorics to have surged during downswings. The evidence in figure 12.4 broadly supports this hypothesis.

Figure 12.4 displays, as parallel timelines, an averaged estimate of the eras of expansion and contraction (given in table 12.2), as well as our estimate of the eras

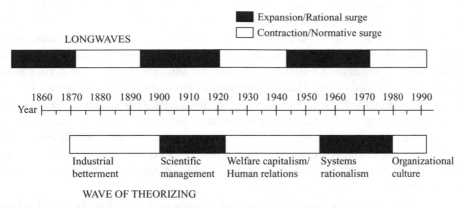

Figure 12.4 Correspondence between ideological surges and longwave expansions and contractions

during which each rhetoric surged (given in table 12.1). Shaded portions of the two timeliness signify periods of expansion and rational surges. Unshaded portions represent contractions and normative surges. If the allure of rational and normative ideologies mapped precisely on to expansions and contractions, then the shaded and unshaded portions of the two timelines would coincide. Visual inspection of figure 12.4 reveals a reasonable approximation of coincidence. Surges of normative and rational theorizing occurred, respectively, in conjunction with periods of contraction or expansion. Although more difficult to pinpoint with the available data, the estimated timelines also seem to indicate that changes in the tenor of managerial discourse generally lagged the beginning of an upturn or a downturn, thereby raising the possibility that the latter may have cued the former.

Discussion and conclusions

The data suggest that organizational scholars ought at least to consider the possibility that American managerial ideology has evolved rather differently than commonly hypothesized. Rather than having progressed steadily from coercive to rational and then to normative conceptions of control, managerial ideology may have been elaborated in surges of rhetoric that alternately celebrated normative and rational forms of control. Moreover, an interplay between broad cultural and economic forces may have underwritten these alternations. Specifically, deeply rooted but opposing images of Gemeinschaft and Gesellschaft appear to have constrained the collective imagination of the managerial community by dichotomizing the range of acceptable images of organizing. New waves of rational and normative theorizing have, in turn, been associated with long-term expansions and contractions in the economy. Rational rhetorics prospered when the economy expanded; normative rhetorics surged when the economy contracted. Thus, one might postulate that culture has set the substantive and structural boundaries

STEPHEN R. BARLEY AND GIDEON KUNDA

within which managerial discourse has developed but that economic forces have determined when new surges of theorizing occurred.

Such a claim at once violates and bridges traditional accounts of ideological change on two fronts. First, most scholars have advocated either an idealist or a materialist explanation of ideological change. Idealists have argued that new ideologies arise out of tensions endogenous to the system of ideas itself (Sutton et al. 1956; Gramsci 1957; Douglas 1966). In contrast, materialists claim that ideological change is triggered by exogenous events such as wars, immigration, changing economic conditions, climatic shifts and so on (Marx 1906; Harris 1979). Not only have idealists and materialists generally portrayed their perspectives as mutually exclusive but the purist tendency has solidified [...] with the rise of postmodernism and the realist backlash it has occasioned.

Social theorists have long counselled that ontological purism is too rigid to account adequately for social change (Bendix 1956; Weber 1968; Giddens 1984). However, most attempts at synthesis have been cast at the level of abstract social theory. What we have attempted to show, in however a rudimentary manner, is that by pragmatically combining idealist and materialist explanations, one can account more fully for the dynamics of ideological change in at least one domain, American managerial thought. In this arena, cultural arguments are necessary for explaining conceptual constraints, while material arguments are crucial for explaining the timing of trends. Either explanation without the other would leave an incomplete account of the pattern's unfolding.

Second, our analysis of American managerial discourse blurs the long-standing distinction between strain and interest theories of ideological change. Strain theories assert that ideologies enable collectives to cope with contradictory social forces (Parsons 1951; Sutton et al. 1956; Johnson 1968). But since all ideologies contain inconsistencies, they eventually prove inadequate either because social conditions change or because the ideology sows the seeds of its own destruction. For whatever reasons, once contradictions have become apparent, a new ideology arises to redress the previous ideology's inadequacies. In contrast, interest theorists (Mannheim 1936; Marx 1976) have argued that because all ideologies champion the concerns of their purveyors, ideological change signals either a change in the dominant group or a change in the dominant group's interests. Our reading of the elaboration of managerial ideology suggests that any sharp distinction between these two perspectives is unwarranted, since both may be necessary to explain the dynamics of ideological change.

Specifically, the role of cultural antinomies and economic change in the evolution of managerial discourse is broadly consistent with the teachings of strain theory. Cultural antinomies generate inherently unstable interpretations of social life, and economic cycles occasion social tensions that highlight the antinomies' contradictions. However, the existence of contradictions and strains does not lead automatically to a new ideological surge. Instead, the contradictions provide ammunition for the formulation of an ideological alternative by members of an insurgent interest group. With the exception of the most recent ideological turn, each surge of managerial theorizing was championed by members of a specific subgroup: industrial betterment by owners, scientific management by mechanical

332

and industrial engineers, human relations by personnel administrators and systems rationalism by financiers, accountants and mid-level managers with management-science-oriented MBAs. Portions of various ideologies and certain of their associated practices ultimately became institutionalized because of the actions of these groups.

Several concluding clarifications and caveats are in order. First, to say that rational and normative ideologies of control have swept over managerial thought in alternating sequence is not to say that adherents of rational ideologies 'outnumbered' adherents of normative ideologies in some eras but not others. Nor is it to say that rational and normative ideologies have alternately become 'dominant', at least in the traditional sense of the term. In fact, there is considerable evidence that rational ideologies have always 'dominated' the managerial community, in the sense that they are more prevalent and more tightly linked to managerial practice. For this reason we have been careful to avoid a language that might suggest the cyclical rise and fall of hegemonic regimes. Instead, in our view, the ideas, beliefs and practices that inform the managerial community cluster around two broad themes: organic solidarity and rational control versus mechanical solidarity and normative control. The first cluster may be the larger (and perhaps more influential), but for both socio-economic and cultural reasons, the second cluster periodically attracts considerable attention in the managerial community. This is not to say that rational theories disappear, nor even that rational thrusts do not also occur during normative eras, but only that rationalism will be tempered by and perhaps will even justify surges in normative theorizing. For instance, in the 1980s as the rhetoric of culture and commitment surged, the economy was overhauled by a wave of mergers and acquisitions justified in some managerial quarters by a hyper-rational ideology of financial ruthlessness. Rather than cast doubt on our claim that this period was characterized by a surge of normative theorizing, the presence of this hyper-rational ideology could be variously interpreted as the culmination, the continuation or even the institutionalization of the previously surging rhetoric of systems rationalism. From this point of view, the rhetoric and practice of mergers and acquisitions may actually have fuelled interest in the rhetoric of corporate culture. It is certainly the case that even as they implemented their hyper-rational vision of industry, proponents of this point of view also sought justification and legitimation in the rhetoric of values, motivation and morality characteristic of the concurrently surging normative ideology. Interestingly enough, industrial betterment's popularity also mushroomed in conjunction with the first wave of acquisitions and mergers to shake the American economy (Brandes 1970; Chandler 1977; Edwards 1979).

Second, our analysis has focused on ideational phenomena. We have not sought to address the relation between ideology and practice. Conceivably, the two might co-vary, or they might be completely unrelated. The alternatives have very different implications for a theory of ideology. Co-variance would indicate that ideology has an impact and that ideas may even play a causal role in the development of practice. Independence would be consistent with the claim that ideology is largely window dressing. While management theorists typically assume the former and labour historians the latter, the issue remains an empirical question that begs for further analysis.

Ultimately, the power of any social–scientific theory lies not only in its capacity to explain the past but in its ability to predict the future. Ignoring social science's less than illustrious record of accurate predictions, if our analysis has merit, one would expect the current emphasis on normative control to be followed by a resurgence of rationalism. Moreover, this surge should occur in conjunction with a long-term expansion in the economy and the rise of a new paradigm of automation. The implications of such a suggestion for organization theory are sobering. Some believe that organizational theory develops progressively, while others believe that shifts in the tenor of our theorizing offer an opportunity for greater understanding. But to the degree that trends in organizational theory mirror trends in managerial discourse at large, our efforts may be neither cumulative nor pathbreaking. Instead, in the long run, the tenor of our theorizing may amount to little more than the turning of a small cog within a larger socio-economic clock over which no one has control.

NOTES

From S. R. Barley and G. Kunda (1992), 'Design and Devotion: Surges of Rational and Normative Ideologies of Control', *Administrative Science Quarterly*, vol. 37, pp. 363–99.

1   The relation between managerial ideology and practice is hotly contested. Some histor-
    ians argue that despite shifting rhetorics, managerial motives and practices have
    remained stable (Braverman 1974). Others argue that ideological fads only affect the
    practices of the largest corporations (Brody 1968) or those in innovative sectors of
    industry (Edwards 1979). Still others suggest that practices have varied so widely in all
    eras that any generalization is unwarranted (Licht 1991). Our own view is that manage-
    rial practice is now, and always has been, highly variegated. Yet a disjuncture between
    ideology and practice does not invalidate the study of ideology itself. On the contrary,
    studies of managerial rhetoric are important, for they enable scholars to link the world
    of business to the larger culture of which it is a part. Examining this link is our primary
    objective. Consequently, although we use data on events and practices to identify eras,
    we certainly do not intend to imply that managers have practised what they have
    preached.
2   A welfare secretary functioned much like a social worker. During the late 1800s welfare
    secretaries were often employed by industries. Ultimately the job of the welfare secretary
    evolved into that of personnel director.
3   Maybury-Lewis (1989) identified two other general strategies: (1) integration and (2)
    social or spatial segregation. Cultures pursue the former by devising ideologies that
    embrace both poles of an opposition simultaneously, as in the Taoist notion of yin and
    yang. Cultures that pursue the latter allocate each pole of an antinomy to separate
    realms of social life or to different groups (moieties) and then periodically perform
    rituals of integration.
4   Personal communication.
5   In 1980 the Reagan administration ordered the Department of Labor to compile data
    only on strikes involving 1000 or more workers. Figure 12.3 therefore plots data on all
    strikes as well as on strikes of over 1000 workers, so that the two curves can be

compared and general trends can be examined over the entire 118-year period. The Department of Labor also collected no data on strikes between 1906 and 1914 and incomplete data for 1915 and 1916. Using data from five states, Griffin (1939) developed a procedure for estimating the missing data. Edwards (1981) has shown that, if anything, Griffin's procedures underestimate the number of strikes that actually occurred during those years. We have used Griffin's estimates to calculate the number of strikes between 1906 and 1916.

6 Longwave theorists have measured cycles of expansion and contraction using aggregate indices of price and production. Until the 1950s the two types of indices tracked each other. Since then, prices have steadily risen while output has followed the expected pattern. Most analysts concur that the change in the price data reflects the growth of Keynesian economic policies. Consequently, most recent longwave analysts, with the exception of Rostow (1978), consider price data to be a muddy measure of economic performance and rely almost exclusively on output data. For this reason, Rostow's estimates of the number and the timing of longwaves depart radically from all others'.

REFERENCES

Abbott, A. D. (1990), 'Positivism and interpretation in sociology: lessons for sociologists from the history of stress research', *Sociological Forum*, vol. 5, pp. 435–58.

Aldrich, H. (1979), *Organizations and Environments* (Englewood Cliffs, NJ: Prentice-Hall).

Amon, R. F. (1958), *Management Consulting* (Boston: Harvard University Graduate School of Business).

Archibald, R. D. and R. D. Villoria (1967), *Network-Based Management Systems (PERT/CPM)* (New York: Wiley).

Baker, E. L. (1980), 'Managing organizational culture', *Management Review*, vol. 69, pp. 8–13.

Baritz, L. (1960), *The Servants of Power: A History of the Use of Social Science in American Industry* (Middletown, CT: Wesleyan University Press).

Barley, S. R., G. Meyer and D. C. Gash (1988), 'Cultures of culture: academics, practitioners, and the pragmatics of normative control', *Administrative Science Quarterly*, vol. 33, pp. 24–60.

Bellah, R. N., R. Madsen, W. M. Sullivan, A. Swidler and S. M. Tipton (1985), *Habits of the Heart: Individualism and Commitment in American Life* (Berkeley, CA: University of California Press).

Bendix, R. (1956), *Work and Authority in Industry: Ideologies of Management in the Course of Industrialization* (New York: Harper & Row).

Beniger, J. R. (1986), *The Control Revolution: Technological and Economic Origins of the Information Society* (Cambridge, MA: Harvard University Press).

Bice, M. D. (1984), 'Corporate cultures and business strategy: a health management company perspective', *Hospital and Health Services Administration*, vol. 29, pp. 64–78.

Bluestone, B. and B. Harrison (1985), *The Deindustrialization of America: Plant Closings, Community Abandonment, and the Dismantling of Basic Industry* (New York: Basic Books).

Boulding, K. E. (1956), 'General systems theory: the skeleton of science', *Management Science*, vol. 2, pp. 197–208.

Boyle, R. J. (1983), 'Designing the energetic organization: how a Honeywell unit stimulated change and innovation', *Management Review*, vol. 72, pp. 20–5.

Brandes, S. D. (1970), *American Welfare Capitalism: 1880–1940* (Chicago: University of Chicago Press).

Braverman, H. (1974), *Labor and Monopoly Capital* (New York: Monthly Review Press).

Brody, D. (1968), 'The rise and decline of welfare capitalism', in J. Braeman, R. H. Bremner and D. Brody, eds, *Change and Continuity in Twentieth-century America: The 1920s* (Columbus, OH: Ohio State University Press), pp. 147–78.

Brown, T. L. (1982), 'Managing in the 80s', *Canadian Manager*, vol. 7, pp. 14–15.

Buckley, W. (1967), *Sociology and Modern Systems Theory* (Englewood Cliffs, NJ: Prentice-Hall).

Buder, S. (1967), *Pullman: An Experiment in Industrial Order and Community Planning: 1880–1930* (New York: Oxford University Press).

Burack, E. and R. B. D. Batlivala (1972), 'Operations research: recent changes and future expectations in business organizations', *Business Perspectives*, vol. 9, pp. 15–22.

Business Week (1980), 'Corporate cultures: the hard-to-change values that spell success or failure', 27 October, pp. 148–60.

Cameron, E. H. (1960), *Samuel Slater, Father of American Manufactures* (Freeport, ME: Bond Wheelwright).

Chandler, A. D., Jr. (1977), *The Visible Hand: The Managerial Revolution in American Business* (Boston: Harvard University Press).

Cooke, M. L. (1910), *Academic and Industrial Efficiency: A Report to the Carnegie Foundation for the Advancement of Teaching* (New York: Carnegie Foundation).

Cooke, M. L. (1920), 'Discussion', *Bulletin of the Taylor Society*, vol. 5, pp. 28–130.

Coombs, R. W. (1984a), 'Long-term trends in automation', in P. Marstrand, ed., *New Technology and the Future of Work and Skills* (London: Francis Pinter), pp. 146–162.

Coombs, R. W. (1984b), 'Innovation, automation, and the long-wave theory', in C. Freeman, ed., *Longwaves in the World Economy* (London: Francis Pinter), pp. 115–25.

Crowther, J. G. and R. Whiddington (1948), *Science at War* (New York: Philosophical Library).

Cunningham, M. (1981), 'Productivity and the corporate culture', *Vital Speeches*, vol. 47, pp. 363–7.

Dandridge, T., I. Mitroff and W. Joyce (1980), 'Organizational symbolism: a topic to extend organizational analysis', *Academy of Management Review*, vol. 23, pp. 77–82.

Davis, M. (1986), *Prisoners of the American Dream: Politics and Economy in the History of the U.S. Working Class* (London: Verso).

Deal, T. E. and A. A. Kennedy (1982), *Corporate Cultures* (Reading, MA: Addison-Wesley).

Derber, M. (1970), *The American Idea of Industrial Democracy, 1865–1965* (Urbana, IL: University of Illinois Press).

Donnelly, R. M. (1984), 'The interrelationship of planning with corporate culture in the creation of shared values', *Managerial Planning*, vol. 32, pp. 8–12.

Douglas, M. (1966), *Purity and Danger: An Analysis of the Concepts of Pollution and Taboo* (London: Ark Paperbacks).

Drucker, P. F. (1954), *The Practice of Management* (New York: Harper & Row).

Durkheim, E. (1933), *The Division of Labor in Society* (Glencoe, IL: Free Press; first published 1897).

Edwards, P. K. (1981), *Strikes in the United States: 1881–1974* (New York: St. Martin's Press).

Edwards, R. (1979), *Contested Terrain: The Transformation of the Workplace in the Twentieth Century* (New York: Basic Books).

Eisenstadt, S. N. (1989), 'Dual organizations and sociological theory', in D. Maybury-Lewis and U. Almagor, eds, *The Attraction of Opposites: Thought and Society in the Dualistic Mode* (Ann Arbor: University of Michigan Press), pp. 345–54.

Ely, R. T. (1885), 'Pullman: a social study', *Harpers New Monthly Magazine*, vol. 70, pp. 452–66.

Emerson, H. (1912), *The Twelve Principles of Efficiency* (New York: Engineering Magazine Co.).

Emerson, H. (1914), *Efficiency as a Basis for Operation and Wages* (New York: Engineering Magazine Co.).

Etzioni, A. (1961), *A Comparative Analysis of Complex Organizations* (Glencoe, IL: Free Press).

Federated American Engineering Societies (1921), *Waste in Industry* (New York: McGraw-Hill).

Fish, E. H. (1917), 'Human engineering', *Journal of Applied Psychology*, vol. 1, pp. 161–74.

Follett, M. P. (1918), *The New State: Group Organization, the Solution of Popular Government* (London: Longmans, Green).

Follet, M. P. (1924), *Creative Experience* (London: Longmans, Green).

Forrester, J. W. (1973), *World Dynamics* (Cambridge, MA: MIT Press).

Forrester, J. W. (1977), 'Growth cycles', *The Economist*, vol. 125, pp. 525–43.

Fry, L. W. (1976), 'The maligned F. W. Taylor: a reply to his many critics', *Academy of Management Review*, vol. 1, pp. 124–39.

Galbraith, J. R. (1977), *Organization Design* (Reading, MA: Addison-Wesley).

Giddens, A. (1984), *The Constitution of Society: Outline of the Theory of Structuration* (Berkeley, CA: University of California Press).

Gilman, N. P. (1889), *Profit Sharing between Employer and Employee* (Boston: Houghton, Mifflin).

Gilman, N. P. (1899), *A Dividend to Labor: A Study of Employer's Welfare Institutions* (Boston: Houghton, Mifflin).

Gladden, W. (1876), *Working People and their Employers* (Boston: Lockwood, Brooks).

Gordon, R. A. and J. E. Howell (1959), *Higher Education for Business* (New York: Columbia University Press).

Gramsci, A. (1957), *The Modern Prince and Other Writings* (New York: International Publishers).

Griffin, J. I. (1939), *Strikes: A Study in Quantitative Economics* (New York: Columbia University Press).

Haber, S. (1964), *Efficiency and Uplift: Scientific Management in the Progressive Era 1890–1920* (Chicago: University of Chicago Press).

Halsey, F. A. (1891), 'The premium plan for paying for labor', *American Society of Mechanical Engineers Transactions*, vol. 22, pp. 758–65.

Hannan, M. T. and J. Freeman (1987), 'The ecology of organizational founding: American labor unions 1836–1985', *American Journal of Sociology*, vol. 92, pp. 910–43.

Harris, M. (1979), *Cultural Materialism: The Struggle for a Science of Culture* (New York: Vintage).

Hertzberg, F. (1966), *Work and the Nature of Man* (Cleveland, OH: World).

Hollingworth, H. L. and A. T. Poffenberger (1917), *Applied Psychology* (New York: D. Appleton).

Hopkins, H. C. (1951), *History of the Y.M.C.A. in North America* (New York: Association Press).

Hounsell, D. A. (1984), *From the American System to Mass Production 1800–1932: The Development of Manufacturing Technology in the United States* (Baltimore: Johns Hopkins University Press).

Hoxie, R. F. (1915), *Scientific Management and Labor* (New York: Appleton-Century-Crofts).

Jacoby, S. M. (1985), *Employing Bureaucracy: Managers, Unions, and the Transformation of Work in American Industry* (New York: Columbia University Press).

Jacoby, S. M. (1991), 'Masters to managers: an introduction', in Jacoby, ed., *Masters to Managers: Historical and Comparative Perspectives on American Employers* (New York: Columbia University Press), pp. 1–20.

Jacques, E. (1951), *The Changing Culture of a Factory* (London: Tavistock).

Janis, I. L. (1972), *Victims of Groupthink* (Boston: Houghton Mifflin).

Johnson, H. M. (1968), 'Ideology and the social system', in *International Encyclopedia of the Social Sciences* (New York: Macmillan), vol. 7, pp. 76–85.

Kanarick, A. F. and D. L. Dotlich (1984), 'Honeywell's agenda for organizational change', *New Management*, vol. 2, pp. 14–19.

Kanter, R. M. (1983), *The Change Masters: Innovation and Entrepreneurship in the American Corporation* (New York: Simon & Schuster).

Kleinknecht, A. (1987), *Innovation Patterns in Crisis and Prosperity: Schumpeter's Long Cycle Reconsidered* (New York: St. Martin's Press).

Koerner, P. (1984), 'Professionalism means sharing', *National Underwriter*, vol. 88, pp. 11–24.

Kondratieff, N. D. (1935), 'The longwaves in economic life' *Review of Economic Statistics*, vol. 17, pp. 105–15; first published 1926.

Koontz, H. (1961), 'The management theory jungle', *Academy of Management Journal*, vol. 4, pp. 174–88.

Koontz, H. and C. O'Donnell (1955), *Principles of Management: An Analysis of Managerial Functions*, (New York: McGraw-Hill).

Korman, G. (1967), *Industrialization, Immigrants, and Americanizers: A View from Milwaukee* (Madison, WI: State Historical Society of Wisconsin).

Kubr, M. (1986), *Management Consulting: A Guide to the Profession*, 2nd edn (Geneva: ILO).

Kunda, G. (1992), *Engineering Culture: Control and Commitment in a High Tech Corporation* (Philadelphia: Temple University Press).

Kuznets, S. (1953), *Economic Change* (New York: W. W. Norton).

Laslett, J. H. M. and S. M. Lipset (1974), *Failure of a Dream: Essays in the History of American Socialism* (Garden City, NY: Anchor).

Latta, S. W. (1906), *Rest Houses for Railroad Men: How the Railroad Men Regard such Conveniences* (New York: Welfare Department of the National Civic Federation).

Lawrence, P. R. and J. W. Lorsch (1967), *Organization and Environment: Managing Differentiation and Integration* (Boston: Harvard University Press).

Lesieur, F. G. (1958), *The Scanlon Plan: A Frontier in Labor Management Cooperation* (Boston: MIT Press).

Lévi-Strauss, C. (1963–7), *Structural Anthropology*, 2 vols (New York: Basic Books).

Lewin, K. (1951), *Field Theory in Social Science: Selected Theoretical Papers* (New York: Harper & Row).

Licht, W. (1991), 'Studying work: personnel policies in Philadelphia firms: 1850–1950', in S. Jacoby, ed., *Masters to Managers: Historical and Comparative Perspectives on American Employers* (New York: Columbia University Press), pp. 43–73.

Litterer, J. A. (1963), 'Systematic management: design for organizational recoupling in American manufacturing firms', *Business History Review*, vol. 37, pp. 369–91.

Locke, E. A. (1982), 'The ideas of Frederick W. Taylor: an evaluation', *Academy of Management Review*, vol. 7, pp. 14–24.

Louis, M. R. (1981), 'A cultural perspective on organizations: the need for and consequences of viewing organizations as culture bearing milieux', *Human Systems Management*, vol. 2, pp. 246–58.

Luthans, F. (1973), 'Contingency theory of management: a path out of the jungle', *Business Horizons*, vol. 16, pp. 67–72.

Malinconico, S. M. (1984), 'Managing organizational culture', *Library Journal*, vol. 109, pp. 791–3.

Mandel, E. (1980), *The Longwaves of Capitalist Development* (London: Cambridge University Press).

Mannheim, K. (1936), *Ideology and Utopia* (New York: Harcourt).

March, J. G. and H. Simon (1958), *Organizations* (New York: Wiley).

Marquand, J. P. (1961), *Point of No Return* (New York: Bantam).

Martin, J. (1982), 'Stories and scripts in organizational settings', in A. H. Hastorf and A. M. Isen, eds, *Cognitive Social Psychology* (New York: Elsevier North Holland), pp. 255–303.

Marx, K. (1906), *Capital* (New York: Modern Library; first published 1876).

Marx, K. (1976), *The German Ideology*, vol. 5 of *Karl Marx–Frederick Engels Collected Works* (New York: International; first published 1846).

Maslow, A. (1954), *Motivation and Personality* (New York: Harper).

Masuch, M. (1985), 'Vicious circles in organizations', *Administrative Science Quarterly*, vol. 30, pp. 14–33.

Maybury-Lewis, D. (1989), 'The quest for harmony', in D. Maybury-Lewis and U. Almagor, eds, *The Attraction of Opposites: Thought and Society in the Dualistic Mode* (Ann Arbor: University of Michigan Press), pp. 1–18.

Maybury-Lewis, D. and U. Almagor, eds (1989), *The Attraction of Opposites: Thought and Society in the Dualistic Mode* (Ann Arbor: University of Michigan Press).

Mayo, E. (1930), *A New Approach to Industrial Relations* (Boston: Division of Research, Graduate School of Business Administration, Harvard University).

Mayo, E. (1931), 'Psychopathologic aspects of industry', *Transactions of the American Neurological Association*, vol. 57, pp. 468–75.

Mayo, E. (1933), *The Human Problems of an Industrial Civilization* (New York: Macmillan).

Mayo, E. (1935), 'The blind spot in scientific management', *Proceedings of the Development Section: Sixth Annual Congress for Scientific Management*, vol. 3, pp. 214–18.

McGregor, D. M. (1960), *The Human Side of Enterprise* (New York: McGraw-Hill).

Mensch, G. (1979), *Stalemate in Technology* (Cambridge, MA: Ballinger).

Metcalfe, H. (1885), *The Cost of Manufactures and the Administration of Workshops, Public and Private* (New York: Wiley).

Miller, E. J. and A. K. Rice (1967), *Systems in Organization* (London: Tavistock).

Mills, C. W. (1951), *White Collar* (London: Oxford University Press).

Montgomery, J. (1832), *The Carding and Spinning Master's Assistant: Or the Theory and Practice of Cotton Spinning* (Glasgow: J. Niven, Jr.).

Moreno, J. L. (1946), *Psychodrama and Sociodrama* (Boston: Beacon Press).

Needham, R. (1973), *Right and Left: Essays on Dual Symbolic Classification* (Chicago: University of Chicago Press).

Nelson, D. (1975), *Managers and Workers: Origins of the New Factory System in the United States 1880–1920* (Madison: University of Wisconsin Press).

Nelson, D. (1980), *Frederick W. Taylor and the Rise of Scientific Management* (Madison: University of Wisconsin Press).

Newman, W. H. (1951), *Administrative Action: The Technique of Organization and Management* (Englewood Cliffs, NJ: Prentice-Hall).

Odiorne, G. S. (1965), *Management by Objectives: A System of Managerial Leadership* (Marshfield, MA: Pitman).

Olmstead, V. H. (1900), 'The betterment of industrial conditions', *Bulletin of the Department of Labor* (Washington, DC: Government Printing Office), no. 31, pp. 1117–56.

ORSA Committee on Professional Standards (1971), 'The nature of operations research', *Operations Research*, vol. 19, pp. 1138–48.

O'Toole, J. J. (1979), 'Corporate and managerial cultures', in C. L. Cooper, ed., *Behavioral Problems in Organizations* (Englewood Cliffs, NJ: Prentice-Hall), pp. 7–28.

Ouchi, W. G. (1981), *Theory Z: How American Business Can Meet the Japanese Challenge* (Reading, MA: Addison-Wesley).

Ouchi, W. G. and R. C. Price (1978), 'Hierarchies, clans, and theory Z: a new perspective on OD', *Organizational Dynamics*, vol. 7, pp. 24–44.

Owen, R. (1813), *A New View of Society, or Essays on the Principle of the Formation of the Human Character and the Application of the Principle to Practice* (London: Richard Taylor).

Park, R. E. (1934), 'Industrial fatigue and group morale', *American Journal of Sociology*, vol. 40, pp. 439–46.

Parsons, T. (1951), *The Social System* (New York: Free Press).

Pascale, R. T. (1984), 'Fitting new employees in the company culture', *Fortune*, vol. 109, pp. 28–43.

Pascale, R. T. and A. G. Athos (1981), *The Art of Japanese Management: Applications for American Executives* (New York: Simon and Schuster).

Pennock, G. (1930), 'Industrial research at Hawthorne', *Personnel Journal*, vol. 8, pp. 296–313.

Peters, T. J. (1978), 'Symbols, patterns and settings: an optimistic case for getting things done', *Organizational Dynamics*, vol. 7, pp. 3–22.

Peters, T. J. and R. H. Waterman, Jr. (1982), *In Search of Excellence* (New York: Harper & Row).

Pettigrew, A. (1979), 'On studying organizational cultures', *Administrative Science Quarterly*, vol. 24, pp. 570–81.

Pettigrew, A. (1985), *The Awakening Giant: Continuity and Change in Imperial Chemical Industries* (Oxford: Basil Blackwell).

Pierson, F. C. (1959), *The Education of the American Businessman: A Study of University College Programs in Business Administration* (New York: McGraw-Hill).

Piore, M. J. and C. F. Sabel (1984), *The Second Industrial Divide: Possibilities for Prosperity* (New York: Basic Books).

Pondy, L. R., P. J. Frost, G. Morgan and T. C. Dandridge (1983), *Organizational Symbolism* (Greenwich, CT: JAI Press).

Roethlisberger, F. J. and W. J. Dickson (1934), *Management and the Worker: Technical versus Social Organization in an Industrial Plant* (Boston: Division of Research, Graduate School of Business Administration, Harvard University).

Roethlisberger, F. J. and W. J. Dickson (1939), *Management and the Worker* (Cambridge, MA: Harvard University Press).

Rogers, C. (1961), *On Becoming a Person: A Therapist's View of Psychotherapy* (Boston: Houghton Mifflin).

Rostow, W. W. (1978), *The World Economy: History and Prospect* (New York: Macmillan).

Rostow, W. W. (1980), *Why the Poor Get Richer and the Rich Slow Down* (Austin: University of Texas Press).

Salvati, M. (1984), 'Political business cycles and longwaves in industrial relations: Notes on Kalecki and Phelps Brown', in C. Freeman, ed., *Longwaves in the World Economy* (London: Francis Pinter), pp. 202–24.

Schein, E. (1969), *Process Consultation* (Reading, MA: Addison-Wesley).

Schein, E. (1985), *Organizational Culture and Leadership* (San Francisco: Jossey-Bass).

Schumpeter, J. A. (1934), *The Theory of Economic Development* (Boston: Harvard University Press).

Schwartz, H. and S. M. Davis (1981), 'Matching corporate culture and business strategy', *Organizational Dynamics*, vol. 10, pp. 30–48.

Scott, W. G. (1959), *The Social Ethic in Management Literature* (Atlanta: Georgia State College).

Shapiro, K. P. (1983), 'Corporate culture can be changed three ways', *Business Insurance*, vol. 17, p. 30.

Sheldon, O. (1923), *The Philosophy of Management* (London: Pitman).

Shenhav, Y. (1994), 'Manufacturing uncertainty or uncertainty in manufacturing: managerial discourse and the rhetoric of organizational theory', *Science in Context*, vol. 7, pp. 275–305.

Silverzweig, S. and R. F. Allen (1976), 'Changing the corporate culture', *Sloan Management Review*, vol. 17, pp. 33–49.

Simon, H. A. (1960), *The New Science of Management Decision* (New York: Harper & Row).

Sterman, J. D. (1990), 'A longwave perspective on the economy in the 1990s', *Bank Credit Analyst*, vol. 42, pp. 28–47.

Stern, R. N. (1978), 'Methodological issues in quantitative strike analysis', *Industrial Relations*, vol. 17, pp. 32–42.

Stevens, G. A. and L. W. Hatch (1904), 'Employers welfare institutions', in *Third Annual Report of the Commissioner of Labor* (Albany, NY: New York State Department of Labor), pp. 225–329.

Sutton, F. X., S. E. Harris, C. Kaysen and J. Tobin (1956), *The American Business Creed* (Cambridge, MA: Harvard University Press).

Taylor, F. W. (1895), 'A piece rate system: a step toward partial solution of the labor problem', *American Society of Mechanical Engineers Transactions*, vol. 16, pp. 856–93.

Taylor, F. W. (1903), *Shop Management* (New York: Harper).

Taylor, F. W. (1911), *The Principles of Scientific Management* (New York: Harper).

Thompson, J. D. (1967), *Organizations in Action* (New York: McGraw-Hill).

Tolman, W. H. (1900), *Industrial Betterment* (New York: Social Service Press).

Tönnies, F. (1957), *Community and Society* (New York: Harper & Row; first published 1887).

Towne, H. R. (1886), 'The engineer as an economist', *American Society of Mechanical Engineers Transactions*, vol. 7, pp. 428–32.

Towne, W. R. (1889), 'Gain sharing', *American Society of Mechanical Engineers Transactions*, vol. 10, p. 618.

STEPHEN R. BARLEY AND GIDEON KUNDA

Trahair, R. C. S. (1984), *The Humanist Temper: The Life and Work of Elton Mayo* (New Brunswick, NJ: Transaction Books).

Trefethen, F. H. (1954), 'A history of operations research', in J. F. McCloskey and F. H. Trefethen, eds, *Operations Research for Management* (Baltimore: Johns Hopkins University Press), pp. 3–36.

Ulrich, W. L. (1984), 'HRM and culture: history, ritual, and myth', *Human Resource Management*, vol. 23, pp. 117–128.

US Bureau of Labor Statistics (1919), *Welfare Work for Employees in Industrial Establishments*, Bulletin of the US Bureau of Labor Statistics, no. 220 (Washington, DC: Government Printing Office).

US Department of Labor (1942), *Handbook of Labor Statistics* (Washington, DC: Government Printing Office).

US Department of Labor (1980), *Handbook of Labor Statistics* (Washington, DC: Government Printing Office).

US Department of Labor (1989), *Handbook of Labor Statistics* (Washington, DC: Government Printing Office).

Uttal, B. (1983), 'The corporate culture vultures', *Fortune*, vol. 108, pp. 66–72.

Van Duijn, J. J. (1983), *The Longwave in Economic Life* (London: Allen & Unwin).

Van Maanen, J. (1979), 'The fact of fiction in organizational ethnography', *Administrative Science Quarterly*, vol. 24, pp. 43–101.

Van Maanen, J. and G. Kunda (1989), 'Real feelings: emotional expression and organizational culture', in B. M. Staw and L. L. Cummings, eds, *Research in Organizational Behavior* (Greenwich, CT: JAI Press), vol. 11, pp. 43–104.

Van Zelst, R. H. (1952), 'Sociometrically selected work teams increase production', *Personnel*, vol. 5, pp. 175–85.

Von Glinow, M. A. (1988), *The New Professionals: Managing Today's High-tech Employees* (Cambridge, MA: Ballinger).

Vroom, V. H. (1973), 'A new look at managerial decision making', *Organizational Dynamics*, Spring, pp. 66–80.

Walton, R. E. and R. B. McKersie (1965), *A Behavioral Theory of Labor Negotiations* (New York: McGraw-Hill).

Weber, M. (1968), *Economy and Society* (Berkeley, CA: University of California Press; first published 1922).

White, A. T. (1879), *Improved Dwellings for the Laboring Classes: The Need, and the Way to Meet It on Strict Commercial Principles, in New York and Other Cities* (New York: G. P. Putnam).

Whitehead, T. N. (1936), *Leadership in a Free Society: A Study in Human Relations Based on an Analysis of Present-Day Industrial Civilization* (Cambridge, MA: Harvard University Press).

Whitehead, T. N. (1938), *The Industrial Worker: A Statistical Study of Human Relations in a Group of Manual Workers* (Cambridge: MA: Harvard University Press).

Whyte, W. F. (1955), *Money and Motivation: An Analysis of Incentives in Industry* (New York: McGraw-Hill).

Whyte, W. H., Jr. (1956), *The Organization Man* (Garden City, NY: Doubleday).

Wilkins, A. (1979), 'Organizational stories as an expression of management philosophy', unpublished PhD dissertation, Stanford University.

Wilson, S. (1955), *The Man in the Grey Flannel Suit* (New York: Simon & Schuster).

Wren, D. A. (1972), *The Evolution of Management Thought* (New York: Ronald Press).

Editor's Bibliography

Booth, A., M. Francesconi and J. Frank (1998), *Glass Ceilings or Sticky Floors?* (University of Essex: Institute for Labour Research).

Boseley, S. (1998), 'Radical reform urged on killer poverty', the *Guardian*, 27 November.

Bowdon, S. M. (1991), 'Demand and supply constraints in the inter-war UK car industry: did the manufacturers get it right?', *Business History*, vol. 33, no. 2, pp. 241–67.

Bowles, S. and H. Gintis (1976), *Schooling in Capitalist America* (London: Routledge & Kegan Paul).

Braverman, H. (1974), *Labor and Monopoly Capitalism: The Degradation of Work in the Twentieth Century* (London: Monthly Review Press).

Buckingham, L. (1998), '£1 million-a-year salary club swells to 49', the *Guardian*, 6 August.

Cowan, R. S. (1989), *More Work for Mother* (London: Free Association Books).

Foucault, M. (1977), *Discipline and Punish: The Birth of the Prison* (London: Allen Lane).

Franks, S. (1998), *Having None of it: Women, Men and the Future of Work* (London: Granta).

Gallie, D., M. White, Y. Chang, and M. Tomlinson (1998), *Restructuring the Employment Relationship* (Oxford: Oxford University Press).

Gorz, A. (1997), *Misères du présent, richesse du possible* (Paris: Galilée).

Grint, K. (1994), 'Reengineering History', *Organization*, vol. 1, no. 1, pp. 179–202.

Grint, K. (1997), *Fuzzy Management* (Oxford: Oxford University Press).

Grint, K. (1998), *The Sociology of Work*, 2nd edn (Cambridge: Polity Press).

Grint, K. and S. Woolgar (1997), *The Machine at Work* (Cambridge: Polity Press).

Harrington, R. (1998), *Railway Spine* (York University: Institute of Railway Studies).

Lukes, S. (1974), *Power: A Radical View* (London: Macmillan).

Rifkin, J. (1996), *The End of Work* (New York: Jeremy P. Tarcher/Putnam).

Rosener, J. B. (1990), 'Ways women lead', *Harvard Business Review*, November–December, pp. 119–60.

Rowley, J. (1998), 'Deadlier than the male', *The Mail on Sunday Review*, 27 December.

Sajer, G. (1993), *The Forgotten Soldier* (London: Orion).

Thomas, K., ed. (1999), *The Oxford Book of Work* (Oxford: Oxford University Press).

United Nations (1998), *Human Development Report* (New York: United Nations).

Wainwright, M. (1998), 'Delia causes a stir with omelette pan endorsement', the *Guardian*, 21 November.

Ward, L. (1998), 'Ethnic minorities pessimistic over race relations', the *Guardian*, 10 September.

Willmott, H. (1993), 'Strength is ignorance; slavery is freedom: managing culture in modern organizations', *Journal of Management Studies*, vol. 30, no. 4, pp. 515–52.

Index